Secret Paths: Women in the New Midlife

ALSO BY TERRI APTER

Altered Loves:
Mothers and Daughters during Adolescence

Working Women Don't Have Wives:
Professional Success in the 1990s

SECRET PATHS

Women in the New Midlife

Terri Apter

W. W. Norton & Company
New York London

To the continuing memories of Gillian Mirrlees

The text of this book is composed in Adobe Garamond
with the display set in Adobe Garamond
Composition and manufacturing by the Haddon Craftsmen, Inc.
Book design by Beth Tondreau Design

Library of Congress Cataloging-in-Publication Data
Aptar, T. E.
  Secret paths : woman in the new midlife / by Terri Aptar.
    p.   cm.
  Includes bibliographical references.
  1. Middle aged women—Psychology.   2. Middle age—Psychological
aspects.   I. Title
HQ1059.4.A68   1995
305.4—dc20   95–2151

ISBN 0-393-03766-5

W. W. Norton & Company, Inc., 500 Fifth Avenue, New York, N.Y. 10110
W. W. Norton & Company Ltd., 10 Coptic Street, London WC1A 1PU

1 2 3 4 5 6 7 8 9 0

Contents

Acknowledgments

Throughout the four years during which this book was written, I have received tremendous help and support from a number of people. Elizabeth Garnsey offered encouragement at the project's conception, and has since been helpful in the framing of my research. The Betty Behrens Research Fellowship at Clare Hall, Cambridge, has supported my work during the past three years. The President of Clare Hall, Anthony Low, and his wife Belle Low, have helped provide a wonderful working atmosphere. The psychology seminar in the Cambridge Faculty of Social and Political Sciences that ran in 1992 and 1993 also provided crucial support. The comments of Carol Gilligan, Jim Gilligan, Judy Dunn, Dale Hey, Janet Reibstein, Martin Richards, and David Good were particularly helpful. Carol Gilligan and Michelle Stanworth provided useful comments on the manuscript, as well as invaluable encouragement. Mary Jacobus, Jane Marcus, and Shelley Fisher Fiskin engaged in fruitful and continuous ruminations with me. Judy Barnard provided not only a sounding board for various ideas, but also an excellent cutting service. Nancy Chodorow, with whom I discussed this project in the very early stages, offered insights that became increasingly relevant as my research progressed. My agent, Meg Ruley, made use of her enthusiasm and expertise to find the book a good home. My editor at W. W. Norton, Jill Bialosky, continually amazed me with her ability to make non-drastic but transformative suggestions.

The greatest debt I owe is to the women whose development is described in this book. Their willingness to collaborate with me, to follow lines that interested me, and to lead me when I was stubborn and slow, involve an incalculable generosity. I can only hope that the immense pleasure I had from working with them and writing this book has been shared by them.

Preface: Secret Paths

On my fortieth birthday, two women with whom I had been close friends in high school announced that they had several hours' stopover in London before traveling on to Frankfurt. To maximize our time together, we agreed that I should drive to Heathrow, meet them as they came off the plane, find somewhere to eat, and then take them back to the airport. Then they would not have to travel to Cambridge—a journey which would have eaten away half their time in England. This arrangement, however sensible from one vantage point, was not fully appreciated by my family.

"Don't mind us. It's only your birthday," my older daughter assured me with barbed magnanimity.

Her younger sister fought her own disappointment to protect me: "She can do what she wants. It's her birthday."

"Yes, like I said. And she doesn't want to spend it with us." Her saucy grin broadened as she saw her little sister's heated response.

"You always try to make her feel *bad*," she protested, close to tears because that big girl would always have the last word.

But it would have taken more than this to make me feel bad. The prospect of meeting these friends, whom I had managed to see only five or six times during the last twenty-five years, drew me back to those years upon which I was inclined to reflect anyway. This birthday, in particular, was a marker which demanded a question and answer period. But I had avoided this aspect of it, and was merely pleased that it promised to be without trauma, pleased that forty, now, was much younger than I had ever supposed it would be. The arrival of my girlhood friends, however, highlighted those peripheral reflections I had been putting to one side. I felt an eerie distance from the last-minute negotiations involved in clearing my schedule both at home and at work. There was a more important agenda to attend to.

As I made the tedious journey along the congested, and increasingly icy, roads to the airport I felt the warmth of memories so vivid that I wondered where all the intervening years had gone.

At fifteen, life had been hell. What had centered this hell was a sense of inadequacy too shameful to be voiced. Instead, it was patched over with flippancy and bravado. Knowing I would eventually disappoint anyone in that other world—that world in which people with real knowledge and real skills moved effortlessly—the friendships I managed to form felt like temporary planks on the brink of collapse. My daily life consisted of the pretence that I did not know I would soon crash into the pit below. My connection with these women, as girls, had been different. They had witnessed my inadequacy and knew my fear, but found them causes for amused concern rather than revulsion. Always, one or the other had stood on the far side, smiling with confidence, or urging me on, impatient with my doubt. Whether it was enduring the humiliation of poor exam results or tending wounds from another girl's snub, they were there to make my sojourn in that isolated, competitive boarding school bearable. My final years at that school—since they were older than I—had been marked by their absence, a definition so palpable that it emptied the faces and hearts of all who sat next to me in the cafeteria or the classrooms. No one could touch me, once my real friends had left.

Now we were all women in, or approaching, midlife. Those adolescent terrors were left behind. The chasm of self-doubt had, after all, been bridged, one plank at a time. Yet its echoes remained. It was no longer dragging me down; but it was still part of me. I heard it now, more clearly than usual, because I was recalling the past, because I was now forty, really grown up, and should no longer hear it. Yet it formed a running commentary—on my driving, my inadequate timing, my trouble in finding my way from the car park to the terminal. I found myself listening with a new curiosity. I felt I was eyeing up a returning enemy, which I would lure into the open in order to attack.

Moments before such reunions are often dreadful. As I waited outside the customs area I could see that the freezing rain had congealed to thick snow. I despaired of their plane ever landing. I rang my home to check in, announce my safe arrival, and explain the uncertainty. My older daughter sounds younger on the phone. Her voice is thinner, less expressive, and loses its capacity to tease. "We're making the most beautiful cake in the world," she told me, and in the background I could hear her sister's squeals as she discussed the icing decoration with her father. They seemed days, not hours away, so that even when the plane I awaited was announced as "landed," I felt lost in the dull terminal, and worried about the difficult drive home.

My excitement turned to doubt as I scanned the figures emerging through the exit. Would I see in their middle-aged faces the young girls who had meant so much to me? And would they see, in my face, the girl who had been sustained by their affection? Might we not, in the ten years since I had last seen them, have become strangers? Had I made a worthwhile journey? Did I really want to see them?

I need not have worried. Faces of friends change even less than do our own in the mirror. It was only gradually, after our celebratory embraces and exclamations, when we were settled in a restaurant, that I could recognize the mature women they had now become. As the snow thickened, we delighted in our marooned state. The news that their flight was delayed a further four hours seemed like a gift, for we now had more time together; but they were too drained, after our lively meal, to keep up the pace of conversation. We decided to see a film, after which they might be refreshed. Our choices were constrained by film times and cinema locations, but the choice was apt, as such things which signal turning points often are. We decided on *When Harry Met Sally,* with Meg Ryan and Billy Crystal, scripted by Nora Ephron.

The scene that struck me like a whip in its timeliness was Sally's despair when she learns her former boyfriend is getting married. She feels time speeding by, and protests, "And I'm going to be forty." Harry pauses as the comic surprise sets in: "When?" he demands.

Sally gestures impatiently. "Some day . . . What does it matter? It's there, staring at me. A big dead end."

As the film ended, I put my dissatisfaction to my companions.

Judy sighed, burdened by the need to explain something so simple. "It's funny." Her voice had a feigned patience. I was, as always, slow on the uptake. But the pleasure I took in noting my unchanged role as ingenue among these larger and wiser women did not distract me.

"I know it's funny, and it's cute, but it's disturbing." Yet, as I watched a range of thoughts play on Judy's face, and heard Pam's low chuckle, it was difficult to feel disturbed. These women, now in their mid-forties, had, since I last saw them, undergone an exquisite change. The strength they had always carried was fine-tuned to a new tension, and they looked down upon that image projected by Sally's despair with a majestic indifference.

"You see," she continued, wearied by my need for further explanation, "Sally says it as though it's tomorrow, as though she really has to worry, but of course she doesn't. It's a formula in romantic movies: The distressed heroine, just when she's on the brink of her best future, feels the greatest despair. She feels 'old' or 'unloved' and then turns out to be neither." Her mouth straightened in irritation and her eyes filled with affection, as she watched me brood over this explanation.

"But 'dead end' is such an awful term. Think about it. 'Dead' and 'end.' Like you're racing towards something and then there's no where to go, and you just die."

"Remember, she's forty today," Pam interjected, and Judy's eyes widened; she nodded in appreciation, and kissed me. "Congratulations!"

"So it's not a dead end, is it? And why is it that Nora Ephron, who's past forty and gaining strength with everything she does, can write that it is?"

"Because it's good copy," Judy repeated.

"But doesn't it offend you that it is good copy? And that people who know better make use of it?"

"It's our secret," Pam explained. "We undergo a metamorphosis at forty—or so, but don't tell anyone about it."

"Really—." I was undeterred by their conspiratorial amusement at my expense. "But why? Why is it so secret?"

Judy shrugged. "It's too hard to explain. To start from scratch. It must be a long story, and it's not easy to tell. Of course some people try . . ."

"Do they get it right?" I asked.

"No," Pam announced, but as she turned to check the flight information board she guffawed: "Oh no, she's going to write about it!"

Their amusement was suddenly overlaid with interest. A silence fell among us as we acknowledged that some decision had been made. "Okay," Judy consented, eyeing me steadily, "you can change the copy. Reveal how we tunnel out, around the dead end."

It was time to say good-bye. The string that tugged inside me as they proceeded towards the security check unraveled a pattern I could not yet discern. What I knew was that the story of that secret development had to be told by many women, by the many different kinds of women now merging into midlife. A new kind of listening would have to be achieved, as we wiped the copy clean.

I watched them dump their bags onto the conveyor belt and walk through the metal detector. Their gestures, their facial expressions had, for me, that mythic quality which stemmed from the discrepancy between my knowing them so well, so deeply—and yet being unable to account for that knowledge. Watching them, I could see how that center within them had shifted, gaining weight and power. I could hear the silence of their new strength, but I refused to respect that silence. Partly, I could not resist exploring the developmental path that lay ahead for me; but I was also impatient with that secrecy, and convinced that every woman's journey would be easier if it were shared.

THIS EPISODE OCCURRED two years before I was even to begin the studies which form this book. Now, five years later, I look back on the work's conception, and realize that I had only a dim idea of how taxing it would be to disclose that silence. Development in infants, children, and adolescents is much easier to see: It is more rapid, more hectic, more physical. In those developmental stories dramas are enacted on a broad stage, observed by an enraptured audience. At midlife, women's development appears muted. It is far more private, and there are fewer players. Its silent but sure pace has led many people to believe that midlife change is hormonal—another byproduct of women's reproductive system. But psychology is a listening science, and in listening to women I could trace a deliberate acquisition of self-determination and self-definition—a matter of psyche, not biology. Instead of seeing themselves through others' eyes, or through the maze of social images, they took steps to forge their own vision and gain greater control over the precious second half of life. For they saw mid-life as a midpoint, a turning point, wherein they could strike out in new ways. The "dead end" was a tangled knot of unresolved fears, lingering constraints, and distorted images. During their forties it became disentangled, then transformed into a myriad of paths towards new challenges, new pressures, and new anxieties. In confronting these, a new certainty was born. This book charts the story of women's journey through that occluded passage—wrongly conceived by some as a "dead end." It tells the story of a developmental leap which has hitherto been achieved in silence.

Secret Paths: Women in the New Midlife

Introduction:
Crisis of a New Breed

In a society of unprecedented stability, women have experienced upheaval. Women who are in their forties and fifties today have participated in a social revolution which has changed their ways of living and their ways of thinking. While many markers of women's lives remain in place, their meanings have been transformed. Marriage, motherhood, fertility, and sexuality are concepts jam-packed with questions and a decreasing store of answers. As women either welcome or resist change, they engage in a struggle to define who they are and what matters to them. Every conclusion a woman reaches is hedged with doubt, challenged by a bombardment of ideologies and expectations alongside the urgent requirements of daily life. The cataclysmic changes experienced by this generation of women have oriented them to new psychological developments which, in midlife, elicit a new crisis. This crisis often feels like a catastrophic breakdown,[1] yet is in fact a turning point wherein women capitalize on what they have gained through new challenges and struggles. A new midlife awaits women at the far side of this journey.

The women who are in midlife today faced, as children, a divided social history. For many of them the games and teachings and examples set in childhood prepared them for what was then the traditional female world: They would grow up to be wives and mothers; their place of work would be the home; and their goals would be to produce and maintain a family. Their aims were to be loved and to be chosen, and then to care for others through their love. "Feminine," during their childhood, had a special meaning, and evoked a powerful control over their behavior, their wishes, and their needs. It was not something they had thrust upon them simply by virtue of being born female. It was something they had to work at, and something their behavior could endanger. Ambition, competition, independence, strongmind-edness could threaten femininity. With femininity threatened, they faced the unacceptable alternatives of exclusion, loneliness, and ostra-cism.

Yet this generation of women entered adulthood with very differ-ent ideas about what a woman should be, what she could be, and what she wanted to be. However little the world around them changed, however rigid were career structures, family practices, or personal hab-its, these women had different ideas about themselves, and faced new challenges to their self-esteem and their sense of identity. The dissolu-tion of old norms seemed to offer freedom; but with this freedom came anxiety. As in any social revolution, no one knew which hopes were realistic, or what the consequences of change would be. And, as in most revolutions, certain things changed more quickly than others, so that women's new hopes were hitched up with old habits. Thus, op-portunities at work expanded while practices within the home were static. More women were welcomed into male professions, but discov-ered a maze of male prejudice therein. Couples praised equality, but practiced old forms of dominance and submission.

Twenty years ago, the move towards equality seemed inevitable. It seemed then that with a mere modicum of good will on each side, sex-ual division would travel a smooth path to a just meeting point. Few women who are now in midlife had any idea how hard their lives would be and how difficult it would be to be at peace with their life choices. Few of the women planning to be working mothers under-stood just how time-consuming child care and domestic work were. And as they vastly underestimated the amount of traditional maternal or wifely tasks to be done, they vastly overestimated the amount of help with those tasks they would get from their partners. Women with more traditional goals failed to appreciate the costs of fulfilling roles that once appeared an easy option. If being a career woman was diffi-cult, being the wife-at-home could be equally so. As men's income fell between 1970 and 1990, as men's job security decreased, their "homemaker" wives had to sustain family income by finding paid work. At the same time, many women who believed they had some kind of security as homemakers found that divorce had disenfranchised them of financial support or health care for either themselves or their children. Women who had deferred their careers while they raised children found that they were attempting to enter a workplace whose rigidity had increased since they had left it in very early adulthood. Now, with fewer jobs and prolonged working hours and increased demands of employers, the new opportunities that in some sense women did have were lost on them. As women's expectations soared, as certain kinds of achievement became necessary to self-esteem, as the concept of happiness shifted from the more modest version of *satisfaction* to the demanding notion of *fulfillment,* they found life progress confusing. Inherited ideas were not so much replaced but extended. While their mothers before them were haunted by ideals of youth, beauty, and maternity, the adult woman of today has not escaped her mother's ghosts, but added to them. Beauty, charm, grace, and youth are no less important today than they were in the 1950s; but, in addition, women in the 1990s are expected to be smart, successful, and powerful.

Throughout adolescence and young adulthood, women of this generation have grappled with contradictory aims, needs, and expectations. They were under pressure to embody that image projected by one of Naomi Wolf's publicity photos: ambitious yet caring, physically attractive yet unconcerned with time-consuming grooming, intellectually sharp yet yielding to men's desires. The efforts involved in realizing these aims within stubborn social and family structures have been repeatedly recorded in recent years.[2] Women's defense of their life choices and the inevitable pros and cons of any choice, have also been explored.[3] What has not yet been explored is the developmental effect on midlife women of this history of personal conflict.

AS I WORKED ON a book about mothers with young children who were also professional women, most of whom were between the ages of 28 and 37,[4] I noticed that their management efforts led to relentless, excessive attempts to control their lives. They often sustained themselves with the belief that things could be better, even perfect, if only they were more organized, or had more energy. Though they observed, and resented, and resisted external constraints, their commands were directed within: They would make themselves strong enough to over-come constraints. So, while they were courageous and often ingenious in finding ways of managing their busy and conflict-ridden lives, they were also under the spell of the belief that somehow they would estab-lish a way of life in which there were no compromises foisted upon them as women. This is daunting—this belief that their long journey must be justified by ending in some perfect order that accommodates their entire array of needs, aims, and obligations. Under the sway of this ideal, they regularly disguised from themselves the costs of their efforts. On one level, of course, they felt them; but at the same time denied them:[5] they were "temporary"; they were not "really all that bad"; they were "worthwhile." While often suffering great stress, they used whatever mental energy was left over to control their awareness of just how deep their conflicts were. Such awareness would give rise to regret, anger, anxiety, and more stress—which, mentally, they could not afford.

As I returned to the midlife women to whom I had already begun to listen,[6] I found—even among those who, like my younger sample, had young children and careers which were important to them—dif-ferent styles of reflection. Among women in their forties, this control was disintegrating. They no longer sounded so certain or so deter-mined. Questions crept in at every turn: about what an effort was worth, what compromise could be accepted, where she had gone wrong, what she had done right, what she wanted to be, how she had to change either herself or her circumstances. Midlife women were no longer sustained by the fantasy that a perfect balance was to be found. There was a growing resistance to the control they had once worked so hard to sustain. The interviews were framed by competence and con-trol, but as they spoke the surface calm cracked. Anxieties, anger, re-gret, fear, despair dwelt in lively concert beneath their composure. Voices broke with tears, old memories protruded oddly, old pains in-spired bitter laughter, points of impasse became magnified as they swung from self reproach to anger or despair. There was a *sense* of ca-tastrophe; but as these conflicts were confronted, women passed into a new stage of development, wherein they found a new voice for express-ing a suppressed powerful individuality.

At about forty, most women allow themselves to feel those points of dissatisfaction that were once born in heroic silence. Making use of what Joyce Carol Oates calls "looking back time,"[7] they see how past decisions have cut them off from the potential they had wished to achieve, or how past expectations blinded them to the costs their goals incurred. As they took note of their new—really grown up—phase, they felt the panic of self-responsibility, and sought means of gaining greater control over their compromises. But to gain this, they had to see what they had compromised, and what it had cost them or those they cared for most. Regret and doubt are violent feelings, and this was often a violent time. But as I tracked them over the course of four years, and as I included women in their fifties in my sample, I saw that this hectic phase was temporary. However, it did not simply pass, like a bout of nerves. Instead, it gave way to new skills in making assessments and choices. These women had passed through a crisis, and come to a turning point where they could now perceive their own strength and assert their own desire. From this point on they were aware of what they had accomplished and where they were headed. I wanted to retrieve their stories for the women currently experiencing midlife growth, and for the women of the future who may be able to achieve this developmental task with less suffering, as the current strong, loud-mouthed generation of women extend the range of possibilities for women.

THE GENERATION OF WOMEN now in midlife has, like any other, its own special history, experiencing similar events and conditions at certain stages of its life.[8] Each new generation differs from earlier ones "because of intervening social changes of many sorts: in education, in nutrition, in the occupational and income level at which people begin their careers. There is no pure process of ageing. . . ."[9] Our parents' generational identity was formed by the two World Wars and the Great Depression. Now, they are the generation of unprecedented wealth and health in old age, creating new forms and features of longevity. But the generation of women in their forties and fifties belongs not only to the generation of the new woman, but also to a new life phase. "Middle age is the latest life stage to be discovered," writes sociologist Arlene Skolnick:[10] As people expect to live longer, and as their expectations of productivity increase, they do more and demand more of their middle years.

The concept of aging itself has been a special problem for this gen-

eration: first, because fewer women in midlife today feel they have attained their goals—because their adult goals have been formulated in a
social context that does not foster them; second because youth and its
potential are so peculiarly and highly valued by contemporary culture.
It is more difficult to experience the end of youth when its promise is
not fulfilled. It is also more difficult to accept one's maturity when
being young has such enormous value, and being mature has none.

Those who came to adulthood on the crest of the cult of youth
have now learned that aging is not optional—it is a reality. This can be
seen in the recent focus of the media and society on menopause. The
long-overdue attention this physical change is now receiving has put
the spotlight on midlife, but has left its real psychological story lost in
the shadows. Germaine Greer, in her book *The Change,* sees women's
release from reproductive cycles as leading to a golden, luminous phase
that frees them from all previous constraints. Gail Sheehy, too, in *The
Silent Passage,* sees menopause as the last taboo, something that is
feared and yet which mysteriously releases women's energies. While
the issues surrounding menopause remain of enormous importance, to
put this at the center of midlife development is as unsatisfactory as
placing the onset of menstruation at the center of adolescent development. Such physical markers often have a psychological impact. They
may jolt a woman into reflection and reassessment. But they remain
only one reference point in her individual and social history, which was
begun long ago and which she daily creates anew. The still-neglected
story of this generation's female midlife development rests on the clash
between ideals accumulated in adolescence and early adulthood, on the
one hand, and the edging out by society of a woman's significance in
midlife, on the other. For as women's lives changed rapidly, and as the
contradictory demands on them increased, they were driven forward
by the ideal of perfect integration: Everything they wanted to be both
personally and professionally, both psychologically and physically,
could be achieved if only they were tuned to some perfect pitch. The
inherent contradictions in the expectation that they could remain the
women they wanted to be and make it in a man's world were suppressed by this ideal. As the women living through this social upheaval
matured, they saw that the contradictions could not be so easily mastered. As this gradually accumulated knowledge intersects with the
threat of being marginalized as a middle-aged woman in a culture in

which only young, attractive women are visible, women at about 40, in self-defense, rise to the challenge. There must, they reason, be a way through this threatened dead end. The hope of new development sustains them through doubt and despair. For in midlife, when women are freed of the supposition that someone else has the answer, when they are no longer shadowed by a need to please a parent, when they are less anxious about standing in opposition to a partner, when the fantasy of the ideal of who they should be is shattered by the mature reflection in the mirror, they grow strong enough to listen to their own answers to the questions they pose. Thus, women gain strength to engage in this crisis and conflict because they have gained the confidence that they could come up with answers. While crisis at midlife is now thought by many psychologists to characterize only a minority of adult men,[11] women engage in it as a normal developmental stage. For men today, midlife is less threatening than it was twenty years ago. The male midlife crisis tends to focus on fears of diminishing potency and adventurousness. As health and physical activity tend to be sustained well into their sixties, as men are encouraged to broaden their notions of success and achievement, as a wider range of roles is opened to them, men now enjoy the changing pace of midlife. At forty or fifty a man can become a "new man," discovering emotional expression and the pleasures of connection and freedom from the pressure always to be strong, to be certain, to surpass others. The "new woman" cannot be so easily realized; both family and career time have to be created by her over a much longer span. The costs of both connection and independence tend to be higher for her, and hence the midlife counting of these costs is more drastic.

Women's construction of a new midlife can be seen as a counterpart to the invigoration experienced by countries such as Japan and Germany in the 1950s, after defeat marginalized them in others' eyes. So, too, do women unglue the labels they know all too well. Highly sensitive to others' views of them, they both register and resist the blankness of others' gaze: They see others dismissing them, categorizing them as middle aged. A secret resistance then occurs. They establish their own knowledge and their own vision. Ripe for significant change, many different things may act to instigate a crisis. It may be the pressures of work; it may be release from domestic burdens; it may be a daughter's impasse, a son's disappointment, a partner's departure;

or, sometimes, deep within her, as she confronts her surprise discovery that her potential must be realized now or never, she retrieves neglected needs and wishes, and finally wages battle against the dragons that have stood in her way. Hence, women, proud of their battle, emerge with a stronger sense of themselves and their own powers.

These clashes and the developmental crisis which ensues usually occur during a woman's 40s, and are resolved in her early 50s—though, as in all developmental stories, individual variation is vast. Recently, however, there has been a large-scale slighting of women in their forties by stronger, more sharply focused women in their fifties. Gloria Steinem[12] looks askance at the jumble of her younger adult self, seeing much of her past self as shallow or misguided or off-center, without appreciating how this shifting perspective was a developmental process. Germaine Greer[13] claims to have "sailed through" her forties. She believes she foundered on the rock of aging suddenly, at menopause, quite forgetting the previous psychological descent and reconstruction during her forties as she traced the steps of her father's life and the images and feelings which, hitherto, had been fragmented and ignored.[14] Gail Sheehy,[15] in admiring the force of women's "second adulthood," notes, but only in passing, the turmoil women in their forties suffer. She uses this turmoil as a point of comparison, to show how much better off women are once they pass fifty; she fails to see that it is an essential step toward that special phase of women's maturity she so eloquently embraces. This book attempts to fill the gap in accounts of development, and to trace the pivotal stage where women come into their own. Surprisingly, this phase, so commonly experienced, is difficult to capture. Having gone through it, women tend to forget the process. Just as a four-year-old has particular intolerance toward a younger child caught in the developmental stages she has recently passed through, so too, apparently, do some older women slight the developmental steps that were so exhausting, so exacting, and so necessary to their new-found self-confidence and self-certainty.

THERE IS A WELL-GUARDED secret about women in midlife that has just begun to come out. Both women and men, both psychologists and novelists, have noted an increase in energy and self-assertion among midlife women.[16] Once this surge of energy was thought to arise from the decrease of domestic burdens: At midlife women were often released from the demands of young children and, hence, had more time and energy for themselves. Yet today's women share no common timed events, except biological ones, which may be why menopause, in the absence of any other common marker, has such a high profile. The current generation is marked and challenged by the variety of its members, as those who, at 45, attend their children's college graduations or weddings, send invitations to friends of the same age who are nursing their infants. Even women whose children are grown face new extended parenting: Their children, through economic necessity, stay at home longer, or return home when jobs fail to be offered, or when income from jobs obtained cannot support an independent lifestyle. Moreover, family demands come from all angles: Children's independence sometimes makes way for demands of other relatives—either of aging, lonely parents, or partners in need of renewed attention and support. These demands often increase in midlife, as does a woman's wish to remain connected to an ever-widening network of friends and family. Today's midlife woman is *less* likely to be freed of family demands than was her mother, whose children left home at a specific time and found jobs and the financial wherewithal to be independent and whose own parents had shorter lives.

Women's lives, once thought to be routine, constrained, and predictable, are now understood to be so much more packed with variety than are men's lives that none of the models sociologists or psychologists have constructed to explain or describe men's life patterns work for women's. Whereas men often concentrate on one special role at a given phase of life, in a society which is structured to sustain the separate parts they play—as lover, as worker, as responsible father, women's roles—as mother, as wife, as daughter, as participants in economic and domestic and community production—fragment their attention. As Mary Catherine Bateson says, they "compose a life" from different themes; they must be opportunistic in developing these themes within varying contexts of time and place. Women's self-confidence, their aspirations, their personalities, and their work lives show far more change over the life course than do men's.[17] There is no doubt that women undergo developments in adulthood that men, on the whole, do not. Why? What triggers this development? How does it proceed? How does it succeed? What happens when it fails? These are questions answered by the women whose voices fill this book.

I T W A S T O A D D R E S S T H E S E questions that, in the winter of 1990, I began a research project on midlife women. Having recently completed a study of mothers and adolescent daughters, I remained puzzled by the ways in which mothers were often knocking over the psychological blocks that their daughters were putting in place. As adolescent girls were becoming more controlled, more circumspect, their mothers were often growing more impulsive, wickedly relishing a new spontaneity. Many mothers, too, I noted, were fired by anxiety about their own lives, and were taking apart the assumptions on which they were built. At the time I thought that this had something to do with the mother/adolescent relationship. Perhaps a mother, aware of a child's new capacity for independence, was exulting in freedom from the vigilance younger children required. I quickly saw that this account was inadequate, as I learned how watchful and caring parents remain of their adolescent children, whose independence often brings terror rather than relief. I wondered whether the mother might be trying, through example, to preserve aspects of her daughter's personality that she saw on the way out. Was she reverting to a childlike directness and literalness because she missed having it around? Was her anxious questioning of her own life a mimic-response to her adolescent daughter's challenges?

I shelved these questions at the time, but brought them back when I turned to the new project on the development of midlife women. What I saw was that women in their 40s, whether or not they had adolescent children, were exhibiting the more impulsive, willful behavior that I had thought was a response to adolescents; women in their 50s had, on the whole, cast aside that anxious challenging. Whereas the speech of younger midlife women is often hedged with queries and qualifications, that of women over 50 is like a direct flow, sometimes with the to-the-point humour that children display. They were more likely to speak their minds, to know their minds. I became more and more curious to see how this new directness was achieved, and to see more clearly what was happening.

As I "studied" midlife women, or worked out ways in which I might be drawn into their world, as participant and observer, as both anthropologist and native, I found two distinct and apparently contradictory things. I found the increased strength that other writers and psychologists had led me to expect. Their energy, and the eagerness with which their interests were engaged, revealed a thrilling, consoling self-confidence. Alongside this I heard something else, which nearly, but not quite, contradicted it. I heard hectic self-assessments, full of doubt and anxiety. I witnessed self-recrimination and self-correction. I heard resentment at the cruel costs exacted in both private and public features of their lives. I heard of defeat and confusion, of change and uncertainty. I heard about the frustration of compromise, of being constrained both from within and from without. I heard, in effect, the language of crisis and the language of conflict and, often, the language of anger. While men in midlife seem to "mellow," and welcome a new flexibility and new expressiveness, enjoying the fruits of their labors or finding compensations for past disappointments,[18] women have a much rougher passage into midlife. Like adolescents emerging into a new self, these midlife women were foraging among their pasts and presents to forge their futures. The pivot of development from anxiety and anger to liberation and energy was defined as women confronted the question: "Why did it take so long to trust myself?" The question could leave a woman bewildered: The people, the images, the models, the advice, the ideals she once trusted might, for a time, seem thoroughly untrustworthy. Posing this question could, for a time, leave her more bewildered, more angry, more anxious as she confronted wasted energy and wasted time. How, indeed, women asked themselves, could they have been constrained as they were, knowing what they did know, but what they somehow ignored? How could they have been guided by ideals that they must have known (they decided on reflection) were false constructions? How could they have foregone either a career or a family and pretended that the compromise did not hurt? How could they have been shadowed by their concern about what others thought, or how others judged them, knowing as they must have known (they decided upon reflection) that the approval they sought would never be gained—or, if gained, never fulfill the function they had imagined.

This query, "Why did it take so long to trust myself?", arises in the wake of a woman's special experience of conflict and compromise. She asks it not in a self-punishing or rhetorical manner, but as a genuine question about the course of her development. It takes time for patterns to emerge. The frustration so many parents feel as they discover they cannot "make their children listen" or "give lessons from their own experience," is a result of the simple human need to learn, some

important things at least, from one's own experience. The lesson that
one's own experience matters, that it provides the best line to truth, is
knowledge we are born with, and then taught to forget, and then learn
anew. Girls and women seem under particular pressure to abandon this
more direct line to knowledge. The archetypal coming-of-age book by
women, about girls growing into women, tells the story of a break between a girl's "innocent" relation to her knowledge and the pressure to
"not know," as Carol Gilligan says, "what she knows."[19]

The most striking coming-of-age books—books about a girl's passage into womanhood—have been written not by women in early
adulthood, newly freed of parental control, newly honed in literary
skill, newly proud of their passage; nor have they been written by
women in the strength of secured maturity. Instead, they have been
written by women at the brink of midlife, women who experienced a
girl's development into woman and who have also experienced the
adult consequences of those steps taken. They have had time to reflect
on the links between girl's suffering and women's psychology. Jamaica
Kincaid's *Annie John,* which charts the fissure between girlhood whole-
ness and adolescent fragmentation, was written—despite its youthful,
angry immediacy—when the author was 35—still too young, perhaps,
to imagine a resolution. Annie John, though outwardly "healed" at the
close of the novel, remains at internal impasse. She cannot, yet, envision an adulthood outside the constraints of social and maternal expectations.[20] Susanna Kaysen's *Girl, Interrupted,* which marks the split
between the clumsy and illiterate descriptions of her psyche by profes-
sionals and her own passionate experience of mental illness, was written when she was 44. It is only at midlife that she can catch the image
of a "young and distracted" girl, who was "looking out, looking for
someone who would see her."[21] Only now can she see through others'
descriptions of her to an abiding, valid reality. Michèle Roberts was 43
when *Daughters of the House* was published. Here, the tortuous course
of a young girl's development deletes memories of a language "Deeper
than English or French; not foreign; her own," which came as "the
underground stream that forced through her like a river, that rose and
danced inside her like the pulling jet of a fountain. . . ." As a teenager
and young woman she colludes with adults' denial of her own knowledge, until in midlife, she must make the journey again, stepping forward "into the darkness, to find words."[22] *Martha Quest,* written when

Doris Lessing was 44, brilliantly traces the link between a girl's loss of her own knowledge and idealization of a feminine future. Martha chatters in a voice she knows is "false" and becomes powerless as she loses touch with her own emotion. As "her childhood . . . said good-bye to her" she idealizes her "new" self and her "extraordinary" future, over which she has lost power.[23] In her nonfiction book *Wild Swans,* Jung Chang at 40 describes with startling simplicity the process that began when she was 12: "I was learning to live with contradictory thoughts and realities, and getting used to compartmentalizing them." As these contradictions are compartmentalized, she comes to embrace the ideals promulgated by her society: In the fast flow of doubt and emotion, she pledges herself to be the ideal woman in the society she pretends is itself ideal. For the more fragmented her knowledge is, the more attracted she is by an ideal of perfect integration. She experiences social control and cruelty, yet cannot trust her experience. Thus, she denies its reality and listens to voices outside her. These voices promise solutions. Believing those promises, she buries her own doubts. She does not unearth them until midlife, when "looking-back time" and a new tolerance for conflicting emotion allows her to judge anew, with her own eyes.[24]

The notable exception[25] to such coming-of-age plots is Sylvia Plath's *The Bell Jar.* Lacking the defenses of those women who waited until they were stronger before they embarked on their devastating exploration, Plath cannot envision a resolution between her individuality and the social experience of womanhood. As Plath's character Esther Greenwood scatters the pretty fashion clothes out the hotel window, resisting the "prize girl" persona, she finds herself empty—for what can replace the superficial lady others want to see? Buoyed by determination and intelligence, Esther forestalled psychic conflict to late adolescence. At this crossroads, however, her knowledge and her social experience cancel one another out, until she is left inside that vacuum of "the bell jar" in which she could not breathe. To prove herself sane, she must succumb to the control of the Other-Eye—or the view others have of her: "The eyes and the faces all turned themselves towards me, and guiding myself by them, as by a magic thread, I stepped into the room."[26] Recognizing those eyes as the ones that had looked at her "over white masks" during her terrifying electric shock "treatment," she accepts them as the authorities that must be placated if she is to pass into "normal" womanhood. Had Plath lived, she may have made a happier, more integrated passage through the crossroads of midlife.

G I R L S   A N D   W O M E N   F A C E   three significant danger points in their development. The first "meeting at the crossroads"[27] is at puberty. Under the influence of their sexual maturity, as they become aware of who holds power, as adults' unquestioning delight in their child's ways turns to new forms of control, their child's eye is blinkered by confusion and disappointment. The need to please, the terror of rejection, which all children feel from time to time, may harden in adolescence to images of perfection. Hence, adolescent girls are cramped by the desire to achieve the ideal form—both within and without. That tense perusal of face and figure teenage girls engage in, searching out one mirror after another for a better look or a more favorable pose, is not superficial: Through attention to their appearance girls are dealing with profound questions of what they must be to become a person others like and a person who feels "right" from within.

Adolescent resistance or rebellion is usually a girl's attempt to maintain contact with her own responses. Even as her thoughts and feelings and perceptions confuse her, she seeks recognition for them. Rather than change and deny her self, she tries to change others so that they will accommodate and appreciate, rather than deny or punish who she really is, who she is becoming.

These resisters may survive adolescence only to succumb at the next danger point: the passage into adulthood. While parents, teachers, and friends may have allowed the adolescent girl her own rough-edged self, the proximity to adulthood may unnerve her. At this second crossroads, pressures to be what she may not want to be again crowd her: She sees the need to make decisions and carve out paths in this adult world, yet she finds there is no pattern ready-made, and that her own inclinations may threaten relationships with both parents and lovers. The successful new woman portrayed by Bridget Fonda in the 1992 film *Single White Female* runs her own business, but is caught out by a dread of loneliness, which makes her the dupe of male deceit and female malice. At this second crossroads, goals and plans and ambitions often lose their once pristine outline. During this phase, as a woman steps out into the world outside the structure of school, college, and family, she often makes far more compromises on behalf of lovers, friends, siblings, or parents than she ever imagined she would.

Experiences of marriage or motherhood, and of the institutions that surround these relationships, form the third crossroads of a young woman's development. During the years between 25 and 40 the pressure of working out those ideals is felt in all its immediacy, as questions crowd in about marriage, maternity, work. Clashes between affiliative needs—to be closely, carefully involved in the emotional well-being of others—and expansive needs—to achieve, to meet challenges, to gain social recognition for skill and competence—create deep fissures in her life. She tries to heal them with a monumental determination, but often the wounds are left to gape beneath the thin skin of her control. Her own hopes and desires may now seem null and void. Her doubts and confusions may slip into a parallel universe. Dissociated from them, she may be "certain" that she can manage her woman's life, or change it, or "certain" that the compromises she makes are right. Hence, her "certainties" and her ideals can create pools that drown her doubts. These ideals may guide her until they are shattered by the crossroads at midlife, when she breathes new life into self-knowledge.

Dilemmas between independence and connection, work and family, cooperation and ambition, are not new. Each generation of women in this century has believed that it stood on the verge of breakthrough—a break away from constraining female images, and a liberation of a broader female humanity. This expectation was described in Mary McCarthy's 1963 novel *The Group,* which opens one week after Vassar Commencement, with a wedding, but a wedding that is special, different, as the couple forego a honeymoon and think about work. The different characters who form "the group" have very different lives in early adulthood—some of them married to men with good careers who support them, some of them married to men who have to be supported, some of them unmarried. All of the young women who form the group value their intelligence and see their education as a door to opportunity. But what they all discover, in various ways, is that after the dawn of early adulthood, they have become typical women: They are individuals, with individual worries and disappointments and triumphs and frustrations but they are enacting women's typical lot. They slot into typical feminine positions—as wife afraid of her husband, as mother terrorized by a child's needs, as wife demoralized by her husband's infidelity, as woman trapped within a confused sexuality. Education gave these women high self-esteem, high ideals, and high goals. As they set out to fulfill their potential, however, they found themselves repeating old patterns. The novel ends with a funeral of the woman who, in the opening scene, was married. There is nothing special about this funeral: It is a "regular burial in the ground." A decade on, these once eager women are now ready to bury the expectation that they can, in their society, be the individuals they had set out to be.[28]

Mary McCarthy's grim narrative, however, leaves her characters when they are in their thirties. The story stops short of women's midlife, the precise point at which past impasses are most likely to be resolved through a crisis. With more experience, more knowledge, and fewer attempts to control their voice and vision, more women can amass the resources to forge their own lives, and to live through their own experience. As Carolyn Heilbrun points out in *Writing a Woman's Life,* authors as varied as Dorothy Sayers and Virginia Woolf created new and distinctive styles in their forties and fifties; with their midlife vision, they wrote about women in new ways, knowing that as midlife women they had to construct new stories as they followed those secret paths to their own strength.

The women who are now in midlife were not in their youth mere dupes of others' whims and wishes; they were far more self-aware and self-determined than previous generations of women, who were more cruelly hedged in by constraints of law, education, and economy. The women who are now in midlife have been more active in fashioning their goals and their identity than any other generation. This splendidly noisy generation of women, ruthlessly critical and deliberate, nevertheless described themselves as having suffered the influence of false ideals. Even those who, from without, appeared fully self-determined, admit in midlife that they had been shadowed by false voices and images. Gloria Steinem describes how, even as a mature woman, even after nearly two decades of feminist activity, she disguised her real self in order to inspire the love of man. Germaine Greer admits that she was highly conscious of and concerned about her appearance, even as an outspoken feminist. Angela Davis has recently reflected that even radical young women in the 1970s sought power through men rather than obtaining it directly themselves; they turned to men, Angela

Davis now realizes, for approval and strength. Midlife development is the process whereby borrowed voices are returned and idealizations shattered.[29]

Ideals have power because they are not simply, not thoroughly false. During certain developmental phases they are necessary: we use them as crutches in infancy and craft knives in adolescence. They support us when we have not yet established an internal world, and they draw vivid pictures of futures we may not be ready to envision.

We are not born with idealized images of others. We learn them, painfully, through belief in our own inadequacy. Babies are thought to develop ideals of the mother or father who cares for them.[30] Powerless themselves, they endow people upon whom they depend with ultimate strength and knowledge. As babies enter the social world of childhood they still borrow from this bank of idealization: A parent belongs to the child, becomes part of the child, who then feels strong through her association with this larger-than-life figure. In middle childhood, however, there seems to be a remarkable window in development, wherein ideals are not needed. A child now registers an inconsistent, imperfect human world. Children accept their own ragged feelings, the mood swings of others, the vast changes in the emotional weather, as part of real life. They observe in order to learn, and they learn from what they observe.[31]

At adolescence, however, idealization regains an important role in development. Parents are loved as deeply as ever, but they come to have more definite boundaries, and more specific "faults." Their inconsistencies become extremely annoying. They do not fill the child's psychological world in the way they once did. Instead, the adolescent feels a new self emerging within her. As this self is fluid, unshapen, but enormously precious, its owner seeks new images, new ideal forms. Now, as she observes the imperfections of the human world, she wants to distance the brand-new self from them. She will be different, better, perfect—but how? She seeks a variety of images, promises, hopes on which to model herself. She desires new, very strong ideals to direct her development. But her need for such ideals is double-edged: These new ideals will offer some strength and comfort, as they did in very early childhood; but they also may fill her with doubt and dread as she sees how far she falls from their standard.

In adolescence, too, girls develop a searing self-consciousness through which they are aware of how they "look"—how others see them, how they might be defined and criticized.[32] They long for a perfection that will protect them from rejection. But how can they achieve it? As they struggle with their own confusion, they seek answers in others, burying the acceptance they had as children of a human world that is edgy, uneven, and volatile.

Enmeshed in the contradictory visions of her future, a young adolescent girl posed this question to the psychologists who had been interviewing her: ". . . is there such a thing as a person who is not necessarily perfect but who has everything together all the time?" Lyn Mikel Brown and Carol Gilligan describe the eerie silence that settled over the room as the girls and women present pondered the speaker's question. Their imaginations stung with the effort of envisioning some person who from the outside can be likable and attractive, and who matches up this outward beauty with a wonderful inner self, who finds that "magical spot" where everything comes together. Layering this question with a kind of dread, is another query: "if the long journey did not end with perfection, what was all this expended energy about and for whose benefit?"[33] As a midlife woman dismantles the false structure this adolescent girl was trying to maintain—as she frees herself from the ideals that the adolescent girl takes on board to carry her to adulthood—she asks this question in a different guise: How can I continue my journey knowing that the map that I have used for so long is not right? The routes different women take through this impasse are traced in this book. Sustained by their determination, guided by the skills they have acquired through long-term confrontations with old and new concepts of womanhood, they find their way to a new midlife in which they make use of the positive changes in this social revolution of women.

Yet the beginning of the journey is difficult. The impact of this initial question—How can I continue my journey knowing that the map I have used for so long is not right?—may arouse so much anxiety that a woman tries to brush it aside. The "devil she knows" may be preferable to admitting how much needs to change. She may wish to retreat to an earlier phase at which her energy and emotions, though not satisfactory, were comfortable in their familiarity. She might resist the challenge of development, and chug along in the old way. Usually, however, women move forward. A new directness and literalness was apparent in the language of the women I studied. There was less "second guessing," fewer qualifications and modification and redescriptions of things said. There was a shift from a role personality—in which they spoke of themselves as mothers, daughters, partners, employers, colleagues—to a subjectively centered personality, in which they spoke about how things felt and how things seemed to them. The balance of identity changed from "This is how I would be described objectively in terms of my position, achievements, and connections" to "Here is a gathering of my thoughts, feelings, and perceptions." When this developmental crisis was successfully negotiated, when they were able to balance their lives so as to fit in with their newly assembled self, there was an enormous gain in power, and a reduction of envy, guilt, and anxiety.

The successful outcome of this developmental phase can be seen as a normal parallel to a cure for multiple personality disorder. In this disorder, whose sufferers are predominantly women, defenses against trauma and pain are constructed by the mind so that certain things that are known and remembered are split off from the "host personality"—or that personality that is closest to being normal and most closely linked with current relationships and activities. The woman who, as a child, suffered some intolerable experience (usually sexual abuse) for which no validation or comfort was provided by the adults around her blocks this pain, humiliation, and terror from consciousness. So intolerable is this part of herself that she cannot acknowledge it. Yet so powerful is this silenced body of youthful torment, that it will not be denied. Hence, a separate "self" is constructed, holding forth in someone else's voice, with a different posture, different handwriting, a different history, a timeless future. Where two personalities exist, more are likely to emerge, all unknown to the host personality, all knowing well what the host personality denies, all highly critical of that unknowing host. Herein is many women's psychological drama writ large. Here, in exaggerated, pathological form, can be seen the contradictions and pressures many normal, healthy women experience, as, in meeting demands and expectations that are blatantly inconsistent, a wedge is drawn between their capacity to meet or even acknowledge their own needs, and a coffer of anxieties about what they as women need to be. The fear of not pleasing a mother, of disappointing a father, of harming a child, of losing a partner's love or approval, of failing to advance professionally, can put a wedge between the real and all those ideals. Guilt and doubt build barriers between layers and aspects of the self. So, even as women make decisions and choices, they often feel shadowed by half-seen ghosts, who hang about them, so their footsteps drag and each step forward drains their energy.

This "dissociated" self, this self with its fissures, is healed not by denying the multiple voices, but by silencing their disruptive, punitive aspects, by ending the wars between different "selves," by breaking down barriers so that each "self" has access to the others. Hence, the self becomes integrated and empowered rather than anxious and defensive in its layered diversity.

In general, men do not have to do this midlife reconstruction. They seem much better at partitioning different aspects of themselves; they seem less driven by needs for integration of the various parts of the self; they also live in a society that is better adapted to meeting their different needs—for love and work and rest and play—so that men's different needs, unlike those of women, are less likely to become conflicting needs. Throughout their lives girls and women are likely to feel the pull between pleasing themselves and pleasing others, between working and loving, between private leisure and communal participation. After the construction work of midlife, women devote the energy they once directed towards meeting idealized expectations to managing their own needs and desires. With far less of that second-guessing and those second thoughts, a woman has a more direct line between wish and action, perception and judgment. If this midlife development is not achieved, then a woman in her fifties becomes increasingly rigid in her defenses against change and growth. She may try to deny the reality of her age, or the difference age makes, or leap from one preassigned script to another. Still mimicking the vamp, or the earth mother, or the superwoman, she becomes a caricature of these ideals, using more and more energy to keep her knowledge and emotion at bay. Like the character portrayed by Shirley Maclaine in the film *Postcards from the Edge,* who is trapped within her fear of aging, such women seek out ways of "beating age" and try to become exceptions to the human plot. When psychological growth cannot be accomplished, defenses are marshalled against change. Such women may become more rigid in their ideals—of beauty, of love, of matriarchy, or of feminine perfection in any other of its many guises. And while some of these defenses remain to some extent within most women, they are, in most women, dwarfed by new growth. For women are now entering a new midlife, determined to engage creatively with new opportunities, and to forge success on their own terms.

THE RESEARCH FOR THIS BOOK involved interviews and observations of 80 women. The sample of women was, at it clearly had to be, mixed. Roughly sixty-five percent were American and thirty-five percent were from Britain. Sixty-five percent of the women were in their 40s, and thirty-five percent were between 50 and 55. Among the American women, fifteen were from Northern California, fourteen were from Southern California, five were from rural Illinois or Wisconsin, ten were from East Coast cities, and eight were from small cities, mostly in Michigan. Of the Northern California women, five were African-American, two were Hispanic, two were Chinese American, and six were Caucasian. The women in England were based in the Cambridge, London, and Manchester areas; two were Japanese, two were Scandinavian, one was Indian, the rest were British. The economic standing of the participants varied widely. I have used fictional names for all the women in my study, and though I have tried to match these fictional names with the ethnic origins of the actual women, I have changed any details that might identify them. We worked collaboratively to construct their stories; but if the description I give in this book does not fit theirs, then they should be protected from the outrage of my written truth claiming more legitimacy than their felt truth.

I contacted the American women through alumni lists and employment lists of two state universities; from the personnel department of a computer company, which provided names both of midlife women who were currently working for them and midlife women who had recently left them; from a community college, which held evening classes and kept lists not only of people who had enrolled in evening classes but also of people who had made enquiries but not enrolled. In Britain, local job centers referred me to various retraining courses through which I was able to distribute a questionnaire, which was really just a means of finding out who would be willing to talk to me further. Several colleges in England and the United States permitted me to approach their older students in a number of ways. Though they were reluctant to supply me with class lists, I was offered access through informal meetings and the distribution of questionnaires.

Different women were approached for different aspects of my study: I needed in my sample some women who were in the process of divorce, some women who were single, some women who had very young children and some whose children were grown. To a great extent this happened naturally—but I sometimes had to take definite steps to redress an imbalance.

I began with a simple interview, which was arranged to last about two hours, but which frequently went on for longer. It was always agreed ahead of time that the interviewee could end the session at any time she wished—but this never happened. There were certain things I wanted to get from each woman—age, age of children (if any), marital status, sexual orientation, brief employment and education history— but from then on the discussion and questions were led by the women's own cues. For some of these women, discussions about the problems of aging were crucial, and for others they were peripheral. There is nothing more boring for a respondent than to be asked a series of questions in which she has no interest, and she may well be disappointed or even insulted when she is cut off or cut short on issues that have an emotive impact for her. The great problem an interviewer has in such circumstances is to obtain from each respondent information that can in some way be compared to other women's responses, yet to avoid a blueprint, a definitive set of questions, because that would prevent exploration of individual leads. In a study like this, which does not begin with a theory to confirm or refute, but whose purpose is to form a theory about development, the interviewer must allow herself to be led by and learn from her respondents. The researcher becomes an interpreter of voices, rather than a tester of hypotheses.

After the first interview session, I arranged two or three days during which I could shadow a woman through her ordinary routines. Questions and explorations often continued during the observation sessions. However important self-reports are, they do not provide the full story. Not only does different information come up at different times, under different circumstances, and in the context of different moods, but also small, passing responses to current events can be as enlightening and revealing as considered reflection. These shadow days were not always chosen at random. The first interview sometimes indicated where more information would be most useful. For women who were going back to school, I wanted to compare descriptions of their domestic life in the early stages of college, with those a year later. I sometimes sought debriefing sessions, so that after watching a woman at work, or in a business meeting, or caring for an elderly parent, or having lunch with a son and daughter-in-law, or meeting an estranged spouse, I could listen to her interpretation of the events I witnessed, and match these to the more generalized accounts she had given in the interview. For women who had suffered some setback or loss, I sought both observation days and interviews at two-month intervals during the course of fifty months. For the other women, I "checked in" at three-month intervals, sometimes in person, sometimes (less satisfactorily) by telephone, again over a period of fifty months. I met at least four times with all the women discussed in this project.

In social psychology there is a term, "saturation," which is supposed to indicate the point at which the researcher has enough information. It is a friendly term, suggesting that the researcher is replete with data; but it is also slippery term, persuading one to slide a little too readily into simplicity. Saturation is reached when further research offers no more surprises, when everything that the researcher is hearing from one subject has already been heard from another, when everything heard can be quickly slotted into a preestablished category.

I have not reached saturation. I always hear something new. Looking at photographs of mature women in a special exhibition at the Cambridge Dark Room, I was struck by the marked differences in each face. Women of the same age seemed steeped in different time scales. Women's eyes expressed different knowledge, and each mouth revealed different expectations. Yet these very differences signaled a similar line of development, for each had attained an individuality in conflict with a society that still offers sparse and spare images of midlife women, which still puts constraints on women's speech, which still slips scripts into their hands, making it particularly difficult to speak their own lines.

What these women had in common was a challenge presented by the social conditions that they experienced as children, and the changed conditions in which they had become adults. Along with increased expectations and increased good health, they experienced new conflict and new crises. The self-responsibility that emerged in midlife as they were liberated from former fears and influences wielded its own terror. With no maps for this new age, each woman had to create a new self and a new future. The hard labor of construction lay on one path, the tedium and stagnation of depression lay on the other. Most women were eager to take the first path.

But is this journey of interest only to women? Soon after this book was under way, I was buttonholed by a male professor at a college meeting about the nature and purpose of my work. How would I collect information on such a wide subject? What was my subject, anyway? What answers did I expect? What indeed were my questions? But before I could answer, he launched into his own narrative about a mother whose remarkable youthful achievements had been cast aside at her marriage, who had been happy in marriage, and who would have described herself as content, but whose frustration burned into his childhood memories; of a sister fiercely at odds with her mother but driven to fulfill herself the mother's fractured goals; of a daughter who puzzled him with a midlife serenity, when love and marriage had suddenly waylaid her hectic career. His aggressive curiosity now signaled passionate interest rather than dismissal. His hope was to discover the story behind the female dramas of which he had been a sympathetic but helpless and confused witness. I caught sight of a new figure in the pattern of women's lives, which in my bias I had omitted. For a woman's story involves the sons and the brothers, the husbands and the fathers. They, too, are caught by the puzzle of what it means to be a woman in our world. Men, as well as women, are awaiting better answers to this question.

AMONG MY SAMPLE OF 80 women, between the ages of 39 and 55, I found four types of midlife women. These types, which I define in subsequent chapters, were linked to past decisions, to definitions and assessments of power, and to female ideology—ideas about what a woman is, what a woman should be, and how being female affects each woman's life. The first group comprised 18 of the 80 women in my sample. These women, who came closest to the dominant ideology of previous generations, I call *traditional*, in that they stayed within the conventional feminine framework, viewing themselves in their family roles—as, for instance, mothers, wives, or daughters. As they shifted from seeing themselves first and foremost in terms of their relationships to others, to viewing themselves as mature women responsible for the courses of their own futures, they addressed questions of past compromises and neglected potential. Though their daily lives were structured by the same roles their mothers had taken, they were aware of living in changed times: The life patterns that seemed inevitable to their mothers were not so for them. They felt both anxious and liberated as they stepped beyond the bounds of habitual roles.

The second group, which I call *innovative,* consisted of 24 women. These were women who deliberately set out to be new career women, to pioneer in a man's world. They felt traditional women's roles were threatening: Even though most of them did marry or have children, they worked hard to transform the patterns of marriage and maternity. Many innovative women entered adulthood with a very strong sense of direction; they modeled themselves on the career man, thinking this model would serve them well, but found ultimately that the costs of keeping to the rules of career success—such as making competitive moves and keeping one's eye on the next rung of the career ladder—were too great. At midlife, they often assess the work they have done on themselves to sustain the positions so eagerly sought.

Innovative and traditional women, who continue to work within the general framework of their pasts, can be distinguished from *expansive* women, who are determined to break with the narrow grooves of their pasts, who feel constrained by lack of skill or education, and who takes steps to expand their horizons. These women—18 in my sample of 80—deliberately form new goals. Some expansive women decide to go back to school, or to work, or to qualify for new types of work. Some construe goals spiritually, and turn with new or renewed vigor to a religion. Some expansive women turn a hobby into a vocation, becoming the poet or artist they always wanted to be. Expansive women tend to keep a careful watch on themselves, suspicious of "lapses" into former patterns of behavior and response. They believe they must change, radically, to be the person they want to become, and so guard against any return to old habits. In many respects these women are doing deliberately and consciously what most women are aiming at, though more discreetly. Some of these women at midlife describe themselves as "having lived in a dream world," others describe themselves as "always looking over [their] shoulder, waiting for a nod of approval," and others describe themselves as "blind to my own needs" or "doing everything in the name of love." "It takes years to get smart," one woman remarked. These women tend to be aggressive in the pursuit of self-interest because they feel they have to make up for lost time. Having finally gripped a sane perspective, they steel themselves against distraction and deviation. For expansive women, control is an important aspect of power because they judge themselves to have previously been out of control. They feel they have been easily and excessively influenced by values and needs and expectations, which are in fact not their own.

I have also classified as "expansive" women who experience upheaval from without, facing external changes, which force them to break with past patterns—women, for example, who experience divorce at midlife, and suddenly realize that their outlook has been too narrow, and that they must change radically to adapt to new circumstances.

The final group of midlife women I could distinguish in my sample displayed enormous eruptions of energy but no specific direction. These women—13 in my sample—I call *protestors* because of their protest at midlife's approach. They were impulsive and enthusiastic, but their impulses and enthusiasms had been curtailed by a premature adulthood. These women, in late adolescence, had faced responsibilities that constrained their first decades of adulthood. Either an early pregnancy or disempowered parents had forced them, prematurely, to assume the exacting responsibilities that can drain a woman at any age. At midlife they sought ways of reaching back to develop the spontaneity and adventurousness they had been forced to leave behind. They were like women calling out their own names, confident that there could be a brilliant response to their call, if only they could mouth the right words. Several of these women spoke about a "parallel self," which had been constrained before reaching maturity. These women, having made contact with that parallel self, experienced an exuberance and power, and daily relished their release from past fears.

WHILE I HAVE GROUPED women into these four categories, it is important to stress that women shared common themes. No rigid boundaries separate women in one group from women in another. Women who have stuck to traditional female roles in the home are still members of the generation of the new women, and few have followed the traditional patterns in the stark ways their mothers might have. An innovative or protesting woman, forward-looking and eager to "write" herself a powerful and original future, may suffer a setback in her emotional or financial conditions, which pares down possibilities and ushers in a period of diffusion, before a new, modified, innovative style can be established. Some women who had followed conventional female life patterns became, in midlife, either innovative or expansive. Many women had something of the protester in them, whatever their life pattern: Many felt that, for too long, a spontaneity had been suppressed, regarded as dangerous to others for whom they felt responsible. All these categories have low walls and flexible boundaries.

Throughout adulthood women are interested in trade-offs, and the conflict between old and new ideals of femininity. In the course of my study I discovered that women in the new midlife follow a pattern: At about 40 their perception of trade-offs was likely to change from seeing them imposed by external force, to seeing their lives as shaped by a series of inner decisions. These decisions were made not between the good and the bad, the real and the false, but between competing values— good career decisions may be poor decisions at home, good decisions made on behalf of a partner may be bad for a child, good decisions for a family may be a poor decision for them personally. The challenge was to deal with conflicting values without cancelling everything out. They sorted and sifted according to the following principles.

They spoke first and foremost about *power, effectiveness,* and *influence* versus *impotence, uselessness,* or *insignificance.* Their sense of power involved being heard, having a say, being able to make a point or make a difference, knowing that their views, opinions, or feelings mattered. When they spoke about power to do something, the emphasis was on the power to act without being distracted, or power to develop their talents. Power implied not power over others, but the ability to act without inhibition or interference; it did not mean overriding others' opinions or needs, but being able to put weight on one's own. As women referred to these issues, they expressed a wish to be considered sufficiently valuable to be able to make a contribution. This was crucial to their self-esteem, which they insisted could not be attained in isolation. It was "a social thing," an "interpersonal affair," not something "you can go to work on in an armchair," not something "you can sort out by yourself," but a state attained by "living as yourself in the world."

They spoke about control, too, but this was distinguished from power. Control meant self-control, which primarily involved the ability to make choices they were happy with. They did not have control over other people's demands or expectations of them, and they often felt they did not have control over their own responses to other people; but they could gain control by having some ability to bring their judgment to bear on their decisions, and to have a grasp of priorities.

They also saw control in terms of their ability to understand and gauge their effect on others. They felt out of control when other people responded to them unpredictably. They were not aiming towards control over others but having some ability to read other people. Control involved knowledge of how the world worked and how they fit into it.

Women in the new midlife spoke, too, about *attachment, responsiveness, commitment,* and *connection* versus *isolation* and *loneliness.* They seemed clear-sighted about the costs of attachment as well as its benefits, which for most of them were as necessary as the air they breathed. They spoke about achievement, reward, and acknowledgment versus anonymity and invisibility. Lack of achievement splintered into issues of power: When a woman judged herself to have achieved very little, she was likely to describe herself as "slow to speak up" or "left out of the real world." Some women dismissed what they had achieved, insisting that what they had done "didn't count" or "didn't amount to anything" or "didn't matter," either because they felt their achievements were unrecognized by society, or because they felt they had not done what they had really wanted to do, but instead been too strongly influenced by others' expectations of what they *should* do. The challenge in midlife became one of finding a way to meet one's own "real needs."

Women spoke about *movement, direction,* and *freedom* versus *confinement* and *stagnation,* which was linked to imprisonment—"being stuck" or "confined" or "hemmed in." The ability to grow and to change, to seek out new directions and follow where their own interests led them, constituted their concept of freedom (and what was frequently referred to as "bliss" or "heaven"), but virtually every woman insisted that her freedom was limited and was likely to remain so. Only one proved an exception, declaring that now she was going to do just as she wanted, and at the same time, she acknowledged the she would "have to grow old with the consequences of [her] own selfishness."

Midlife women spoke about *useful energy or time,* versus *wasted energy or time,* about *acceptance* and *hope* versus *anger* and *regret,* and about *balance* versus *bias* and *clear sight* versus *distortion.* This last cluster underwent many fluctuations, as time first marked "wasted" was later redefined into something that was "necessary" or "worthwhile" or "not lasting all that long anyway." Criticism of her past, or regret, could be salvaged by acknowledging the values on which past compromises had been based. Though they spoke, too, about *stress* versus *sanity,* they saw stress as something that had to be tolerated, rather than overcome. Stress arose when a woman lost her "priority list" and was unable "to make spot decisions between various demands." Stress then was the effect of being unable to make choices between competing demands.

These were the issues that emerged as the crisis was in progress. Such stresses had, women said, been "long-term friends," but had recently begun to nag in new ways. As the ideal of a perfect solution or the pressure of others' (sometimes imagined) expectations unraveled, these compromises were more noticeable. As women scrutinized their compromises, they bombarded themselves with criticism. Here, the process of development felt like a catastrophe, a breaking down of all defenses. But the criticisms could only be answered if fundamental psychological fixtures were rearranged, and ideals or the ideas of others no longer sustained control. This painful phase of crisis involved holding onto many negative feelings. The strength to hold and attend to these painful thoughts came from the experience of many previous years' questioning and conflict. The pride gained from past experience led to hope for a new time in a woman's life. This hope led to determination, and the determination led to the realization of a new midlife. This process—from catastrophe to reconstruction—is not an inevitable or predetermined developmental pattern. It is not like the unfolding of a flower, wherein the different phases are preprogrammed. Instead, it involves effort, the overcoming of a natural resistance, and the maintenance of new inner structures. For some women, this process is clearly marked and clearly felt; for others, the effort is like a background hum, noticed most in the thrilling silence that follows. But each woman in my study who emerged into the new midlife emerged through a crisis. This crisis was a phase during which the previous order of her thoughts and priorities and aims was disturbed. It was a phase during which old certainties about who she was, who she wanted to be, and who she should be were subjected to doubt, and thoughts previously silenced were heard—and then answered. These women emerged on the far side of crisis with new skills to address both their doubts and their certainties.

A MINORITY OF WOMEN —seven in my sample of 80—had particular trouble on this journey. In Chapter 7, *Women Who Cannot Find the Way Ahead*, I describe how even the best efforts to grow may be thwarted. Development is an uncertain process, and there are many impediments to it. Some of these impediments are external—our society has many points of injustice, which pinch some far more sharply than others. The backbone of any woman's crisis can be crushed by an unjust social reality, which forces her to "dance" to a meaningless tune. How, after all, can women engage in that essential midlife construction when they have nothing to build with? The second chances that midlife can offer are not assured. We cannot always build our lives according to our talents or our inalienable rights. Some lives are crushed by circumstances, wherein the language of crisis recurs endlessly, and resolution comes not through power but a realization of helplessness. Women who face poverty, face a special set of challenges and questions. For this reason, Marcia Downes was originally reluctant to talk to me. She leaned against the doorjamb of her apartment and demanded why she should waste her time "talking to some fancy feminist." Taken aback, I murmured something about "important decisions in your life." Her face lit up, and I began to smile, thinking I had made some headway, until a stream of derisive laughter filled the hall. Even the ensuing silence was thick with mockery.

"De-cisions, girl! What kind of decisions do you think I made to hoist myself all the way up here? Food stamps stop and Medicaid goes on holiday and welfare keeps changing its dance steps, and I'm here de-ciding how to run my life. Is that it?" Her hand was on her hip and she wagged her head from side to side as she spoke; but as she delivered her final question, she thrust her face forward and took a good look at me. Whether my confusion amused her or aroused her sympathy, she stood aside, admitting me to her home. "You just sit yourself down, college lady, and I'll give you some education."

Her message was loud and clear: Poor women were different from women with money. Poverty formed a class of its own. It was poverty—not race, religion, or class—that made some women's lives differ from the trends I found in the majority of my sample.[34] When you were poor the framework of decisions changed. You were at others' mercy. You felt powerless when you simply could not afford medical treatment for a child. You had to quit your job and look after your mother if the hospital released her before she could manage on her own.[35] You spent "all your arithmetical know how" figuring out how a job would jeopardize welfare payments[36] but constantly looking for work and taking "whatever anyone will give you." There is "no way," Marcia declared, "a woman who gets poor can get un-poor by herself."

The frameworks of choice and power, which "un-poor" women can use, simply do not function among the poor, the hungry, and the homeless. Women have been hit directly and disproportionately by the policies of past governments and by the continuing economic stagnation. The fact that so many women are by themselves, running a family by themselves, supporting and disciplining children by themselves, throws a burden on them that eclipses their choices and reduces the likelihood that their energy will be effective. Wealth was by no means necessary to the midlife growth of the women in my sample, but some distance from absolute poverty was essential in the acquisition of personal power.

THE BROAD SWEEP OF change that most women experienced also resulted in, or demanded changes in crucial relationships. As I show in Chapters 8 and 9, development was often tagged to shifts in the place love and sex took in women's lives. Such disturbance in relationships may cast up new problems and new decisions about personal influence and power: When a partner resists her midlife change, does a woman then resist him, or comply, or compromise? Some women, for instance, who underwent positive change in midlife had to leave behind relationships that were too inflexible to allow them to be what they had now become. Hence, change itself gave rise to further questions, which often gave rise to further change. During this phase, too, there was marked movement in a woman's relationship with her own parents. These passionately experienced attachments have been seen as central to the development of young people, but their growth in maturity has largely been overlooked.

In the last chapter of this book, I write about women's friendships, because in midlife friends play an important role; they often provide that counterculture women must establish to sustain their pride in midlife. The strength and energy of midlife women is remarkable—and it has repeatedly been remarked upon. Carolyn Heilbrun notes that few women in midlife suffer the burnout that men commonly experience;[37] instead, they are ready to regroup, and advance. As women's lives become even more varied, as their aims and needs resist the confinement of imposed roles, a new culture binds them together. Instead of jostling other women to gain power through men, women may be learning how to develop their power together. If this image-breaking generation is to leave a legacy for their daughters, it must join forces with others who support and fortify women's futures. Many women discovered the euphoria of female friendships at the same time they discovered a midlife strength. This "support network" promised to be the lifeline for the future. As the differences among different women accelerate, and different women learn from one another, it will no longer be possible for anyone else to define women's place, or women's estate. Then, the self-creations achieved in midlife will have more than a life-time's guarantee. What midlife women of this generation require is that their developmental paths not be forgotten, and that the individual work they do for themselves become part of a new culture of midlife growth.

Redefining Beauty and Reclaiming Power

1

When people refer to midlife as the prime of a woman's life, they are employing a tactic well known to the ancient Greeks, who referred to the ocean—to which they had to entrust their lives when they traveled—as "kindly." Such a description is not always false: Sometimes the ocean waters were kind, and carried people safely and speedily to their destination. But the ocean's behavior is unpredictable and uncontrollable. Many people who entrust their lives to it are killed. Its ruthless power inspires a kind of respect: It is what is it, whatever we want it to be.

In describing the ocean as "kindly," the Greeks were giving it a "propitiatory title." They hoped that language would flatter and persuade the thing it described to behave according to its description. The sea just might be cajoled into being kindly because it was so named. What was, in fact, uncontrollable just might be jollied along by positive thinking. The optimistic description sees only the best, and declares the best description to be the most accurate. The propitiatory title aims for appeasement rather than accuracy.

This way with words persists in our culture. Contemporary praise of midlife as "prime time"[1] or "choice years"[2] appeals to the power of positive thinking. Many magazine and newspaper editors have jumped on this bandwagon. Aware of the growing numbers of midlife women whom they must address, many try to supply bright shining images of today's midlife woman. These new popular images tend to be excessively optimistic. The journal and newspaper articles and features, which acknowledge that now women are reaching middle age with more health, confidence, and energy than in previous generations, tend to have a "Hurrah" attitude: This is prime time; you can look and feel as good as you did at 20; here are examples of women who achieved starry success after 40. These articles are like cheerleaders, supplying something between a tonic and a taunt: Here are examples of midlife glamor; if they can achieve it, so can you.[3] But, as midlife women are praised for their appearance and their youthfulness, the assumption that they are worthy of interest and attention because they are "still attractive" or "still young" remains intact.

The idea of midlife has, previously, been so frightening because society prizes female youth and beauty, and is often blind to the self-confidence and power women attain in midlife. Many attempts to reassure women about their appearance in the new midlife reveal imbedded cultural prejudices against this midlife growth. Many "upbeat" messages seem to offer hope, yet in the language of despair. When women are assured that they can still be attractive in midlife, that peculiar rider "still" implies that attractiveness is an unexpected remnant. Furthermore, the suggestion persists that to be attractive, to be of interest to others, a woman has to compete with younger women, and pretty much on a younger woman's terms. The implication that physical signs of aging are flaws to be mastered remains unchallenged by many allegedly positive messages. Through willpower, women are expected to conquer age. They are encouraged to grip youth between their teeth, and throttle signs of change. The language of the pep talk ignores women's ripeness for change, and denies that they will gain from these changes. Yet, in my sample, women were forward-looking, eager to take charge of their lives in new ways. The steps taken toward gaining power over their image were essential to midlife growth. Since the women in my sample had, throughout adolescence and adulthood, become increasingly aware of the influence cultural images have on women, they were able to confront these conflicting images as no previous generation *en masse* has been able to do. The skills they developed play an important role in their new midlife.

The cult of youth pervades many attempts to manage aging. Midlife, especially for women, continues to be seen in terms of loss. The developmental task of the midlife woman is still conceived as adjustment to loss. Even writers highly sympathetic to woman can reveal rigid prejudices of midlife experience. The midlife woman must let go of her children.[4] She must let go of her youth.[5] She must let go of her sexuality.[6] She must let go of her appearance.[7] In a tepidly positive light, she is seen as free to do just as she pleases, because no one needs her, sees her, or cares for her.[8]

In grim resistance to these expectations and images, contemporary women, at about 40, begin to challenge anew the social construction of their identity. In their new midlife, they cast aside negative images of the maturing woman. As they embrace more fluid, flexible, and feisty images, they free themselves from a whole range of ideals that often, in previous times of their lives, have nibbled away at their energy and gnawed at their nerves. As they conquer the doubts and distractions of others' views, they are ready to resolve further conflicts as they arose in their midlife crisis.

IN MANY WAYS, I am the worst person to write about middle age. From the very beginning of my awareness that this person who was "me" would grow older, the prospect brought no eagerness, only dread. At some prehistory of the self, as I was attempting to adapt to a grotesquely conceived future, I plotted my escape from aging. The simple solution I came to was that when I discovered my first grey hair, I would pull it out and then kill myself. I imagined how I would lie, on the carpet of my childhood bedroom where this chill thought found me. I would be discovered, dead, before anyone could disclose the evil secret of my maturity.

I cannot date this bizarre fantasy. There are no signs to help me— no coinciding memories of toys, or wallpaper, or events to mark a before or after of that grim "decision." But I recall the air of petulance. The isolation in which these thoughts arose must have been due to some punishment, which most frequently occurred when, at nine and ten, I was declared to be "so difficult [I] might as well be a teenager."

Why should a single grey hair have triggered my child's imagination in this unwholesome way? Beauty and the attractiveness of youth never featured strongly in my family's value system. My mother noticed her grey hairs, but only in passing, and did not bother to dye them. I think what I found abhorrent, and indeed unthinkable, was the notion of change as decay. For a child, change is growth, advancement. I felt loved as a developing child in whom every action, gesture, and expression was seen as an indication of future worth. For my parents, I felt, my worth was in my future. It was my future in which their hopes would be realized, and which made sense of their present investments. Even my sister's love for me hinged on my youth. I was sometimes adored, and generally tolerated, because I was yet unformed, and uninformed of maturity. I could not conceive of a self, or rather of my self—for I never found age or any of its manifest signs distasteful in other people—separate from my position as young, indeed as the youngest. What I had learned to value was potential, and youth was blessed with a hoard of potential in contrast to the miserly nuggets of realized achievement. Folded up in one of those unguessed drawers of a child's mind lay an unexamined contradiction: Promise held immense value, which no realization of that promise could match. Here was one of those subconscious burdens that many girls carry as they move toward womanhood.

Adulthood eclipsed promise, replaced it with some tasteless substance called reality. But, like most young people, youth seemed my proper possession, a permanent part of my identity, and hence my little suicide scenario barely disturbed me. It was a rapid conclusion drawn up to deal with a possibility I happened to envision rather than the solution to a problem I truly believed I would one day face.

TUCKED NEATLY AWAY DURING adolescence, the impasse of my imagination ceased to trouble me. As I did age, I was more concerned with other things, with specific demands and compromises, with managing the moment, and reducing the costs. When I did contemplate "getting older" as an adult, I was more impressed by aging's slowness than its speed. At 30, I was amazed by how young I still was, and at 40, when I knew I had unwittingly slid into a different phase and a somewhat different identity, I did not experience any loss. Having never had beauty in my possession, the loss of youthful attractions made no significant impact on me. Yet it was in these terms—"still young," "not much lost"—that I conceived aging. I grew accustomed to thinking that my students were outlandishly young—that they were the aberration, not me. I took for granted that invisibility an adult has among younger people, or among older people seeking out the attractions of youth. I grew used to pretending, in the presence of very young adults, that I was a different kind of being, that I knew more, that I knew so much and had changed so much that I no longer felt exactly as they did. As they sat opposite me, the adult, who corrected their weekly essays, I would pretend to have an adult's innocence of youthful embarrassment. I grew accustomed to my mask.

The childhood plot to preserve my youth forever was virtually forgotten, as memories are that lose the sense they once had; but one evening, as I was preparing to teach a subject on which much mental dust had settled, I was stopped cold by these lines of John Dryden: "I am resolved to grow fat and look young till forty, and then slip out of the world with the first wrinkle and the reputation of five-and-twenty."[9] The casual, but vicious determination of Dryden's character reopened that sorely problematic fissure—the fissure between youth and maturity, between potential and actuality. A version of "Die young, and leave a good-looking corpse," it enlivened that nightmare in which the natural and inevitable process of life is seen as a monstrous onslaught against personal identity. And it came right on target. The "accidental" jolt occurred on my forty-first birthday. Having braced myself for being 40, a sharp aftershock came at 41, when I realized that aging would not stop at this milestone, but would keep on going. How, for so long, had I believed this would not happen? How was I so unprepared to meet my future self?

Had I wanted to turn away from this question, or shelve it, I was prevented by my youngest daughter. An artistically talented ten-year-old drew two pictures for her, one of her and one of her sister as she envisaged them 50 years from now. These beautifully executed sketches were hideous images of women with skinny legs and swollen knees, with protruding noses decorated by warts, with mouths twisted into malicious grins. As this ten-year-old's imagination turned the clock forward, it saw only caricatures, which blotted out personal feeling and personal value. These sketches were held in my daughter's hand like a party bag as we took her home. "You have the biggest wart," she proudly announced to her older sister.

For a child who has a sign on her door prohibiting the entrance of monsters, ghosts, vampires, and "anything scary," she treated these visual predictions with distinct calm. "It's a joke," she explained as her falling tears made wrinkled patches on the little gifts with which she had sought to entertain us. Rigid in my condemnation, I listed the people she knew and loved who either were past that age already (her grandparents) or who would be within a span she could acknowledge as hers, reminding her that her father would be 58 before she was 20. Even in the heat of anger, I could not bear to admit that it alluded, also, to myself.

The deep offense I took to these sketches was double-edged. I did not want my daughter to be repelled or alienated from me as I aged. But my offense was on her behalf, too. She should take more care with her future self, and work harder for its preservation. Her maturity should not be an end or a degradation, but an opportunity and an achievement. Yet what was the likely shape of her future reality? Why were its forms, both to me and to her, muted and uncertain? Why were we both so ignorant about midlife?

SOME TIME AGO, WHEN I was studying professional women who were mothers of young children, I spoke to schoolgirls about their future. I wanted to discover how the girls of the 1980s plotted and planned for their future womanhood. The range of goals varied enormously in content, clarity, and determination. Some girls spoke forcefully and decisively about a future that they would carve into the world. For these girls, certain goals and ambitions were beyond negotiation. For other girls, personal matters had to be decided before other things could be considered; they could not see ahead without knowing more about future attachments. For them, plans were collaborations. Some girls wanted to "wait and see" what opportunities would be available to them. But whether they saw themselves as fierce achievers or tender nurturers, whether they were brashly cynical or determinedly romantic, girls always spoke about love, marriage, and motherhood. These were indelible marks on their maps, whether they were to be approached or avoided. I heard varied stories about work and children. Some stories involved sublime balances and integrations. Some depicted careful avoidance of distracting romances and demanding infants—at least until they were "much older." But being "much older" was an empty concept. The progressive focus slipped. The narratives of their futures got stuck. They frequently spoke about being forty years old, as though that marked the final definition of identity and maturity. "I want to marry a man who will still love me when I'm forty," one girl said. "Love is not love which alters when it alteration finds," Shakespeare wrote; and this young girl imagined the alterations to herself at 40 as a test case. Another girl remarked that she did not want to marry, yet could not imagine herself "still unmarried, at forty years old." Yet another said she wanted to travel and work at odd jobs while she saw the world, but did not think that she would feel the same way when she was forty.

Their imaginations could not reach beyond forty. Forty formed a barrier between their present and future selves. The epilogues they recited, in which they had become grandmothers, sitting in their leafy gardens on summer days, surrounded by loving grandchildren whom they regaled with tales of adventure and woe, were cheeky—a pert and non-serious coda to a "real" life that could be lived only in youth. A silence was cast upon the middle of this life. Their youth was envisioned as fiery and romantic and brave; maturity negated all this. Whatever maturity replaced youth with was beyond speech. What they could not foresee was that midlife would provide its own speech, which would give it interest.

Girls mature into women with a foreshortened future. The narrative of midlife remains unfinished, peculiarly empty. We can read and learn of the confusion, trust, and vividness of childhood, of the shocks and hunger of adolescence, of the determination and fierceness with which the young adult seeks her way. We have, more recently, gained access to other women's stories of how motherhood provides both fulfillment and bondage, how "the mother knot" provides profound satisfaction and meaning, yet can frustrate other desires and ambitions. The telling of these stories is never finished, and no one's story can be told for her, but a woman's access to others' experience serves her well: She can fit together her feelings with pieces of other narratives. There is a tradition to draw from, a set of pictures to hold and help frame one's own image.

This is not the case with middle age. The description of a woman's construction of a new and different self has been ignored. This developmental phase remains hidden, partly because women who go through it, do so on their own, using their own judgment and energies as never before. Even if midlife women did not walk this path in such privacy, however, it would be difficult for others to spot. Younger women cannot foresee it, because, lacking that essential "looking back time," they do not understand how self-awareness will change as patterns of compromise and its costs emerge. Psychology "experts" do not see it because of the strong cultural bias: Midlife women are marginal and "invisible."[10] The very foundations of modern psychology are rife with blindness towards the midlife woman. Freud saw her as virtually used up, dried up, by the awful adjustments that being female required. Whereas a man of thirty looks forward, Freud noted, ready to embrace the challenge of his future, and "to make powerful use of the possibilities for development," a woman of the same age "frightens us by her psychical rigidity and unchangeability . . . There are no paths to further development."[11] Since then, the marker age of 30 has moved on, but that type of prejudice remains. At a 1993 conference about women, a therapist proclaimed that a 56-year-old woman was not worth working with, since she was "too old" for developmental change. Yet I found the opposite: The psychological growth women tend to undergo in their forties makes change much easier, much more fluid, much more under their own control.

A woman's careful training in seeing herself through others' eyes makes her quick to pick up on others' dismissal. Where is she to go, when psychological experts tell her there is no place for her to go? "The significant fact about women," writes Carolyn Heilbrun, "in fiction as in life, is that after youth and childbearing are past, they have no plot, there is no story to be told about them."[12] What has gone unnoticed is the sheer energy released by this absence of plot. As women come to a road forked by liberation on the one hand, and the terror of meaninglessness on the other, they free themselves from the tyranny of that critical, overbearing reflection. As they are thus freed, they embrace their own vision.

Mirror, Mirror:
The Reflection versus the Self

Our sense of being seen by others, the awareness of our "looks," involves a dramatic psychological story. This is a specifically human skill,[13] a product of mental capacities, molded by culture. It is not something the child can do from birth; it is experienced and learned. The point at which a child recognizes what she sees in the mirror as a reflection of herself is a crucial point in development.[14] From that point, known as the *mirror stage,* the recognition of the self in the glass refashions her self-awareness. She is not only the thinking, feeling, reacting person she knows her self to be; she is also an object, which others see. She learns, moreover, that others see her in ways she cannot, directly, see herself, so they have information about her that she herself does not have. Thus drawn into the world that others see, she learns the power of the Other-Eye—the sense of how others see her.

This stage in development is, initially, the same for both girls and boys. Both girls and boys are shocked into a new sense of who they are as they see themselves viewed by others and realize that others respond to their appearance on the same terms that they respond to other people. But a girl's "looks" soon take on more powerful meanings. As girls stand and stare at their reflection, they may be thought to be lost in admiration; but in truth they are in search of some judgment, some other person's response to their appearance. "Am I pretty?" a girl may ask of the mirror, not "Who do I see, and what do I feel about her?" She addresses some roving eye, which observes all women, indifferent to individuality, judging her according to beauty alone.[15]

During adolescence, self-consciousness takes on a cruel force. Studying and exploring their changing bodies, maturing girls feel censored, just as Anne Frank's objective rendering of her naked body was deleted from the published diary.[16] Often girls censor themselves as they take cues from others.[17] They are the same person as they were six months ago—yet physical development is so rapid that they cannot keep track of who they appear to be. They notice that others respond to them differently. Some people are more interested, and some less so, granting them, in their sexual maturity, a cruel new privacy.[18] Do others notice, they wonder, these pubertal changes? If so, then, which ones?—for some are very private, and some are obvious. But are they obvious to others—who may pretend not to see, but respond as though they do see? How can a girl know what someone else sees? How can she measure these changes without knowing what others see?

As girls at puberty learn more about the social realities of womanhood, they are subject to the "Over-Eye"—the term Dana Crowley Jack uses to describe the internalization of others' expectations, which a girl may embrace in order to gain others' approval.[19] This judges her from within and without, using that girl whom everyone likes to be with and who has everything sorted out, both inside and out, as the measure. The awareness of being an observed self joins with a heightened awareness that her appearance is judged according to ideals of beauty, sexuality, and personality. Soon girls become too sensitive about what they *should* look like to be able to see themselves directly and honestly. Young adolescent girls speak with pathos about the trials and tribulations of being a visible object in their world. Sara, 13, said that when she walked into a room full of people their eyes pressed into her like barbed wires. Another girl said that even among her family— in gatherings with grandparents and aunts and uncles and cousins— when people hugged her and showed her warmth and love, she felt she had to defend herself against them. "I kind of put on a mental suit of armour. I clamp myself in it, and then walk into the room. Grandma opens her arms up and cries 'You're beautiful! Isn't she a beauty? Look at my beauty!' and I want to scream. I feel like my nipples are sticking out for everyone to see, and I can feel my thighs sticking together, and I think of little things, like whether there are any of those gooey specks of dirt between my toes. That admiration is excruciating! It swoops down on you. Oh, suit of armor, where are you now? How can you defend yourself against it? All those eyes on you, thinking 'Ooh, ah— hasn't the little girl gone and got all developed?' An animal at a zoo gets more respect. You know, how you kind of snigger at a masturbating monkey, but feel sorry too. Well, no one's feeling sorry for me, as they scratch away at me, snorting and giggling."[20]

The raw exposure, the sense that in being observed she is having her defenses snatched away, that in maturing physically she loses the "armor" her undeveloped body provided, the sickly balance between being aroused and repelled by others' admiration, the awareness that their admiration involves an intrusive curiosity and a desire for control—these feelings, characteristic of adolescence and bound up with adolescent ambivalence and uncertainty, gradually fade, but remain within us. These distorted body images can lead to anorexia or bulimia, as a girl tries to control her body with punishing diets and denial of nourishment; or they can remain silent partners until at mid-life we catch them out and, like Gloria Steinem, declare: "It's taken me twenty years to realize I might have asked: Where did that woman in my mind come from?"[21]

At about forty this uneasy relationship between a woman and her appearance may feel worse—on its way to getting better. For now she sees not only an image that is to be perused critically, but an image of the person she is not used to being—not ready to be. Feeling "young inside," she may be amazed by the reflections that disguise rather than reveal her. The "great secret" we share, Doris Lessing said, is that "your body changes, but you don't change at all. And that, of course, causes great confusion."[22]

Throughout our youth, midlife women are other women—our mothers, our teachers, our parents' friends. They are not us—until suddenly they are, or we are they. Being included in a group whom we have always defined as "other" comes as a jolt. "I used to watch my mother's hands as she talked," Deborah Lim, 43, explained. "I knew they were veined and spotted. It meant nothing to me as a sign of age—they were just hers. It never occurred to me than mine would grow into hers. It's the oddest sensation—seeing her hands starting, just starting, to show that one day I'll see her hands on me! I thought I knew the difference—she was that physical person, and I was a different one. I was younger! That's how I saw me versus older women for so long. I was young, and they weren't. Talk about the gender gap—well, it's nothing to the age one. When you're 20, someone who's 45 is in a different world. And then you see you've become the physical person who's part of that world. But you feel the same, and you don't know whether this is some nasty trick, seeming to be something you're not, or whether you've all along belonged to a whole set of people you thought were so different from you."

To ourselves we remain largely the child we knew—until we are jarred into relearning ourselves. At midlife comes a "new" objectivity, a new mirror phase. Deborah saw that she, too, was "other," in the way she had previously thought only older women were. "I'm still the same," she thinks, and yet sees that in some ways she is not the same. She has to address questions about what meaning this identification has, and who it is she now has become, and why she cannot immediately get to know this new self—in whose existence she only partly believes.[23] She shares with many women the belief that her mature body disguises her true self, that her maturity is mythical, even deceitful.

But this strangeness, this awareness of a discrepancy between the meaning of the reflection and our sense of who we are, can be ultimately constructive. Anita Brookner shows the pride combined with the awareness of marginality as a woman peruses physical change. The mirror image is transformed from a narcissistic mourning to a confrontation with a changed identity and a confused meaning of self:

> I ran a bath, took off my clothes, and looked at myself in the long glass. That was when I saw the softness at my waist, the lines around my neck, the loosening flesh of my upper arms, the widening of the hips, the ashy hair. I had not felt these things happening. The process, so far, had been benign, but inexorable. I shed a tear then, not out of vanity but from sadness that touched me and that had to do with women who still thought of themselves as girls, even after their youth had gone.[24]

Brookner's character Fay weeps "not out of vanity," but out of the incongruity between what she thinks herself to be, and what she sees reflected in the mirror. She has failed to see the change. Now that she sees it, she is shocked into reassessment. "Why didn't I know before who I was?" she is asking. "Why didn't I look, and see myself?" Then begins the road to a new self-construction.

Seeing oneself as older is very different from finding some flaw. It provides a stimulus to correct and expand one's vision. Culture has taught women to fear aging because, for women, aging is associated with loss of power. The discrepancy between this expectation and her gradual experience of her own new power is the first stage in the midlife disengagement with others' expectations and assessments. For as women in their new midlife experience a new power, they realize that they can escape the power of an external gaze. Away from its constricting influence, they are ready to define themselves in their own terms.

SHEILA FISHER, AT 44, sees others' expectation that she wants to stay the young beauty she once was:

> I know people look at me, and see this face . . . because, you know, people made much of me then. Not in lights, not stardom, but I was known to be beautiful, that was just a fact about me, which everyone seemed to acknowledge—my friends, my parents, and the modeling was just a sideshow, compared to how much everyone else made of it. So . . . it's always this face, compared to what it used to be.

There's the image they have, which I sort of sympathize with, but isn't mine. And they see my daughter . . . One woman even said to my husband, "How wonderful to have such a daughter. It's like getting your young wife back again." Because she looks like me, but the idea he doesn't have me anymore because I don't look just like I did! And all this . . . it's as though somehow they're all opening the door to envy, real wide, and I have this sense of me walking through it, right in the thick of it. But it's not me doing it, just some image they have or what they expect me to feel. So even while I know it isn't me walking right into that envy trap, I see myself . . . as though I was doing it, and I have to sort of shake myself, my mind, to say, it's not me, that's not what I feel. Not only about myself—but my daughter, whose beauty, let me tell you, isn't giving her a whole lot of joy. No one lets her forget that she's a beauty. Just walking down the street is harder for her. Ask her, and she'll probably say it's more fun. Ask her friends, and they sure will. But that happens and—it can make you lose your steadiness. And when I think how hard life was for me then . . . like suddenly I was off balance . . . not because of anything specific, just because it is at that age, and that goes—doesn't it?—with that kind of beauty. But you still have to kind of turn around and say, "Well, are you sure?" Because it's not easy, you know, finding all those boundaries, knowing where your feelings are.

As Sheila puzzled over her own feelings, she still had to negotiate her way through others' expectations. Labeling others as "wrong" or "mistaken" was not enough. ("Because it's not easy . . . knowing where your feelings are.") She admits that beauty does not necessarily feel good (her daughter's beauty, she confides with authority, "isn't giving her a whole lot of joy"), but she still has to work to sustain her own view, since others expect her to wish she still were beautiful—or beautiful in the way she was at eighteen.

Sheila is feeling her way around various attitudes towards her "looks." She is presented with how others see her and she has to deal with this view as others talk about it. As she senses how others see her, and how their responses to her "looks" influence how they feel about her, she confronts the "Other-Eye." She also deals with the Over-Eye, which belongs to a god-like judge, who doles out approval or disapproval according to some feminine standard of goodness *and* beauty.

The Over-Eye is not a particular person's view, but an accumulation of images and expectations, "a cultural consensus about feminine goodness, truth, and value."[25] It dictates what every woman is supposed to be, regulating her anger or her ambition, her desire or her disgust. Sheila brings her own sense of self versus her looks into play—but is confused by the ghostly whispers of an external judge. She is well on the way to locating the importance of the Inner-Eye (the ability to rely on her own vision) as she sees that her daughter's beauty "does not bring her a whole lot of joy." She sees how the admiration her daughter receives disturbs her "steadiness"—her ability to be centered, and she remembers, too, how being a beauty as a young woman had knocked her "off balance." The Other-Eye distracts, especially when it is widely reinforced; for a girl, thinking that beauty is good, needs years of experience to defend herself against it. Yet Sheila cannot immediately take possession of the Inner-Eye: She is still partly the woman "walking right into that envy trap." She is at an early stage in this process of disengagement, waiting to be sure of her own boundaries, and the path away from concern with how she is seen and judged by others.

But can she find that path? After all the years of learning to be appearance conscious, can she turn away from the reflections so often present in her mind? "A woman's being," writes art critic and novelist John Berger, "is split into two. A woman must continually watch herself. She is almost continually accompanied by her own image of herself. Whilst she is walking across a room or whilst she is weeping at the death of her father, she can scarcely avoid envisaging herself walking or weeping. From earliest childhood she is been taught to survey herself continually."[26] This male supposition of woman's experience ignores a woman's resistance to this split. It ignores a midlife woman's new interest in her body as something that is her own, whose meaning she constructs. Berger does not see how she learns to look at it with her own eyes. He ignores the reality of midlife development wherein she resists pressures of a judgmental gaze. Like many men both before and after him, Berger discounted the possibility that a woman might mature to heal this divided vision.

"WHEN I WAS FORTY —that was a big thing, something very difficult for me," Dora Lane, now 46, reported. "My mother, too, has always fought aging, and when I was forty said, 'What's the problem?

Forty is young. You have no idea what I would give to be forty again.' But I remember her when she was forty—or so—and she still felt too old. I remember clearly, at dinner one evening, her eyes were roaming around, so young and dark looking, while the rest of her face was immobile. She always looked so much older when her face was still. Maybe I didn't see this right away, maybe it's one of those things you understand more in remembering something than at the time, because she then started to talk about how it was in the spring she always noticed her wrinkles deepening and her eyes sinking. Her birthday was in May, so that must have made her count the years, too—but what sticks in my mind is the way we were all talking—my brothers and my Dad, and I was watching her, thinking at first that she was eyeing them, that they were doing something wrong. And then she said this about her wrinkles and the spring, and it seemed that while everyone was talking about something else, she was at the dinner table just thinking about her mirror image. 'Don't say things like that—you're making me lose my appetite,' my father joked, and that really summed up my thoughts, because her and wrinkles just hit me at the pit of my stomach."

The image of her mother's stare, drawing her away from the family conversation, the self-involved musings that deaden the family's fun, the father's jocular but brutal dismissal of the feelings that give rise to the mother's remarks, the daughter's isolated sympathy, which will haunt her own maturity, sketch a minute but common pathos. Looking back to the time she was thirteen, and her mother was in her forties, Dora wanted to break the pattern: "Now I have to face coming up to fifty, and what I have to tell myself is that if I don't get over this now—if I don't accept this—then I'll have spent my entire adult life wanting something I know I can't have—wanting to be younger."

Dora could count the cost of her mother's fear of aging and wanted to resist it. But how? It was not a matter of simply determining that looks did not matter, or even that her looks were just fine as they were. The struggle involved understanding how her mother's fear had been a fear of floating away from the center of her life and of losing power.

The women in my sample who view a mother as powerless have an extra task of reconstruction in midlife. It pushes them to the question, "What do I want out of my life now? What, all these years, have I been wanting?" Dora knows her values have not been centered on "a pretty face and pretty figure"; but she discovers a reluctance to accept an identity as a mature woman. This impasse is also described by Anita Brookner as her character Fay once again reflects:

> Old times, sad times. I feel better about them now than I did then. Then I felt like a girl, bewildered, although I was of an age to know better. This girlishness of mine, persisting in spite of the evidence of my body, had proved my enemy to the end. For it was the end of something, and I knew it. No more excitement, no more expectation, no more power. The old are disempowered. I caught sight of myself in a plate glass window . . . I reminded myself of someone, but someone I had not seen for a long time. It was not until I was in the flat and smoothing my hair in the glass that I recognized myself. I looked like my mother.[27]

Loss of youth is associated with loss of power only when one has no power—when one is unable to experience the potential power female maturity can offer. Both Brookner's character Fay and Dora know that the inner girlishness is their enemy, for this "girlish" personae cannot grow up. She has no access to the Inner-Eye: she sees only the excitement of pleasing and attracting others. Dora knows she must overcome her fear not by managing to stay young looking, but by ceasing to fear maturity. Dora could see the solution, but she could not, immediately, adopt it.

A woman's concern with beauty—or a youthful appearance—can stick fast even though she in her wisdom discards it. She may persist in thinking that a youthful appearance can give her things—like self-esteem and power—which, in fact, it cannot. She can state a sensible position vis-à-vis youth and beauty: but we cannot always take the position she judges to be right. Yet I could not believe, given her deliberate struggle against it, that Dora would be condemned to repeat her mother's impasse. "It's a concern which gets much smaller," she laughed when we spoke about this a year later. "But it's more than getting used to the idea. I simply don't see myself as I once did. You know, I saw wrinkles on my face when I was twenty-five—no, even at nineteen I worried about moving my forehead too much. I could see the lines on my friend's faces. This sounds as though I only think about looks—which isn't so—and it sounds like I'm extreme, which I might agree with, except that I think so many women are extreme on this issue, aren't they? I got used to staring at myself in a certain way, spotting things that were going wrong with it. I don't want to give you a list—I'm too ashamed . . . I don't know how I managed to do this to myself—look at myself like this—for so long . . . I can see that, as I go about living, there's so much else to think about, and the times my face stands still like that in front of the mirror get fewer and far between."

Dora's "extreme" concern was not, in fact, unusual. The strong commercial structure of our society and the celebrity of glamour, foster dissatisfaction and tempt us with promises of disguise and renewal. She is partly ashamed of her concern, yet captivated by it—willing to speak about it, to magnify it for a moment so she can see its proper place in the rest of her life. She now sees, when she looks in the mirror, not the flaws or signs of aging she is looking for, but her eyes looking anxiously at their own reflection. Seeing this, she is appalled at the wasted effort. She sees her own eyes as collaborators against her.

She had taken a big step up from her initial despondency, when she wished but was unable to resist her mother's despair at the aging process. As she spoke, it was clear how difficult it was for her to talk about it, since she both sees how unimportant her concerns are, yet feels their significance. Many women who will talk about virtually any subject, however intimate, however controversial, avoid direct discussion of their appearance and their attitude toward it. As soon as they speak about their appearance, their language is dominated by the external structures that set standards for a woman's appearance and the importance of appearance in a woman's life.[28] As they use this language, they know that it is ridiculous, shameful, in its falsehood. Yet, it can take years before a woman hears this in her silence. Dora sees how she has been sustaining these false structures by looking at herself in order to criticize and to worry. She recalls her dread, at nineteen, of the red marks from her nose to the sides of her mouth which prefigured her laugh lines. Like so many women, she asks, "Why did I create these problems for myself?" and, like so many midlife women, she asks the crisis question, "Why didn't I see what I was doing?"

Now she looks at her looks in a different way: not as a single static image in the mirror, but as a living, multidimensional being. Just as Gloria Steinem's careful studying of her face lines and liver spots[29] is an attempt to restructure her vision of her midlife body, Dora wants to give her own meaning to what she sees. She creates a new tool kit of images based on new sensitivity to her own responses to others: "I look at other women's faces now very differently. I don't like them all, but I like so many of them, and see so much more in them. It feels much better seeing other people in this way . . . I can't begin to tell you what I must have not seen before."

As a woman retrieves her own way of seeing, she redefines beauty. This is one of the skills that women acquire on their secret path through midlife crisis. "I used to always be tracking how pretty some girl was," Linda Gerson, 52 said. "It's amazing the thought-time I wasted as a teenager over that. Was so and so really pretty? Was she prettier than me? Me and my friends would sit down with *Seventeen* [magazine] and take a face apart. This model wasn't really pretty— look at her nose. Another one had eyes that were too small, or a funny mouth. I'd whittle things down so that some girl had to be perfect to be called pretty. That made me feel better, thinking that there wasn't too much that was pretty prancing around. Now all sorts of people seem attractive. It's where you look—what you look at. I see my daughters' friends and realize that lots of those faces I'm admiring today I would have been real critical of 20 years ago. You just come to realize that all sorts of faces look good. It's a matter of seeing what's inside—all those little movements—surprise, amusement, doubt. I used to automatically erase those things, while I weighed up the shape of the nose and the mouth. Big deal! Even Madonna's face is going to fall to pieces that way. Now I couldn't even begin to answer that kind of question—who's pretty?"

Linda realizes the enormous effort she had once put into seeing women through a false judge's eyes. She did not simply look and respond to what *she* saw, but stared at another woman's image, erasing her own response until she could grasp what she supposed was a "real" judgment. She would "whittle things down" to see what someone else would see. Making her way through the path of midlife crisis, she resists her residual concern with stereotypes of beauty and frees herself from the internalization of others' views. In so doing, she understands how much work it took *not* to see things for herself. Now she looks around her with relief, through her own eyes.

THE STEPS A WOMAN takes to repossess her own image are often slippery and uneven. The women in my sample had tried throughout their lives to make this journey. Even in midlife they found no simple step up, no final perch. But they did develop skills in dealing with the backsliding they experienced. In fact, at the initial stages of crisis, concerns about their appearance were often heightened as a prelude to a better resolution. One symptom of the onset of this crisis is that concerns about appearance become shifting and inconsistent. A woman might be satisfied one moment, and dissatisfied the next. She might be pleased in one context and displeased in another. Appearance was painfully important one minute and irrelevant at another. Like the numerous magazines, which in recent years have juxtaposed articles about how good it is to be older and how we must make friends with those wrinkles alongside hints on how to disguise the "ravages of aging" and ads for age-retardant cosmetics or plastic surgery, women themselves reveal blatant inconsistencies in their attitude towards appearance. Of the multiple images of herself that the midlife woman now sees in the mirror, those that alienate and judge her will return from time to time. Often resistance is made in half-steps: the vision is strong, and then it blurs. Micky Riley, who had stopped smoking as "a present to my future self on my fortieth birthday" had gained fifteen pounds in the past eighteen months. "When I see myself in the mirror, all fresh and naked, I think—how really sexy I look, how luscious . . . ," and she opened her arms to the side, inhaling her delight. She sighed, and placed her elbows on the table. "Then I see myself ready for work, and I think—what a frump."

When these negative images return too often, a variety of strategies are employed to chivvy the process along. One strategy is humor. The novelist Angela Carter, at 50, when asked to describe a typical day, made many references to her appearance: Aware of the discrepancy between the privacy of her daily domestic and working rhythms, on the one hand, and its public "snapshot," on the other, she summoned up an image of herself, which both endorsed and challenged the expectation of what a good and famous woman should try to look like: "I put on this egg-stained dressing gown and become instantly squalid as I make breakfast."[30] The self-denigrating humor is both mocking and exultant. She accepts others' labels of a frumpy middle-aged woman, but preempts them by using them herself. "Egg-stained" and "squalid," are challenges tossed to the public, as she presents them with her normal, working, contented self. The television personality and writer Joan Rivers engaged, at one time, in comedy routines that mocked her aging female body. This was a hit with so many women because, in laughing at those images projected by the way a woman in her maturity may appear to others, they felt temporarily liberated. Rivers was saying on their behalf: "I know how others see me and ridicule me because I am getting older, but I can go one better: I can make fun of myself before they do." Laughing at the odd, usually unspoken awareness of aging, women felt the comfort of togetherness and the relief of humor. But though this reappropriation of the language of ridicule provides momentary relief, it leaves a disturbing aftertaste: How long can women counter images that demean them by mockery alone? For midlife growth involves more than rejecting others' views; it also involves constructing one's own. There comes a time when exposing others' prejudice is insufficient. To emerge triumphant from this journey, a woman needs to lift the blind on her own new vision.

Many women assumed that *other* women found it much easier to negotiate the aging reflection than she did herself. Biting on the knuckle of her hand and smiling playfully above it, Amy said that when she saw her reflection in the mirror or caught a glimpse of her reflection in a shop front window, she would think, "Yes that's how I look in the mirror, but that's not really how I look." Her half-serious reasoning was that people wouldn't be as friendly to her, as appreciative of her, if she really looked as she did in the mirror. What she thought was merely whimsical, however, was a genuine attempt to deny the structure of the reflection and to create her own image.

The denial of how one looks as one looks in the mirror is not as bizarre as it seems. I noticed that when an adolescent girl passed a mirror, her eyes met her face's reflection directly at the reflection's eyes, and then roamed all over the face. At forty, women are inclined to glance somewhat lower, at about chin level, or maintain their glance firmly at eye level. Either they were *less* interested in or they defended against an overall view of their face. Fifty-year-old women, however, look at their faces quite differently. An innocence of gaze returns, a spontaneous sweep over the entire image. The adolescent girl does not see her gaze when she looks in the mirror: instead, she sees eyes—of a certain colour, shape, and setting. At forty, women begin to be more guarded. Though, in fact, they are less critical of their appearance than younger women,[31] they also work to avoid a return to that "cage"—as Dora described it—of self-consciousness. Remembering all too well how, in adolescence and early adulthood, she was dominated by her looks, she knows how self-consciousness can lock up one's responses and feelings. At the onset of midlife crisis, as new awareness of conflicting images and expectations comes into focus, many women in my sample were concerned that there would be a return to previous worries about their appearance. But, in fact, their increased concern was a sign of growth. It was a way of bringing together loose ends, for a final confrontation. Among the fifty-year-old women that fear had gone: The internalization of other's judgments was now so slight and skewed they noticed it only in passing. They looked upon themselves instead with the Inner-Eye, which looked to understand and learn and respond, rather than to criticize or judge according to someone else's standard.

But the route is not easy. Rhea Jarvis, who had a mastectomy at 42, worried that, from one side, an imbalance in her figure was noticeable. When she spoke about cancer, she spoke of this new self-consciousness, which made her hold herself a little differently when she walked across a room, or made her try to present her right profile to her students as she lectured. It reminded me so much of adolescent girls' excruciating self-consciousness in which an angry, losing battle is waged against external images, a battle that gives feelings like embarrassment more weight than issues of life and death. Rhea had faced major problems of illness and pain and the prospect of death, yet what preoccupied her on a daily basis were the superficial ones. Her concern about the visibility of her absent breast was, however, not separate from other, more profound images of the "bodily harm" done to her in order to preserve her life. These were "shadowy, ghostly fingers" which "sometimes came in dreams, or just crept into [her] thoughts"; without specific shape, they "drew horrible pictures" of the invasive threat to her health.

Compared to death or illness, the removal of her breast was minor, but it served as a constant reminder both of the illness and its cruel cure. "I know it's beyond all reason," she admitted. "I know I should feel grateful, because things really seem to be going well. Every time I have a test the doctor bounces about like it's a party, things look so good. But at the same time, there's this mark, this scar. I don't ordinarily talk about it. When people ask me how I am it's always the good news I tell. But while they're asking and I'm answering I'll always be looking away or turning away because I want to cover up. I know it's not shameful, but it's so private—that part of it—that . . . well, I do—I do feel ashamed."

She struggles towards admission, then deals with further problems this admission gives rise to. Her response is not "right," yet it is nonetheless what she feels. Her vulnerability comes from being unable to have, as yet, her own body image. Therefore, others' image, or her vision of others' image, threatens her, more powerful than her as-yet unformed one. The shame she clearly feels, even though she knows "it's not shameful," comes from being unprepared to counter others' views with her own vision. "Shame," writes Erik Erikson, "supposes that one is completely exposed, and conscious of being looked at: in a word, self conscious. One is visible and not ready to be visible. . . ."[32] The transformation from a susceptibility to this kind of shame, on one side of the crisis, to a confidence based upon a strong internal vision, on the far side of crisis, occurred in the midlife women I studied.

Two years later, Rhea, like Dora, found the problem smaller, but for her, too, the improvement was not merely a matter of getting used to her body, but of changing her way of seeing: "I feel I'm in a strange place now. I'm in the ordinary world in one sense, but I'm also on this ledge, where time and physical things are different. I'm proud of where I am—the difference, the sense that it's deep here—that's nice," and she held her breath, as though holding it before her, unsure whether to expose it to me further. "But sometimes, when I'm in the ordinary world, and it comes out from someone else—the way you just do catch people looking at you, or the way I know I look at other women—then it's unsettled again, and I feel the shame, but also, now, I'm angry at that, because, really, I'm not ashamed."

In less drastic circumstances, too, women had to deal with feelings that seem beneath them. "I know it doesn't affect the person I am," 47-year-old Judy Mann insisted, "or what I can offer someone else, but the summer comes and I might have a lunch appointment in the Park and I see my thigh spread out along the bench like a half-rolled pie crust. One minute I'm the person who's talking to another person, and the next minute I'm that woman with the crepe paper thighs. I keep the conversation going but my mind keeps snapping from the person who's talking and has these ideas to someone who just has these thighs. It's like one of those pictures that plays optical tricks on you—one minute the blocks are coming towards you and next they're going away. One minute I'm a design consultant talking to a client, and the next I'm a woman who's—you know all those terms—long in the tooth, no longer a spring chicken—and should have covered her thighs."

Like Rhea, Judy struggles with feelings she knows to be beneath her. She knows the limitations of an external vision, but it continues to focus her vision. She knows who she is, but her knowledge slips from one external definition to another ("design consultant talking to a client . . . a woman who's . . . long in the tooth . . . "). She struggles with this vacillation because she cannot—yet—steady her own vision. Like Micky, who thinks that one minute she is sexually "luscious" and the next minute sees herself as a "frump," both the good and the bad images come from outside. These women are struggling with the cheerleader's language, the pep talk, which may give them a buzz for a moment, and then leave them stranded. As they become aware of their shifting perspective, Judy and Micky are beginning to resist others' images. Such resistance is the first stage in growth.

"MY FACE NOW BETRAYS me," 50-year-old Anna Klaus declared. "People say 'What's wrong?' or 'Don't you like what you're eating?' or 'I guess you didn't agree with that,' when they've just said something—and I don't know what they're talking about. Then sometimes, just when I'm bending down, you know, to wash my face, I see this angry woman coming towards me in the mirror, and I realize that the way my face has gone—these lines, this drooping around my mouth—make me look as though I'm disagreeing—or disagreeable!—when I'm not. So here I am stuck with this face which won't show what I feel, but keeps showing something different." At first, she thought she would do exercises to build up her facial muscles, but, six months later, she noticed what her face did when she saw other people. She realized that as she expected someone looking at her to think how she had aged, she would tense, and try to rearrange her face, or hide it by turning away. She half-expected that acquaintances would no longer recognize her (feeling the invisibility many midlife women spoke of) and so she was slow to greet them. People, she was sure, did not notice her, and therefore she had "blanked out as people passed." It was these defensive responses that made people comment on her changed face—not the specific depth of lines and hollows. What Anna had to learn was how she carried the mirror around with her and how it got in the way of her responses to other people. "Can you believe I was so stupid? Why? When I'm not that shallow? But there it was—this mirror in front of me when I saw someone else—that made my face freeze up because I didn't like what they were going to see."

Still in their forties, Judy and Micky vacillate between external definitions: as professional, as no-longer-young female. The vacillation registers the first stage of disengagement, when the reflection begins to lose the meaning and the power it once had. Anna, a few years older, is further away from the anxious stage of vacillation. What Anna identified and rejected, was the impasse Germaine Greer identified and resisted in midlife: "there in my mind's eye was I."[33] The "I" that Greer once saw in her mind was not her own vision, but the image others had of her. Always, Greer reflects, she was trying to embody an image that would attract others; even as a radical force, she was concerned to meet the restrictive standards of female beauty. In fact, Greer believes all women are compelled to think about themselves in terms of how others see them—until midlife. For as a woman realizes that simply by being mature, by being herself, and by being more powerful she can never be what the accumulation of cultural norms and images dictates she should be, she makes a deft, defensive move. As she makes this move she discovers the ability to see herself anew, and create her own judgments. As she develops this skill, she steps into that new midlife in which she has far greater control of her decisions and compromises.

In her novel *Mrs Dalloway,* Virginia Woolf beautifully describes this process of resistance and growth in a 52-year-old woman. Packing a character's lifetime experiences into a single day, Woolf describes as occurring within a few hours a process that, in reality, takes years. Preparing to meet a former lover, who represents that overseeing judge (memories of him "started up every day of her life as though he guarded her"), Clarissa wonders whether he will think she had grown older. She looks into the mirror:

How many millions of times she had seen her face and always with the same imperceptible contraction! She pursed her lips when she looked into the glass. It was to give her face point . . . That was herself when some effort, some call upon her to be herself, drew the parts together, she alone knew how different, how incompatible and composed so for the world only into one centre.[34]

That "imperceptible contraction" (like the facial tightening Anna affected when she looked into the mirror of others' eyes) assembles an image that is not herself, but which others will see as her. Clarissa Dalloway tries to focus herself into one thing—giving it that static image, which Dora noticed she gave to her reflection. In so doing, Clarissa also falls prey to that moral dictator of what woman should be; for now, as a single, static reflection, Clarissa is someone who "had helped young people," someone who hid "faults, jealousies, vanities, suspicions." She feels she can only show what is appropriate to cultural norms—the nice, helpful, radiant woman. But she knows this is not really her, and it is only for the world that she assembles herself into one being. She knows herself to be layered, with a dazzling multiplicity of thought and feeling. Since this complexity cannot be captured by the mirror, she does not view herself as the thing seen by others. Now, more and more often, she has "the oddest sense of being invisible; unseen; unknown." The dominance of this Inner-Eye is assured when she is able to defend herself against the fact that, as an older woman, she is a potential target for ridicule: she is "a narrow pea-stick figure; a ridiculous little face." But this view of herself as ridiculous is, she knows, wrong, and in resistance she develops her own privacy, her own self-knowledge, and her own vision. This is what I observed happening over the four years I tracked my sample. Women were not simply changing, magically, under some hormonal influence; instead, they were taking an ordered series of steps towards new growth.

Through the Looking Glass

The process of dealing with appearance is only one segment of the midlife crisis, often worked upon in tandem with the more profound dramas I will describe later that bring about positive change. Yet dealing with issues about appearance is often easier for women in the new midlife. Most midlife women of today look far better—healthier, younger, more active and appealing—than did women of the same age in previous generations. Most women at 40 and 50 and beyond look far better than they had expected to look at this age. Nearly 60% of the women in my sample felt that at their current age (between 40 and 54) they were (or would be, since many of them were not single) at no greater a disadvantage as a potential marriage partner than they were at 27, and 25% believed that in their 40s or 50s they were more attractive to men than they had been as young adults. As women come to value their own vision, they are less daunted by negative views of others, and quicker to register others' positive views. "At many of the parties and conferences I go to," Joyce Ferelli reported, "there are not many women, but there are several younger ones. This does not prevent men from wanting to talk to me, too, and in my friendships with men I often feel something extra there—the possibility of something more, were I ever to become available."

Whatever the midlife woman believed about the *general* probability of marrying, her personal experience of men's responsiveness was far more important to her assessment of whether *she* was likely to marry. Several women in my sample ridiculed the notorious predictions about older women's chances of marrying, thus resisting the fear that such reported statistics might otherwise have inspired.[35] Several women insisted that they thought they looked better now than they ever had. "You should have seen me when I was 20!" Gabby Steller exclaimed. "I had frizzy henna hair, and weighed 25 pounds more than I do now. I'll gladly take a few wrinkles as a trade off for that gleaming blimp I used to be." Rachel Barlow felt that her face, with its large, pronounced features, suited a middle-aged appearance more than it had suited her in looks. "I feel I'm growing into myself . . . I'm gaining, not losing my looks." Other women felt better equipped to make their appearance effective. "I feel I use my appearance more," a 47-year-old medical administrator said. "It's not a matter of womanly wiles, but there is a female charm at work which I use to communicate certain things." Like Gabby, Naomi Katz described herself as having "a poor physical image" when she was younger. The confidence of age brought release.

Many African-American women, who age incredibly slowly, felt wryly superior as I broached the subject. "Don't let these few grey hairs fool you—I'm much older than I look!" Lucy Bell laughed. "But my skin isn't going to crinkle up all of a sudden like the pink and yellow stuff." Felicia Able, 52, also black, felt relief from the ways in which prejudice had acted as a harsh judge of her appearance when she was younger. She believed that now black could really be seen to be beautiful. A host of tiny things influenced her physical self-confidence. "I walk into the Twenty Eight Shop in Marshall Field's, and the saleswomen no longer exchange glances and wonder what the hell I'm doing there. I'm allowed to look and buy or not buy. Twenty years ago they would ask me whether I was there to pick up someone else's package." The easing of social prejudice and the staying power of her good looks allowed her to savor her appearance. "You have no idea how different things are—for me anyway. Maybe it's a narrow view of what's happened to my people as a whole—but isn't every personal triumph a general 'Hurrah'? I walk down Michigan Avenue and I don't feel that I'm some black woman treading on white people's territory. I go to my office, I do my work—things like that make me want to dress up and *swagger.* You think I'm going to be cowed because I'm fifty instead of thirty?" As women feel empowered themselves, the view of others loses its dominance. Still aware of how others may see her, Lucy stares this image down. As a woman gains self-confidence, the disapproval of others loses the meaning it once had. This provides the freedom to get on with her life in ways younger women can, on the whole, only vaguely imagine.

NEVERTHELESS, THE *IDEA* OF aging can haunt women, whatever their age. A woman's fear of aging, Susan Sontag wrote, is "the longest tragedy" of every woman's existence.[36] The French feminist Simone de Beauvoir reflected, "Long before the eventual mutilation," she noted, speaking perhaps of menopause, or of death, or simply of a wrinkled face, "woman is haunted by the horror of growing old." But what is it that she fears? Men, too, have become middle aged after a youth, which endorsed a cult of youth, but they do not face the same battle. For men have always known that the significant question is not, "Who can attract others?" but "Who can act and think as he wants?"[37]

De Beauvoir understood that fear of aging occurred when beauty was seen as power, and that when beauty and youth are seen as power, women themselves have no real power. For when a woman gains power through her beauty, she is depending on others' responses to her, rather than on her own ability to enact her wishes and express her thoughts. A woman is enthralled by the way others may see and judge her when she is subservient: She must please someone else, be chosen by someone else, gain power through someone else, when she has none herself. Her knowledge that she will age dwarfs her horizons when her world is small and weak, when she seeks power only through men. "She has gambled," de Beauvoir writes, "much more heavily than the man on the sexual values she possesses: to hold her husband, and assure herself of his protection, it is necessary for her to be attractive, to please . . . What is to become of her when she no longer has any hold on him? This is what she anxiously asks herself, as she helplessly looks on at the degeneration of this fleshly object that she identifies with herself."[38] Beauty and power are linked only when one identifies that one-dimensional reflection with a multidimensional self. The idea that beauty gives a woman power is derived from her belief that she cannot herself be empowered.

But one reason so many women felt duped—angry and frustrated that it had taken them so long to see that this "fleshly object" is not something someone else can assess, not some object obliged to pass quality control—is that women in fact do not lose power when they age. Instead, they gain it. They gain it through self-confidence and through self-knowledge. They gain it by their new directness, and by their refusal to repeat past patterns of compromise. The fact that mature women have more power than younger women is both widely known—and unknown. It goes against social expectations, and yet emerges in more controlled studies of people's attitudes. Perhaps some find that power unsettling, and marginalize the mature woman in order to protect themselves from her increasing power. Perhaps they judge mature women to be less attractive, or even unattractive, because they feel safer with a less powerful femininity. As she matures, a woman may come to look more authoritative, more wise and knowing.[39] Perhaps this, the Over-Eye declares, is not what she should be.

Or, perhaps, others do not see it because it is at odds with their expectations.

If this generation can change those cultural images, then subsequent women will walk into midlife with an easier stride. New research shows that women have new sources of power, and new interest in self-assertion[40] in midlife. Research further shows that other people see this. There is an increase in the perceived strength, confidence, and interpersonal power of women relative to men in the second half of life.

One method that has been very fruitful in the study of women's images of themselves involves use of the Thematic Apperception Test, which is really just a systematic way of listening to stories someone tells about a suggestive but indefinite picture or story "cue," such as an opening sentence. The themes and images used by the participant to construct a story around the incomplete cue can be analyzed to reveal her expectations and assumptions. Such studies strongly support what I found in my sample. While I found that women in midlife discover new power, studies using this method show that older women are seen by both men and women to be stronger than men. Moreover, both men and women see younger women to be relatively powerless.[41] In looking at pictures of women of various ages in a vaguely sketched picture, participants in this study were far more likely to see the older woman as authoritative and following her own wishes, whereas younger women and older men were seen to be more influenced by others' wishes and by fear of others' anger or distress.[42]

The balance of power shifts between man and woman over the life span.[43] In fact, as I found in observing my sample, older women feel relatively less dependent on their partners, and older men become relatively more dependent on theirs.[44] Older women become more assertive and more content. But the precise process whereby women are able to express in midlife the previously suppressed powerful side of themselves has never yet been traced. This is the thrust of my work in this book, which not only observes the new midlife in women, but shows the psychological steps taken to achieve it. This painstaking process will now be described.

2 Traditional Women: Changing Times, Changing Conflicts

Women who have made different life choices approach midlife crisis from different angles. Traditional women are those who have identified themselves primarily as wives and mothers and who believe that their family's needs take priority. Had they lived in previous generations, these women would have been typical. Today, they often feel abnormal and obscured by the high-profile images of the career woman. It is in the context of a contemporary culture in which they feel outmoded and under-powered that traditional women undergo a crisis at midlife, in which they a confront the desires they have daily suppressed and the personal needs they have so long neglected. This confrontation feels like a catastrophic collapse of the structure of their lives, yet ends in integration and growth. As the traditional women in my sample passed through this crisis they learned to voice new feelings and thoughts. Their responses, brought into focus, gained a powerful dynamic. No longer apologetic for past compromises, they nonetheless gained new skills in controlling their future.

There were three different points at which the traditional woman's midlife crisis was targeted. The first was a woman's identification with a husband's ambition, an identification that silenced her own needs—until, at midlife, she acknowledges what she has previously ignored. Resolution involved accepting regret, and finding a new perspective from which her own vision was central. A second sore point was the time and energy a traditional woman had poured into her family: Perhaps her family was very large, or had a nomadic lifestyle, linked to a husband's career in the diplomatic or armed services; or she may have been particularly taxed by an ill husband or handicapped child. For these women, time had to be managed in new ways so that they could be relieved of the mechanical scheduling of their thoughts and feelings. The third target for midlife crisis was the empty nest: As the tasks of motherhood become less intense and less central to their daily lives, some women were flooded by a surplus of time, in which they confronted a lack of direction and purpose. The emptiness, initially experienced as a catastrophe, ushered in awareness of neglected dimensions of themselves. They discovered, as their long-valued roles changed, a new subjective core.

The crisis for traditional women occurs within a revolution of ideas about what women should and could be. Most women who were born in America between 1939 and 1954 have a fairly strong idea of what a traditional woman's life is like and what a traditional woman is: Her identity is centered on being a wife and mother; her thoughts, wishes, and actions are weighted towards this center. Many women born during these years fought against this traditional mold, feeling its pressure, frightened that they were being conditioned or programmed for a life they did not want. In the women's groups that met throughout the U.S. and Europe in the 1960s and 1970s, members were on guard: words and phrases, once innocuous and unquestioned, became signs of subversive thought. Femininity was seen as a malicious concept, a network of control and repression, whereby a socially acceptable woman was pliant, eager to please others, devoid of ambitions for herself—a reed on which others leaned. In the view of many young women who were determined to be New Women, being feminine meant being less than a mature adult. It meant being in men's power. It meant serving men domestically and servicing them sexually. It meant neglecting one's own needs and one's own identity. Young women in those decades pounced on any turn of phrase or gesture that cast them in a feminine role. Like a ruthless cat on a bewildered mouse, they attacked hidden expectations, whether they discovered these in themselves or in others. To be free was to be free of what women had traditionally been.

During consciousness-raising meetings, women often worked together to locate the little strings that kept tripping them up in their daily battles for equality and independence. I remember how we whipped up anger against men who offered to "help us" prepare the dinner. We tore apart such polite offers, as though they were direct attacks, outraged by the assumption that participation in preparing a meal, which everyone would eat, was *help* to *us*. Such an offer, rather than providing support for the new womanhood, manipulated us into thinking of ourselves as responsible for the dinner. The assistance so gallantly offered was a subversive denial of joint responsibility. Nor were men the only culprits reinforcing old expectations. Some young women felt their mothers were feeding them poison when they spoke about the importance of marriage and children over other goals. I remember how traditional women's roles haunted us like monsters, green-faced, fanged, nipping our heels in the form of others' innocuous comments and questions. "Can I save you a job? Can I iron [your husband's] shirts for you?" one woman reported her mother-in-law as asking; and we booed in unison at the criminal assumption that such a job was hers.

We felt exhilarated by our ability to pin these phrases, like pictures of wanted men, to our mental bulletin boards. Yet we worried that they might, nevertheless, insinuate themselves into our thoughts, like parasitic aliens, popping subversive phrases onto our lips, phrases like: "I am happy to do this for you"; "What I want most is to be with you"; "You are the most important thing in my life." We wanted to be shrewish Kate, untamed, but we were frightened; we knew how the play ended.

Nor did we understand just how ungiving were the social and domestic and economic structures we thought our consciousness-raising would overcome. We had not quite located either our weaknesses or our strengths. We knew we were capable of more than those roles usually allotted to us, but we did not know what it would be like—for us—to extend those roles. Raising children, caring for our children, maintaining domestic and family life, seemed, in those days, when the voice most clearly heard was the voice of youth, like tasks ready and waiting to be restructured. We could change it all, share it out, deal a new, equal, hand of cards.

The world for women has not changed as rapidly as many thought it would. The roles of homemaker and mother that women typically took when today's midlife women were girls, continue to have a magnetic pull. It has been far more difficult than anticipated to change these roles. Yet there have been enormous changes. Women's lives have become so varied that there are now no markers along the way to make one feel, "Yes, I'm going along life's path just as I should." In previous generations, developing one's looks, finding a boyfriend, getting engaged, then married, then becoming a mother—of one, two, and three children—marked the rightness of women's path. Whatever else a woman did—whether she went to college, took a job, traveled—these other markers showed whether she passed or failed her test for normal femininity. Now women have no normal life pattern. Though criticism for deviating from past prototypes is still common, it is easier for women of this generation to decide not to marry, not to have children, or to bear children in midlife, to espouse grand ambitions. But with a woman's greater freedom comes anxiety about whether she has made the right decision. For when we feel dissatisfied with what we have done, and other people we identify with or measure ourselves against—sisters, cousins, friends from school—are all doing different things, we may think, "Why didn't I do what *she* did?" At different times, and in different ways, all contemporary women ask this of themselves. For the traditional women in my sample, this query could uncover regrets that had been controlled or denied. This disclosure then allowed them sight of the impediments that took difficult choices out of their control.

WOMEN WHO FOLLOWED A traditional feminine pattern were distinctive of their own generation. Even as they centered their lives on the roles of wife and mother, changing images of women forced them into a distinctively contemporary awareness of what they were giving up. Women who led conventional women's lives—who spent their time caring for children, driving them to school, to swim lessons, to hockey games, who moved from city to city where their husbands' jobs took them, who did iron shirts for them, and asked for "help" doing "their job" of cooking for the entire family, valued their family commitments. It was rewarding work, but it was also costly work. At midlife, the sum of these costs was confronted.

There is no longer a universal cultural shroud over women's needs to extend themselves beyond home and hearth, to explore different worlds, and to challenge previously male domains. Today's women do not become homemakers as women of previous generations have done—by having little choice or awareness of other options. Awareness of expanding options, however, often makes traditional women feel defensive, and in their defense they often suppress their dissatisfaction. Traditional women who did not have careers knew that many other women saw them as different, as limited, as inferior. They spoke about feeling "marginal" or "small" or "useless" or "foreign" in the presence of professional women. In defense, they labeled career women "selfish." They judged that such women were ignorant of the stamina and perseverance and generosity necessary to cope with their own demanding lives. They guessed that career women cost their families "too much" or more than they wanted their own families to pay. They argued this when they saw professional women, when they thought about them, and when they thought about themselves. Their battle to feel comfortable in these roles that were once considered the soft option, gave rise to a continuous internal dialogue, which, in their early adulthood, went round in circles, skirting many of their real feelings, which at midlife are addressed directly.

The psychological energy women in their first years of adulthood employ to keep their regrets at bay and to deny their dissatisfaction has been repeatedly documented in the past decade. Women who decide, after the birth of children, not to return to work, engage in "cognitive manoeuvres" whereby they minimize both the financial and personal costs of their decisions.[1] This decision, with its huge impact on career prospects, is described as temporary, and hence a chunk of adult life is conceived of as an "interlude." The costs of such a decision are too high to admit, so mental work is done to make it seem smaller, less drastic. Here often begins the suppression of desires and needs, which stimulate midlife crisis. This suppression continues as women in young adulthood try, but fail, to enlist a husband's help in the home. They often develop appallingly self-effacing methods to cover their frustration: A husband does "his share," one woman insisted; but on further questioning, her husband's "share" was about one-tenth of the whole.[2] Taking on the mothering and wifely tasks in the home, women cut their hours of work, or drop out altogether. They may see their decision as conscious and logical; yet the terms of this compromise are often beyond their control. When the demands of work and family cannot be balanced, when a woman sees herself as primarily responsible for the family's well-being, she may "decide" to meet the needs of her family while denying her desire to work. The terms of her decision may be pushed underground because she does not want to see what she is giving up. Why focus on regret, when she cannot do anything about it? The terror of harming her marriage, or being labeled a poor mother, controls her options.

Virtually all the traditional women I interviewed harbored ambitions and achievement identities—a sense of themselves as potential achievers, which ticked, in counter time, to the real time in which they passed their days. Each day brought arguments and counterarguments in defiance, and then compliance with their roles. "Not a day goes by," Mai said, when I first interviewed her at the age of 47, "when I don't think about what I might have achieved, and how that would have felt. I look the part of the perfect wife and mother, and it's a part I play with all my heart. But I chose it because I did not see, for me, a way of doing more, which doesn't mean I didn't want to or don't want to." As midlife struck, with that mingling of dread and liberation, women confronted their compromises in bolder ways. First, they acknowledged those anxiously suppressed regrets; second, they demanded of themselves how they had failed to see what they had suppressed; third, they asked the crisis question, "Why didn't I see this before?" thereby confronting the dangers of self-repudiation on the one hand, or further reburial of dissatisfaction on the other. If they resist these destructive alternatives, they can free themselves from the internal inhibitors to gain a more powerful and confident perspective. Their new midlife is a turning point away from the wasted energy of suppressed wishes and denial of regret, towards an ability to make use of the multidimensional self they now acknowledge.

Olga Pearce, now 46, had been taught by Germaine Greer in 1970, when, in her classes at Sussex University, she was airing the ideas that were to be published in *The Female Eunuch.* "The energy in that room was electric," she explained. "Everyone was summoning up whirlwinds of hatred against her mother and her boyfriend and society for those stupid expectations they all had of her as a woman. There was a conspiracy afoot, and we had to flee it. We were told—and we felt we were really seeing the truth of this—that the notion of raising children was a fiction to keep us home and keep us down. Children grew up anyway, without being raised. The great investment society expected us to make in our children was debilitating all round—to mothers and children alike. I listened to this, and felt that lightning—everyone around me felt it, too. But while it made them feel good, I felt smaller and smaller inside—the one mature woman in the class, the one woman stuck in a completely typical woman's grind, thinking how I'd have to run straight home to get the children's tea. Actually, I didn't want to talk to the others anyway. I was old, a different generation. Twenty-*four* was old then! I saw the truth of what [Germaine Greer] said, how we should all just turn our backs on the things that kept us down. But I knew it wasn't that easy. You can't just walk away without leaving yourself behind. But I knew whatever I might say—about how difficult, really, it is to leave—would just be heard as socialized guilt. I'd lost my language for explaining how I felt."[3]

In previous generations, the birth of children and the love and care they generate, were simply normal markers of a woman's predicted life course. "On time" in one frame, Olga felt "off time" in the Sussex lecture hall. Newly ambitious, she discovered that she could not, after all, finish her degree while her babies played and slept. She had learned to value intellectual achievement in a domestic and emotional structure. She could not enlist either voice in self-defence, because each silenced the other.

Silence and alienation were common themes in traditional women's stories. They felt de-voiced by what they perceived as the louder voices of the new woman. Some believed that at the time they were forming those family bonds that are resistant to change, they simply had not taken on board the other possibilities. At 41, Meg O'Casey explained that she "had reached the giddy heights of a third-rate secondary modern education and had [her] first son at 19. Where, exactly," she demanded, "was I supposed to get my heightened awareness of women's true potential from?" Like Olga Pearce at 24, who alternated between hope, regret, and shame as she heard the call of feminism, Meg, at 25, "began to educate [her]self, not least in feminism." While she was learning she was still living with people she loved, and who had got used to her traditional domestic roles, "fastened into a whole structure that makes it difficult to break from without alienating those who are nearest and dearest . . . We do not live in a vacuum." The sense of something being "too late" even in very early adulthood was confusing and sometimes enraging. Patty Anselli, now 46, described the upheaval in her small college community. "It wasn't so bad," she explained, "when it was just the young unmarrieds spouting their slogans, but when I saw my friends, my neighbors, walking out on husbands and children, seeking some almighty grail of self-fulfillment, I felt like everything was being turned up-side down. I had a good marriage, but sometimes it seemed that it now consisted only of this out-worn format—the husband at work, the wife at home with the kids. I didn't know how to prove that the format wasn't the whole story."

Some of these women had already established traditional marriages and patterns of motherhood when they felt the push of women's revolution. Already seeing the costs mingling with benefits of their roles, they watched warily as women whose "commitment slate" was still clean, changed more easily with the times. They created their own culture of resistance. "People today describe us as playing at happy families, and really being miserable," Patty noted. "And of course we were not happy all the time. But the community of women who did remain at home, looking after their young children, formed a terrific group. The sociability we offered for our preschool children, and the support we gave one another, and all the community activities we arranged over weekends. That's a vanishing world, and that's a shame. You know, it's easy enough to ask whether that was all there was to life, when you refuse to see how much there was in it."

Repeatedly, traditional women slipped in reminders that the old forms had value: They were buffeted by their own doubts, but wanted to show the legitimacy of their past decisions. A bitter edge arose from the expectation that they would not get a fair hearing. Midlife signaled, Olga told me, that "it's time to get the story straight—for me, because it's not enough to say 'I'm right? You're wrong.' This doesn't get me anywhere. I want to run toward the rest of my life, but there's this awful sinking feeling . . . I want to know whether I was really conned, or wasting my time, or fooling myself. Do you know what I mean? There's this excited feeling because I feel a kind of inner storm gathering, but I need some kind of steady hold on what I was . . . Does any of this make sense?"

The perfect sense it made was that the defensive arguments of her younger adulthood no longer worked. The issue could not be seen in terms of "'I'm right/ You're wrong" because what mattered was her role in her future choices. She was not "right" because she knew the constraints involved in her traditional roles; but she was not "wrong" because she "could not walk away" from her children "without leaving yourself behind." Like Patty Anselli, she insists that those who are critical do not see what is real and good; but she nonetheless feels anxious about the costs, confused as to why she was compelled to pay them. She could not, at 24, have her say, since her two perspectives then balanced one another out. Now she needs to break that dissociation wherein the two views were at deadlock. She needs to gain "a steady hold" on her past, which will address the crisis question, "Was I really conned?" She needs to weather the blows of this question before she can enjoy "this excited feeling" about the rest of her life. For she has to understand what may have conned her, and who she is when she is free. Then, the midlife transformation does seem like being born again. As her different thoughts and feelings can now be acknowledged, as her own story is validated, her energy can turn outwards rather than waste itself in defense and denial.

ONE TENDER SPOT, ONE source of suppressed regret, which a traditional woman's midlife crisis can expose, is her belief that her husband has a reality or significance, which she herself lacks. Perhaps his earning power, his talent, or the sheer fact of being male have given his thoughts and feelings precedence. Under the power of this assumption, a woman's own needs are often shunted aside. At midlife, the assumption and its costs have to addressed.

Mai Collins, whom I interviewed for four years, from age 47 to 51, tread at first a delicate line between seeing and denying her past misperception. At first, her speech is meticulously balanced, always edging towards an elegiac acceptance, until she retrieved memories of what, at the brink of adulthood, had been eclipsed. As the rhythms of her language change, she feels new power.

Mai had come to London from Korea to study at the Guildhall School of Music when she was 19 years old. Ten months later, she married. Her husband was already an accomplished pianist when she met him, but real success was "a little slow, given his remarkable talent." Within six years of their marriage, however, his success became worldwide, and in many ways, even with young children, it was "the most important thing in their lives."

> We had a sort of pact, we knew the world out there, with the critics, agents, and audiences, was tough and you just had to be extremely good but also lucky to get inside it. What other people see as the musical gravy train, is a roller-coaster, and you have to keep jumping up and down until you look back to see whether you're moving along fast, or standing still. Jeff, with all his talent, had been trudging along slowly. He would give concerts in church halls for fifty pounds, and the local women would fill him up with roast beef and that funny pudding the English serve with it, an hour before he was supposed to go on. He wasn't in a position, then, to say, "No I'm not going to eat before a concert." When I met him, things were just starting to get better. I was a singer, but my voice was really going through a rough time. There was a range in the upper register that could desert me at any time—and you can't go on stage with that. I was advised to wait, put no strain on it, not drink or smoke. It was worse than being pregnant!
>
> We weren't wealthy then. Sometimes money was so scarce that we'd have to count our pennies to see who would take the bus and who would walk to work that day. So when he started doing so well, it was exciting for us all, and yes, I wanted help with the baby—yes, once upon a time there was only one!—but I could never say, "No, don't go to Milan" or "Please stay home this week." You have to say yes to everything that looks good, and then you have to say yes because you're losing so much money if you say no. And I was happy, really, at home . . .

As Mai first tells me her story, she keeps regret under control. She presents herself as aware of what she was doing, and why. Yet the effort to manage her feelings shows through. She explains what she cannot say to her husband, and why. She balances the constraints of pregnancy with the constraints on her as a singer. Her dissatisfaction is further highlighted by her perfunctory denial, "And I was happy, really, at home." Her story, at our first interview, was that of a reasoned and fair choice: Any one path precludes others; we all make trade-offs.

Six months later, Mai's story began to change, and new accounts of her motives emerged. She began by saying that she had felt, recently, that she was holding back an impulse to change. "I feel this very young woman keep coming back into my personality, when I talk to Jeff mostly, but also to other people. I'm so used to being young, you see— younger than he is. It's a little disturbing to see how I have aged, though everyone tells me how young I look, I know I look different, even if it's not older. And then I have these young children." At 48, her youngest child was only 4, though she had started having children at 20. She had two children, and then, when they reached puberty, she had a third, and eleven years later, she had her fourth child.

My children are an important part of my life, but if I look back to why I had the second lot, I know it was from a kind of fear of facing the emptiness when the first two left home—because they were going to leave fairly early. They're studying music now in Germany, even though the younger one is only 15. But it was also [my husband's] excitement at fertility or propagation—it really fills him up, seeing things grow. This garden—which everyone praises, meaning to praise me—is his, and he just loves planting things and seeing them grow. I can see now how I was trying to live up to that—no, not quite that silly, that's just one part of it, and I don't regret it—it's just that in the last few years, I've come to face what I did give up. I haven't been cheated of anything. No one could possibly feel sorry for me, any more than I do for myself, but it's a different life from the one I envisaged when I worked so hard at my singing when I was a teenager. And you know how my parents supported me, encouraged me, but then they were equally pleased because I was marrying him. I can't blame them, but I see now that their enthusiasm for what he was and what he was doing, gave me permission to let go of my own plans. It all seemed to go together then—his success, my cutting back on my own music, the children, my happiness. And now I've weeded it out a little. I'm glad of what I can give him in our marriage, and I wouldn't give up our marriage for anything—but his success isn't mine, in the way I once thought it was. I'm still stunned when I hear him play. Every time there's something new, something deeper and better. But what I feel now isn't pride, because it isn't mine, and this has been a little hard, shifting from feeling myself successful because he is, and realizing that I'm really something else, that what I have is more personal, but it's not success.

Here was the pivot of her crisis, the emerging pattern, showing consequences of *her* choices. As Mai confronted her knowledge of what she had given up for her husband and what she had given to him, she saw what this had not given her. The layered perspective—what she saw then and what she sees now—threatens to cancel out the meaning her behavior once had. Even the birth of some of her children was now explained in terms of her wish to compete with her husband's other interests. What was unseeable before can now be admitted, as such admissions cease to vex her in the context of "a standard I all along thought I was living up to, and now see I was only borrowing."

As Mai was absorbing the shock of what she now saw about her past, she sometimes edged away, trying to deny it. But she caught herself out: "I'm so often so busy—going to concerts, traveling, meeting people—that I have no time to think. And while I'm not thinking, I hear myself whispering, 'This should be enough. This is marvelous. I have friends. I have . . . this admiration.' Because when I'm this busy and tired I can take cues from other people, and I hear their effusive compliments. 'Doesn't she look divine!' But this background noise makes me feel even smaller. It smothers the bigger questions I really do want to ask. I don't want to keep smiling like some aging hostess, gobbling up the silly compliments of my guests. I want something more, something I can locate in me."

THE POPULAR (AND OUTDATED) image of a traditional woman is of a wife, mother, and homemaker. She is the woman behind the man, the woman whose energies are devoted to supporting and directing his energies. Her ambitions are satisfied through his goals. Within this framework, a woman is often seen to be confronting achievement, success, and power at one remove. According to some, such a woman, without direct access to money, prestige, and influence, is exploited and her life is a cheat. According to others, such a woman is preserving the family, society, and fulfilling her proper purpose.

Neither account of the traditional role accurately describes the traditional midlife woman's subjective experience and assessments. These women, like Mai, were not less autonomous than other women. They carefully sifted out self from husband. A new sense of self was taking shape, so that though they once felt "so proud of what [a husband] was out there doing," they were, at midlife, aware that "his success isn't mine." This realization forms the crisis that traditional women confront: Their own needs must be met, their own desires must be satisfied, their focus on others has eclipsed attention, which now must be given to themselves. This shift away from vicarious satisfaction stimulated questions about fulfillment and meaning.

Mai's inability to say to her husband "No, don't go to Milan" stemmed from the pact that they had, because they knew entrance into that magical kingdom of professional musicians was tough. She identified with his goal in two different ways. It had been her goal, too; she knew what it felt like, how strongly it beckoned, and how tricky it was to realize it. She knew that there were few second chances, however talented one was. How, then, could she hold him back? Though there is a time at which someone who had "made it" can afford to decline invitations, that time is not easily identified. The insecurity of the beginning of a career sticks for a long time. The insecurity of an inherently insecure career, such as professional musician, sticks that much longer.

She also identified with his ambition in the way in which anyone who loves someone identifies with the other's desires. Knowing how badly he wanted success, Mai wanted it for him. As he faced opportunities, and she confronted an arrest in her own (in the advice: wait, don't strain your voice), she found it reasonable to stay home with the children, and to offer him the freedom to pursue success. Her own push towards achievement increased her sympathy with his; her expansive needs, rather than drawing her into her own work, influenced her to act on behalf of her husband.

Like many decisions made in early adult life, the consequences become clear much later. Whereas, at the time, Mai had seen herself as "setting things aside of a time," she gradually redescribed her decisions as "giving up one thing and doing something else." Mai found her husband's success a constraint: The more successful her husband became, the less flexible her own life became. Though the money was available to pay for services that might increase her freedom, the nannies, gardeners, cooks, cleaners, and even private secretaries, could not cut down social meetings, constant relocation, and participation in her husband's musical world, which "was exciting, though [she was] usually a hanger-on."

> With most other people, I'm his wife, and that's how they see me. When we go out, it's to a concert he's giving or to one a friend of his is giving. It's not that they don't like me, or even appreciate me—they're willing to see the slightest thing I do as some sign of talent, just to make sure I'm worthy of him—but it's not the same, and somehow inside this busy exciting life, I've had to hoard for myself something private and very personal, that no one else knows about.

Here, her personally centered vision, is defended from how others see her, as she retreats from the public definitions of her, which are both flattering ("Doesn't she look divine!") and alienating, since she is usually seen as a "hanger-on," a side-kick to her husband. The ways in which Mai, and other women, too, spoke of this private space as a precious commodity, alongside their difficulty in explaining its content and its specific effects, reminded me once again of midlife Clarissa Dalloway in Virginia Woolf's novel. Organizing and fussing over her party, Clarissa takes a few minutes alone in the drawing room to mend her dress:

> Quiet descends upon her calm, content, as her needle, drawing the silk smoothly to its gentle pause, collected the green folds together and attached them, very lightly, to the belt. So on a summer's day waves collect, overbalance, and fall; collect and fall; and the whole world seems to be saying "that is all" more and more ponderously until even the heart in the body . . . says too, that is all.[4]

The seductive language that describes Clarissa's reverie, the passivity and peace alongside the activity of "drawing the silk smoothly" together and attaching the folds "very lightly, to the belt," echoes her desire to preserve the "thing there was that mattered," a thing usually "wreathed about with chatter, defaced, obscured . . ." and which can finally be assembled in awareness of a single self among the multiple aspects of one's life.

This secret place that preserved the self was mentioned by other women as a "safety value" or "restorative." Dana Crowley Jack, in her study of depressed women, observed that in the process of recovery, women sometimes sought a secret place as "a withdrawal from the authoritative voices and from the critical gaze of present, past and imagined others in order to be with the 'I' . . . Such a withdrawal can offer a safe, incubating 'egg place'⁵ of creative darkness, waiting and transformation, where new understanding and new strengths are found."⁶

My last interview with Mai took place when she was 51. There was less of that balancing act and cautious sifting among her feelings. Instead, she approached her conflict directly. "For so long, I realize now, I was thinking that not becoming a performer myself was a cop-out. That was what I was afraid I would see when I confronted my disappointment. That's the shadow that's been hanging over me . . . dragging me back . . . so I felt I didn't want to take a good look at things, but at the same time I did—badly—want to look. The relief of seeing, even though there are all kinds of regrets—and anger, yes anger, too—and what I thought I was doing, and how I could have thought that . . . What I now understand is that while I was supporting [my husband] so that he could make it in that strange world of music, I was appalled by what it took. So cutthroat, beyond the jokes we all told, about competitors putting razor blades between the keys during an audition, or singers spiking a competitor's drink with some kind of acid. Yes, the domesticity froze me, but there was something else, the sense that I was too private for all this. Seeing that I had some reason, some justice, in not performing is such a relief. I used to think that cold fear was bad—childish. But it was me . . . yes, childish, but that was me. If I had believed in my own judgment then, I might have done more. It would have been easier to decide to do something else with music. What slowed me down was not a fear of success—as I used to think—but my refusal to see how that was justified. Making friends with all those feelings I thought were wrong, gives me an enormous sense of power. Of course it isn't simply a matter of seeing myself as wholly in the right. I was too unsure, too confused, really . . . what I say I felt then, isn't really all I felt, and I've added to it so much of what I know now. I'm talking about inklings . . . so I'm understating the confusion. The big difference is that I used to feel I had to apologize for my life. I don't now."

The marker between the 40- and 50-year-old self is not always so sharp, but in Mai's case, the clarity was startling. She travels back along that "river of development"[7] to unearth turning points. She recalled that "sinking feeling" when she knew she could not harden herself to the life of a performing artist while living the life of a wife and mother. She sees that she had buried her regrets at not developing as a performing musician, but that, though buried, these regrets had an underground life, which constantly challenged her self-esteem. "Frozen" by domestic commitments, and confined by the pact she had made with her husband, she managed her life by not feeling the ambitions she once felt, by refusing to ask what she had given up, and why.

Aware of her fear at looking too closely at what she has lost, she wonders whether a new assessment of her past will devastate her and destroy the life she has established. As she gains the courage to confront her regret, however, she also uncovers the legitimacy of her earlier "inklings" as she stood on the verge of adult life and gazed, appalled at the entry price to "the magical world of the professional musician." It was cutthroat and tense. Her fear of these challenges, alongside her genuine revulsion at some of the costs, motivated other decisions to care and support family life, while her husband did pursue that career, which in many ways she would rather not have for herself. Her protection of him (by her acceptance of the pact by which she would not let domestic concerns intrude upon his career), she saw, was partly "an intense pity that this was still his joy."

> Going back to this, and feeling it again, has let me pick up something else. What I really wanted to do, always, was to show people what the voice could do, how music can be transformed by vocal interpretation. That was always what I wanted to do. I imagined that it had to be as a performer, But I could only see that, because I couldn't deal with having given it up—I couldn't really think about how I had . . . The unhappiness, over that, was . . . quite something. Feeling it now, as I do, isn't easy, but now I see how I have to do something else—not that, because it is too late, it just is . . . the voice ages . . . there's no time for that now, but there is time for something else. I've started holding sessions here at home. Young musicians come, and older people. They come for all sorts of reasons. To see Jeff's house. To take a look at me. But they also listen. They want to

hear what I can teach them to hear. I'm using, now, what I haven't used for so long, and what I feared was useless. I don't know why it took me so long to see . . . that there was a way forward.

As Mai places the regret alongside her concern for her future, the way forward seems easy, and she cannot understand why, once, it seemed so difficult. Free of the idealization of what she might have been, and free, too, of the voices that compliment her and control her identity as the perfect wife and mother, what once seemed shameful is now acceptable. No longer under the shadow of or dragged back by an internalized judge who demands that she be only what, in the best possible world, she might have been, she moves forward easily.

How Women Manage Regret

For Mai, as for most traditional women in my sample, the successful resolution of midlife crisis rests on her ability to manage the regret she feels at having suppressed her own needs without denying what she had given up. Traditional women have a tendency to rationalize their choices—to overestimate what their families actually need of them, to underestimate their own ambitions, to gloss over their frustration and magnify their satisfaction. At midlife, when the internalization of what a good woman should be lessens its control, when domestic demands on them tend to decrease, recognition of how much of themselves they have suppressed becomes a stimulant to crisis. I have coined the term "regret control" to focus on the way women in my sample tread that fine line between management and denial, and to trace their paths through this crisis to confidence in the way ahead.

Women often engage in enormous efforts to control the regret they are inclined to feel. These efforts are special to women because society is far less friendly to them than it is to men in providing ready-made patterns to accommodate their different needs for love, family, and personal development. At the brink of adulthood, many women make decisions on the basis of the belief that the division between work and home, the public and the personal, the old male roles and the old female roles, can be healed. They expect to combine a variety of goals, but instead are likely to find themselves confronted by unexpected priorities. They believe themselves to be making a single choice, but find that each decision about work and love is tightly "packaged,"[8] engendering a range of obligations. The packaged consequences of single choices took many women by surprise: Unexpectedly, they found themselves following typical patterns. Since, in midlife, patterns appear with greater clarity, the realization of what one has done, and what one has become, can be a shock. Questions about lost hopes, neglected potential, atrophied skills are extremely difficult to pose to oneself. They churn up the possibility of terrible answers: of a wasted life, of being cheated, of being set adrift, with neither a meaningful past nor a rich future. "Why," their crisis question is, "did I not see what was happening?" or "Why did I let this happen?"

AS TRADITIONAL WOMEN ADDRESS these questions, they often tread a delicate, dangerous line between management and denial. We often try to manage or manipulate our feelings, to make them less antisocial, less destructive, less painful. Throughout our lives we are accustomed to using and offering "feeling rules." As children, we are taught them; as parents, we teach them to our children; as adults, we try to impose them on ourselves. "Don't be so upset," we tell our children. "Have some patience!" we implore them. We count to ten when we want to control our anger. We try to relax our muscles when under stress. We also employ techniques for keeping at bay the circumstances or thoughts that disturb us. "Don't pay attention when you're being teased." "Just ignore her." These techniques for self-management link up with strategies to control or manage others. "If you ignore her, she'll stop teasing you." "When my boss starts to shout, I go blank. I automatically nod and he's still shouting but I can tell he's less angry because I'm telling him he's right." "When a customer is difficult I know I have to be extra nice, or compliment him in some way." We also teach children, or persuade others, to endorse certain values through feeling reminders: "You should be ashamed of yourself," we tell a child or friend or partner. "You should be proud." "You should be pleased." Feelings do not simply occur. We work on them: They are interpreted, redescribed, encouraged—and sometimes denied.

Sometimes we manage our feelings by changing our environment. We march outside the house when, inside, we feel so tense that we fear our feelings will become destructive. We treat or pamper ourselves, by

eating or shopping or seeing a film. We may elicit satisfaction or comfort from the notion that we have earned something. We *deserve* a new
dress. We *deserve* an ice cream sundae. We construct others' desserts,
too. A child deserves a scolding. A friend deserves to be ignored. The
notion of "deserving" something is, as Hamlet aptly noted, somewhat
arbitrary and dangerous: "use every man after his desert, and who shall
'scape whipping?" Such assessments of who deserves what, are usually
informal and impulsive; they may simply justify out whims.

How we feel about something is linked to how we think about it,
or how we see it. Sometimes we mold thoughts, or shift our perspective, in order to change our feelings. "My husband shouts when he's
hungry" is a means of deflecting the pain that the shouting causes. By
making it into an expression of hunger rather than seeing it as a personal attack, we are less likely to take offense. "She's teasing you because she's jealous" might be a way of persuading someone to feel good
and strong, rather than inferior and helpless, in the midst of playground bullying. The comforting story is one that convinces us we are
victimized because we are superior. In her fascinating study of flight
attendants, for whom being pleasant is part of their job description,
Arlie Hochschild found that women redescribed difficult passengers to
themselves in order to suppress their anger. One attendant described
how she would see an irate passenger, drunk and verbally abusive, as "a
little child." In response to this label, she could avoid the inconve-
nience of her own anger.[9]

We all have to find ways of seeing and feeling through which we
can function. Yet, when we find these, we may be doing one of two
very different things. For psychologists, managing anxiety or any negative emotion usually implies repression: Emotions are managed when
they cannot be accommodated, admitted, or confronted. Management
may involve getting on top of the problem, or it may involve obscuring
and burying it. The borderline between self-deception and self-forma-
tion is often blurred. Whether what we are doing falls to one side of the
border or the other may have to be established through trial and
error—a matter of what feels rights, or what, ultimately, works. Some
people have a special knack, either for one mode or the other. Integrity
and "being honest with ourselves" involve such delicate and unstable
operations because of the way our identity and judgments are
constructed.

As we look at women reframing their lives, we need to pick up on distinctions between management and denial. Is a woman confronting difficult feelings and integrating them into her self-awareness? Or is she turning away from them, and molding them into a more tolerable shape? The first is at the center of midlife development; the second stalls it. As women find their secret paths through midlife crisis, their skill in distinguishing the line between these two tactics increases, and they take this knowledge into their new midlife.

How Lack of Time
Leads to Suppressed Desires

Traditional women tended to talk about how little time they had for themselves, and how stressful and pressured their lives were. The fact that they avoided the role-overload of working mothers did not leave them with more time *for themselves*. Instead, they felt at everyone's beck and call. Several traditional women in my sample said that in their daily lives they felt like a machine working hard to keep on schedule. The space they require for their new mental labor—that confrontation with regret and that increased access to their wide-ranging responses—was not easy to come by. This is the second point at which the crisis of a traditional woman might enter: Being mechanized by others' needs, she becomes aware that the natural rhythms of thought and feelings, which should define her self, have been suppressed. She must find ways of voicing her needs and changing the ways she controls herself.

Though the overload of work and the absence of time for oneself are more likely to be associated with a "superwoman" who combines two full-time jobs—in the home and at work—they were common in the traditional women in my sample who felt required to be serviceable and responsible to others. Indeed, the superwoman image itself is really grounded in the feminine mystique: The adage "Women's work is never done" was heard long before women entered work outside the home. The traditional woman whose thoughts are dominated by domestic duty, by jobs to be done, by others' needs, is more mechanical than the woman who flies from home to work on the wings of superwoman's cape.

The absence of time and of mental space can become woman's worst enemy, as pressure to perform without self-reflection and self-responsiveness dissociate her from herself. Many traditional women spoke about the mechanical running of their lives, of maintaining control by keeping lists of things to do, of racing through the days, and trying to run things "like clockwork." Everything is cut fine, as everything has to be to fit in. They spoke about the rage they felt when something went wrong, when a job done had to be repeated, when some accident or inefficiency rendered their efforts ineffective. They spoke about the high they felt when things were running smoothly, and the sense of power they had because when things ran smoothly they felt in charge: They were both directing their lives and "coasting."

I was struck by how similar their language was to that of the working-class women in Margery Spring Rice's *Working Class Wives,*[10] written in 1939: Their days consisted of an endless series of tasks, cleaning, caring, mending, cooking, all fitted together, so that "leisure" lost its meaning and became time for sewing and shopping and less routine household jobs, and that "an hour's fresh air" was a rare luxury. Their minds are full of lists of jobs to be done. Their thoughts are dominated by the routine, the organization, the need, endlessly, to "keep up." The novelist Jane Rogers describes an unmarried but traditionally dutiful woman resorting to this strategy as she tends her ailing mother:

> Alice Clough was always busy. When she wasn't looking after her mother, or cleaning, or cooking, or washing or ironing, she would sit by the kitchen window, sewing or knitting . . . The only way to cope was to be efficient. Do what needed doing—meticulously, everything. Be a machine. Alice woke in the morning with lists of duties in her brain, and the list carried her from one task to the next, one hour to the next, day after day.[11]

This technique allows her to function, but at the expense of experiencing and valuing her life. Time becomes her jailor, to whom she succumbs. The day's routine imposes emptiness upon her. Yet, dominated by routine, she does not see her own emptiness. Endlessly, she waits for time to be hers. The superwoman syndrome has been misappropriated as a pitfall of mixing career and motherhood. It is a traditional female pitfall, created by overload. Woman's work is never done because there are always people around who want things from her, and she is likely to respond to their wishes. In her focus on others, she has lost a gauge for what is fair to her. She has no vantage point from which to say clearly: "This is for me and this is mine."

Yet "switching to automatic" is something we all have to do sometimes. We all have to do things we do not enjoy, whose meaning is only in the completion of the task. "Going on automatic" or "switching to auto" is a strategy used to suppress the process of making choices about what one does. Things have to be done and one does them. One's own preferences and needs and impulses are suppressed. The objections: "I don't want to do this; I'm too tired: I'd rather be doing something else," get pushed aside. This is precisely what "being taken over" means or "having one's work take one over" or having one's family "take one over." But normally, when the hours or days or weeks of overload are at an end—when the builders have finished or the child recovers or the relatives leave—we can return to being ourselves. For some traditional women, however, the pressure is continuous. They feel centerless, no more than a resource of others and cannot find that rhythm of thinking and feeling and responding, which defines our subjective individuality, which makes us a responsive, learning, knowing self. Many women suddenly saw at midlife that this was how they were living, and this recognition aroused their resistance.

AS A COLLEGE UNDERGRADUATE, Nell Godwin was indistinguishable from her peers, who then went on to pursue careers. She studied art history, and then took an apprentice course in restoring damaged or dirty paintings. Her work, her sense of ambition and creativity had always been important to her, but she also knew, from very early adolescence, that a close relationship with a man and children of her own would be a crucial part of her happiness and essential to her well-being. She worked for a city museum until she married in her mid-thirties, which, given her long-term desire to marry, was "late." Her husband was in the U.S. Army, and she moved with him from Germany to England to Virginia. By the time she was 40, they had three children. "If you ask me about my plans," she explained, "I will tell you how I plan to get through this day. My mind is filled with domestic stuff, and there isn't room for anything else."

She felt both frustrated and resigned: "It hasn't been easy, but I see why it happened. That's not everything, but when something goes wrong you want to make sense of it. There's comfort in that—don't you think?—you can hold on to things when you see why they happened. I was desperate when I thought I might not marry. I simply could not conceive of a future without a husband and children and even grandchildren. It was overpowering—a real personal need, you know, not just someone else's idea. I do look forward to having more time for other things, but I don't have that time now. I know how meagre this seems to my friends from work and from college, but I could not go back to being alone, and this hectic lifestyle came with my husband."

The idealization of family life with which she had begun marriage signaled a genuine need ("I could not conceive of a future without a husband and children . . .") but it also locked her into a compromising position, which she both defended and perceived ("I know how meagre this seems to my friends . . ."). She then suggests she did not have control over her choice ("This hectic lifestyle came with my husband") but subsequently confronted the contradiction between seeing herself as constrained and knowing that she is ultimately responsible for what she does. "I panic now, when I think of another move, and all the energy that goes into that, all the things I'm leaving behind. It's always someone else calling the shots—not me, not [my husband]. You know I have a special word for it: going into 'gut gear,' that's what I say I have to do when I have a whole bunch of things I hate doing and have to do. But now when I feel this—well, at 45, you can't go around saying you don't know what you're doing. But deciding how to make things better so that you do have more say . . . I don't know, I get into a spin . . . I haven't worked this out . . . it's still pressing. I can't take it all for granted, like I once did."

For Nell, the crisis of responsibility is carried by the idea of what it is to be an adult: "at 45, you can't go around saying you don't know what you're doing." Her idea about what it is to manage her feelings is reframed. Previously, she managed by grinding her feelings down. She would act without thinking, simply do what she had to do. She did not protest because, if she protested, she would have to change. If she were to change, what would she change, and who would be harmed? Would she then be responsible for stopping her husband's career? Would she damage the marriage? Would she find that if she were to speak out, he would punish her in some way—if not by "putting her down" then by "just not hearing, not caring"? Or would she hurt him, she wonders and contemplates his helplessness: "He doesn't want to move any more than I do. He's not in control any more than I am." Addressing her own dissatisfaction arouses intolerable anxiety, as she wonders, "If I admit this, then what will change, and what will I lose if things change?" Hence, Nell says she is "in a spin"; she has not "worked this out." So much energy is devoted towards minimizing or denying regret that every attempt to get beyond the crisis question is blocked by its denial.

The turning point came at a reception at which she was one of the "old" army wives entertaining the "new" wives, who had more recently come to the army base. As she was "doing the welcome routine, and offering all that information and chit-chat, one young woman started ooh-ing and ahh-ing about this big exhibition that had come to the art museum in the nearby city. I mentioned that I'd studied with the painter—and there was this—," and she mimicked the young woman's gasp, " '*You* studied with him!' I smiled politely and nodded, but felt as though she'd punched me. Why was it so surprising that I had once done something interesting? Who was I—who was she looking at? I felt what she saw—a middle-aged woman with ash-grey hair and glasses, someone who is perched nice and comfy on this little niche here. And I'd been feeling . . . so far from that. It made things worse, seeing what a nonentity I was to her." Nell experienced the jolt of seeing another's view of her. Feeling the insult of being "a middle-aged woman with grey hair and glasses," she summons up her resistance, strengthening a personally grounded vision, to counter these blows. Yet this process is not immediate, and she found herself, during the next few weeks, "in another of those depressions, where I seem to be floating further and further way from any grip on myself."

Nell then remembered that this feeling of being at an unsafe distance from what mattered to her was familiar. She had endured similar feelings of dislodgment throughout her adolescence. "All the time I was doing these fancy things in high school and in college, I felt a craving for something. All I wanted was to be grown up, so that I could have a husband and a family. Nothing else felt safe. So it didn't make sense to question what I had to do to keep it safe." Yet in midlife, the revving of her "gut," which once silenced her own desires, directs her to look at what she had been suppressing. She feels that push in adult development that psychologist Roger Gould described—the reworking assumptions about one's world that have been brought forward since childhood. Gould found that age 45 and over brings the challenge of creating new ways of being in the world based on the emerging assumption, "I own myself."[12] This determination to assume ownership of oneself is a step towards the resolution of midlife crisis. But as traditional women take this step, they are flooded with new anxiety as they ask, "How can I preserve my role as the linchpin of the family if I admit just how much this role has cost me?" The way forward, then, is to discover how a differently centered self, one in touch with her own responses and desires, can retain what she values most in her traditional life without continuing to suppress many aspects of her self.

Six months after Nell described herself "in a spin," she said she had decided things had to change.

> This is far more frightening than anything I've ever thought before. It's easier to say, "I'm going to bear with this, however awful it feels." But time is rolling on, and—well, once I saw what I was doing, how I was controlling things, it was clear that I shouldn't have to. At first, when I brought it up with Jim, his response was "Life is difficult; we can't all do what we want; being in the army isn't easy." There were little dismissals. "It's not so bad" and "Life's not fair." The sort of thing you'd say to a child. But that's what I'm not. I'm not a child. And I've kept pushing. I'm going to touch base—we can compromise, we can decide together, but no more of this moving around. I look at the young wives do it, with their kids, and I can see again how hard it is, how I really don't have to keep doing this when I can see that I don't want to. I don't know why I didn't see it before. I don't know why I didn't start from here. But I do know that this certainty gives me more say in this marriage than I've ever had.

Her path to power lies in seeing what it is she wants. Previously, arguments had disintegrated as, in response to her husband's dismissals, she felt unsure of what she wanted. As she listened to him tell her that her expectations were too high and her complaints exaggerated, she feared that her own wishes were destructive. Fearing her own desires, she suppresses them and runs in "gut gear," acting out of that anxiety she suffers in the pit of her stomach rather than from her own wishes or judgment. As she sees how much power the need for a perfectly-run family had over her, she takes new control. The young woman who had mistaken her for "a middle-aged woman with ash-grey hair and glasses" had triggered Nell's fear of remaining forever at a distance from her real self. No longer afraid of her own desires, she can barely understand the control that fear once had: "I don't know why," she reflects, "I didn't start from here." Now that she can give a voice to hidden and suppressed desires, she is no longer isolated from her own needs. With her new midlife voice, her own wishes take a prominent role in family life. The specific outcome of these new dynamics may be uncertain, but her control of the way ahead gains a new certainty.

How Traditional Women in the New Midlife Cope with the ''Empty Nest''

In her eloquent book on traditional midlife women, Lillian Rubin[13] explores their response to the "empty nest"—or the shift in their lives as their children, in their late teens, leave home. Though previously it had been widely supposed that women who were particularly involved with their children and devoted to mothering roles often became depressed,[14] Rubin found that, in general, women discovered new sources of energy as domestic burdens eased. Other researchers too have found little evidence for the once wide-spread assumption that the empty nest is problematic for women;[15] instead, it has been recognized that they are far more likely to embrace the "loss" of maternal roles as an opportunity[16] to foster their own neglected needs. Rubin found, in fact, that fathers were more likely to feel disturbed as their children left home—for college, for marriage, for a distant job—because they, unlike the mother, had not been prepared for this separation by watching the incremental steps of the child's independence. The mother, closer to her child than the father, saw the separation coming. She was as prepared, as was her child. Ripe for change, anticipating new opportunities,[17] she suffers more distress when her growing child *fails* to leave home.[18]

The traditional woman of today anticipates, like the women studied by Rubin and others in the 1960s and 1970s, new opportunities arising from time to herself as her children leave home. But the changes today's traditional women have experienced, and the changing experience of their children, create different patterns and different problems. The markers of family time have changed. Many children do not leave home when they reach adulthood. The empty nest is often a "cluttered nest," as young adults cannot afford to live away from home when they attend college, when they find jobs, or even when they marry.[19] "My daughter takes up more of my time now, at 20, than she ever did as a teenager," Rachel admitted. "She's depressed about her future, about still being stuck here, where she thinks nothing's ever going to happen to her . . . I hear her weeping at three in the morning and sit beside her, trying to stuff some of that old youthful glory back into her heart. But I know I add to her problems. I'm the boss here, but she's ready to be her own boss. We live as best we can . . . but the nerves will get jumpy, no matter how hard you want to try."

Even harder may be the "revolving door" syndrome, wherein children who left home to go to college, return, unable to find a job that will support a separate home, or unable to find work at all. Then the family, having grown accustomed to an empty nest, finds a new adult in its midst. Expecting to have time, now, for herself, Amy Richards at 47 found herself "still a mother, primarily. Children are forever, and now forever's longer than it was for my parents. And maybe I shouldn't say this—well, maybe it's not so terrible, just odd—because I'm relieved, relieved to know that I can still be useful to my children, and more than useful, like lending them a hand, but still pretty essential to their well-being. I know women who would say I'm copping out with all this, but it's not my fault that the job market's so shaky. I'm not keeping them here, am I? So I like it, okay?"

Amy's argument shows how that critical gaze, dictating what a woman should be, has changed. These women are not only being judged by feminine norms but also by feminist ones. The feminist oriented judge, whom she has internalized, tells her that she is copping out. She establishes her innocence—she is not responsible for children's continued dependence—before admitting that it gives her satisfaction. The relief she feels registers her anxiety at being called upon to do something "significant" with her time—an anxiety that embodies new expectations about what achievement is. "There are these women who have done so much . . . but, well, my mother was greatly admired because she organized wonderful block parties, with these fantastic processions the kids took part in. She designed the kids' costumes, and they were just gorgeous. And people marvelled when they saw their old curtains turned into king's robes and such. But that sort of thing has just gone, and for me, whatever I could do now, is so small . . . I'm not going to turn into a big career woman, just because I have some free time, so whatever I do want to do—well, it doesn't seem so terrible to let it wait a little while . . . does it?"

The freedom that traditional women in the 1960s and 1970s felt at empty nest time has, for contemporary midlife women, been spiked by anxiety. Expectations of what achievement means have increased, so that the development of hobbies, interests, and talents, which were once admirable, now may seem insignificant. Some women felt that without immediate feedback from their children—without their company and their demands—they would be pushed to face what they had not done, and that they would be looking into an abyss. They spoke of slipping into a diffuse state wherein "free time means I have no energy." For these women, the empty nest stimulates a crisis, which seems like a downward slide, but it is often more like a padded room in which ordinary perceptions are dulled so that new psychic arrangements can be made. Jasmin Falil described how the house had changed when her 18-year-old son left home. "I go into his room and I stare at it. I know I shouldn't. I know I'm being morbid, but I stare at the bed and the desk and the wall posters until they take on a life of their own, and there are seconds you know when I go kind of crazy and he's sort of there haunting it, and that makes him seem closer but it also makes him seem almost dead. Then I realize he's not dead, and I'll be seeing him when the semester's over. It's like suddenly being given something, this realization that he's alive and well. The worrying habit will stick with me throughout my life, but as I do more and more other things, it will ease a bit."

In missing her son, and vacillating between mourning and reassurance, Jasmin is testing out the transition between a woman who feels responsible for her son, and a woman who is free to move on to other things. The empty nest—like the empty room—takes some getting used to, but few women get stuck in this transition. The gap felt by some women when their children do leave home presents a new range of questions, along with its opportunities. The freedom that the absence of children gives to women who do not already have too much to do, presents a puzzle, which may initially feel threatening.

Corinne Simon, whose youngest child was 17 and had just gone away to college, said, "I wake up and the day is stretched out like a long blank sheet of paper. I can taste the emptiness on my tongue. I swallow it with my tea. 'You're a free woman now,' my husband says to me. 'Enjoy it.' But that freedom makes me ashamed."

Three months later, Corinne described how her free time made her vulnerable to "be at the beck and call of every last person in this family." She saw she had to protect herself by "making a quick decision." She took a job as a saleswoman to "protect that new independence." Empty time had to be taken and defined as hers; without definite steps it would be usurped for others' use. Women have to work hard and fast to preserve the space offered by the emptying of the nest.

Time and control over time remain crucial issues, even for empty nesters. From being dominated by an overfilled schedule, a woman might suddenly feel imprisoned by an empty one. Some women feel marginalized by both a standard of judgment that dictates they should be giving of their time, and one which denies them importance because they have not done the "right sort of thing" with their time. Some women wonder whether they have a right to make counter-claims against the feminine judge, when they cannot do so with the feminist voice. Perhaps at no other time has midlife been so challenging for traditional women.

"The whole world is spinning around me, and I'm governed by it. There is no time out, no time for me, and I'm too busy to think about what I am." Or, "My day is like a ray of dust motes. I just sit and watch all the minutes dance away in front of my eyes. I get in a kind of trance. There's nothing that connects me more to one decision than another, so my life is just suspended in midair."

Time separated these women from themselves, and they did not see how to make the connection between time use and self-expression. Time is useless to them either because they cannot act constructively within it, or because they have too much to do; they feel overloaded and cannot do anything well. For other women, depression threatens, through lack of power to do what they want, to achieve what they want, or to discover what it is that they want. The sense of being "gobbled up" or "drained dry" by one's family may persist, as a woman finds other family demands rising to the surface as soon as one evaporates. A husband, or her parents, expect more and ask more, as her children require less attention. The expectation that now, in midlife, time will be her own, is frustrated as others usurp this "free" time. She may then realize that time will never be hers without a deliberate preservation order on it.

IN THE COURSE OF the next two years, I interviewed these empty-nesters at three-month intervals. The first few times I heard the vacillation that I was accustomed to hearing—Rachel's daughter's depression improved, Corinne found a new rhythm in which her free time made sense, Jasmin took a part-time job in a local store; the anxiety of the crisis diminished as they simply got used to the way things were. But this push into marginality had a definite effect, which emerged more clearly at the one-year mark. Rachel said, 'I felt awful then [a year ago, when her daughter was so depressed]. I don't know if I said how awful it was . . . I felt this dread, this sense that I was being measured up, and found short. That kind of thing makes you think— when it goes on like that, on and on. And when I started being able to sleep again—because my 21-year-old baby could sleep through the night without crying!—I thought, 'Who is this, who's getting me down? Who's wagging this finger at me—tut-tut?' So, was I picking up her depression? Well, I can't say, but you know, what I really thought was that I had to get better for both of us . . . I had to get better because I deserved it—not this ratting on at myself. Why? For what? There was this sudden freedom, when I realized I didn't have to take that wagging finger. I'm a grown woman. What has anyone else got to say to *me?*" She laughed broadly at her own question, and at the reexperience of relief, remembering how that "wagging finger" was shaken off. The question, too, is bright in its simplicity: Who is it who is ratting on at her, and what has that judge got to say to her, that she cannot say for herself?

For Jasmin, the absence of her son was "still like a hole" inside her. "Some would say I loved him too much. I know that . . . but I can't agree, not really. What's too much? What I have to do, is find . . . well, it's like finding out who you are again. Maybe because I had kids so young, that it's not easy to go back to who you were. But I'm making more friends now, just feeling my way. I'm not sure I ever did that before. It's sometimes a little scary. But I can do it, just feel about in my own way. It's pretty neat."

Like Rachel, Jasmin argues away the disembodied judge that blames her for missing her son. She guesses that others would say she loved him too much, but dismisses their measure ("What's too much?") and feels she is learning from her own experience, which is sometimes scary but the activity itself, new as it is, gives her confidence: it is "pretty neat."

At midlife, as they confront their suppressed visions and voices, many traditional women have to get to know themselves anew. Never before, in their adult lives, have they had direct access to thoughts and emotions. Previously, each thought and feeling was vetted and judged according to its right or wrong. Until they entered their new midlife, some traditional women barely bothered to distinguish between a thought that was considered appropriate to what a wife and mother should think or feel, and the multidimensional thoughts or feelings they actually had. As the gaze of that external judge dims, the freedom of access to a wide variety of responses may be scary; but as their midlife crisis is resolved, they embrace this new freedom, knowing it is the best way forward.

IN RECENT YEARS, the orderly and rhythmic course of women's lives that was taken for granted in previous generations has fragmented. This generation shares no notional time line, or what Ravenna Helson calls a social clock pattern,[20] which sets targets for milestones, such as marriage, the birth of children, writing one's first book, being promoted, and so on. Within a single generation, women have suddenly been confronted by enormous differences among them: Some marry and have children "on time"—between 18 and 25, which once marked women's window of marriageable opportunity. Some women are haunted by newer versions of old time lines, and worry about not being married at 25 or 30 or 35 or 40. For some women, 25 is judged as "old to have children," whereas some women do not feel ready for motherhood until 40. These variations are not mere idiosyncrasies among a few women; they are new trends, new life patterns. No single pattern of getting married, working, having children has that comfortable (if constraining) inevitability shared by women of previous generations. Whatever unhappiness these women's mothers had, they at least had the kind of equilibrium that goes with the sense of not having much choice, whereas contemporary midlife women often see themselves as having had more choices than they were able to take advantage of, and many of them feel that every choice they made has involved a series of compromises over which they have not had adequate control.

Different choices, or the different influences that directed their choices, give rise to uncertainty. The inevitable bouts of disappointment and dissatisfaction that accompany any life course no longer seem inevitable. Different pockets of unhappiness would have pitted a different path, but the unhappiness we do not experience is often judged less severe than the unhappiness we feel. Dissatisfaction breeds easily when other people, people very much like us, are doing very different things. We are easily tempted to think: "I might have done something different, and avoided this."

Because uncertainty about the rightness of one's path or the legitimacy of one's choices is now an inevitable part of contemporary womanhood, the task of midlife is to uncover regrets that have been controlled or denied, and gain sight of the impediments that took difficult choices out of our control. As the closing chapter of youth leads to a future that must be reinvented, traditional women engage in new battles against the voices and visions that had edged out their own. Once these were identified, they looked round the battlefield, bewildered, as Mai was when she asked, "Why did it take me so long?"

It all seems simple as she reaches the resolution of the crisis and takes control of her future. But the process is far from simple. The traditional women in my sample were thrown into crisis as their habitual management of regret no longer worked. They felt an impending catastrophe as once-suppressed wishes and thoughts flooded them; but what felt like devastation was really a path toward new growth. We have seen how they took deliberate steps toward learning how to voice their neglected feelings. At the resolution of midlife crisis, they are empowered by new access to those thoughts and feelings and responses; no longer will they be blind to the impediments that once took difficult choices out of their control.

Traditional Women: Signs and Signposts of Midlife Crisis

The lives of women in this category are, from the outside, very like those of the traditional homemaker of the previous generation. Yet, the growing knowledge these women have—that their feminine roles have been upheld within times of social change and that these roles have involved sacrifices for which they come to hold themselves responsible—leads them to confront questions about how best to change their life patterns to allow, in their future, fuller self-realization. The following lists mark out possible routes in their midlife path. Women who see themselves in this category may be able to use this list to identity their stage in midlife passage—though this is a rough guide, not a detailed map.

Previous orientations:

1. Roles of wife/partner and mother have been crucial to one's identity and happiness.
2. The needs of the family have had priority over one's own needs.
3. Ambitions and skills have been channelled into domestically useful activities.

In a pre-crisis state, the goal is to fulfill these orientations to the best of one's ability. Efforts may be controlled by ideas of what a "good" or "valuable" woman is.

Signs of approaching crisis:

1. increasing frustration with the pressure of others' demands
2. anger at the inability to focus on one's own desires
3. panic at the distance between how others perceive one and who one thinks one really is

These feelings are not entirely new to a traditional woman, but previously she has worked harder to control them, and defend herself against them. Now, mounting doubts arouse acute anxieties as to the value of what she has done and how to proceed with the rest of her life.

Resolution of crisis:

1. gains more control over the extent of one's responsiveness to others' needs
2. forges a strong link between what one wants and what one decides to do
3. connects with that "unseen" self, often through having more private time

As she confronts self-criticism and dissatisfaction, she extends her capacity to trust her own judgment. Released from the pressure of external ideals, she finds a more flexible, confident self.

3

Innovative Women: Plans, Pressures, and Resistance

Innovative women have, during the past three decades, ridden high on the crest of the wave of change. These are women who set out to compete in the man's world of work and to gain equal status. Many of them had, at the brink of midlife, attained their goals, and those who had not, still had made significant advances towards them. Yet the women in my sample, who had come so far, were halted by a crisis, which forced them to reassess the work they had done on themselves to achieve their aims, and the stilted futures they might face if they continued to follow ready-made career patterns. For innovative women, who as young adults had stormed the male preserve and sought success on men's terms, discovered at midlife new resistance to the male cultures of the workplace. As they ran into the contradiction between their genuine ambitions and their equally genuine resistance, they met, head-on, their point of crisis.

To make her way through this impasse, the innovative woman redefined her goals and found ways of refashioning her career, freeing herself from the long-held assumption that to succeed she has to follow established standards of career success. In resisting the assumptions that directed her throughout young adulthood, an innovative woman often feels that everything she has built up now threatens to topple. But as she works through the contradictions in her desires, ambitions, and values, she is working to create new professional and personal patterns. As innovative women question the structures that have been fashioned by men, to suit many men's preferences and needs, they discover their own vision—distinct from that of women in the past, and distinct, too, from what they had expected as they set out to achieve their ambitions. Thus empowered, the innovative woman in her new midlife transforms her future.

THE INNOVATIVE WOMAN'S MIDLIFE crisis is grounded in the most powerful new image to arise during the past decades. The woman of the new age is forward looking, forward moving, slicing through the businessman's jungle with such ease that it is difficult to believe there were ever any odds against her. She is competent, confident, controlled. She has shed any internal impediments to success at work. She has conquered external biases against her. Her admiring husband works alongside her in the precious few moments they both spend at home. Her life is full rather than hectic. She has time for what matters. Her maternal devotion is, like everything else she achieves, efficient and effective. In short, her life is a perfect unity, a smoothly woven tapestry.

Though each woman may know that her own progress towards balance and equality has been uneven, unsettling, and to some extent unsatisfactory, she is likely to retain the assumption that someone else has got it right. The dream of a conflict and compromise-free life for the woman-who-has-it-all is a staple of our cultural diet. In the early days of the Clinton administration, an article in *Time* magazine concluded, "Perhaps in addition to the other items on her agenda, Hillary Rodham Clinton will define for women that magical spot where the important work of the world and love and children and an inner life all come together."[1] The blind faith that there is some magical spot wherein each part of a woman's puzzling life finds its perfect fit has stimulated much courage and much suffering. As most midlife women have not achieved quite what they set out to, as they found the going much rougher than they expected, the promise of some finally solved equation has persuaded them to keep trying. As each woman knows that she herself has not come up with the right answer, she may believe that, though missing figures still elude her, they are easily calculated by someone else. At midlife, women count the costs of this assumption.

THE   WOMEN   DESCRIBED   IN   this chapter devoted their early
adulthood to bringing innovative ideals to life. Those ideals provided a
strong sense of direction and purpose, but could become destructive
and distracting as the difficulties of attaining them were minimized.
Faith in that magical spot where all her goals come together perfectly is
highly confusing: For, as a woman learns how difficult it is for her to
make her way into high-powered careers, fit into the workplace, and
sustain the private life she values, she wonders, "Is the problem her
own? Is she not smart enough, not lucky enough, not blessed enough
to read the magical map?" Until the crisis of midlife disentangles those
male and superwoman ideals from her own realities, she may search,
half-blinded by the bright image of the ideal woman. Until then, she
will imagine her, read about her, or construct her from her own circle
of acquaintance.

Angela Heath, 44, is—for me—one such woman. My daughter
and her daughter are friends, and we sometimes swap our children during holidays. Her daughter will join us for a week during the spring
break, and my daughter will spend part of the winter holiday with her.
But the delivery of these children is complicated. We live in different
parts of the country, and meet midway for the change-over. The last
exchange took place as I took my daughter to London, and dropped
her, near the close of the working day, at Angela's office on the South
Bank. The guard phoned her from the entrance. "There are two young
ladies to see you," he reported, awaiting her assent before giving us our
visitors' passes. My skewed collar and bulky shoulder bag eclipsed my
forty-year-old face: For him, female maturity involved more dominance and polish than I could muster. Angela was, as always, polite and
gracious. She chuckled at the guard's description of me and my daughter; but her vast office, its prestigious view of the Thames and the
Houses of Parliament, its two paper piled desks, and her elegant work
clothes, all conspired to enforce the guard's diminishment of my
maturity.

As my daughter keyed in to the computer, to be entertained for
the last half-hour of Angela's day by the games that frequently saved
her from a child's distraction, she thanked me for the "delivery" and
apologized for the time it must have taken. "Oh—it was fun," I assured her. "We wanted to see the Christmas windows anyway." I fal-
tered in my protests that the day had not been wasted. My daughter

was already off school, and so work that day would have been touch and go; but this implication was lost in the look I saw, or thought I saw, leap into Angela's face, before it was politely swallowed. "A day to take a girl to London?" I imagined her thinking. An unscheduled day off work just to see the Christmas window displays? I believed she was marvelling at the distance between us and our different meanings of time. I saw my own work sizzling and wailing in meltdown, like Dorothy's witch, after inadvertently pouring this water on it.

For me, Angela is the new woman who knows, and has always known where she is going. Her husband, like most partners of corporate women, admires her as a professional woman. Tensionless, they share those domestic chores that they do not allocate to paid employees. Yes, she feels responsible for the burning garlic bread, and she goes out to buy the croissants in the morning, but the meal preparation is fairly evenly divided, and the clearing up is a well-orchestrated joint effort. All this is purely weekend stuff anyway. It is hard to catch her out in traditional women's roles. The time she spends with the children is time spent together as a family, doing things they all enjoy. She is innocent of women's drudgery and women's constraints, as elegant outside as within. Whereas my mother, in such a woman's presence, might have suffered the same self-defeating gawkiness I feel, she would have felt it because Angela is tall, thin, and blond; I, a contemporary woman, feel it because she is corporate, managerial, and highly paid. To my mother, the outside trappings of appearance might have offered proof that inside herself Angela was all set up, that she had the key or knew the combination to that magical spot. For me, the idealized image has changed, but what is idealized—that perfectly organized, assured self—remains the same.

I do not trust myself to see her clearly. On the one hand, I idealize what she has, what she does, and what she is; on the other hand, a grudging nature insists that though I cannot see it, some debt lurks in the wings of her life, awaiting payment. Can her children, I wonder, really need so little of her? How does she manage to need so little of them? How does she manage to ride out the political storms and the terrible hours of corporate life?

I know many other highly successful women, who are profoundly committed to their careers; but they have all been through the wars of early adulthood, and however triumphant they have emerged, they are not unscathed. I can locate a commonality of effort and tension, a knowledge that plans are fragile things, tightly hedged by varied circumstances.

But Angela is not a woman I could use in my research. As a social acquaintance, I cannot ask her to pick at the threads of her life until we see where they are weak and shredded, where they are strong, and how they are woven into a fabric that minimizes weaknesses and utilizes strength. I cannot guess this, because I do not know her well enough. My ignorance is not due to any reserve or disguise on her part, but to the way she matches up with an image I cannot fathom. What I fail to understand is not how it all works, but why its working is so well for her, and so creakily for others. What is it that usually goes wrong, but is going right for her?

My puzzle signals an impasse in my own vision. Idealization, as I learned from this study, kills perception. If I could make that transition from acquaintance to researcher, I would doubtless find that Angela shared the more complex, rugged picture of the women I interviewed. If I could achieve the midlife growth, which so many women in my sample achieved, then the puzzle would be resolved as my focus changed. Ideals of the perfectly run life were eroded by the pride of midlife, as a woman looked again upon herself as someone who can learn best from her own experience. But to reach this vantage point, a woman had to redefine her own goals, and free herself from the established assumptions about what it takes to be a success.

ONE OF THE FIRST, FORCEFUL lessons of the second wave of the women's movement was that young women should, like ambitious young men, have special, life-shaping plans. At that time, girls were criticized for failing to develop career strategies, for being too easily distracted, or too dependent on others' expectations or wishes of them, and for not taking sufficient responsibility for themselves.[2] It was not brains, or even education that girls lacked, but foresight and determination. For it had been found that if you knew the standard intelligence measurement (or I.Q.) of a very young man, then you could predict his future professional status. You cannot be absolutely precise, but you can form reasonable expectations on the basis of his intelligence.

For women, however, no such predictions could be made nor expectations formed. A young woman who scores high on intelligence tests in college might have no professional standing whatsoever at forty. Even if you took her ambitions into account, you could not predict her future career. Her abilities and her potential did not work together with her plans, decisions, and actions in the way they seemed, on the whole, to do for men. Even as women increasingly embarked on postgraduate courses, even as they entered the professions, they rapidly "disappeared"[3] in midlife. This generation of women could, they were told as young adults, make the breakthrough to equal work, if and only if they held onto their plans with sufficient ferocity. Their dreams of achievements would have to rule over all other dreams. When they married, whom they married, when or whether they had children would be secondary considerations. Events that once marked out a woman's life course would now have to be slotted in between career markers. The women discussed in this chapter took this challenge to heart. They pledged their intelligence and ambition towards forging new paths in men's territory.

The swings and roundabouts of that social revolution are only now coming into focus. As the burden of proof was put on these young women, the working world they entered grew far more demanding than the working world they envisaged as very young adults. The integration of women's different roles and goals has been much harder than anyone anticipated. Just as young women's expansive ambitions came to life, a new ethos of hard work, of consuming work, spread throughout businesses and the professions.[4] The nine-to-five *Organization Man*[5] was a man of leisure compared to the contemporary worker, with his laptop computer replacing the newspaper during his commute, with his car phone allowing his office instant and constant access, with his home computer on which he can study flow charts during sleepless moments in the night.

Nor have demands on parental time decreased. Though many midlife women, as teenagers, judged their mothers to be over-engrossed in motherhood, and overinvolved with their children, society now seems so unfriendly, even dangerous, to children, that the protection—in terms of education, control, and care—the family can offer is judged to be of increasing importance. With its special features of fertility and nurturance, a woman's life is still more seasonal than a man's, more attuned both biologically and psychologically to changes around and within her. The special course of women's adult development is not accommodated by the rigid career structure, which is based on the supposition that workers are not responsible for the young, the old, or the ill.[6]

The working hours of all Americans have risen sharply in the last few decades.[7] For women at senior career levels, the pressure to work long hours is especially strong. Since the occupational ladder is a pyramid, with far more workers at the bottom than at the top, the top admits only those who put prodigious efforts into the corporation. This is not a matter of simple punctuality, or staying on an extra hour. It is a matter of putting in more hours than anyone else. It is a matter of being seen to work, being present at the work place, proving each day and each night that work comes first. It is a matter of using one's leisure time in work-related activities, such as networking. It is also often a matter of having someone else devote herself to family and domestic matters, of having someone else organize the pedestrian details of one's life: Such hard work often involves the back up of a wife. The majority of male managers have "nonworking" wives—wives who work, unpaid, at home. No woman has a wife.

The midlife generation working at such a pace today belongs to the generation who, in their youth, called the slower pace of their parents a rat race. The working demands of today's corporations are too high for anyone's good. The number of working hours has been set high for a variety of reasons. The rat race is contagious. When one corporation's employees overwork, then others have to follow suit, in the great competitive spirit. Time is becoming a scarce resource, bullying us with its demands. Employers ask more and more time from their employees. It is a badge, a proof, a token of commitment. Many feel its demands and its costs, yet few realize what a useless token it is. Increased hours at work do not necessarily increase production, but often—especially over the long term, decrease it, with burn out, with ill health, with stress. The link between time and productivity is outmoded, based on a simple model of the production line, wherein longer working hours lead to more things produced. Yet companies continue to be "manned" twenty-four hours a day, seven days a week, as they respond to increased volume of work and the manufactured belief that it is necessary to remain in continuous contact with every other country, whatever its time zone. Time becomes "a proxy indicator for performance, based on some crazy assumption that the more time, the better."[8] When unemployment threatens, no employee can afford to work less hard than another employee. When financial rewards are offered for long, constant work, then long work seems like good work, even though it may not be productive. When corporations believe, however mistakenly, that it is more efficient to work its employees hard, then people who want to be employed have little choice.

Eighty-five percent of male heads of household surveyed believe that they do not have a say in how many hours they work. Eighty-five percent of married men believe they are faced with a dilemma: either work this job at the hours that do not suit you, or be dismissed from your job.[9] In this take-it-or-leave-it position, men take it. If women want to work alongside them, they have to take it, too. In pursuing their achievement goals through work, in making use of the freedoms they have gained, "women come to recognize the cruel irony that the opportunity to have a career does 'liberate' them from traditional roles and expected behavior, but at the same time the only real opportunity this freedom allows is for women to adopt a male career model."[10]

Women are often unwilling or unable to "take it" like a man. Their ambitions have not been blinded and blinkered by generations of harsh training. Yet, most career women see work as necessary to them—either financially or psychologically. Women, for the most part, no longer have a choice whether to work or not.[11] It is becoming increasingly difficult to rely on a male breadwinner as rates of divorce and male unemployment run high. More commonly, too, a viable family income depends upon the income of two adult workers. Nevertheless, necessity does not constrain women's outlook to the extent that it seems to constrain men's. Their "outsider's" view[12] allows them to see the quirks. As outsiders, they are more likely to resist conditions, which to insiders seem inevitable. As women still feel ultimately responsible for their families, still crave close relationships with children, still have partners and friends they wish to nurture, they see the costs of single-mindedness and the single-track, which men, typically, do not. Women's marginal position is in many ways highly underrated: For this marginal position, when joined with a critical and confident perspective, permits sideways glances round the constraints and conditions, which men often reify as forces without potential for change.[13] Throughout their working lives, women are more likely than men to question the existing status of the workplace precisely because they are outsiders. In their first years of adulthood, innovative women often question workplace practices to discover what it is they have to do to fit in; in midlife they are more likely to take up the challenge to change the conditions under which they work, and to create work conditions in which they can thrive[14] and to find ways of working in which they can both do what they want and like who they are.

Women's career goals and resistance during their first years of adulthood have been frequently charted, as the dilemma between women as workers and as mothers has been extensively explored. Researchers turn again and again to *young* women's decisions about work and family, or to the way women in their thirties balance child care and career.[15] Rarely has attention been given to ways in which accumulated conflicts between personal and professional goals emerge in midlife crisis.

For midlife women, whether or not they have young children, the conflicts and their underlying assumptions change. The "breather," which the idea of being 40 threw in their path, led women to ask: "Who do I want to be?" and "How do I want to continue?" They took a new look at the ways that they were managing themselves to suit their work. They reconsidered the means by which they had been protecting their families from their professional ambitions. These more sensitive assessments of their personal and professional lives created a host of new problems. The precise configuration of their crisis and its resolution depended on the ways that the feminine and feminist ideals had been accommodated. Had they suppressed their personal needs to pursue their career goals? Had they put brakes on their professional energies to nurture others? Had they worn themselves out trying to balance that impossible equation between a demanding career, which eats up personal time, and a family, which still tends to assume the mother will be its linchpin? Had they suppressed their spontaneity to fit in with a rigid working atmosphere?

Twelve of the twenty-four innovative women in my study made drastic career changes in their forties. Those who exited from careers, told stories layered by opposing feelings. They felt competent, but wary, as though always on trial, never fully accepted. Having tried for so long to groom themselves to fit in with their professional environment, they came to resist this male mimicry. They would rather come into a stronger sense of self and leave a workplace.[16] Recent research has confirmed the general trend of my sample. Women in their forties have a high dropout rate at senior career levels.[17] Women in their fifties who are at a senior career level have distinctive zig-zag career patterns—in contrast to the single-track pattern of their male colleagues. As a result of previous struggles, they could more quickly identify the sore spots and deal with stressful situations without feeling personally attacked or personally deficient. There is a progression: In their twenties, women try to find the career that is ideal for them; in their thirties, they try to fit in with their chosen career, working hard on themselves to come up to employers' or clients' expectations; in their forties, they spot the unsatisfying patterns and move towards the phase at which they find (or create) an environment in which they can do the work they want.

FOR THE INNOVATIVE WOMEN in my sample, crisis was stimulated by one of five often interconnected things: the stress of overwork; a new awareness of an imbalance between professional and personal needs; the pain of prejudice; frustration with ambitions that had been muted or disguised; or the increasingly tense conditions at work. Any of these could be the sore spots exposed by midlife crisis. As a woman entered crisis she had to rethink her goals and the strategies she had been using to attain them. Her rethinking sparked the fear that she had lost all sense of direction, but it eventually led to increased self-assurance and skill at refashioning the way forward.

When stress about time triggered a woman's crisis, extremely minor hitches—such as being forced to cancel dinner with a friend, or having no time to prepare a room for a guest or help a child with a homework assignment—could unleash major questions about what she wanted to do with the rest of her life. When lack of time cramped her and left no room for maneuver, when she realized the fun had fled with the flexibility, she saw a catastrophe, but gained control of her decisions. Katrina Pieters reflects

> So often, now, my goal is to just get things done, clear my desk, keep things running smoothly. So when something else comes up—no matter how small, or how important, I can go haywire. The other day I had to take my daughter to the doctor. There was just enough time

in my day to do this, but I fretted over it—you know that moaning thought—Ugh! I have to do this as well. I knew we would have to wait when we got there, so I brought work, and I dived right into it, as soon as we took our seats in the waiting room. Immediately, I regretted not having the forethought to bring something for my daughter. She's doing a patchwork now—I could have brought that. It sounds like a little thing, but it wasn't then. I hate waiting, having nothing to do, and I know how happy my daughter is when she is busy. Bringing along her patchwork would have been like offering her a gift. Instead of sitting there, suffering boredom and self-consciousness—you know how you sit in a waiting room and are sure everyone else is watching you—she would have been pleased by people watching her keep busy. It seemed to me then like I might have been able to offer her a whole new self, but I hadn't been able to do that because I was focused on myself and my time, and resenting the time I had to take up with this appointment.

The discrepancy between bringing along something for her daughter to do and "giving her a whole new self" is comic: The mother exaggerates both what she might have given the daughter, and what she has deprived her of. Yet her "thoughtlessness" was seen as a symptom of stress. Stress was making her into something she did not want to be: grudging, brusque, and selfish. But this irritation was called up to defend herself against the unease she still sometimes felt about not being a traditional, stay-at-home mother, always available to her children, always second-guessing their needs. She felt this guilt, however, because she did easily focus on her child. Sympathy with her daughter's self-consciousness and boredom opened a well of dissatisfaction. Her sympathy and regret combined to question what she was giving to her job, and whether it was allowing her to be the person she wanted to be. And, as so often with mothers and daughters, the question broadened into one of social reproduction: What example, she wondered, was she setting? "Will she have to sit with her daughter, feeling the same things?" Katrina asked. "I see her sulky face—mad at me for being mad about having to do this with her, while I'm mad at my husband because this sort of thing is still *my* job. You suddenly see . . . well, it isn't just him and her and me. I mean, is her life going to be the same, this hand to mouth affair?" She shrugged and raised her hands, which then fell onto her lap. "I mean, can we make it better?"

The extreme reaction Katrina had to this minor episode signaled the onset of a crisis. Irritation broadens into wider significance: What will she pass on to her daughter? she asks. A minor incident is magnified to allow her to see the problem more clearly. Minor details of conflict often became cues for vast reorganization. Impatience and anxiety are taken as proof that change is urgently required. The juggling acts practised throughout her thirties, she saw, were not getting any better. "I've kept saying to myself things like: 'When Bridgit starts school, things will get better.' Or 'When the kitchen's redone, I'll have more time.' It goes on and on, but things aren't going to get easier unless I do something. Well—I'm a cautious person. I'll start slow and small, and just keep track. But I know now there will be a change—a real change. I'm just watching out now—for that answer about how to do it. But knowing that I will—well, there's both dread and excitement."

How the Innovative Woman in Midlife Creates a New Balance

The reassessment triggered at midlife can lead an innovative woman to a new careful tracking of where she is going. Often, career men at midlife enjoy a rest after their youthful scramble up the ladder. Secured in a high position, their labor takes up less energy because, with experience, it functions smoothly. Successful men in midlife often lose their brashness because their position is so strong. Women seldom have this luxury because they remain wary at work, and each step up has to be fought for and then guarded. As the innovative women in my sample realized that they had come far, but the battle would continue, they took stock of their futures, and realized that they alone had the power to refashion their work and their goals to suit themselves.

At 46, Nan Grodsky, the in-house lawyer for a commercial bank, made a deliberate decision to change the framework of her choices. Seeing that, in personal terms, she did not have what she wanted, that her close relationships tended to "fizzle out" or "go cold," she began watching herself, trying to spot and then correct the pattern that repeatedly brought an unsatisfactory outcome. "When you tell someone every weekend that you have to work, and cancel a date every time something comes up at work, you're not giving a relationship a chance," said Nan. She decided that she would change, because she did not want to spend the rest of her life alone.

> For 20 years I've either been looking ahead or behind. How do I get there, and how do I stay there, and who is the challenge ahead and who is the threat from behind? Now I'm looking ahead again, but in a different direction, and the future is empty—no husband, no children, no family of my own. All those images of families, of groups of couples, which hit you the minute you open a book or turn on the television have barely touched me until now. Before, they were clichés I was determined to resist. Then it hit me that I really wanted what I thought I was mocking. You see something about yourself, and you're never the same again. I no longer want to be alone. I'm no longer sure I ever wanted to be alone! So I'm taking a calculated risk. Maybe my career will manage without so much input. Maybe I'll miss the next good promotion. But the greatest risk I can take is to keep putting my job first.

The dual risk of losing her position at work and being alone required her to accept a risk, which in earlier adult life she would have "pushed aside like a frilly party dress." Under the pressure of time left for what she wants to do, she reassesses her aims. Now that she can see the pattern, she gains greater control over her decisions and admits the long-denied appeal that more traditional women's roles have had for her. In early adulthood, when she "was determined not to lose control over the career I wanted," she kept tabs on how she was seen by others at work and whether she was adhering to the standard laid down by the ideal of the perfect career woman. Her belief that she was in control is disturbed by a recognition of what she was missing. As she sees this, her language becomes more extreme. There is a youthful angst, with loneliness and longing, dramatized in the rhythm of her speech ("All those images of families, of groups, of couples . . . "). She sees she was "pretending to mock" what she really wanted. Having seen this, then, she is pushed to question her goals. This is the nub, the turning point, when she sees something she will never *not* see again. Then the question becomes a practical one: Given what she knows about the consequences of her lifestyle, given what she knows now about what she ultimately wants in a relationship, and given her beliefs about how much time she has to reach her new goals, she sees that some things have to change quickly. Having reached this vantage point, she is careful not to deny the negative consequences her changing priorities may have. She does not want to uncover one thing and bury another. She wants to behave "like I always thought real grown-ups did. Remember how they seemed to know what they were doing?"

While Pat Deloughery, at 41, had made a similar decision to "take the risk of going part time" in order to "put time into her [new, first] marriage, and lay those important foundations," Nan recognized that she would not get the opportunity to establish a valuable relationship unless she first took a "side bet." To do this, she looked at her tendency to put the career first, to find it unthinkable that a personal decision would precede a professional one, and noticed how this had counted against her. Her determination not to step onto a "mommy track" meant that she was available to sit on every work committee, to travel to any meeting anywhere in the world, and never to decline a project on personal grounds. In making sure she would never be a "typical woman," she was so controlled by the way others at work assessed her, that she did not see what else she wanted.

As Pat sought ways to reengage herself in the world of love and commitment, she still felt uncomfortable about how she would appear when she did what she wanted. She also felt that she risked the charge of letting other women down. She would be setting a bad example: "And this really puts me in a bind, because I don't believe the example I'm setting is bad—it will just be used that way. I think it's reasonable to refuse to work those hours . . . the hours I work. I think more men should, but they don't, and they just don't feel the same pressure. So there it is. I wish I could argue my case outright, but I can't. You know, it would be good to sit down and say, 'You're going to see things this way, and you shouldn't.' No one will admit that they will 'misuse' my refusal, so I can't explain that they will be using it unfairly. I have no platform here to justify myself." The tension in her voice dissolved suddenly; she proposed disarmingly, "Can I leave that to you?"

Not working at full steam, and not aiming at the highest rung, are, for some women, as difficult now as work and ambition were for women a few generations ago. Having fought so hard for equality in the workplace, they have ignored the work they have done on themselves to adapt to work conditions that are increasingly hard on them. Freer from the control of the Over-Eye, which judges them according to the standard of that magical spot wherein a woman is expected to find the perfect means of fulfilling her career and personal goals, they ask whether they want something more or something different. More and more women, who have devoted their first years of adulthood to establishing their career, cautiously reassessed at 40—the marker of midlife, the marker of real adulthood, and the mark of the last decade of fertility—their once-certain sense of direction. Among the 80 women in my sample, fifteen had at least one child after 40, and eight had their first child in their forties, and of these eight women each had planned her pregnancy. Carol Rogers, at 44, reflected,

> A few years ago my husband bought me one of those silly badges, with a woman putting her hand over her mouth and gasping, 'Oh, my God! I forgot to have children!' It wasn't really funny—just apt. I thought I would want to have—well, something . . . something like a child, eventually, but it was so nice not having them, being free, as my friends weren't, and just doing what I wanted—because my work is what I want to do. You have this identity, which seems to work so well, and feels comfortable—just no problems, really—but when you look forward—I mean, when you look forward and you can see something, not just that huge empty space you see when you're 25— something changed, very fast. It's frightening at this age, taking such a leap, but I dreaded keeping on as I was, even though I was very happy as I was, and life certainly was simpler then than it will be now.

The idea of being forty made Carol take a new look at her future, and in so doing, her priorities shift. The need to achieve, to be her own person, were guiding features of her first adulthood. Now she sees the inconsistency between being her own person and controlling her impulses to the extent that she has. In her new midlife, she will seek a different balance, one which is less weighted by her fear of not conforming perfectly to the fast-track woman who avidly pursues each and every career opportunity.

How Innovative Women
Lift the Mask on Their Ambition

The first thing that struck me about innovative women—those women deeply committed to their careers in ways ambitious men are—was how impossible it would have been, twenty years earlier, to predict their professional progress.[18] Whereas many women living traditional life patterns had, as young adults, harbored strong professional goals, several innovative women had been, as young adults, highly traditional. Their plans were traditional women's plans: They would be "good" wives, they would be "good" mothers, but above all, they would be nice and pleasant to be with and a source of comfort to all around them. Yet, very early on, they found themselves on a different track. Pretending that they were preparing themselves for the roles of good wife and mother, they meticulously fostered their own talents. Lacking superwoman's exultation in her achievements, they could nonetheless, like superwoman, accommodate both the traditional feminine goals to establish a family and the new feminist goals to develop and exercise their talents in the workplace. What was distinctive about this particular group of innovative women was that they acknowledged their traditional goals, but disguised or masked their innovative goals, even from themselves. Like superwoman, they would be both the woman who achieved and the woman who pleased. While some of these woman admitted to being ambitious, they wanted to modify the term. They had goals, but not "tunnel vision"; they wanted to achieve certain things, "but not at any cost." Their ambitions had boundaries, and they could step back to consider where they might be placed in the general scheme of their lives. They were not "driven" or "blind." They frequently spoke of "the risks of being too ambitious" or of "not putting their personal life at risk." For these women, midlife brought a crisis whereby they learned to acknowledge their aggressive or achievement-oriented voices, and bring a more powerful sense of self into their relationships.

"I always wanted to do well," Kay Plackett admitted, "but doing well gradually changed from doing well like a good Daddy's girl, and not wasting all that money he was pouring into a private college, to doing well because I was getting a great big kick out of it. And even then, I was still stuck in that bobby-sock mold. I'd keep working so that I could be worthy of the type of man I wanted to marry. I'd make my husband proud—that sort of thing, and then I went into economics, thinking how my husband and I could discuss flow charts in the evening, and he'd be so proud, in his polished brown leather shoes, because his wife knew so much." Her 46-year-old mouth drew itself together in an imitation of a young girl feigning wisdom. She then laughed gently, seeing how slow I was to spot her self-mockery.

As adolescents, many of us have visions of futures that are as hilarious, when we take them out years later, as the clothes carefully packed in store boxes and the hair styles that once seemed both comfortable and necessary, but that now stare out at us from school photographs like stiff hats. But the ridicule we cast upon these past selves may be superficial, and disguises our clear memories of just how we chose such items, and what use they were to us. What Kay had done as a teenager was to explain her achievement goals to herself in ways that slipped in to another, more acceptable framework. She screened, rather than repressed her knowledge. Her urge to achieve wound its way, crudely but conveniently, around the image of herself in the role—which once upon a time seemed straightforward—of the obliging daughter and accomplished wife.

In her early forties, Kate grew amazed that she had "got away with this for so long." She began to notice how hard she worked to keep her pliant, nonthreatening side in place.

When I saw friends—even good friends—I'd just put work out of the conversation. I wouldn't even think about it. After all, I worked in a huge company, which has an enormously complex hierarchy of jobs, which are graded by both numbers and letters. I could be a very low number, for all they knew . . . I'm ashamed of this, how I did it, barely noticing what I was doing, because it wasn't simply modesty, either. I see how it implied that I was really better than them, but had to tone things down, otherwise they would envy me. Well, now that I am a director, other people do envy me, though it's mostly the men—and it hurts, but I also want to fight it. I no longer can be that nice young woman, who pleased them so much. Not only because

I'm now 46, but because I see now how, for me, that was so ineffective. And it's not only at work—this feeling that I'm changing, and I have to keep up with those changes. I noticed, too, that as I was promoted, the tone in which my husband expressed his pleasure started changing—and more important than that, how that frightened me. He's in business, and it looks as though he's in for a rocky time for the next year or so. He has always supported me in my career, which was a very nice surprise, because he had every reason to expect something else of me, but the seriousness of my job is something that is not easy for him, especially now when things aren't running very smoothly for him.

As Kay receives the age-40 signal (which actually comes anywhere between 40 and 45) to look back, she is surprised that her disguise worked so well for so long. But this is not self-congratulation. Her awareness of what she is doing leads to shame: She asks why she had thought it necessary. She feels that in playing false with her friends, she has insulted them. Hiding the extent of her professional success, she may have avoided envy, but forgoes the support and appreciation she might have received. "It meant I had to be careful, and keep my distance, which seems so strange when I know we have so much in common."

In noticing her husband's changed tone as he congratulates her on her promotion, she regrets her collusion. It was she, after all, who had persuaded him that she was "not really ambitious" and "not really trying to get ahead." This leads to further questions about how she maintains her place in the family. "I now hear other things—so often now, I hear my own voice," and she rubbed her hand against her throat, as though it were sore. "It was flat, controlled, somebody else's. At work, too—though there I see what I'm doing, constantly reassuring them that I'm not an excitable woman, that I'm in control, competent, and self-confident. That's all right. I see that, and I pass on that. It makes me more effective—and it *is* work. But why I've been doing it at home too . . . ? And what am I afraid of? What am I trying to be in this marriage?"

Noticing how the the judge, who in its feminine guise declares that a good woman is pliant, and without ambitions of her own, has constrained her, she remains cautious in handing over power to the

Inner-Eye: She is "not quite sure what else [she's] not seeing, or what will happen when [she] stops being afraid." Once she sees her fear, everything else becomes uncertain. Pushed from the safe certainty of her role as submissive wife, she wonders what she does want to be. Nor does she know whether her fear at her husband's changed voice is more her problem, or his. How much will she be punished by striding forward in her career? How much does she have to leave behind to go where she wants to go? Crisis questions generate further questions, and the answers may be slow in coming. Yet, as these questions are addressed, innovative women see the need to take new charge of their futures both at work and at home. As the crisis is resolved, they develop the power to bring new voices into relationships.

A year later, during my final interview with her, she described the fear, which had so disturbed her as she discovered it, as no more than a "remembered nightmare—except that I'm so sorry for what it did." For whereas she once saw herself as protecting her husband, she now sees that the false aspects their relationship left him more vulnerable to insecurity as his business prospects foundered. The strict ways in which she "gave him the last word," playing the submissive wife, deprived him of her strength when he felt threatened. "I thought the disguise was so thin that it didn't matter. After all, I was doing well. It wasn't holding me back. But how unnecessary it was, and how damaging, I think—but I didn't notice it until it *had* to wear thin." She also felt that she had deprived her son of "seeing how well at least one of his parents is doing." When I asked her the question that other women had put to themselves, "Why had this taken so long? Why had she only seen this recently, and done something about it?" she laughed and shook her head. "What can I say? I guess I thought that those rules about who I could be were necessary. And I was breaking enough of them already, simply by working as I was. But there comes a time— doesn't there?—when you just see through those rules, because things have changed so much and no one else can define your place for you."

Innovative Women's Response to Persistent Inequality

Some innovative women believed, as young adults entering male careers, that they were participating in a superbly successful revolution in the lives of women. They felt fully supported by their families, their schools, and by society at large. To fail in their careers would, these women judged, be to fail the changing networks that had supported them. Throughout their first years of adulthood, they may have continued to believe in the basic possibility of equality, however many blips and bumps they encountered. These, they thought, were exceptions; these, they hoped, would be undermined by the general trend. The shock at midlife was to discover that the equality of respect, opportunity, pay, promotion, and prestige was illusory. As they were no longer offered the attention, encouragement, perks, and promises many young women in the workplace are offered, as they had enough experience to spot the pattern, they saw clearly what they had felt for so long: The conditions under which they worked were not equal. Ashamed and angry not to have known this before, they had to develop new means of managing their self-assessment.

Ilsa Havig, 45, works as a marketing manager in a large department store in Finland. Her children are now teenagers, but when they were born she had eighteen months paid maternity leave and the assurance that her job would remain open to her even if she should decide to extend this leave, unpaid, up to three years. When she fell ill after the birth of her second child, she had a home help who looked after both her and the children. While her children were small, she was allowed days off work if they were ill, or a home help would come to look after them. Hence, the stinging series of questions that many working mothers put to themselves: "What if my children are ill? What if I have to take them to the dentist? Who will look after my children if I am ill?" were answered through social policies.

In Finland and other Scandinavian countries, which are well advanced in their social policies and offer working mothers enormous support, more women do work, and more women rise to the top; but wage gaps and glass ceilings continue to characterize much women's work.[19] Institutional child care does not pick up the entire maternal tab, nor does it change what goes on within the home, as women continue to feel primarily responsible for domestic organization. In Finland and Sweden, policymakers are concerned to correct this, but they cannot pinpoint the causes as to why jobs remain segregated—why there are still women's jobs and men's jobs, and hence inequality of status, income, and opportunity.

Less formal structures within the home are not significantly different in these countries than in America and Britain. Ilsa's husband does not do much housework, and when the home help cooked and cared for Ilsa and the baby, he was somewhat put out to be told that he would have to cook for himself, since caring for the husband did not come under her job description. The husband's conservatism, however, seems a mild drawback, one surely counteracted by the supportive social practices. It remains surprising, and puzzling, that Ilsa's working life shares many features of women's working lives in other countries. Ilsa has discovered that she has met a glass ceiling—an invisible edifice, which presses her down at a fairly low rung in middle management. Throughout the 1980s, when management posts became open to and occupied by women, the term *manager* gathered a weaker meaning.[20] The centers of power were transferred to other areas. Ilsa is called marketing manager, and her job has some prestige and many perks. Since she has some say in the store's marketing policies, she is invited to trade fairs, to openings, to dinners. But she is not well paid, she has no access to a secretary, and she will never move to a higher position, "where the men are."

It took me by surprise, and seemed to happen suddenly. I was a bright, hard-working young woman. I got praise, and regular promotions—though now I see the incremental steps were pretty small. But suddenly—I can mark the day on the calendar—I came up with a wonderful promotional idea, which I could carry through if my position were stepped up a grade. My boss used to enjoy my bright ideas, even if he didn't carry them out. He used to be tickled pink, just to talk them over. This time I got a cold blank look. "Wild," he said. Sort of a joke, or what we call a non-response. "That's not your area," he said. As I saw how different he was looking at me, I understood what I should have known years ago. I wasn't a bright young woman any more. I was middle aged. And I wasn't going anywhere fast.

Ilsa finds that her perception of herself through the eyes of others, which used to be fun, is now against her. No longer buffered by her youthful appeal, she comes up against the harsh structure of employment.

This silent, and probably unacknowledged, policy does not provide a comfortable working atmosphere in her female-run department. The women are often competitive with one another. Having no direct access to power, lacking any prospect of promotion based on a fair assessment of merit, they compete for the attention of the male bosses. Ilsa found this type of competition "draining"; it demanded "negative energy." She liked her work, but the atmosphere in which it was done aroused deep dissatisfaction. "If I were twenty years younger, I'd play ball with them. I remember what it was like—thinking you'll be an exception. Now I know I'm not, and that nothing will change for me unless I make a change."

As Ilsa observed her younger women colleagues, she confronts the danger of defeat and stagnation.

They spend all their money on clothes. We don't have a high salary, but we make just enough so that you can dress well, if you put your money to that. And it's the dress and the hair and the face and the nails, and even a bunch of flowers now and then for the male boss. No—you smile—like me, I thought it was silly. Who could fall for that? And we older women have different things to spend our money on—our families, our homes. How could this dressing up matter? But the men love it. When these young women started glitzing into our office, we thought they were writing their own tombstone. Who could take them seriously? But there it is. I complained because a young women had been promoted over me. The boss said she was so good at her job, and—yes, he said this—so good looking and so nice . . . I don't want to live day in and day out with this anger.

At a different stage of her life, Ilsa would have worked to suppress this anger and despair. "I must have seen all this before, but I'd just work harder. 'Hold on. Hold on' I'd whisper this to myself until the pain went. Then I'd just put on a brave face and hope that I'd be the lucky one next time." But, now, she resisted that solution of calming herself down. With the "looking back time" of midlife, she saw that patterns of prejudice would recur. She now redefines her own goals as she sees the contradictions in the workplace between its lip service to equality and its prejudicial practices. As she addresses these contradictions, she is aware of changes within herself that increase her confidence. "To everyone else I probably seem worse than I was a year ago. I'm more on edge. I'm not so nice. But I feel better. I feel more in control because it isn't so easy to lie to me." Pushed up against this crisis point, she refuses to "help the system out-maneuver" her, and gains a new sense of her power to make her own truth known.

Fighting a younger generation of women, who did not see how they participated in reenacting stereotypes, was particularly disheartening for the innovative women in my sample. One managing director who decided, at 48, to resign from an engineering design firm, explained that her greatest difficulty was in dealing competitively with the many younger women who were joining the firm. Grace Hogan felt there was a "generation gap in the gender group"; as young women "acted out their packaged version of the new woman," they behaved like "cute tigers clawing their way to promotion and success. I may have been a lot like them at one time," she admitted, "but I'm not now, and I don't want to be. Looking at them I sometimes wanted to laugh, to say 'Come on—you don't mean this,' but I realize they do mean it. At first I thought they wouldn't be taken seriously, or their tactics wouldn't work, but they're hanging in there—those who stay, stay the same. I can't fight them, and I don't want to wait until I'm stabbed in the back. It's not a very large firm, as these firms go, and I had built up a kind of trust and a good working atmosphere. But all that is changing. The recession makes all the employees feel mean and scared, and I don't want to continue giving so much of my time and my life to this kind of thing."

Grace's impasse brings together a range of problems. She looks at the younger women in her firm with a double vision: She sees how she might have been like them at one time; yet simultaneously, she cannot believe in their "act" or believe that they believe in it themselves ("I sometimes want to laugh, to say, 'Come on—you don't mean this').

Yet she also realizes they do mean it, that they see themselves through a new gaze, which judges them according to how aggressively they pursue a career; hence, they fully believe in the image they are trying to project—the contemporary career climber. To work alongside them, in these particularly threatened economic conditions, she will have to peg her consciousness to theirs, guessing their tactics and protecting herself from them. This is something she would rather not do ("I don't want to continue giving so much of my time to this kind of thing"). As this reassessment begins, other problems and questions and potential disappointments follow at a hectic pace. She is disappointed that more women in the firm have not brought forward the changes she had envisioned. She is concerned that she is opting out, and by so doing will leave the status quo unchanged. She also asks the more personal question, "What am I going to do instead?" Halfway through the interview sessions, Grace, like Ilsa is still in the dazed phase of crisis, as questions continue to proliferate and answers continue to elude her. Thrust into this whirlpool of questions, she is at the turning point of the new midlife for women, wherein change will be elicited. As the force of these questions subside, she will be transformed by a new ability to address such contradictions and take control of her own path through them.

Corporate Crises and Increasing Prejudice

A changing work environment can spur a crisis in innovative women, who may previously have been running on automatic. Corporate roulette, for these women, brings dissatisfaction to the surface and stimulates questions about what they want to do during the next phase of their lives. The innovative women in my sample were often surprised by their willingness to diverge from long-held plans. They were empowered by a new ability to change the blueprints to which they had meticulously referred for all previous decisions. Now, their own vision gained clarity as they assessed changing goals and the changing contexts in which they could be attained.

The recession, as Grace said, made everyone nervous. It made many people work harder. In large institutions, especially, it is often very difficult for managers to gauge the productivity of employees.[21] So they work longer, harder, and more competitively. This generally is easier for men to do than for women, who still, far more than men, engage in family sustaining activities, while their partners put in more working hours.[22] When firms have to cut down on employees, it is easier to make women redundant: Usually women do not have the seniority that men do, often because they have started later, or took time off. When more and more men are out of work, or in unpromotable positions, it becomes harder for each woman who loses her job or who is not promoted, to claim discrimination. Though women's employment did continue to grow during the recession of the 1980s, this was not a sign that prejudice against women in the workplace was abating. Instead, women's employment then continued to grow because employers preferred to employ those who would accept disadvantageous jobs—without security, with poor pay, and with little chance of promotion.[23]

The managerial world has changed, as has the nature of competition, as has the volume of work, as have corporate structures, since the women who are now executives entered the workplace. In what Rosabeth Moss Kanter calls the "global corporate Olympics," companies have to seek new means of survival. The leaner and meaner policies of many corporations make life tough for everyone. Employees have to work harder, under greater pressure both from a sense of competition and from a sense of job insecurity. These conditions are precisely the conditions that many women feel unable to work well in. These are precisely the conditions in which their behavior seems like "fear of success" as they remain immune to a daggered motivation. It has always been convenient for those who wish to impede women's career equality to insist that women who leave high-powered positions do so from personal choice, rather than in response to a system riddled with contradictions for women—denying them time to nurture the rich range of personal relationships they value, or to organize the homes and families that everyone else expects them to oversee. Furthermore, as the atmosphere at work becomes highly competitive, the intrinsic pleasures of the job—such as taking time to do one's best, train others well, listen to others' opinions—are forfeited. It is an atmosphere that can be highly inefficient, as others try to run alongside every other runner, rather than find their own means to their own ends. When women see themselves as having a choice, they cannot see the point. Herein, a crisis enters for many innovative women, as they refuse to follow the old ideals of what it is to be a career person, and they forge new paths through their futures.

As the workplace becomes less hospitable to everyone, women can be more easily edged out. Prejudice retrenches as those men who feel weak try to hold on to their declining powers. Kanter vividly describes what restructuring feels like for *any* employee of the firm: It can make people feel "helpless, anxious, startled, embarrassed, dumb, over-worked, cynical, hostile or hurt."[24] Restructuring, which has become necessary for all firms, is not a one-off event, a crisis that then settles, but a continuing process, shaking the foundations and the past certainties as severely as a divorce may upset a child's vision of adult stability. The effects, which can easily persist for three years, are "bizarre": "Some people come to work in an almost catatonic state, starting no new programs; others who have been let go continue to come to the office."[25] In these conditions, everyone feels that membership is in question—and women, as newcomers, as people sensitive to bias, are likely to suffer more from this common threat of exclusion.

Women in corporate life are not simply trying to enter a man's world. They are trying to enter what was previously a male domain, but that is rapidly changing and casting doubt upon men's membership in it, too. Everyone's career expectations have changed, and that makes everyone wary of membership. The corporate ladder is not as stable as it once was. It also has fewer rungs.[26] A common organizational policy known as "demassing" eliminates middle management positions, so that there are simply fewer places a woman can climb up from. The new opportunities open for women have come up against the narrowing opportunities available for corporate men. Though women's position in general is expanding,[27] it may be only the very determined, the willing sacrificers, who remain as competitors in the corporate world. The innovative women in my sample who did stay on in an aggressive working atmosphere were guided by a mission to show that they could perform well under pressure. As I shall show in the next section, these women gained power through their ability to influence the male preserve and felt that in their new midlife they were taking on responsibility to transform their working environment—either by finding different work or changing their current workplace.

PREJUDICE IN THE WORKPLACE has been much harder to abolish than was initially estimated when the innovative midlife of today began their careers. Many of these women believed that together they could shatter prejudice, and sweep away the broken pieces. They were aware, as a minority, that they represented women, no matter how individually they acted. As they made new types of decisions in midlife, they themselves were freer of careerist ideals, but they still had to confront the ways that others perceived them—not because they were afraid of criticism, but because they were aware that how they were perceived at work would have consequences for other women.

"I never want to let anyone down," said Lynn Fairn, 44, as she faced a decision "I never thought I would consider making"—that of turning down a partnership in a law firm.

I work fifty hours a week as it is, and now I'm facing an eighty-hour week. I know that. You just walk into a firm like that and disappear. That is not for me. I'm sure I wanted it as much as any young person now hooked on the glamour of *L.A. Law,* but I've learned, maybe the hard way, that it isn't for me. Work like that changes you—I've seen it change people. I've known this for a long time—it was clear, I guess it was clear from the beginning, but I thought I could be different there, too. I don't think—no, I don't think I can, because of the pressure and the speed and the sheer number of hours. You have to internalize that way of thinking. It has to become part of you to work. I know a lot of people would disagree. I know people who say you just have to switch modes. But I don't see those people switching off. You can't cross-examine a nine-year-old girl and try to knock down her credibility and then switch off. And that's the kind of work they want me to do as partner—not everyday—but I'll be for them the female attorney who can be tougher than a man because she'll be seen as sympathetic because she's a woman. I also know that in turning [the partnership] down, (she paused, and made an effort to regulate her voice) I know I'm making it much more difficult for the next woman. They'll see themselves as having tried. "See we tried, we offered it to a woman, who was too chicken to take it on." But though I feel real bad about that, I can't let such a consideration rule my life. It's hard to say—I'm being selfish, maybe I'm being selfish, or small minded. I think it's more like being personally minded. Because for me, though I wanted it once—the partnership, the responsibilities, the involvement, the work—the money!—I now want other things more. I can't face what I would become—something, not myself—if I stepped up my hours, and for my personal life, what I've now decided I have to work to keep, I would lose more of it than I can accept losing.

The discovery that she does not, after all, want the type of career she believed she had wanted for so long bewilders her. She skips over her own disappointment and focuses on its potential meaning and consequences. In the past, she felt successful as a representative for the innovative woman. Now, her individual gauge finds a different measure. Is she being selfish, she wonders, in failing to be a good representative of the type of woman she knows women should be allowed to be? In being "personally minded," she not only has to slip away from the imagined critic who judges her according to her ambition and dedication, but also from the views her colleagues have of her, towards which she has a political relationship: Working to change others' expectations of women has been high on her agenda. But as she watched others rise in her profession, taking notes on how to make her own way up, she saw something that for some time she had sought to deny—that you cannot succeed on these terms without becoming different. Furthermore, she feels that time demands would change her ("I would become—something, not myself"). Nor is she willing to fill the role others have in mind for her. This is not as easy to reject as it may seem. As Lynn later reflected, "Anyone can understand my not wanting to tear apart the testimony of a sympathetic witness, but you have to realize that this means I'm leaving it to the men." For Lynn, the question about what her own goals were, was overlaid with the concern about how much worse things would be for other people—for example, the child witnesses whose testimony she challenged—if someone else, and not she, did her job.

While younger innovative women are more likely to work hard and do well to prove themselves,[28] midlife women wish to prove themselves capable of defending what they value, instead of feeling they have to adapt to male standards of the workplace. Though they are much freer than younger women from concern about how others at work see them, they still know that, as women, as newcomers or outsiders, they are constantly on trial. While midlife crisis has commonly been conceived as a total break and change from past commitments, its configuration for innovative women is highly complex: As illusions are smashed, the consequences of resisting colleagues' and clients' expectations or prejudices has to be reassessed. This reassessment then leads to questions about how much to change, how much to preserve, and how much, still, to accommodate those other voices and other visions. Lynn, at 44, is still at an early stage of the crisis that deepens a midlife woman's sense of self: Knowing what she knows, she refuses to join the partnership, but she cannot yet envision ways of compensating for the loss or damage her resistance sustains. The path ahead will be forged as she emerges from the other end of the crisis.

SEVERAL INNOVATIVE WOMEN WERE forced into crisis as they saw that in following the male rules of the workplace, they were themselves actually colluding in prejudice against other women, or against men and women who were "different," not "one of the boys," not "the right sort." This problem arises for midlife women for various reasons. It is in midlife that women become senior enough to be perpetrators of prejudice. They are in positions of power, and influence hiring, promotion, and redundancy decisions. They also have more experience of working practices, and so can see the repeating patterns of policies. Their crisis comes as they see the ways in which they are reproducing unequal conditions in their workplace.

When I first contacted Beth Geist, she had recently become a vice president of a pharmaceutical company. She asked to be interviewed in her office. She allowed me the exact time we had agreed to before the interview. She was thoughtful, composed, and, I felt, fully in control of what she revealed and what she reserved. Her job was to explain her rapid success and the trick of being the first woman vice president in this firm. She was 45.

The next interview, three months hence, was cancelled. She was too busy to keep the prearranged appointment and would be traveling soon after. Six months after the initial interview, she suggested that she drop out of the study. Things were changing too rapidly, she explained, for her to be able to talk coherently about herself and her work. She did not think what she had to say now should go "on record." I tried to persuade her that "off the record" stories had to be told. If they were hidden, then other women would think their "off the record" lives were freakish. The experience of this new generation of midlife women should be shared.

"That's not what I want to hear," she laughed.

"Why?" I asked.

"I guess you'd better come, so I can explain."

This time, too, she sat behind her desk, facing me. But instead of resting her folded hands on its top, she fidgeted with papers, paper clips, and pens, and wheeled herself constantly first closer then further away. "I don't think I have anything more for you," she began.

"But you do. I know you do. Why do you think you don't?"

"Because," and she sighed at my slow uptake, "I'm going to be resigning. So," she continued impatiently, "I'm not exactly your model career woman."

"*My* model . . . ?"

"Well that's why you're here, isn't it? To find out how women become successful?"

"No. It's to find out about midlife women."

She held my gaze for a moment, and then laughed. "All right. Here it is."

Beth had "fought long and hard" within the company, particularly on the issue of hiring and promoting women.

After a series of interviews we sit down to decide who will get the job. Now I'm not working with a bunch of archaically minded men. They know it's important to admit women into the firm. They know it's important for fairness, and for their image. But when they sit down to decide any individual case, they go haywire when discussing a woman. Their criteria keep changing, and they don't even see what they're doing. We need a woman in to manage one of our regional branches. We all agreed beforehand that we wanted a woman, because in that particular branch there are so many women employees, and there have been a series of complaints and problems, linked either to the fact there is a male manager or no woman there to oversee the problems. But of course we can't advertise the job like that. We have to advertise it straight, so we have lots of men applying, too. The procedure's got to be fair—oh, they're very careful about fairness when it comes to making sure they're not discriminating against men! They start picking each female candidate apart. She's very good, but she also has a family, so that means she probably won't be able to spend informal overtime, which every firm needs to take for granted. If she isn't married then she is either considered too young, or not the sympathetic sort. When I try to point out what they are doing, I'm told that I'm veering towards reverse discrimination. I'm labeled a feminist, so everything I say in appointment discussions is undermined by that. I have this unwarranted identity thrust on me, and it means that whatever I say is counterproductive. Everything I say is heard with that assumption—that I'm going to be rooting for a woman just because she's a woman, so anything I say in defense of a woman is just brushed aside. I'm not really talking any more, just mouthing words. The feeling this gives me—it's not a feeling I want to live with. After the last batch of appointments I decided to distance myself from it all, and I've realized that means I'll have to leave the firm. If I'm going to stay sane, if I'm going to wake up each morning without chips sloughing off my shoulders, then I'll have to find something else to do.

She wheeled her chair forward and launched into what sounded like a defense against an imagined accusation. "You have no idea how hard it will be to give up this job. Okay, I'll find something else. I'm not giving up work. But to walk out—when I think how much it's meant to me. But you can only say 'Things will get better' for so long. And once you see they're not, you keep seeing them, and asking yourself . . . It's a headache, let me tell you."

Initially, Beth was so deeply committed to a standard of a successful careerist that she could not imagine that someone would want to see the person who might be at odds with that personae. The set of feelings and experiences and needs that were at odds with her corporate life were assumed to be of no interest, not to be spoken of. She was receptive to my argument that women's disappointments or rough edges or "off the record" stories should be heard because she was already distressed about her collusion in sustaining unequal structures. Her argument to me ("You have no idea how hard it will be . . .") is typical of an early crisis phase, in which others' judgments are still internalized and must be argued against. Like the adolescent girl who, in her mind's ear, hears her mother's remarks before they are spoken and fights her mother on these imagined grounds,[29] Beth imagined in me the objections she was beginning to overrule.

The problems women have with prejudice are many and varied. Sometimes they are denied jobs because they are women. Once in a job, they are often expected to adapt to a male-fashioned workplace. As they do so, they themselves may be expected to show prejudice against other women—and it is at this point that many women face that crisis in which they reassess their goals. Beth did not experience prejudice at firsthand, but suffered from it nonetheless: As she spoke up on behalf of female job applicants, her credibility with her male colleagues was diminished. They put her in a bell jar and labeled her "feminist," and nothing she said could be heard through those glass walls. Grace felt threatened by the "hard male model," which younger women in her firm adopted, and then exaggerated as they tried to be more aggressive and obviously ambitious than their male colleagues. She, too, felt her resistance was doomed to be ineffective: "The more I fight, the more invisible I become in this firm. This is not an efficient use of my time and energy. I am still capable of doing some good in this world, but not here, not in this capacity . . . not unless I can change something here."

WOMEN'S INTOLERANCE INCREASES WITH age. Their intolerance increases with their confidence, and with their new expanding vision. Many career women changed career course at midlife as they became more critical of the conditions under which they worked and the rewards they were working for. The high incomes and prestigious offices and glossy managerial titles, which in early adulthood had been the key to their ideas of equality and success, lost their appeal—not because they did not like the work but because they did not like the working conditions. No longer enthralled by the mystique of the career world, they continued to value the skills they had developed, but left if they were unable to put those skills to good use, or if they had to become what they did not want to become in order to preserve their success. For as women who set out to break new ground in careers, they were accustomed to creating new patterns both in their personal and private lives. Unlike men who, in pursuing fast-track careers, follow ready-made patterns, innovative women have to create them. The qualities that earn these women the term "innovative" give them, in their new midlife, enormous flexibility. If a man, at midlife, feels dissatisfied with the atmosphere in which he works, then he does one of two things. He either bands together with other men to press for changes in the workplace, or he withdraws and seeks distractions. Women can seldom do the former, because there are simply not enough of them. The number of high-powered career women is increasing, but these women tend to be scattered, so that each, individually, is isolated. At midlife, a woman may be reluctant to distract herself with outside interests or compensating pleasures because she remains aware of herself as a pattern-maker, and her dissatisfaction is a stimulus to create yet another pattern. Women who leave their place of work at midlife are far less likely than a man who leaves his work at midlife to think of themselves as failures; instead, they feel empowered by their embrace of their new, higher standards of self-fulfilment.

MANY INNOVATIVE WOMEN in my sample tried to find ways of transforming their workplace so that they could stay and find voice there for their new midlife. Neither Grace nor Beth permanently left her place of work. Three years into the interview sessions, Grace Hogan did resign from her firm, and then spent eight months as a freelance consultant, but accepted the position of branch manager when her firm opened offices in Hungary. "I feel as though something in my life has changed, and there's a new rhythm to it. The last five or six years have been rough—a balancing act every bit as bad [as] when my kids were young. When I resigned I felt an awful disappointment—a real letdown—but I also felt this was the only thing I could do to keep sane. I was at deadlock with my colleagues, and everyone was edgy. That restructuring was really something. We'd lost twenty-five percent of our staff, and the pressure to compete was even greater, so there was no lessening of workload. Anyway . . . I've been through all this. What I now feel—and I think this is working—is that I don't worry so much about how other people see me, but I also try to be more careful. I want to be effective, rather than right, and my tension doesn't help anybody. It's wonderful to feel this distance from my work, and still be able to do it . . . so I'm personally protected, and yet can give myself to it. It's the sort of thing I know I should have learned how to do as soon as I stepped into management—but you just can't learn everything right away."

Now 51, Grace saw the crisis in the past, as she stepped into a new mode of management. This is how she moves into the new midlife. She would be careful with how others could see her, but not be ruled by that. The new distance she was able to put between herself and her work eased the tension that she found so ineffective.

Beth's window on the future was more circumspect. She had not, after all, resigned her position, but she felt that her decision to stay on had "weathered her." She was far less trusting of her colleagues' good will, but hoped that, in however small a way, she might make the difference she had always hoped to make. "When I was appointed vice president, I thought I was 'there,' and then I realized that the real climb had just begun. What I felt, when . . . you know, when I wanted to drop out of these meetings, was . . . well, I think it must be the type of depression a high-flying man suffers when he feels he just doesn't have what it takes. You have no idea—," she began, and then broke off and laughed with me as she heard the defensive shift in her voice. "I'm still surprised at how difficult these past few years have been, because I had so much of what I'd been working all my life for. But how can you predict . . . ? Well, you just can't. You have to see for yourself." Thus, Beth steps into the new midlife refusing to make predictions on the basis of ready-made patterns, but with the skill to make judgments according to her own vision.

Some innovative women do leave their place of work—but only to find another job in which they enjoy greater autonomy, or a working atmosphere in which they feel less wary. Or they find ways of working independently—for example, by starting their own business, medical or law practices, or working on short-term contracts. Whatever specific job decision they made, they tried to use "voice" rather than "exit."[30] That is, they stayed in careers in order to change things. Financially and personally, they could not retreat from the workforce—which was, in any case, the best platform for change.

THE DILEMMA INNOVATIVE WOMEN often face between what they see as personal well-being—wherein they feel comfortable and relaxed—and a duty to fight for their rights and the rights of others, is often harsh. When innovative women chose, for their midlife path, the stony one of duty, they made their journey meaningful and enjoyable by amassing different support systems. As Frances Conley

felt her colleagues shun her, she identified more closely with the suffering voices of other women, and defined her task as converting "this
private commiseration . . . into public action."[31] Battles often could
not be fought alone, but were made possible by membership in an underground, or a network of voices, which validate and confirm one another. Instead of feeling that they must turn inward to preserve their
sense of right, they find others who think as they do, confirm what they
see, and listen to what they say. Grace and Ilsa had supportive, sympathetic husbands, but partners cannot always be partners in battle. Partners consoled and commiserated, and then encouraged them to exit. It
takes other women, with similar experiences, to help midlife women
remain to fight. The women who stay to fight on in midlife are women
who feel the power of their potential influence, and who feel a passionate connection to those who are likely to benefit from their battles. The
women in my sample who fought all kinds of battles with corporations
or universities or local government were fuelled by the visible results of
their influence and the feedback of respect and the fun of interdepen-
dence. The anger and frustration and outrage and insult, which persuaded some women that it was time to leave or time to stop, were
buffered by the atmosphere of support that their battles generated.

As Alecia Fox took her university to court against its decision to
block her appointment because she was too old,[32] she "discovered the
best friends in the world. These are friends for life. They are intelligent,
hard working women who willing to take time out to testify for me.
And this wasn't just ten minutes for a kind word. This was days of
preparation, getting their testimony together, finding out who else
could testify. I was bowled over by the generosity. It has convinced me
that every battle for equality is worth whatever it takes." The support
she had experienced made her determined to "pay them back by giving
others the same help." Before her own case was heard, she "was just
not a political animal. I did my work at the lab, and that was all I had
time for besides my family. The women who helped me fight my case
opened up an entire new way of going about things."

For Megan Howard, the energy for her use of "voice," or stay-in-
order-to-change approach, came as her work led her to construct an
underground of support. Her first job was to compile a list of qualified
black women computer programmers to counter a corporation's claim

that they had to hire a man in spite of affirmative action laws because no qualified black was available. "I was stunned when they backed down. You could have knocked me over with a feather. I did it thinking I could take it somewhere else, maybe to a local paper, where it would get some attention. I saw its potential as no more than a whining factor. But they backed down. They hired a black woman on my list. That thrill will never go away. I saw that I could fight. I could learn those rules. I'm known now as someone to approach when black women need me. I'll never be too old and weak to resist that."

This joy of resistance was gained by midlife women who embraced apparently contradictory aims: to succeed in what was once a man's domain without becoming prisoner's of men's dreams. The personal configuration of their crises bore a public face. This then ushered in further crisis questions: "How much do I want to fight?" turned into another question: "What will happen if I don't?" "What will happen to women if I decline the mad hours that a partner puts in a law firm?" Lynn asked herself. "What will happen to other women if I don't?" she then asks. And yet how can they "stand up and be counted," as Majorie Fiske remarked that the middle-aged are now "old enough" to do, if, as in Beth's case, she feels that as a woman, she will neither be counted nor heard? Her personal crisis is resolved as she seeks a way to break through the bell jar that often leaves her silenced. As she learns to speak anew, the innovative woman in midlife can change more than she dreamed of in her youth. As she redefines her own goals, she leaves behind both the male ideal of the career person and the image of the superwoman who finds that magical spot, in which everything can be achieved and nothing sacrificed. As she confronts, in her midlife crisis, the discomfort of the male preserve and the impossibility of a life without any compromises whatsoever, she gains new control over the compromises she makes. In the new midlife, she is able to find new paths through old patterns along which she can take possession of her strengthening vision and voice.

Innovative Women: Signs and Signposts of Midlife Crisis

The life patterns of innovative women are in several ways similar to the life patterns of career-oriented men. For these women, personal success is measured to a large extent in terms of professional attainment. In the first years of adulthood, they come to realize how much they, their families, and their colleagues, have to change in order for them to realize their goals. At midlife, they question the value of such effort and such extensive change, and search for new variations on fulfillment. Their searches and discoveries are often conducted along the following lines—though for many women, the onset of crisis begins many years before the resolution, and for others, the dissatisfactions are only felt immediately before the resolution.

Previous orientations:

1. has strong career ambitions
2. guards against distractions
3. works hard to minimize traditional feminine roles and characteristics

In her pre-crisis state, an innovative woman feels single-minded and determined. She works hard both at home and at work to prove and enforce gender equality.

Signs of approaching crisis:

1. sudden pangs of doubt as to the value of long-held ambitions
2. panic as one sees that guilt about the rejection of traditional feminine roles has not been resolved
3. feels trapped by one's own compulsion to control the contradictory pressures between career and personal life

In the conflicts and stresses of the first half of adulthood, innovative women experience many ups and downs as confidence and energy and optimism fluctuate; but their goals of success along the lines of a typically successful man remain intact. Now these goals are questioned, and an enormous amount of mental energy is expended on sifting out real from borrowed ideals.

Resolution of crisis:

1. Goals are reassessed, usually with a shift in emphasis, rather than a complete reversal.
2. Feminine roles and characteristics are redefined, and those that are valued are accepted with a highly individual slant.
3. The setting in which one pursues one's goals is transformed so that goals are now pursued on one's own terms.

4
Expanding Horizons and Radical Changes

T he path through crisis to a new midlife often remains un-marked by obvious change. A woman may feel enormous development within herself, but those around her may be oblivious to this transformation. Some women, however, cannot find their way ahead without achieving radical changes in their lives. The women in my sample who felt they had lived the early years of adulthood in a narrow corridor, confined by lack of skill or confidence or self-awareness, saw midlife as an opportunity to expand their horizons, to break out of that narrowness, which had once seemed natural and safe to them. To make use of the new opportunities presented by midlife, these women—18 in my sample of 80—made deliberate efforts to expand their horizons.

Expansive women take a specific series of steps on their journey. They first have to identify the impediments to growth. They then have to ask themselves how they are going to overcome those impediments. They must also assess the risks of failure and the risks of change. Will their attempts to extend their boundaries be successful, or will they again confront the doubt or inadequacy that dug them into those ruts in the first place? If they do succeed in expanding their horizons, how will these changes be integrated into their lives? As they test possible answers to these proliferating questions, they find their way to a stronger future.

For some expansive women, the urge to make radical changes

arises from that midlife assessment during which previous dissatisfactions are confronted. Ready to take charge of their own futures and less distracted by the judgments of others, they resist the narrowness that was enforced by limited training or education. Other expansive women see the need to extend their self-knowledge and to abolish the buried fears that have limited their emotional horizons. Now these women set themselves the daunting task of building new skills and gaining new knowledge. The need for expansion can also arise from changing circumstances: A divorce, with its emotional and economic upheaval, may make a woman aware of a narrowness that before she barely noticed. Now, she has to change radically in order to adapt to her new situation. Whether the stimulus for crisis arose from her own sense of timing, or from an external upheaval, the expansive women in my sample reviewed their pasts to find the place at which their potential was curtailed. Once found, they moved forward into their new midlife with skills and strengths they could never have imagined in their first years of adulthood.

The starting point for a woman who seeks radical changes is the conviction that she cannot move into the next phase of adult development as she now is. Seeing the potential that her future should offer, she feels impeded by some dull and pressing weight. Her awareness of being at a crossroads, and her need to reequip herself for the journey ahead, can be seen through the thoughts of Elaine Risley in Margaret Atwood's novel *Cat's Eye:*

> This is the middle of my life. I think of it as a place, like the middle of a river, the middle of a bridge, halfway across, halfway over. I'm supposed to have accumulated things by now: possessions, responsibilities, achievements, experience and wisdom. I'm supposed to be a person of substance.
>
> But since coming back here I don't feel weightier. I feel lighter, as if I'm shedding matter, losing molecules, calcium from my bones, cells from my blood; as if I'm shrinking, as if I'm filling with cold air, or gently falling snow.[1]

Elaine Risley makes the journey through midlife crisis. Aware of a new maturity, she reviews her past—not to sum it up, as an elderly person might, but to get a better view of her future. The long-forgotten pain of girlhood, the achievements of young adulthood, all give her "weight," but not the "substance" she imagined maturity would offer. She feels contradictory things; she feels lighter as she sheds part of her youthfully assembled self, but within this lightness she feels a counteracting weight; she does not rise, but descends. In midlife, as she sheds that controlled and protected personae of youthful adulthood, she senses a return to an earlier phase of development. Though this is necessary to future growth, it threatens her: She feels "dragged downwards, into the layers of . . . liquefied mud." She has to return to her past, but protests about getting stuck there: "I don't want to be nine years old forever."[2]

Some women have, at midlife, a particularly fierce battle with their pasts. They must return to that crossroads wherein they lost the lines to their futures. It may have been at puberty, when they felt the cruel constraints of femininity. It may have been at the brink of adulthood, as they lost the protective environment in which the world could be explored forthrightly. It may have been through the experience of marriage and motherhood, with its contradictory needs and constraining attachments. At some point in their development, they stepped not up, onto a higher rung, but into a shackle.

Such women must, at midlife, take determined, drastic steps to correct their pasts. Weighed down by this task, and by their uncertainty as to how to proceed, they feel the double edge of new opportunities and old fears. They may be tempted to foreclose the move forward because the long-buried fears are so great. In the early phase of midlife crisis, expansive women described how images of childhood became far more vivid than they had been in the early years of adulthood, when they denied their vulnerability. "It's the shock of seeing that I am grown up that makes my childhood seem so close. So many times I know I've said to myself 'Good, now you're at this stage, no longer at that stage.' There was this kind of marking . . . here was maturity you could measure. But somehow, that idea hits you, that you really should be all grown up by now, and then you see how you're never going to get away from that childhood, no matter how hard you try. And that's . . . eerie, but it makes you think: 'How can I get to where I want to go?' Because you're not going to get there on the path you're on now."

Women like Amanda Hill, who feel they have to do something

radically different to get to where they want to be, are most easily identified as going through a crisis. They seek abrupt changes as they realize
that the course they are currently on will not allow them to become
who they want to be—the person who they will be when they are all
grown up. They confront a "specter of despair over lost opportunities"[3] alongside the fear that they have not been true to their innermost
feelings, goals, and ambitions.[4] They may begin to "act out"—become
impulsive, aggressive, and tense—as they come to realize how they
have been confined by their own ignorance or fear. For the women in
my sample who felt that they lacked the skills or knowledge or confidence to move forward, progress was often difficult and scary. Yet they
seemed impelled forward by the need to forge a better future, and by
the determination not to waste the gathering of midlife strength. I
found that however many setbacks these women had, they made steady
progress towards expansion.

WHETHER AN EXPANSIVE WOMAN'S crisis was stimulated by
internal or external forces, it followed a similar course. First came the
critical realization of her own impatience with the status quo. This was
followed by anxiety as to change. Anxiety could be so acute that a
woman would retreat to the pre-critical state, in which she may not
have noticed how unsatisfactory her condition was. She would foreclose on the crisis, rather than endure the anxiety of change. When this
retreat was rejected, she had to deal with continued anxiety about what
she might lose through the change, and whether the change would be
effective. As she begins to take definite steps towards change she often
experiences a relief, which releases enormous energy. Hence, she may
seem, to others, wild or scatty or irresponsible. Yet such carelessness is
superficial: At each point of change, I found the women in my sample
asking, "How much should I preserve?" and "How much should I
shed?" Anxiety and caution are close at hand, even as she seems irre-
pressible. The crisis is resolved not when she has gained everything she
has hoped for, but when she feels confident in her ability to sustain her
upward stride.

CHANGE FOR THESE WOMEN was often sought through reedu-
cation or retraining. This step itself led to a series of changes: As they
went back to school, or enrolled in a training course, they met new

people, and felt themselves interact with others in new ways. They not only learned new facts, but gained new perspectives. In learning how to run a business, for example, some women felt they were gaining access to an entire range of concepts that they had previously thought themselves incapable of mastering. In studying social theory or psychology or literature, they gathered new tools for reflecting on the problems that had long plagued them. Moreover, the new knowledge and new skills would, they hoped, lead to new opportunities for further friendships, further self-confirming experiences, and make further knowledge possible.

It was not so long ago—less than 20 years—that I heard a distinguished psychiatrist speak at a conference about the problem of overeducating women. He was noting a problem that arose in his women patients. Women were dissatisfied because they had trouble putting to use the knowledge and qualifications their education had offered them. He did not see himself as arguing against education for women. He did not see himself as dismissive of the value of women's intelligence. He saw himself as sympathetic toward his patients' unhappiness; but he saw the problem in a way that withdrew the sympathy just as it was offered.

No woman identifies *herself* as "overeducated." This is not something she feels from within. It is a fault someone else identifies to explain her dissatisfaction. It implies that women's roles are final or fixed; and that women who cannot adjust to them have some flaw, some excessive need stimulated by "too much" education. Women themselves, however, are far more likely to feel that the roles are at fault, and they would have greater control and more choices among various roles if they were indeed "overeducated." But the cultural environment in which the psychiatrist formulated his version of the problem was the same environment in which many women, now in midlife, grew up. Some had been actively discouraged from continued education. One woman's father had refused to pay to educate a child on whom it would be wasted. Another's mother had declared that should her daughter go to college, she would be so uppity that no one would want to marry her. A teacher had blocked a young girl's musical education since "girls could not be percussionists." Other women had found the passive discouragements sufficient to dissuade them from further education. Seeing few career opportunities for women, they had not seen the point to education. Others, still valuing education, had dropped out of college to support a husband's further education, or had left school to move to a husband's place of work. Some, at the time, barely noticed what they had given up; while others felt a loss, which, they promised themselves, would at some future date be restored.[5]

Standing on the bridge of midlife, these women felt muffled. They felt that if only they knew more, they could see more clearly. In *An Unknown Woman,* Alice Koller speaks of her wish to leap out of the "safe inadequacy" of what she has learned and to see with her own eyes; yet she does not know what to look for inside her, and she does not know how to identify her feelings.[6] As she discovers that she can be the source of her own knowledge, she confronts a new puzzle: What responses count, what gives her information about her world, and how does she name, or describe, or define the feelings she has? Many of the women in my sample who wanted to make radical changes sought education not so much as a means of learning more, but as a means of learning how to give voice to what they already knew.

PREOCCUPIED BY "WOMAN'S BUSINESS," Trina Roberts, 41, had not previously thought that her knowledge could be communicated or exchanged. She had the adult experiences of marriage and motherhood, but, she felt, something within her remained static: "My mind," she said, "hasn't budged since I was fifteen." She thought she knew "only about children and people" and had "imagined [her]-self pretty competent, though not really smart, in the usual sense." Gradually, however, she began to notice how dissatisfied she felt with other people's knowledge and, at the same time, how it would "wipe away" her own thoughts. Her desire to correct this surprised her as much as the people around her. "I walk around and smile at people and we're talking nicely together, and then—I don't always see it happen, just feel it after it's past—someone's said something that just casts out what I might have said. Do you know this feeling, too, or is it just me? There's what you say, which can be made into nothing, because it doesn't have the right stuff behind it. And what I catch myself doing is smiling more and feeling young. You see it used to make me feel young, that's it, really, and I didn't even notice before how much it hurt."

Seeing that feeling young was no longer appropriate, Trina noticed that it was hurting. When she noticed the pain, she also felt insulted. As Trina described her decision to return to school, she beautifully rounded out the point of crisis. "I tell you all this like it was one thing, you know, a kind of flash. But what's so strange is the way things you've always known keep coming up until they add up. So I can't really say I ever didn't feel the pain and that it wasn't real insulting to have what I said swept under the blanket, because it was just like dust you wanted to hide quick. But what happened, I guess, was that I'd just hide underneath my little smile, and I thought for a while that was okay, that I could be safe there. But it gets lonely, you know, and that quick getaway to the place behind the smile was a little too easy to get to. And what I remember—maybe this isn't right, but it's how I see it now—is a flurry of excitement. That came before any ideas about going back to school—to real school—I mean, to college. It was the rush of excitement first, so that when the idea came I wanted to laugh it was so ridiculous, but I couldn't get rid of it, and because of that excitement—well, sure, I was afraid, but turning back seemed more ridiculous than anything else."

Here, the relatively straightforward idea of going back to school at 41 becomes an analysis of midlife development. From her awareness that she was not being heard in the ways she thought she deserved, she came to notice both the insult of this and the defensive ways she had been handling it. But, in seeing this, her defense—her "hiding"—no longer worked. In seeing what she had previously ignored she was already taking the step away from defensiveness towards growth. But to take this step she had to extend her idea of herself. She wants to laugh at the "ridiculous" idea of her going to college, but self-ridicule is countered by the absurdity of her fear. Like many women at this point of crisis, she counters the fear of what will happen when she changes with the greater fear of what will happen to her if she does not change.

Dealing with Doubts

The initial stages of an expansive crisis were, for the women in my sample who sought radical change in their own ways of thinking, sore and tender. A woman must confront the sense of inadequacy or incompleteness or dissatisfaction she has been harboring, and sometimes hiding, throughout adulthood. For, in early adulthood, we try to develop those skills and patterns that make us feel competent. In midlife crisis, we have to turn back to neglected, thwarted themes, and try to develop them. To sustain impetus through the strategy phase of the crisis—addressing the question, "What am I going to do about what I now see and what I now want?"—a woman may exaggerate the negative side.

When I first met Trina, she described herself as "shut out" from the knowledge and experience "which counts for something." She described herself as "knowing nothing beyond these four stupid walls" or "knowing only about things that don't matter." At 41, she had just seen her older daughter married and her son promoted in his first job. Though she still had two children at home, her restlessness convinced her husband that she should "find a nice little job." She resisted his dismissal of her plan to "take some dumb courses." She then began to notice how much of her self was "in hiding." At the same time, she felt the stirring of a new confidence.

To help themselves over certain hurdles, women at the initial phase of this developmental crisis summon up others' views at their very worst. They challenge potentially negative views of themselves, practicing their own resistance. The vivid imaging of how she seems from the outside can actually ease the control that others' views have over her. Among the group of midlife women returning to education, several described how, during the initial stages, they saw themselves as they might have seen a middle-aged woman when they were young. Having been young during a time when being young in itself was considered to be of paramount value, they still "caught glimpses of a past self among the young ones, looking at this strange middle-aged woman trying to do young people's things." Some worried about being "stupid seeming" and "trapped by this strange body." They were haunted by memories of how they, as young women, had seen older women: "not quite real," "sort of strange," "unsure whether they're going to turn on you, disapproving."

The fear of being too old was paradoxically accompanied by the sense of being a novice. "It's like going back to square one. I worry about things I can't remember giving a second thought to when I was in high school. Like not being able to find the right room. Like forgetting to put on shoes and looking down at my feet to discover I'm wearing slippers. Like being handed a text book and suddenly realizing it's in the wrong language, or that I just forget how to read."

Irrational fears—of forgetting how to read, of being too nervous to speak, of "falling apart on the first day" or losing one's way and "not being able to find the classroom"—were typical of those strategic exaggerations, which pushed women through the earlier crisis phase as they proved that change was needed. These exaggerated fears also seemed to play a role similar to that of "the examination dream." Freud noticed that people who dream about their miserable performance on an exam were, in fact, highly competent. Freud believed that the aim of the dream was to experience a delicious relief on waking, as the dreamer realizes that he has already successfully completed the exam. For several of the nine women returning to education, their irrational fears served this function. They began with exaggerated fears, then felt a rush of pleasure and confidence quite soon after embarking on a course. Once the decision to return to school was taken, most women then spoke about how well they expected to do. Their main concerns became practical—not being able to work hard, not having the time to study, not finding a way of concentrating and learning.

The next stage was to introduce change to their families, who would have to accommodate their expansive goals. Women returning to college often had more trouble with this than did women returning to work. In taking a job, or shifting from part-time to full-time work, a woman's domestic roles changed; but this was far less likely to disturb family dynamics than was a return to school. Adaptation to a working day is easy compared to a family's adaptation to a working mind—nor can a student ease the disruption with a paycheck. Both husbands and children find it easier to deal with an absent wife or mother, than with an absentminded, or otherwise preoccupied one. Being tired after a long day's work was easier for the family to accept, than needing time to write an essay or prepare for an exam. Women returning to college had two distinct strategies for dealing with their families: They would either share their new life with their families and persuade the families to change, too, or they would hide their changing lives, and allow the family to stay the same.

MY OWN MOTHER WANTED TO return to college when my sister and I were teenagers. She was hardly a novice—already she had a medical degree and had passed the board examination in her speciality.

So we all knew what it was like when she was studying. It wasn't nice: The preoccupation, the anxiety, the silence she demanded of us confined us to our rooms and cast a gloom throughout the house. When she put this idea of pursuing a graduate degree in physics to my father, he paced up and down for a moment, then held up his hand to declare, "You can do it as long as everything in the house remains the same."

She nodded solemnly. I knew they were both playing roles—traditional roles that made them feel good, though on the whole they were quite out of character. My father always has liked women with what he calls "their own interests and their own lives," yet he sometimes cannot resist an invitation to assume the patriarch's role. As an exploitative, chauvinist child, I was on my father's side. I did not want things to change. But I saw what she would do: She would run away with the permission slip and scatter the condition under which it was offered ("as long as everything in the house remains the same") to the winds.

Nothing was the same when she went back to college. The house froze at exam time, and the morning mail, with her grades marked on little cards, popped through the letter box like slices of fresh Wonderloaf. We waited for a signal of relief, so that we could all be happy for her, or at least be free to set our minds on our own tracks. "You're not going to keep on with this if it makes you feel like this," my father declared, but his declarations had lost their bite. Like electric shocks in a heated house, they were forgotten the moment the startling blue white light faded. "Humph," she said, just like Mary Poppins, and he did not venture to "protect" her again.

We listened to her at dinner each night, talking about the students, the teachers, the work. Her degree was as much a part of our world as of hers, yet to her it was an opportunity, and to us, an obstacle. When she found the answer to a physics problem, we could talk to her. When she finished compiling a computer program we could have dinner. When her exams were over, we could go on holiday.

For my mother, this midlife challenge and her ability to meet it was miraculous. I still feel puzzled by her self-doubt and her self-delight. Why was it so extraordinary for her to take this step? It was only when I listened to other women—my age now and the age she was then—speak about their new opportunities, their new hopes and their new terrors, that I began to understand her year-long celebration after she was granted her degree.

What seems normal and ordinary to one woman may be miraculous to another. We hold our achievements up to the light and admire their gleam, though many others glance at them and see only bits of cheap glass. For us, our achievement may be a big chunky fact, while for others it is so small that it barely registers. While men may be more prone to see their abilities reflected at twice their size, women often view the skills they make use of each day, which they exercise and develop, as miniaturized, barely worth mentioning. They feel "untested" in that real world, yet keen to take the challenge. And alongside this keenness is terror of failure and rejection and ridicule. Alongside a sense of her own intelligence and competence may lie bewilderment as to how to proceed. My mother's success was far more than a stroke of luck, it was vindication: What she had always known about herself could now be known by others. If this knowledge were justified, then so, too, could a much wider range of personal knowledge. Some women, like my mother, wanted to bring their new self into the family. Some women learn that this integration is highly disruptive.

A recent study of mature women students of different races and classes found that women going back to school or college had two different styles in dealing with their new situation.[7] These have been described as the "student mode" or the "mommy mode." The women who followed the "student mode" expressed their student identity in their home life. They talked about their courses, and the new ideas that emerged from them. They tried to introduce new topics of conversation, and to display their new skills in discussion. They believed that now, within the family, they had a greater claim to "being heard" or "having a say." They wanted to explore, in new ways, a partner's ideas; they wanted to share their new ways of thinking.

Other women kept their new world private. Those following the "mommy mode" separated their college from their home life. Learning was something that took place behind the domestic curtain; they would not shake it out in full view of their families. They were "the same old Mom" at home, but felt "totally different on campus." They were aware of speaking in different ways, and even using different gestures. This seemed odd but, nonetheless, was the most comfortable way of changing, without changing more than they wanted to change.

The women who separated their student lives from their family lives had much less trouble at home: There were fewer threatened marriages and family quarrels.[8] The women who introduced their student selves into their homes were far more likely than those who separated student and mother to be criticized by husbands for lower standards of housekeeping or of neglecting the family. Many of these women recognized that "permission" to expand was bought at the price of reserve. Family harmony was paid for by a divided life and a double shift. From many women's point of view, the double shift was easier to take on than battles with the husband, or attempts to change his attitude. "It's easier to change alone," Fiona decided.

"My husband would take the mickey out of me if I recited all I'd learned about historical explanations," 46-year-old Mary Anne admitted. "But when my daughter was doing Tudor history at school I could help her with her course work. She looked at me like—'Wow, I didn't know Mom knew about that!'—and I just said something like 'Well, I did it at school, too.' It made my day, but I wasn't about to boast to my husband."

Mary Anne knows that she separates her student and family life because she anticipates punishment: Her husband will "take the mickey out of" her if she talks about her work. In assuming any authority, she will be mocked. Elsbeth, who had not anticipated her partner's punishment, learned the hard way that the "mommy mode" was safer. "I expected everyone to be dead pleased," she said. "My kids were growing, all doing exciting things. My husband was tied up in his work and his politics. They encouraged me. They didn't want me to be moping at home while they were gallivanting about. But when it turned out this was more than a little women's institute course, that I was really going for a degree, my husband's encouragement cooled down faster than a cup of tea with an ice cube dunked in it. Now he starts telling me I'm neglecting the boys, neglecting him, the flat doesn't look right, I don't look right—and here's a man who's home maybe an hour before going to bed, and in that hour he's just watching the telly, and he's never taken one blind bit of notice before about how tidy the flat is or whether my hair's been combed."

When Sean, at 41, began a degree course at a community college, she found that her husband got so angry at "seeing the books cluttering the kitchen" that she learned to hide them behind the cereal boxes. Another woman said that she took money for books and courses out of the housekeeping money. "The excuses are automatic now. I invented a broken thermostat the other day, and an emergency plumber's bill. He didn't even ask to see the receipt. He's as trusting as a lamb as long as he thinks I'm not going to college."

The need to separate the different aspects of their lives came as a shock. For many of the women returning to education at midlife, their aims had been to heal an abscess of self-doubt. They had hoped that their expanding minds would make them more worthy of the love they already had. Having supposed that her husband only needed to feel included in her new life to accept it, Sean took him to see her classroom, because, for her, this was a magical setting. "He stomped about the room, in and out of the rows of desks, and laughed at everything. He sat down at one desk, and made fun of anyone who would sit there—you know, squirming like he was being told off by the teacher. All the way home he kept saying that it was just like any old schoolroom, and there must be something about those jerry built desks to con you into thinking you're doing something when you sit in them."

She then brought some of her fellow students home, thinking they would convince him—if she could not—that college was not just kids' stuff. "It didn't take long to see that he didn't want to be impressed. Who was I trying to kid? I used to think that when he complained I was ignorant, he wanted me to be different. It's a shock to realize that someone who's supposed to love you doesn't want you to improve yourself—no, worse, doesn't want you to feel better about yourself, and then, I don't know, locks himself off from what you're doing. It was a shock, and it hurt, seeing he wanted to dismiss me, and that he had to be so defensive, when I was trying to reach him. The one comfort—if you can call it that—because it's really not comforting, is that he only dismisses me because he wants to, not because of me . . . of what I deserve."

Whereas Sean's desire to bring her excitement into the home is an attempt to reach her husband, he cuts her off, defensive, threatened by her new horizons. While she wants to extend the relationship, he tries to limit it. Thinking that his dismissal of her views was based on her mental inadequacy, she viewed further education as a way of earning his regard. Instead, she finds that he does not wish to hear her or respect her: This is the "comfort," which does not feel comforting. "It feels strange, now, being with him and knowing that he wants such a small part of me. But I can't give it up. Once you feel part of yourself that before you haven't, can you really give it up again? I wouldn't. So I have to keep it down—close to the surface, so I can always feel it, but I don't let it show."

The women in my sample who sought radical change were most likely to experience resistance to change from their partners for the simple reason that it was new. People who were close to them were used to these women as they once were; many partners felt safer as a woman buried her doubt, and lived with it, without challenging it. Unlike innovative women, whose families learned over time to accommodate their goals for achievement and self-expansion, these expansive women were opening themselves up in entirely new ways. The self-doubt and fear, which once had governed their lives, were now lifted. Several partners were appalled by these radical changes: Their underlying question was, "What will happen to me if she no longer needs me to be strong or unafraid for her? What will I be for her, if she can be these things for herself?" Some women, seeking to reassure a partner that the relationship would continue, put their new horizons behind a screen.

This compromise, between staying in touch with this newly discovered part of her mind and hiding it, was rejected by older women. Jaimie, at 52, described how she used to "go easy" at home about her student life, but "couldn't be bothered with all that now. The energy I put into that tightrope walk really got to me. At first I felt I was doing what I had to, to protect [my husband] from all this stuff. I'd hold study groups in our living room and try to keep everyone quiet. At first we'd try to switch round from house to house, so no one family would be put out too much, but for various reasons it became clear that my house was most convenient for everyone. So they just kept coming here. The other day Allen said, 'No one else would have given you as much freedom as I do.' I burst out laughing. I just couldn't help myself. The idea that *he* gave me freedom—when I just went and took it . . . because I'm at a point in my life now, when I'll take it from anyone."

So often, in the women who were over 50, there was a breath of fresh air, something positive and pure, which contrasted starkly to the piecemeal deliberation of the women in their forties who were trying to find their way through a maze of new energy and half-overcome fears. There is an impulse, when hearing women in their fifties, to wonder: Why can't all women be like that, why can't women just jump straight into that more aggressive identity? Yet, when I turn to the developmental process of forty-year-old women, the answer is clear: The web of women's lives, in which needs for expansion and attachment are so easily tangled, the inherited images of women, whose sheer weight and subtlety continue to constrain her, are mazes through which each woman must discover her own route. In our time, in this time, for women, it takes a long time to find the right path out. When expansive women did find this path, they experienced elation at the way ahead. Often, at the end of crisis, expansive women stop suddenly, in their new easy stride, and reflect with wonder at the constraints they once felt.

BUT THE PROCESS IS not easy. Change involves risks. Some attempts fail, and some goals are mis-aimed. The expansive women in my sample often had to deal with false starts. This might bring them back to "point one," where they would make one of two different assessments: First, they might decide that, after all, no change could be made; second, they decided to make a different change.

The women who wanted further education, who got as far as starting a course and then decided that they could not finish, had a tough time. To summon the courage for change—and then embark on unsuitable changes is disheartening. Rosa Cortes, 44, had been in California for fifteen years, having come at that time from Mexico with her young husband who was also looking for work. With her children grown, she wanted "to go through the rest of her life with more than [she had] right now." But she found it more difficult than she had expected.

She had mixed messages from her husband and older son, who said they "liked her cute English." Initially, she thought her son, who had been educated in American schools, might be able to help her. "But all these things—pronouns and reflex—whatever, he didn't know, either." She believed that though her husband teased her about her course, he might have been secretly pleased and proud. However, given the demands at home and in her job, and her difficulty with the course work, she decided "it was all too much. Finally I told my husband I couldn't keep up with everything—him and the housework and the job I still take cleaning houses. I wanted so bad—to learn my English better. I work hard, but I can do this and that. I can't get no job as a receptionist or secretary. To work in a nice place, a nice office, where you meet people, you have to speak nice. My husband's English isn't too good. He made fun of me, trying to get better. I know that's not right. He's a baby. He makes fun of me trying to be better. When I stopped, though, he was kind. He hugged me and said we were O.K. I tried not to say how hard it was. I didn't want him to know I couldn't learn those things."

Rosa is tempted by the comfort of her pre-crisis self: As her husband hugs her and tells her they are fine as they are, she wants to deny the humiliation of defeat. He drew "something sweet" out of her, which was confusing and made her "want to cry." When I interviewed her eighteen months later, the disappointment was still sharp, but she resisted returning to that "safe inadequacy" of her familiar world. "The day I decided to stop the course is like yesterday, so clear in my mind's eye. I thought I'd just get over it, but something's different now. [My husband] was so nice, but I felt . . . I felt stuck, and that made me cry, like I wasn't going to move from here. Eh, well, it was so hard . . . to start it, you know, and then to give up. So other things I do—I work at them harder than I used to. There's something inside me . . . ," and she drew a shape in the air with her hands, "which has to be answered. I feel something . . . different from what he sees, what others see. My self, which I have to answer. Not just the little woman my husband sees."

The "failure" to break through to greater skills and greater confidence has a strong residue of success. Rosa feels an "unseen, unknown" part of her self, separate from and stronger than the "little woman" her husband sees. Though she can still respond to his protectiveness, she finds it more important to answer her self. For it is only by addressing "something inside" that she can move away from the smallness that encloses her as her husband comforts her. She continues to protest at being stuck here, where her husband's view overpowers the inner shape she draws in the air. Six months later, this inner shape has gained greater clarity: "I keep feeling it—this push to do more. I am not that 'little woman' any longer—not even for [my husband]. I wait—you will see—it will come out." For that urge to expand has already shifted the barriers around her, and she will keep trying until she finds her path into her new midlife.

Expansive women often deal with false starts and mistaken directions, but in so doing they may discover one problem hidden behind
the screen of another. I contacted Jeri Coppersmith as a "returner":
She was recently divorced, and had enrolled at a community college in
northern Virginia for an accounting course. I was given her name, as
one of a list of seven others, by the business coordinator of the college
to whom I appealed for names of newly enrolled midlife women. I
wanted to explore their reasons for embarking on what was a fairly
ambitious course at an advanced stage of their career, involving a two-
or three-year commitment. If someone simply had wanted some accounting skills to aid her in her business or secretarial work, she would
have chosen a less demanding program. I wanted, at that time, to trace
the different motives for making a long-term commitment at midlife,
as opposed to a more straightforward attempt to upgrade one's skills.[9]

What I found was that, in two of these women, extensive ambitions accompanied a need for radical psychological change. These two
women became a pair: They were drawn together by some unconscious
recognition. The first felt that she needed a career change to accommodate an already completed psychological change; whereas the other
woman "screened," or disguised, her need for psychological change
with a career change. The stories of each cast light on the other, and
each listened to the story of the other as though she could read her own
answers from it.

IN CHILDHOOD, ABUSE AROUSES pain, but not moral out-
rage, which might offer protection in spite of the pain. Nicola Campbell recalled "on and off" an episode in which she had been abused by
her father's brother, who often looked after her, since he was unem-
ployed and both her own parents worked.

"I didn't see it as something I should remember, any more than
you remember every scolding. And sometimes when I thought of it
. . . it was like a puzzle magically falling into place, and sometimes I
couldn't fit it up with anything else, so it floated in limbo, like some
fallen angel." She described it as "a little piece of light" that could turn
on or off quite suddenly, and once it was out it was "invisible."

She felt that, all her life, she had been held back by her fear of
people. When they were nice to her, she saw their face as masks and
wondered what they were really like. She described how her young

uncle had changed when he started beating her and "touching me in places I didn't know I had." She remembers she smiled at him, at first thinking he was teasing, and how when she saw his mean angry face, "the whole world rained down on top" of her.

Nicola had functioned well enough as an adult: She had worked all her life and had raised a child, but she had always tried to make her world "as small as possible. You know what I mean? If I knew one route to the grocery store, I wasn't about to go looking for a short cut, or find a cheaper store somewhere else. And if I had a nice boss, I wasn't going to leave that office for somewhere else. And I had this real mousey manner—so nervous, everyone felt sorry for me. It kept them away, or made them protective." She had functioned—but within a narrow realm that had offered her safety. She longed to extend it, but was afraid and confused.

"When I was coming up for forty, I felt . . . this jolt. I could either live like I was forever, or get help. So I went—real late—into therapy. I heard all the things I knew, but it was still nice to hear them. That it wasn't my fault, even though I thought it was. That it really had happened. That these things do happen. That considering all of that, I was doing pretty well. So I started to see myself as strong, and that really surprised me. But once I saw that, I wondered why I hadn't seen it before. Because I was really very strong, because I'd survived that abuse, and it wasn't likely to happen again, so what did I have to be afraid of? That feeling of strength was so sudden—like a showering of grace."

The difference between the world raining down on her as it did when she saw her uncle's angry, aroused face, and the midlife showering of grace, was a sense of her own power and competence. "I felt now I could decide how afraid I had to be. I wasn't afraid to try, and I wasn't so afraid of failing. I wasn't so afraid of being with people—that opened up a whole new outlet, I can tell you."

When Personality Changes Are Necessary to Expansion

Jeri Coppersmith, Nicola's classmate at the community college, looked up to the younger woman as someone who had miraculously found the means to build a new adulthood from a broken childhood. Nicola was taking the course to celebrate her achievement, whereas Jeri, at 52, was embarking on it to disguise her sense of failure. She wanted a new career to make a new person inside herself. Though she had a realtor's license, and many years of successful business experience, she "wanted a change, something different from the hard sell approach"; she wanted something where she could "feel quiet and accurate and in control." There was nothing specifically wrong with what she had been doing, except that now she wanted to do something else: She wanted to do something else, she said, because she "wanted to be someone else."

When I first met her, she could barely talk about her studies in accounting. Instead, she spoke about her divorce—nonstop, but haltingly. She would break off speaking and put the first and second finger of her left hand to her temple where she pressed hard, as though in pain—but, she corrected me when I asked, it was not to touch a pain, but to press so hard that she might create a different pain, distracting her from "the one that's churning up [her] insides."

> I pushed him away. You know, just pushed him. I thought we were talking things out, like you're supposed to, and all the time I was doing this I could see myself just pushing against him. I couldn't leave him alone. He'd be sitting watching the tube, and I'd see something on the program and I'd start going on and on. And everything that he did, seemed to be something else, like it was a sign for something else, and he was maybe trying to tell me something. You don't have to tell me I'm crazy. I know all about crazy. That's not it. I'm not crazy—that way. Just something was driving me against him. But what was even worse was that I also saw myself with my first husband doing this same thing, and there they were, all these visions of me crowding all around, and I kept doing what I knew I didn't want to do . . . Yes, I've been married before. God, this is—was—my third husband. And I can't go around like some ladies talking about what shits men are, because my men weren't. They were nice guys. I get really nice guys.

Her third husband, though, had been "the love of [her] life," someone she "could never believe [she] was lucky enough to marry." She repeatedly referred to him as "an educated man," someone with "a good education" with two grown sons who were "college educated" and who had always been "like gentlemen" with her. They had been married for eighteen months, when the older son had visited them with his wife and three-month-old baby. "It lit a fire in me, seeing [her husband] with that woman and her baby. Maybe mine grew up too fast, or I was too young—I don't know, but it was like bombs going off all around me, that group sitting right here on this sofa and playing and laughing, and it just made me cry inside."

Jeri could identify her envy as she saw her husband enjoying his son and granddaughter. She understood that her problem may have been that her own children grew up "too fast," making it impossible for her to have with them the rapport she saw her husband had with his son. But what was even more disturbing than her envy and sense of exclusion, was the way in which she wanted to destroy her husband's happiness—to punish him for loving his son—and in so doing, she could see, but not stop herself from destroying her marraige:

> I couldn't sit down with them, not even for a second. I jumped up, and I was fussing around—I started picking bones like nobody's business. I kept wondering how I was going to get through this visit. And then the whole thing started to fall apart. I just couldn't keep that marriage together, and I was throwing a tantrum before I could count to two. And when he tried to make things good for me, I only pretended to be calm, because I gave up trying to say what was wrong. For the last six months of that marriage I was in hyper-irritation . . . flying in a rage just because he was happy about something, and when it was all over all I could do was look around me, and even though I was kind of relieved, I was also just banging my head—like—What have I done? As soon as he walked out the door I said to myself: 'You've done it again, kid.' It was so frightening feeling those two things—my stomach hitting the floor because he left and that other voice laughing and slapping my back like, what a good a job. Two people inside me—now that's what real loneliness is. I said to myself 'You don't make another move. You don't speak another word—until you get help. And I mean real expert help, sorting out that mind of yours.'

The psychological constraint Jeri had to address was not apparent in her daily life. She was a confident businesswoman, who could deal effectively with people and with day-to-day problems. Yet she was caught in mental grooves, which made her repeat patterns that threatened her happiness. Now, she required a radical revision of her own responses if she were to find a good route forward. She needed to return to the point at which that narrow track was set down, and to find ways of expanding it. This, she saw, required expert help.

Some women, like Jeri, gain competence in early adulthood by forgetting past suffering. The developmental urge in midlife to break down the barriers between different aspects of oneself can smash this competence, and leave even the strongest woman bewildered. Jeri could now see the two people inside her. As each was opposed to the other, she discovered the true definition of loneliness—not knowing who inside her was speaking. The sleeping dogs many women let lie until midlife are awakened as women stand their ground and stare them down. But some women, badly silenced by denial and pain and family conspiracies, needed expert help.

Jeri's parents divorced when she was four, and three years later, her mother had a severe schizophrenic episode, which led to her hospitalization by the time Jeri was seven. Her aunt, who had two young children of her own, agreed to look after Jeri and raise her until Jeri's mother was "on her feet again." Though Jeri's mother did eventually recover to the extent that she could cope outside of a hospital, she never recovered her ability to look after her daughter. When her mother was ill, she was unavailable to Jeri, unresponsive, and, as Jeri described her "holed up with all these creepy nightmares that she preferred to me." When she was well, or better, and able to notice Jeri, she begged or demanded reassurances or proof of love, and then, when they were given, rejected them. "Her memory was selective—I learned that word in therapy—and distorted. She listened to me say how much I loved her, and just when I thought she was mollified, she would bring up something I'd done in the past—how that proved I was really wicked and rotten, and that maybe she was sometimes crazy but she wasn't stupid enough to believe a word I said. I've always thought that someday I'd find some way of proving that I do love her and make her happy—you know, get her trust. I know, I know, it's a pipe dream, and it's not doing any one a bit of good."

For some women, the special vulnerability of childhood harbors huge losses, sadness and, shame. They suffered unfairness, insults, abuse, or neglect, which they saw as part of the rough justice of the adult world, and which then dominated their adult hopes and fears. All of us have borne some losses or disappointments or slights or injuries, which become part of what we both learn to expect and try to avoid as adults. Knowing how a parent's shouting terrorized us, we try to use other techniques in dealing with our own children. Knowing how painful we found their lack of communication, we may try to be more open with our own children. But the compensation we seek as adults may not always be positive. Instead, we may seek to exercise over others the powers that once victimized us. Some people learn, as a result of having been bullied as children, more about how to bully than how to cooperate. Some people, having suffered abuse, grow up to abuse others. However sincerely we want to make up for childhood losses and injuries, we do not always employ the right strategies. And, it seems those who have lost the most in childhood, and been hurt the most, have the greatest trouble in finding strategies that restore losses and put an end to sorrows. It was such women who worked hardest in midlife to retrieve childhood experiences, to disclose past deceptions, and to link up with old pain in order to make way for a new future. But they could not always do it alone. Jeri wanted to be different from the mother who constantly attacked and criticized her. She wanted to be someone who gave love easily and unconditionally. Yet when she did love, the pain she had suffered at her mother's rejection was activated: Fearing that the person who loved her would reject her, she became the one who rejected first. In this way she would protect herself, her unconscious reasoning went, so that he could not reject her. This was the narrow cycle her love life followed.

At 52, Jeri acknowledged that midlife reassembly was past due, and was in despair because she could not see how to begin. Her previous efforts at fortifying relationships or diminishing her vulnerability had failed. "All my life," she explained, "I've wanted people around me to love, and instead they keep dropping away from me like dead flies. I can't keep anyone. Not even my own mother. You should have seen me with my mother. Even at 40, I was always thinking how I was going to get her that little thing from the store, and take her on this particular outing. Boy, I was going to give her a good time, and she was going to love me for it. Over and over again I thought about how I could make her love me—make her happy, and she'd love me for it. All that I'd been told over and over about her condition went in one ear and out the other. I was going to make her better. From 4 to 40 there was just no development in that area."

Implicitly, Jeri admits that something should have happened at 40 to change this. She did at that time undertake a determination to change things. New tensions developed between herself and her (now grown) children: She was quick to take offense, quick to guess that they were rejecting her, and eager to shut the door in their faces before they had the chance to shut the door in hers. She had decided, at 40, to change things: "All my life I'd been on a high wire doing tricks to get people to love me. I decided I was finished with that. I just put my feet on the sidewalk, just anyhow, and those that love me can stand by me, and those that don't can leave me. I can't tell you how many times I've thought with someone, 'Now nothing's going to ruin this,' and then it all just goes right down the drain. Why should I break my neck to make things work?"

This determination may seem like the initial step in a midlife crisis. She sees how much effort she has been putting into pleasing others, and she sees, further, that such efforts will never get her the secure attachment she craves. She sees that her fear of loss cannot protect her from loss. The force with which this hits her is indeed a crisis question: "How could I have wasted my time?" she demands of herself, and "How could I have thought it would work?" But, the steps she took after this crisis realization ushered in a false resolution. She engaged in a new rigidity, a cruel stance: "Take me or leave me." Since she cannot prevent loss, she decides that she will be careless. Since she cannot please others, she decides she will offend them. She throws them the challenge: "If you are going to stay with me, then you'll have to prove yourself by putting up with a very difficult person." Any criticism, any distance, any disappointment throws the whole relationship into question. Instead of gaining greater access to the different parts of herself, instead of retrieving that pre-idealizing ability to tolerate the ups and downs of the human world, she defends herself with a new rigidity.

These new principles, for a while, seemed to work because many people close to her were willing to put up with her even when she made attachment difficult. Her children learned that "When Mom says 'jump' you'd better do it." Her husband learned that if he wanted to keep her home after an argument, he had to "beg her to stay." But threatening others with losing her did not give her the proof she sought. Her new strategy, she saw, was out of control. Her real crisis question, ten years on, was "How could I have thought this would protect me? How did I not see that this was making things worse?" The repetition of broken relationships and false resolutions, catapults her into a belated, panicky crisis. "If I lose this [marriage] now," she said, "I'll lose everything, because every last bit of hope goes out the window, too. The rest of my life will be lonely and empty. I'll drop every last jewel I ever held in my hand. I can see a bitter old woman just waiting to swallow me up and become me. How do I keep away from her?"

Seeing where the narrow path, on which she now walked, would lead, she resisted its course. While some of the women described in this chapter turned to colleges or courses to help them expand their horizons and learn new strategies for growth, Jeri turned to an expert who could help her understand her own mind and enable her to learn new ways of responding to those she loved.

IN THERAPY, AND IN friendship, Jeri learned to affirm her own feelings. "I used to think of my childhood and want to bellow, but somehow whenever I thought about it, I'd whisper. I wanted to keep it quiet. I wanted to feel that it simply didn't matter any more. But there it was, weighing me down, and directing every important move I made." As she heard Nicola's story, she felt that this whispered experience gained a hearing. "Having this kind of ally has been great. I heard about Nicola's childhood, and I realize that there's a whole story that we can tell about ourselves, and we don't have to keep fighting other people's versions of it." Yet this confidence spurred her to further investigation. "Nicola started talking to her brother to find out more about her childhood. It seemed such a reasonable and simple thing, but I'd never thought of it before." Her work in therapy "only tied up things inside my head. It didn't show me whether they were right or wrong." What she needed was to "find the facts," to discover what had really happened, to know whether she was "overreacting" to her experience or justified in feeling deprived. To gain further control "over this inner tiger," she felt she needed to know whether her sense of unfairness was justified. "It's not enough to go over and over your own way of seeing things. You have to get some handle on them in the real world." The validity of her subjective feelings could be sustained, and extended, through objective investigation.

Soon after Jeri's separation from her husband, while she was wondering whether she "dare try this relationship again," she contacted her cousin, whom she had seen very little of during adulthood. "It's hard to find out about your past, when everyone is protecting someone else, and when they know you have no comeback when they say, 'No that never happened.' God—how many times I've heard that. It's like *Gaslight,* you know, like they're trying to make me think I'm out of my mind. But [my cousin] is amazing. I never saw this in her—how it all meant a lot to her, too, and she tried to figure it out, and how she sometimes cut herself off from me, deciding we must be different, because if the things that were happening to me had been happening to her, she would have caved right in."

The memories of different family members can be grossly mismatched, and discrepancies in family narratives can have cruel effects. A parent's insistence that what you thought happened, didn't happen, or that it happened an entirely different way, can feel like theft of part of yourself, denying your memories, and your mind. A child's memories are thought to be shaky, because a child's perceptions are often partial and skewed. The validation of Jeri's memories offered her power over them. "It's like being introduced to the person who's inside you, and who keeps stepping in to act on your behalf. You can finally listen to that inner child, still speaking inside you, and also say, 'That's enough for now. It's the grown-up's turn today.' "

When I saw Jeri ten months later, she said that she and her former husband were "trying again. It won't come together like magic. But it's going in the right direction. What was so frightening, before, was knowing that I was getting older and not moving ahead, not even leaving any of the bad stuff behind." She had to accept a new kind of self-doubt: The "tough lady," who had kept vulnerability at bay, was no longer brought in as a useful guard. Instead, she had to accept an unguarded self: She had to "be brave enough to be like a child again—you know, admitting that I need him, and that things can still go wrong."

Here is the tricky task of return and reconstruction—to go back, but without getting stuck; to regain a child's skill and tolerance, yet sustain a woman's knowledge. Jeri needed to retrieve memories and see her childhood anew. She had to address the inner child that was afraid to come out. She had to regain the lost child's skill of trusting attachments and accepting their day-to-day variations. She did not want to retreat to childhood, but move forward, having retrieved lost skills.

Expansive Woman and Divorce

"I'm 43. I thought, year by year, I was building my life. I was married. I had children. I worked at a variety of jobs while I raised my children. Eight months ago—if I'd talked with you then—I would have said that my life was pretty good, pretty secure, pretty much a success. Now I feel I have nothing—no security for my children, no home that's mine, no health coverage, no pension—in fact, I simply don't know what I own, and I have no control over my future. For the last twenty years I knew who I was, and I felt happy about my future. Now, suddenly, I have nothing I thought I had, and no way of knowing how to start again."

Joann Mason can, she said, "stand for thousands of women who thought they had their lives sorted out, until their husbands decided to leave them." The series of decisions, which seemed fair and reasonable in the context of a stable marriage, can come to an abrupt end in the context of divorce. She had worked, but in part-time jobs, with flexible hours—hence, with low pay, low prestige, and low security.[10] "It all made sense at the time," she explained. "He earned more than I could, he was going places, and so we lost less as a family if I stayed with the kids and he worked. At the time," she repeated, "it was perfectly reasonable."

Joann's explanation of her personal circumstances have a strong backing in economic theory. The traditional roles in the family—the wife doing unpaid work at home to service the paid employment of the husband—are "economically rational."[11] Since her husband could earn more and succeed more easily in his career, it was more efficient for him to engage in paid work, while she does the unpaid work at home. Were he to spend more time in the home, on family oriented tasks and activities, then he would earn less and climb the promotional ladder less quickly. He, in effect, buys her domestic services with his earning power, and she buys his earning power with her domestic labor. This is more efficient, according to one economist's model, than sharing work inside and outside the home, for two reasons. First, it is seen to be more efficient for each person to specialize and gain expertise in one area. Second, because two part-time jobs would fail to give a family either the income or the prestige or the security of one full-time job in the workplace: Part-time work is poorly paid, has few promotion opportunities, and has far less security than a full-time job.[12]

What this model of economic efficiency neglects, however, and what Joann discovered, is that this type of exchange is only effective when the marriage works perfectly. When it fails, the inequality of these exchanges become obvious: The partner who does not have direct access to the family wealth, who does not have the earning power, who does not own the pension and the health coverage, is the person who, as the marriage ends, loses the most.

AS A GIRL, JOANN was warned by her mother of the dangers of spinsterhood. She was encouraged to finish college, but not to become the independent-minded woman men would not want to marry: isolated, unloved, she would be a marginal figure in society, impoverished by women's pay, and unadorned by women's proper roles. In adulthood, a different warning bell tolled: Marriage is not forever, do not believe a man will always look after you and your children, be independent, financially and emotionally, because you can depend upon no one but yourself. "I loved reading the feminist stuff, and I loved talking it. I felt independent because in my mind, in myself, I felt so. But I valued Richard's career more than mine, and so I gave up more of mine to look after the kids. I was a fool to do this," she told me at our first interview. "And any other woman who does it is also a fool. She'll get nothing for it. Her children will get nothing for it, and her husband will not thank her for it."

As she dismissed her past, she despaired of her future. "If I were in this position at any other time of my life I would know what to do. Earlier on, I could build up a career. Later on, a court would allow me more maintenance. If my children were older, I wouldn't have to worry so much about their college fees.[13] If they were younger, they would need me more, and I would be more use to them."

Neither the old fashioned warnings against spinsterhood nor the contemporary warnings against economic dependence take into account the contradictions in women's adult experience as workers and mothers. Financial independence within marriage can be hard to sustain, as a wife's domestic and emotional services are often "bought" by husbands who work "for the family" outside but not inside the home.[14] The wife then never builds up the financial or human capital that will allow her fair participation in the workplace should the marriage dissolve. As career opportunities for midlife women are far less than for younger women,[15] as the pension prospects of women who embark on a full-time career path at midlife are poorer than for younger women, as the economic consequences of divorce are sometimes judged by sociologists to be the primary trauma of divorce,[16] the crisis of divorce is more intense at midlife than in early adulthood. And yet each woman asks herself, as she makes decisions about family and work: "How much can a financial possibility in the future affect my decisions about my family, based on what I know they need now?" Many divorcing women must also ask, "How much can financial difficulty affect my personal decisions?" Joann, to escape her destructive bitterness, has to reconceive past decisions in ways that make sense to her now.

WHILE I WAS WORKING with women who were in the process of divorce, going through and picking out the strands that had bound them to their decision to separate and then divorce, I was surprised by the minor constraint that financial dependence played in that decision-making process. Though women do more adapting or "emotional work" to sustain a marriage,[17] though they worry more about their own and their husband's happiness within the marriage, thought they are willing to change and to compromise their own wishes, they also have higher standards for marriage. More than 85% of divorces are instigated by women. Valuing the relationship more, and investing more in it, they are often harsher judges of its quality. The twenty-two divorcing women in my study, aged between 40 and 52, spoke in terms of the relationship having "no future," of the relationship being "dead," of "being unable to function when I'm always put down," of having "lived too long under the awful shadow of his hatred," of feeling "oppressed and oppressive," of having been "stuck for far too long," of being "bored and unhappy and angry," or "being much too hurt to go on."

The relief at having come to a final decision seems to give women, however precarious their financial situation, some self-confidence and determination to get their lives in order and develop the new skills that may now be demanded of them. They hope that divorce will be a new start, and they work hard to create oportunity. When the women in my sample did divorce, they often delighted in their independence. Other researchers, too, have found that divorcing women discover an individual identity and capacity for assertiveness and self-care. As a painful marriage is dissolved, women are likely to gain both a sense of separateness and individual strength.[18] Once recovered from the shock and the initial pain, 54-year-old Gabby, a year after her divorce, also discovered, "an expansiveness in my days, when I can just suit myself. It's not what I would have chosen, but I have to admit there are new pleasures in my life." Whereas divorcing women are likely to discover their capacity for independence, divorcing men are likely to realize their dependence. Other studies support what I found in my sample: Divorced men said they missed having a lover and a partner; divorced women claimed to miss only a husband's income.[19] No woman in my study regretted her decision to divorce—though some regretted their marriage.

THE SHARPNESS OF REGRET, in its raw state, can be counter-productive. This is what Joann was battling against when I saw her again three months later. To escape from "the locked-in feeling of hatred," Joann worked to restructure her regret. "I can't say I've given my children nothing by spending the time I have with them. I'd like to—oh, it would make things so much easier if I could just see everything I had done as wrong. Then . . . maybe I wouldn't feel so hurt—just stupid. But I know what it was like—making the decisions I did, which have left me where I am. It wasn't because I was stupid or lazy or foolish, was it? No, because I have to go back and pick things up. When something like this happens and suddenly everything seems different, you don't know who you are any more, and what you can do."

Regret can take on an awful punishing force. Under its influence, every path taken, every decision made, every experience can seem wrong. At this delicate phase of development and recovery, there seems to be a crucial difference between disdaining past selves, casting them aside like the old skin of a snake, on the one hand, and seeing them as steps in one's life, however inconvenient and precarious, on the other. A woman who looks back and declares herself a dupe and a fool, feels less powerful than the woman who sympathizes with the legitimacy of wrong turns and mistaken decisions. Embittered, she sees only others' role in thwarting her expectations and needs. In a true resolution of such a crisis, however, she sees both disappointment and potential: She sees herself as the agent of positive change.

For many divorcing women, the task is to expand their skills in order to cope with their new economic position. The practical tactics of finding out what to do as a reentrant in the workforce take precedence over emotional management, yet cannot be separated from them. "If I just sit and stew, then again I'm no good for anyone." Anger isn't profitable or sensible: It's "not the way [she wants] to go." Anger, Joann believes, is wasted energy, and it leads her into a trap: "When these awful feelings wash over me, and sometimes I just can't stop them, I feel they [her husband and his girlfriend] get so close, and because they're so close it's like a dead end—or I'm at the dead end as long as they're standing together, looking at me." To avoid the entrapment of their mockery, or pity, or whatever it is in their consciousness that reduces her to an image she cannot identify as herself, she turns to practical matters as "a relief. Because I need to work on something I can change."

The key to that "locked-in feeling of hatred" is the discovery of her own agency. This discovery that she still has chances and choices triggers that release characteristic of expansive women in crisis. "I'm going forward," Joann told me a year after our first interview. "I'm not wealthy, and I still get angry, but I'm starting to collect things in my life again."

Eight of the women I interviewed were currently undergoing divorce, and 17 more had been divorced in the past nine years. Among the divorcing women in this study, a common characteristic was the sharp drive towards preserving self-esteem, and the will to survive. Those who clung onto their anger did so productively: "I'll show him." So anger welded their determination. Though they sought help where they could—from parents, from siblings, and sometimes from their adult children—the help they sought was not a new dependence, but a base from which they could refocus their goals and reassess their skills. Work became not a luxury or a prestigious pastime but, as it is for many woman, a life-long necessity. Several women in my sample saw divorce as the making of them. Within five years, they had not only recovered emotionally but also economically.[20]

DIVORCE IS ALWAYS A crisis. When a midlife woman experiences it, she meets a network of crises. She is primed, anyway, for a crisis of reassessment as the cultural idea of being forty and no longer young demands new sources of self-esteem. She is primed, anyway, to amass the reality of her experience, finding a new pride in her subjective vision and new ways to validate it. She is primed, anyway, to address conflicts, which emerge more clearly and coherently because she has the strength to hear them and integrate them. But the inner readiness for reassessment and renewed control over the compromises necessary to daily life can clash with new constraints, a new loss of power, and new necessities. Can midlife growth occur in the midst of an externally induced crisis?

The distress of women in the process of divorce seems overwhelming, yet their recuperative powers are remarkable.[21] In spite of economic and social constraints that many women experience as a result of divorce, they tend to recover more quickly than men, and are more likely to use this change as a stimulus to growth. They often discover enormous advantages in becoming head of household themselves,[22] whereas men are more likely to discover the dependencies that underlay their "authority." The women in my sample who were in the process of divorce were well on their way to recovery within eighteen months, and women in their fifties, often supposed to be more vulnerable, to have a sense that prospects of remarriage are virtually nil, were far more eager to adapt to these changes. The process of coping, for them, seemed far more direct. They did not have to go through all the highways and byways filled with that ghostly chatter, which poses the questions: "What did you do wrong? Why didn't you manage to do things right?" The pain they felt was intense, but somehow contained, doing far less damage to their identity and self-esteem, so that the healing process was more localized.

Though Gabby spoke about "layers and layers of pain" and dealt with anger that felt "like being drenched in dirty water," she described herself as "healed" or soundly "rebuilt" within twelve months. Even a woman who had been hospitalized for depression after a suicide attempt (made on the day her former husband's new partner and children moved into what had been her family home) was, two years after the event, free from depression: "It feels like forever," she admitted, "but the dust settles. It feels like the deepest grief, but it just doesn't keep its bite. It's not like death—except that there's an inner rupture, a no going back sort of feeling. The worst thing for me was that he and [his new partner] formed a family. They had a home where my [18- and 20-year-old] children could go, and I had only the bare seedy flat full of boxes I couldn't bother to unpack. But I still meant something to my children, and I still had my own life left. The mourning gradually became more and more inappropriate. I can now look ahead, and work towards my future."

The expansive woman, at midlife, stares from a bridge into a chasm beneath, feeling that her past provides no substance, and yet it pulls her down in "liquefied mud." To walk towards a better future, she must free herself of this weight. To free herself, she must understand what it is that impedes her, and develop strategies for expanding her options. These strategies involve radical changes: She gains new skills or new experience or new confidence or new control.

The impetus of radical change is expressed by Jeri: "I don't want to be who I am," and by Joann's anxiety: "If I were in any other position, I would know what to do and what to feel." To gain access to new horizons, these women reconsider past pains and fears, and find new ways of overcoming old impediments. Whether the retrieval is of a buried fear of inadequacy (as for Rosa) or of childhood suffering (as it was for Jeri and Nicola) or of adult patterns and choices (as it was for Joann) the broken threads of one's life become the reference points of a new task. Expansive women make radical changes in their lives to correct the narrow range of past experience and find new sources of energy and competence.

Expansive Women: Signs and Signposts of Midlife Crisis

Women in this category are sometimes described as "late starters" or "late developers." Their individuality has been curtailed by the expectations others had of them, and by their own internal acceptance of those expectations. They have been "kept in their place," too, by lack of skill, education, or training. Their midlife paths take them back to the point at which they can retrieve a neglected potential. Women in this category may feel that they have much in common with traditional women, but are trying to step deliberately away from their pasts, or they may feel that, like protesting women, they are driven by panic at the passing of time. Many in this category, however, proceeded along the following lines:

Previous orientations:

1. Others' expectations guided one's actions.
2. Familiar patterns and relationships were sought for safety.
3. Challenges were avoided because one felt incapable of meeting them.

Many expansive women feel potentially very capable, yet are easily put down by others. They often have divided opinions about themselves—a sense of competence, and a fear of inadequacy. In early adulthood, they may trust the opinion of others and depend upon others' approval.

Signs of approaching crisis:

1. angry awareness at the unnecessary constraints others impose on one
2. increasing frustration at one's lack of skills or knowledge
3. terror of change—balanced by a terror of stasis

The discrepancy between their two different views of themselves becomes increasingly troublesome. Expansive women now feel desperate to develop skills and talents. Before they have decided how to this, or found a suitable route, they may be irritable, anxious, and impulsive as they try out many different things.

Resolution of crisis:

1. resists the pressures of others' views as to what one is or should be
2. takes steps to expand one's skills and knowledge
3. is thrilled by the long-neglected experiences of development and change

Expansive women measure their success in terms of their new flexibility more than in terms of objective measures of attainment. Their crisis resolution is marked by a determination to pursue different things, filling their lives with variety, rather than seeking a single goal.

5 Protesting Women: Creating a New Youth

There were some women in my sample who waged a war against age. Feeling they still had "all too much to do," they protested against midlife, insisting that they were not prepared for it—not yet, not when they had had so little time to be young. Most of these women—thirteen in my sample of eighty—had been cheated of a time, during late adolescence, to explore, to try out, to play. While, as adolescents, their peers had made and lost friends, played with the fire of passion and stepped back unscathed, found freedom within their families to exercise their youthful lack of wisdom, the women in my sample who protested against the onset of midlife had been catapulted into a premature adulthood—by the death of a parent, by the demands of poverty, or by an early pregnancy. Having been forced to behave responsibly, sensibly, and consistently at a very early age, these women, at midlife, wanted to reach back and grow into the youth they never had.

Protesting women tend to have a strong need to express their individuality. They feel proud of their abilities and confident of their potential, but have been unable to harness their strengths. Some setback or necessity had prohibited them from exercising their taste for spontaneity and adventure. However much they had actually achieved, they felt that they had not done enough, or not precisely what would satisfy them. These women were, at the onset of crisis, keenly aware of a potential history that was parallel to their actual history: They felt closely shadowed by what they might have been, what circumstances have deprived them of being. Though they had functioned well in their first years of adulthood, to do so they had controlled an impetuousness and adventurousness that they identified as an essential part of themselves. Midlife, and the self-assessment it triggered, focused their protest against past controls. Their crisis was impelled forward by panic, lest this time, too, opportunities and second chances fail them. How could they now, at midlife, link up with that more eccentric self they had left behind when necessity made premature demands on their self-control and maturity? For these women, midlife crisis involved a weathering of panic and despair lest the qualities that had been put in cold storage were lost forever. It was resolved as these women learned again what it was like to be spontaneous—not as a child, but as a youthful midlife woman.

THE PROTESTING WOMEN IN my sample were, for all their vitality, the ones most prone to depression. What characterized their depression, however, was not listlessness as much as energy that could find no immediate outlet. Those who were depressed were, curiously, not "glum." They saw themselves looking at a potentially glorious world—but from a distance. At the onset of crisis, they saw, but could not touch a world in which they could realize their desires. This distance filled them with anxiety, and impelled them towards positive change.

"The new life course," writes Arlene Skolnick, "has more twists and turns than it did in the past; new longevity, new health, creates opportunities and new demands."[1] With this increased opportunity span, with the awareness of midlife as a starting point for further development, comes anxiety. Protesting women were anxious precisely because they were hopeful. As midlife triggered an intensified self-assessment, they turned to confront that "parallel" self. Reaching out to it, they saw the gap between where they were and where they want to be. Pressured by the sense that they must do it now—or possibly never—their efforts were often hectic and diffuse. Midlife crisis came in a wild wind that buffeted them this way and that, until, at its resolution, they gained the ability to spend their energies without wasting them.

Wild break-outs are always dangerous for women. In the film *Thelma and Louise,* the two women are still in their first adulthood when they try to take a holiday from the drudgery and fear that bounded their daily lives. But they run into the punishments men inflict upon women who want to have fun. Threatened with rape, hunted as murderers, they keep going. Their story ends, however, not with a leap over that wide canyon, but a death-jump into it. The women in my sample whose adulthood had been informed by a premature need to control their desires and bury their fears, find the prospect of making that leap both thrilling and terrifying. Their challenge is to make good use of both their caution and their courage.

FEMALE DEVELOPMENT CAN BE a series of negotiations around ever-tightening constraints. When families are marked by the death of a member or by financial difficulty, everyone suffers, but it is usually the best functioning woman who does the most work towards sustaining the emotional and psychological well-being of the family. Usually, the best functioning woman is the wife or mother; but sometimes it is a daughter. By the time she was fifteen, Sara Ann Carr had taken over the care of her younger half-sisters and brothers while her mother battled against and then succumbed to drug dependency. Ellen Samuel had left school at sixteen to help maintain her father's motel as his health deteriorated. Monica Selleck became a mother herself when she was sixteen. Throughout early adulthood, each of these women had proved themselves capable and competent. Aware that they had missed out on much of the freedom of late adolescence and the experimental stages of adult life, they looked on their peers as inhabiting a different world, filled with golden opportunities and magical chances. As the gates of youth slammed shut in their faces, they made strong sensible decisions and held their heads high; but however proudly they walked, they felt a stab of regret at having missed out on the trial-and-error stage of late adolescence. They saw themselves as survivors; but all their skills and competence could not give them back the potential they craved. In protection against despair, they felt that some shadow self was enjoying a parallel history that was kinder to their potential personalities. "The person I could have been is right beside me," Ellen explained. "My other self wasn't lost, just put aside for a while." For Sara Ann, a "reckless nature breathed along with every careful step I took. I loved my sisters and brothers and I was glad to look after them, but always there was a secret selfish self quietly watching the door." For

Monica, the parallel was more achievement oriented: "I know, inside me, is an ability to race ahead and do all sorts of things, and still, when I'm with friends, or at parties, I'll be talking about what I do and feel like shouting, 'But all this isn't what I really am!' " Each woman had guarded and tended a parallel self as she met the more urgent requirements of daily life.

These women protested the passing of time because they feared the final loss of the youth they never truly had. "All my life I've been too young to do what I do," Ellen reflected. "Now I'm forty, and old enough for anything. It's suddenly hit me that I want everything I didn't have earlier—all the chances, all the choices. I want it *bad*," she laughed at her own insistence, "and I want it now." Sara Ann felt that her "caring self was plumb worn out": Her own children were now in their twenties, and she was resisting their requests that she care for their children. "When I saw my first grandchild what I felt was not a need to hold her forever, but to make a quick getaway. I just got to . . . I just got to find my own life, before it's too late." Monica, torn between her 26-year-old daughter, who still needed her attention, and a career in nursing, which was in some respects satisfying and in others "frustrating as hell," felt "a new ache, like I never let myself feel before, for more than this, for what I want." Now was the time to catch up with that shadow self, who guarded and tended their potential for spontaneity and adventure. But seeing that the time was ripe for this meeting was not enough: they had to negotiate their way through the habits and commitments and concerns that had informed their actual lives.

Getting pregnant at fifteen was something Monica variously described as a "setback" and "a slap in the face" or "a kick in the teeth." Like many other girls who found themselves pregnant in the 1960s, before any state had legalized abortion, she found termination terrifying—both medically and morally. As soon as she discovered she was pregnant, Monica knew "deep down" that she had to form her future in resistance to the script that this "mistake" had written for her. The pessimistic force against her can be seen in an often-cited forecast about teenage mothers: "The girl who has an illegitimate child at the age of 16 suddenly has 90 percent of her life's script written for her. She will probably drop out of school; even if someone else in her family helps to care for the baby, she will not be able to find a steady job that pays enough to provide for herself and her child; she may feel impelled to marry someone she might not otherwise have chosen. Her life choices are few, and most of them are bad."[2]

There was little reason to suppose that Monica would be an exception to that grim blueprint. She did drop out of school. She did marry someone she would not otherwise have married—and suffered the expected unhappiness and domestic instability. ("I married the father. The father! What a joke. That marriage lasted about two minutes.") She did not, initially, find what could be called a steady job, and her life choices did seem few: Most options involved extreme compromises, and she described her prospects as "pretty poor." The typical structures of work, career, and mothering are, for most women, unforgiving; for a single, and extremely young woman, social and economic facts are more like barbed-wire doors than windows of opportunity.

Given her family background, Monica's narrowing choices were unexpected and cruelly disappointing. Her mother, now retired, had been a teacher at a prestigious private school in Chicago.

My mother wanted desperately to be a part of the educated world. It's funny—she was a part of it, but she always felt excluded. She wasn't quite sure where that magic door was, and which side of it she was on. She was proud of her work, and she loved us kids, but I think she felt trapped, and kept trying to make my dad something he wasn't . . . I used to feel so sorry for him trying to come up to her standards . . . Mom was a tough cookie. She must have been lonely, but it was hard to get close. Here she was, the one black teacher— then—at that fancy school, wanting to be part of the white man's education, but still so proud of being black, and proud of having pulled herself up by her bootstraps to that position. She couldn't have had many friends at the school, and our neighbors weren't any use to her either. They never offered her the respect she kept going on about deserving. Thinking about her like that—boy, I see how I must of disappointed her.

But the real disappointment bit further as she saw the other women in her cohort rise to meet the challenges of changing social expectations for women. "I sat back and watched everyone get what I knew I had wanted all along, but had been too divided or distracted to go after. My friends, who made it to college, were really together, and I was trapped in this mess of my own making. They were moving ahead, while I was following the stereotype of the black girl gone bad. It was so odd—this wasn't me, but it was happening to me. I was really like those college girls, but in another sense I was nothing like them. I knew I could have the same . . . the same range of energies . . . the same confidence in myself, but I didn't know how to bring that potential to life."

At 42, twenty-seven years away from that initial confrontation with the barrier between girlhood and adulthood, she experienced a resurgence of both hope and hopelessness: "I felt like nothing was ever going to happen to me again. There was only this underwater feeling. Then finally that idea . . . walking to work, waiting for the bus . . . nothing's going to happen, and the sense that it's you, only you are going to stop yourself from turning into that old woman nothing happens to." Afraid of becoming "that old woman" as rapidly and as finally as she had become a young woman, she wanted some chance, now, to grasp the might-have-beens she left behind. "I have always been stuck with that 'me' who got pregnant so early, so much against all the advice I'd been given, so true to type—but against the expectations of the people who loved and cared for me. It's a long time for one mistake—if you want to call it that, which I don't any more . . . but for one thing to define you. Not that I haven't been doing a lot—but all the time, there was this river of regret running through me, waiting for the chance to have my future. Turning forty sent me into a panic because I knew it had to be now or never, but I could not see how to make it happen."

EACH OF THE WOMEN who were thrust into the adult world when they were still girls felt that part of their real self was caught in a parallel world, which could not intersect with the one they actually lived. Yet each of these women had, by any objective standards, attained more than would have been predicted from their starting point. Without a high school diploma, Ellen remained employed as a motel manager throughout the harsh recession in the Midwest. Sara Ann stayed with her mother when she married, and cared for her mother along with her own children, just as she had cared for her younger brothers and sisters. With her mother's help, Monica passed a high school equivalency exam and trained to be a nurse when her daughter

entered school. Though each woman had dealt well with potentially
life-disrupting events,[3] she felt burdened by them. Sara Ann said that
there was a "tiny place" wherein she was skillful and competent, yet
this was so small and "so tightly packed" that it often hurt. She felt
there was another self, living and thriving somewhere else, waiting for
her to meet up with it. Monica appreciated the successes and pleasures
of her job, but remained highly ambivalent. Caring for patients gave
her "a great boost. It was wonderful feedback, talking to them, raising
their morale by doing little things. It took all that time for the stigma
to drop away—and that didn't happen—not until my training [as a
nurse]. I would walk onto the ward and suddenly I'm a person—not
the daughter who disappointed her parents, or the mother who was
trapped by her daughter." But, still, there was a gap between her reality
and an earlier sense of who she really was. "It's not a matter of having a
different job—I know how to work on that. It's a matter of feeling I
can harness my energies in a certain way."

These women had built up skills on foundations of fear and frustration. They had believed there was no choice but to rise to the necessary maturity. Ellen remembered how frightened she was when she first
began night duty on the motel desk. She spent hours staring at the
little button that would alert her father if she were in trouble, but however afraid she was, she was more afraid of his despair if the business
into which he had put everything failed. Guests at the motel would
chuck her under the chin, pinch her cheeks, kiss her, or even fondle
her. "My Dad thought I had a recurring eye infection, because I was so
often weepy." Sara Ann said that all the domestic work and child care
tasks had seemed so easy in contrast to the terror she felt when her
mother fell apart. Looking back, they saw the amount of self-management involved. "I kept swallowing down those ideas of what I'd like to
be doing, just thinking about what I had to do," Sara Ann reflected. "I
used to think hope was good. You know, all I wanted was to stand in
the shoes of someone who could hope. I now find myself standing
right in them, but all I can see is how much it hurts. What can I do
with all of this hope?"

The nervous resurgence of potential made Monica feel like an adolescent. "I'm not setting a good example to my daughter. I've been
nagging her because, at 26, she seems so *slow* to grow up. 'When I was
your age . . .' I keep thinking, while she rushes off to South America,

and comes back to flop down with me to save enough money for her next trip. I think *she* should settle down—but what *I* want is to stretch my wings, and not worry about my promotion or my pension or my daughter." It was difficult for these women, grown up too young, matured through necessity, not to feel wild when fear and caution dissolved. "What I used to think about is how much I'd done, how much what I've cared for has been preserved. What I'm afraid of now is how reckless I feel," Sara Ann reflected.

"I don't want to let go, but I'm not sure I can hang on," Ellen said. "I'm afraid of what I do—and then I'm afraid of what will happen if I don't do anything."

"Are you still working out which fear is the worst?" I asked. She thought for a moment.

"No, it's not *that* fear—the child in the dark being a grown-up at the desk. It's just wanting so much now, and not knowing how to go about things. I'm still . . . surprised . . . when I don't feel afraid."

For all their newfound hope and newly established fearlessness, I wondered how they would respond to those external impediments that could make life expansion far more difficult than they, in their giddy release, anticipated. Traditional women are pleased to continue within the family structures they established in their first years of adulthood— as long as they can clear within those structures a private space and a stronger sense of self-direction. Innovative women, chafing against the rigidity of occupational structures, plan their way out carefully, pragmatically. They have built up what economists call "human capital," or employable skills, and make use of these as they seek more flexible, friendly work cultures. Expansive women often find that the education they have gained with courage and effort broadens them "only inside," and leaves them still with jobs that are limited, insecure, and unsatisfactory. Protesting women's desires were intense and vague: Where would their extravagant hopefulness bring them?

Four years after the first interview sessions, when they had spoken about their urgent need to meet up with that once-stalled development, these protesting women seemed transformed. Their gestures were broader, their voices were louder, and they seemed continually excited. Ellen, who was now 44, and Sara Ann, who was now 46, were still strong in their post-release high. "A whole bunch of things seem easier now," Ellen said. "There's nothing big cooking—and I'm still in

the same place . . . but what's changed is that I have a sense of a future
. . . because there's nothing to stop me doing what I what to do." For
Sara Ann, too, her future resided in an ability to act on her own impulses, without fear. "I sometimes hear myself speak out, and I can
barely recognize myself—except it all feels so familiar. I'm amazed at
how safe it feels, just saying what I think and doing what I want."

But was Monica "safe at last in the middle years"?[4] Her laughter
rang out at the question. "Safe? That's what I feel safe from. I worked
in my early years to make things safe. My extreme moods—and my
uncertain future—are my pleasures. The most important thing is that I
feel capable of movement, in a way I just wasn't for so long, and I'm
not haunted by the parallel world in which others are streaking ahead."

In their newly won spontaneity, protesting women often became
"difficult" women—judged by others to be too loud, too sexual, too
assertive. They read others' judgments on them with mingled disregard
and pride. From time to time, behaving just as they wished, they saw
how others saw them. There would be a glimpse, Ellen said, of "disapproval . . . like 'Who is that loud gal?' " or of dismay, as Sara Ann said,
when an old friend say, "You're dressing like a *girl*," or a colleague of
Monica would admonish her, "Haven't you *yet* learned how to keep
your mouth shut?" Their own lack of concern for others' views increased their confidence as they experienced, again, their newfound
freedom. "Every day I catch a memory of that old fear," Ellen reflected, "and then remember I'm free of it. Now all those fears are in
the parallel world, and I don't have to figure out how to meet up with
them. They're now parallel—no, they're *past.*"

Tragic Interference and Protesting Negotiation

The women in my sample viewed midlife as a turning point towards
new opportunities. It was a phase during which the future came into
focus. Midlife crisis and awareness of potential are linked: The pressure
of new opportunities leads to anxiety. The crisis proceeds through a
confrontation with that anxiety and is resolved as a woman forges
stronger links between her desires and her actions. The challenge faced
by the protesting women in my sample was to link up in midlife to the
person they believed they would have been, were it not for specific set-

backs or constraints. Usually the constraints that held such strong influence over the first years of their adulthood were long past: Responsibilities to younger siblings, care for a parent who could not care for children, or care for her own child who was conceived unintentionally and too early, did not currently occupy these women; but they had shaped their early adulthood. The constraints themselves had eased, but many of the coping strategies that had been internalized remained. The task at midlife was to learn how to be spontaneous. What they sought was a new style of response, a new style of decision-making, which would match up with their parallel self.

But some protesting women in my sample forced me to ask the disturbing question: What happens when a woman stands on the brink of that midlife transformation and meets, instead of a clear path ahead, a further constraint? What happens to development when constraints and defeats become worse at midlife? How can the good of this developmental phase be salvaged when conditions that should foster its development are wrecked?

A few women in my sample experienced, in the course of my study, devastating losses, which threatened to stall midlife growth. Such setbacks turned them into protesting women who were bewildered by the discrepancy between their expectations of who they were about to become and their circumstances, which demanded of them something very different. They then resisted the idea that they were now in midlife because they could not see how to move forward. There was a tension in these women's lives between a return to increased control and self-denial on the one hand, and midlife flexibility and self-grounding on the other. Such women had to negotiate these opposing tensions, and find new ways of retrieving power. Like other protesting women, they had to waylay the fear that their spontaneity would be destructive and, whatever their setback, take possession of an expanding future.

DURING THE FIRST SIX months of my study, Margaret Plover's goals and conflicts were in tandem with those of innovative women. She worked in a small pediatric practice. Throughout the first years of her adulthood, she had stretched herself to accommodate her need to have and be with her children, and her need "to do something for [her]self." Her goals had not jelled until she was in her late twenties, and this increased the difficult balance women always face between work and family. She went to medical school while her two sons were infants and toddlers. She did her internship when her youngest child was a year old. "Half the time I was asking myself why I was doing this. Matt [her son] was suffering. Peter [her husband] was in a daze, and I didn't know what harm I was doing to that neglected infant. It was a long haul, and my husband helped a lot—not that I gave him much choice. I just went ahead and did it, just blocked out everyone else's complaints. I felt really tough, and sometimes cruel. The year I was an intern was the worst of all. I was a zombie. I always felt tired, and I mean *tired*. But it was only for a year, and then my residency wasn't so bad. The kids got used to it. I once had a standing joke: 'If you teach your children that you're useless to them, they won't ask anything of you.' There really was a time when I would walk in the door after work, and no one would notice me. It was a relief not to feel missed, but I can't say I felt good about it either." Margaret's expectation of midlife were high.

The prospect of being older seemed wonderful. I calculated my future in terms of how old my children would be, and where they would be in school. Getting older simply meant that my children would be bigger. I felt all the really hard work was behind me—you know, that work of dealing with competing needs, and feeling that every time you do something, someone gets short-changed. Now, I thought, life was going to be easier, because what was *for* me wouldn't be *against* someone else. Dori's accident has changed all that. All of that. It changes things so radically, that what I wanted before, is meaningless now. I can remember wanting those things, but it's as though someone else I knew wanted them. I've become a different sort of person, just like Dori is different. My youngest son says that Dori is still his sister, but she's just a different Dori . . . Just as they have a "different sister," both my sons have a different mother, too, though it may not be as obvious. I can't think of myself as I once did. There's a hump which you just go over . . . I envisioned middle age as a new start, but it's become a strange sort of start. The things I might have done and felt in midlife are very close to me, but not quite at hand . . . I have a strange sense they're waiting for me— or maybe not, maybe this will change everything? And yet, I can't feel that—I don't want that to happen. Some things are in storage while I—while we all—deal with this, and get back for Dori as much as we can—whatever it takes. I want to do what I can . . . all I can, but I'm hypnotized by what was about to happen to me, because I was really set on such a positive course . . . and now I don't know . . . I don't know how to match things up.

The prospect, at midlife, of gaining greater control over the balance between her work and her family has been clouded by tragedy. When Margaret was 43, her nine-year-old daughter Dori was in a car accident, suffered severe head injuries, and underwent a series of operations, followed by intensive and long-term physical and speech therapy. One year after the accident, Margaret said that Dori had made a good recovery, though she did not know how far she would improve. At least one doctor thought that Dori would one day walk again, and Dori herself thought that she would soon return to school and to normality, but Margaret was more guarded: "She's doing well, but she has a long way to go." Alongside all the practical demands was a further question: How much of herself would Margaret give to her daughter, and how far would she travel on the road already begun towards striking a new balance between her own needs and those of others? The renegotiation of a balance already begun formed the backbone of her midlife crisis.

THREE MONTHS AFTER THE accident, Margaret had been shaken and depressed. Her entire life had changed "the second the accident occurred," and everything from then on would be different. She kept swallowing as she spoke, fighting nausea and mastering despondency. Her mouth made a determined attempt to remain firm, but the lines on her lips contracted in spasms whenever she paused. It was impossible to see the person she had been six months before, when the interviews began, so plastered over was every feature with grief. Each train of thought would come full circle to the point of the accident, of why it had happened, what she herself had done to let it happen. The accident became a Chinese puzzle, which fell apart in her hands. Each time she thought it was assembled, she found it odd and unstable, so it was thrown down again, like an unsatisfactory roll of the dice. She had let the girl get into the car, she had trusted the friend who drove it, and she had persuaded her daughter that the outing on which they were embarked would be fun. The blow—to her daughter's head, to her own plans, to her self-esteem—was felt as a global assault. She claimed at that time, "I can't think about myself. I don't want to talk about myself. I don't care what happens to me. All I can care for is Dori."

At the first interview after her daughter's accident, Margaret was in a state of mourning for the healthy daughter she had lost. Such mourning is, of course, not specific to midlife crisis, nor is its accompanying depression, in which the mourner may be unable to take any interest in the world around her. What was specific to the midlife development displayed by other women in my sample was the powerful way she dealt with issues of guilt and control. Guilt threatens to stall her development, shutting down the more powerful control midlife women gain over their compromises.

Margaret initially displayed the special susceptibility women have to feel guilty—of thinking that they have played a crucial role in the bad things that happen to people close to them. This tendency may be linked to "maternal thinking,"[5] whereby a mother's protectiveness toward her children is so strong that she will presume it is her duty to be constantly watchful. But human watchfulness, however vigilant, is never omnipotent. Margaret is not in any reasonable sense of the term responsible, yet she felt culpable. Blaming herself, she suffers a loss of self-esteem. She even feels vindictive towards herself, and her capacity to enjoy anything is diminished, since she believes she does not deserve pleasure or relief. She seems on the borderline between an awful triumph of self-abnegation (she will "sacrifice herself" to Dori) and despair (she cannot "care what happens to [her] now").

The assumption that she is responsible when something goes wrong is potentially self-defeating. It has long been noted that women are much more likely than men to sacrifice themselves to those they consider in need, that they are far less likely to leave a situation in which they see themselves as needed, however awful that situation is. As a result, they seem less well equipped to look after their own rights and needs. But, of course, this tendency to respond to others' needs even at high costs to oneself is not necessarily a weakness. Grace Baruch, in preliminary research on guilt, women, and gender, came to an interesting "pre-hypothesis"—an explanation that is suggested but not yet confirmed by research—that women are especially at risk for "false guilt" or guilt triggered by others' distress or disapproval, by a fear of separation rather than by pangs of conscience. "Vulnerability to concern about disconnection . . . may cause women to convert feelings of loneliness, fear, and especially anger into guilt or to say 'it is my fault.' " If they feel responsible for someone's pain or need, they then have a reason not to turn away from a bad situation or relationship. Instead, they are motivated to increase their efforts to make it good. Research on victimization tells us that one "advantage" of feeling "it is my fault" may be the belief: "I can control this and undo this." In this way, we may indirectly seek some measure of control through guilt. Thus women who are vulnerable to this pattern, rather than suffering from a mysterious deficiency may, in certain situations, be enacting their concern.[6]

At midlife, as her daughter's disability fills her with something that feels like guilt, or a widening sense of responsibility, Margaret's push towards greater control over her compromises is stalled. She protests that she is not ready for midlife, so caught up is she with the emotional and practical changes caused by Dori's accident. "When something like this happens your life splits in two. There, on one side, is how you used to be and how most other people are, and on the other side is your pain and your loss. Even time is different into the two worlds. 'Day' means what you think it means, but for me all I think of is time in which Dori might improve. When she does, time passes, when she doesn't time stays still." The massive confusion Margaret expressed in this interview, only three months after the accident, was to clear. The process of recovery was informed by her negotiation of that midlife protest against seeing an ever-widening gap between her potential self and her actual self. Two years later, she said, "I do what I can, but I see what I cannot do in a different light. I am not willing—there's a very strong resistance here—to give up everything. I can see it— being eaten up, and feeling an awful comfort, that at least I've done everything. I can see how, once, I might have done that, and now I refuse. Because doing all I can still means preserving something for me and the rest of my family. That determination to keep all these things in focus sometimes makes me giddy, but I won't let it go."

This was a transformation that was to save and salvage her energy and self-direction. She had come to accept what Iris Murdock calls "humility," which Sara Ruddick places alongside that ongoing, anxious maternal "scrutiny" in which the mother feels fully responsible for what happens to her child. Ruddick explains: "In a world beyond one's control, to be humble is to have a profound sense of the limits of one's actions and of the unpredictability of the consequences of one's work . . . Mothers identify humility as a virtue, when they recognize in themselves the delusive, compulsive efforts to see everywhere and control everything so that a child will be safe."[7]

Margaret gained power by being able to make a distinction between what she could control and what she could not. Negotiating her way around the tragedy of her daughter's accident and through midlife development, she draws the crucial distinction between power and omnipotence. Omnipotence is the fantasy that one can do everything without compromising anything; power is the ability to act effectively in the world as we know it. At first, Margaret believes it is her job to be punished for not being omnipotent. She then moves to a different sense of power, in which she will gain control over the compromises she makes on behalf of the commitment and responsibility she continues to feel: "However much I want to do for her, I can't think in terms of sacrifices . . . there's such a resistance to that. I can't let those other parts of me die. I won't step back from all I was about to be."

THE WAR THAT PROTESTING women waged against midlife was not a war against change, but a battle to find the right path to change. As their potential had stalled them at earlier growth spurts— Sarah Ann and Ellen in early adolescence, Monica at the transition from adolescent to adult, and Margaret at the turning point of midlife—they saw their last chance to finding a meeting point for their parallel lives. The needs of these women, who initially protested against moving into midlife, were not for stasis, or for turning back the clock, but for finding ways forward. These women found new "selfish" strength and control, as they, in their new midlife, grew into the youthful exuberance they had once left behind.

Protesting Women: Signs and Signposts of Midlife Crisis

Women in this category have spent their early adulthood—and sometimes a great deal of their childhood—being responsible and dependable. They have curtailed their adventurousness and spontaneity because anything that is uncontrolled or unpredictable seems dangerous. They catch sight of their increasing maturity, but protest against it because they have not yet had a proper youth. To negotiate a strong path through the midlife passage, they must find a way to overcome past fears and explore their futures. Many protesting women share paths with traditional women, in that they have assumed traditional roles of obedient wife and dutiful daughter, and with expansive women, in that they are anxious to extend their horizons in midlife. The following list may help protesting women identify their stage in their midlife path, but they may also find the rough guides for other categories helpful. However, most of the protesting women in my sample proceeded along the following lines.

Previous orientations:

1. had an early maturing and possibly traumatic experience
2. needed to be responsible and dependable has governed one's actions and plans
3. suppressed desires and ambitions have always lurked in the background of one's mind

Women in this category have fashioned their lives around others' needs or fears, and they neglect self-exploration in order to remain strong and certain. However strong and courageous they appear to others, they feel that something within them has been constrained by the burdens of early adult responsibilities.

Signs of approaching crisis:

1. panic that one's youth is passing before it has been experienced as youth

2. longs to act irresponsibly, for a change, yet fears that one's desires are dangerous
3. overwhelmed by long-suppressed feelings of regret, anger, and lack of confidence

Some protesting women feel depressed or angry as they enter midlife. These feelings threaten to crush their spirit—until they find ways to make use of new resources of determination and confidence.

Resolution of crisis:

1. sees one's maturity as a door to new opportunities
2. exercises spontaneity in one's daily life without threatening one's well-being
3. retrieves past desires and goals, and refashions them for current use

Changing Rhythms: Menopause

6

Menopause has become, during the past few years, the focus of interest in women's midlife and has come to represent the central feature of women's midlife development. It is an issue that has gathered momentum and aroused awe as both a mystery and a rite of passage. For Germaine Greer, it is an ordeal women must withstand with elemental courage and suffering: On the other side of this turmoil, Greer writes, "is the most wonderful moment in one's whole life . . . that will last forever."[1] In Sheehy's powerful account, too, menopause is a difficult rite of passage, shrouded by a "conspiracy of silence." As "a blood mystery," it triggers midlife change: Passing over that hormonal "hump," women are freed to enjoy their "flaming fifties."[2]

My study of midlife women, however, strongly suggests that menopause is not the cause of midlife development. The changes that have been noticed over the years in midlife women—that they become more assertive, more self-confident, and very often more energetic—result from a psychological, not hormonal story. The "post menopausal zest" of which Margaret Mead spoke is a release of energy that is more likely to come from the crisis and resolution of midlife women's psyche than from biological change.[3]

What my study further suggests is that though, throughout history, women at midlife may have undergone psychological change, the generation of women now in midlife experiences a crisis informed by the special divisions it has experienced. As girls, they were socialized with 1950s ideas and ideals of womanhood. Yet, as they entered adulthood, the concept of womanhood was being revolutionized. The images and roles and morals, which had once seemed stable, were now all open to question. Whether women of this transitional generation embraced brand new ideals and goals, or whether they remained within a traditional framework of womanhood, they were constantly, throughout adulthood, aware of changing ideas and expectations. They felt, at some level, new tensions between the old and the new culture of womanhood. As they come to midlife with a growing sense of unfinished business—either of unmet goals, or of space not yet carved out for their own thought-rhythms, or of unfulfilled potential, or foreshortened spontaneity—they are struck with both panic and determination, and an increased capacity to resolve old conflicts and satisfy suppressed desires. Midlife—the time between 40 and 55 years of age—is now younger than anyone imagined it would be. With better health and longer life expectation, midlife becomes a turning point toward new futures.

Menopause *accompanies* women's midlife, but, in my sample of women—35 of whom had experienced or were experiencing menopause—it did not cause the crises and growth I observed. Menopause played no single, specific role in midlife development. Menopause is simply the cessation of menstruation. It has no universal meaning other than that.[4] It is not a clearly marked event or condition, as are menarche (the onset of menstruation) and pregnancy, but a process that ranges, on average, from a woman's early forties to late fifties.[5] The sensations that sometimes accompany menopause are experienced so differently by different women[6] that researchers have great difficulty measuring what women actually do experience, or gauging how these experiences affect their mood and behavior.[7] Moreover, the sensations that may accompany menopause can be perceived differently by different women. A hot flush may be trivial, or pleasurable. It may cause embarrassment, or send one into a panic. It may be perceived as a symptom—an indication of some disease; or it may be an interesting sign of welcome change. Furthermore, *severe* hot flushes of the kind Gail Sheehy describes are only experienced by 10% of women,[8] and only 5% of Sonia McKinlay's large sample of women found vaginal dryness a problem[9]—the condition that leads Germaine Greer to say that the midlife woman who loses interest in sex is "lucky."[10]

The vast range of women's physical experience of menopause was mirrored by the very different part it played in the psychological development of the women in my sample. For though I am convinced that it was not the cause of the midlife crisis and resolution I observed, nor was it central to this midlife growth spurt, it could stimulate questions and heighten conflicts. The association menopause has, for some people, with endings—of youth or fertility—may trigger concerns about aging. "Not me—not yet," a woman might feel, especially if menopause came before fifty. But since, in this age-conscious, youth-valuing society, so many things—especially for women—trigger this pause in the usual momentum of their lives, menopause plays no special role here. A passing comment, a glimpse of one's changing face in the mirror, a special birthday can activate the same process as easily as changing menstrual rhythms. For women are constantly surrounded by reminders that to be interesting and attractive they have—until recently—been expected to be young, which has, until recently, been defined as under 40. Menopause is only one of a myriad of reminders of aging that can serve as a catalyst to the process by which women, in this new midlife, gain inner strength and greater control over life's inevitable compromises.

The special impact menopause did have in the development of some women in my sample was two-fold. First, menopause could bring a woman into contact with a body of "experts" who would oversee her present and future health. Yet many women rapidly discovered that these "experts" were characterized both by authority and ignorance. The discrepancy between dependence and distrust brought into question her own power and authority, and her control over her own health. This tension could become a focus of a woman's crisis about self-doubt and control; it was resolved as she found a path through the thicket of prejudice and ignorance and assumed control of her own health decisions.

The second type of impact menopause made on the midlife development of some of the women in my sample was through their response to changing biological rhythms. Some women respond strongly to the monthly shifts in mood, or to the different sensitivities and energy surges that accompany the menstrual cycle. For some, the shedding of blood is seen as an event packed with symbolic meaning, linking them to universal rhythms in nature. Menopause, for these women, creates a hiatus in their expectations of their own bodies. This hiatus is bridged as they find new sources of symbolic contact between their daily lives and nature's fluctuations.

COMING AT A POINT in their lives when they were gaining greater power over themselves and greater confidence in themselves, the experience of menopause and the increased reliance many women then feel on medical experts can give rise to doubt as to how much strength, after all, she has gained. Hence, some women's experience with menopausal sensations or with their medical treatment could arouse a mini-crisis mirroring their midlife crisis. How could it be, some of the women in my sample asked, that after all the advances I have made, I can now feel such doubt, such uncertainty, such a sense of being "typecast" and dismissed? Why, having come so far, am I still unheard? For these women, the psychological strength already gained was threatened by a confrontation with those "expert" voices that debased their own.

The issue of the medical profession and women is a long and loaded one. It does not begin with menopause; nor, now, does it end there. The medical profession often creates a structure and a context in which one's own body becomes an object, alienated from one's control and one's own experience. The doctor becomes the expert and the manipulator of the patient under his care and control. The patient puts her discomfort into his hands, and he shapes it into a diagnosis. Whether the fashion is to intervene or to "let nature take its course," the decision is made *by* a doctor *for* a patient. Women are particularly vulnerable to the medical establishment because their normal life cycle requires, or is thought to require, medical supervision in a way a man's does not. Women use medical care more than men do. The birth control they use is far more likely to involve medical supervision and prescription. Childbirth locks a woman into the medical system, as do her children's illnesses and general health care.

Women's clash with medicine and science does not begin at midlife, but it then is reexperienced in different ways. At midlife, a doctor's influence now is over a woman herself—not as breeder of infants, or caretaker of children, or lover of men. She no longer needs to fear that her resistance to medical advice will harm anyone else. "You can try to have a vaginal delivery if you like," I overheard a doctor tell a patient who was resisting a second Caesarean, "but that baby will have to be pulled like a cork out of bottle when your muscles don't contract. You'll be putting your baby through a lot of unnecessary distress." The permission to do what she liked was poisoned. Were she to have acted independently, she would threaten another's well-being. At midlife, a woman is more likely to feel that the backlash will be felt by her alone. She is therefore quicker to resist medical advice and to question medical expertise. She may also find that, at midlife, she is of less interest to her doctor, treated more brusquely, and assumed to be "difficult."

Far too many women—two-thirds in my sample of 80—said that a doctor had, at some time in her adult life, "driven her to tears" or "pushed her to the brink" or "filled her with rage" through his or her lack of sympathy or patience. As a patient's complaints are seen as unreal, imaginary, or silly, she loses power. For the patient who is defined as imagining, exaggerating, or fabricating has no means of insisting that what she describes is real. The private meeting with the doctor, the expert, was often a focus of anxiety: Would sense be made of the strange feelings that were changing her life? Would the "expert" reassure her and, through empathy and treatment, help her negotiate this phase; or would she remain isolated, edged in by awful doubt? However highly skilled or educated a woman was, she might speak of being "irrational" or "terrified" when confronted with a doctor. Women who had earned titles of "doctor" or "professor" tended to make appointments using these titles, hoping they would protect themselves from undue waiting times and undue dismissal.

FROM WOMEN'S OWN NARRATIVES, it seems that women doctors are often little better than men at listening; yet, when I spoke to doctors, I found that women were generally better at learning—if only belatedly. Dr. Eleanor Birks remembers being told by a patient that she felt "as though ants were crawling under my skin." Examining her, and finding nothing, Eleanor tranquillized her. Some years later, she realized her mistake: The itching, crawling sensations were, she now knew, associated with menopause. Can other doctors be counted on to reassess themselves? Can they work with women to explore their own ignorance? What do women have to become to persuade doctors that this is necessary? For many midlife women, this posed a crucial question in their development.

The boundaries of medical interference in child bearing have been curtailed. Information about doctors' treatments of pregnancy and childbirth is more easily pooled, and the range of normal variation—of labor, of weight-gain, of discomfort—is more widely known. There is vastly more sensible literature on the experience and the process of birth than there is on menopause. There are also stricter controls from the patients themselves: Women fight back with malpractice suits when they are not satisfied with an obstetrician's treatment. There is also a history of women—this generation of midlife women—protesting against the medical institutionalization of maternity and taking greater control of the procedures and expectations of childbirth. The issues of aging and menopause are far more isolating—not because the subject is taboo, but simply because there is no established body of knowledge.[11] Of the 17 women in my sample who received hormonal replacement treatment during the course of the interviews, 12 were using different preparations, and each saw a different balance between its costs and benefits. My research on this sample of women was a journey of discovery of the medical ignorance about menopause, hormonal treatments, risks, and patients.

Doctors have fewer answers than they frequently lay claim to. Many hormonal preparations are new, and long-term effects are simply not known. Though there are more than forty preparations of hormonal replacement therapies on the market, tests have been carried out on only one.[12] Any presentation of the known facts takes at least an hour, even with a patient who already knows something about the subject.[13] Many women who accepted hormonal replacement therapy were unsure whether they were taking it to relieve menopausal symptoms (in which case their treatment would last approximately two years) or whether they were taking it to protect their skeletal strength (in which case the treatment would last approximately seven years), or whether they were taking it to preserve a youthful appearance. They often felt dependent on a doctor for information and for assessment as to what would help or harm them. This dependence is frustrating because the issues for each individual woman, and for each individual hormonal cocktail are both complex and obscure.

FEW DOCTORS ARE ABLE to present information openly, co-herently, and sympathetically. Their skills at presenting themselves as authoritative and reassuring (their bedside manners) tend to be better cultivated than their skills at disseminating information. Many doctors are astounded to discover "how little a patient knows" in contrast to their claims about "how much a patient has been told." They blame a patient's ignorance rather than their own communication skills. Yet few doctors allow the patient to make her own decisions because they fail to see how strongly they are influencing her. They fail to see how their impatience increases her anxiety. Audrey Chou, who asked me to accompany her to a doctor's appointment to speak—again—about her physical and emotional discomfort associated, possibly, with meno-pause, said that her doctor was affronted by her continued wish to dis-cuss menopause: "He seemed to think that I was being ungrateful. He had given me access to the best science had to offer. Science was work-ing hard for me. Why was I still fussing?"

Of the six doctors I interviewed,[14] four of whom were women, five complained that patients asked questions to which there were no an-swers, or that they expected the doctor to know far more than she or he did know. "They want to know just how it will affect them, and what will happen if they do have HRT and what will happen if they don't, and what might be a counterindicator of treatment—and they want to know everything—whether being a little depressed is a factor, or hav-ing varicose veins, or having a history of varicose veins, or a grandfather with leukemia. We simply don't know the answers." The impatience with the patient for expecting the expert to know the answer was some-what softened by the more positive conclusion: "We have to work with the patient to try to assess what risks are acceptable."

The sound rhetoric of "working with the patient" is, however, often undercut by the impatience:

"I have this ache—," Audrey motioned to her lower abdomen. "In my cervix—."

"There are no nerves in the cervix," the gynecologist announced. As he dismissed her location of the discomfort, he failed to hear her anxiety. Since there were no nerves in the cervix, her pain could not be there. Her doctor appeared uninterested in discovering where else the pain might be. She tried then to tell him about depression.

"I know, I know," Audrey assured him defensively as he told her

there was "no such thing" as menopausal depression. "But it's the dizziness and the flushes and the weird feeling of not being in control. I
may not be depressed because of them, but I'm depressed about them."

Audrey was the daughter of Chinese immigrants. They spoke very
little English, yet loved their new country, and trusted that their children would fare well in it. Seeing the ease with which Audrey was
"Americanized," they saw her as stronger and more confident than she
actually was; but she, to live up to their image, and help them, suppressed her insecurity and her sense of not fitting in, of being far less
Americanized that she would, at that time, have liked.

> I was so frightened when I took my parents out of the Chinese neigh-
> borhood, and we had to speak English—but they couldn't. I could
> say all the words for them, but sometimes someone would ask me
> something, and I wouldn't know what to say, or how to translate it to
> my mother to get the reply in Chinese. I haven't thought about these
> things for years, but I am reminded of them now, because I feel the
> same way—a cold front coming on me. I have these big fee doctors,
> who charge what they do because they're supposed to be experts, but
> they cannot sit down and tell me what I need to know.
>
> What makes me so angry is the series of moves I know he must
> make in self-protection when I keep asking him things. I know he
> thinks I'm a difficult patient and difficult patients are stupid. But
> . . . how do I make him see that I am telling a story different from the
> one he tells me? Instead of getting help telling my story, I end up
> feeling stupid.

Pushed into maturity by her grasp of a language that her parents
lacked, having suppressed her fears on their behalf, Audrey now suggested that I play the role of interpreter she once took with her parents.
I would accompany her on a doctor's visit to help her communicate in
a language that for some reason failed her. "All this has really shaken
me—because I thought that kind of fear was gone forever. I don't
know how I got away with thinking that for so long. Looking back, I
now see how delicately balanced everything was . . . which is maybe
why all this upset me . . . . " She was seeing how she was still vulnerable
to those "eyes bearing down" on her. She had to do further work to
become the grown-up she knew she should be. Previously, she over-

functioned in the face of fear: She went "rigid inside" and "stared it down," thinking that her fear was easier to tolerate than disappointing her parents, or seeing them unprotected. One means of escape might be to change her doctor—which she knew she should do; but this was not enough. As we have seen elsewhere, women in crisis often magnify a relatively small episode so that certain dissatisfactions become clearer. She exaggerated her weakness because she did not want to ignore it; instead, she wanted proof that new strength was necessary.

Audrey's doctor, whatever his medical expertise, was far less adept at listening to what she was trying to say than he was at finding fault with what she said. Some women do feel a tightening in the lower abdomen, aware of "something" happening, which they cannot always name and to which, apparently, few doctors pay heed. Audrey was not lucky with her doctor—but such bad luck is not uncommon. A recent study of doctor and patient interactions found that patients were interrupted within *18 seconds* of starting to explain the reason for their visit.[15] The sense this gives of being unheard can arouse despondency. By the time most women reach menopause, they see themselves as strong and stable; they may, however, through confrontation with medical expertise and its hidden ignorance, discover old fears of inadequacy, which seem never to have been addressed. She fears regression: She does not want to lose "all this energy, which was just starting to be used, because now I've got over so many of the fears I had as a child." To overcome this secondary, or mini-crisis, a woman had to become her own authority on menopause.

"I thought I would never feel this again," Audrey said. "I felt I had built myself up—was so strong. Now, at 45, to feel . . . like a typical old bag of nerves. It's not something I can just walk away from—like the pain you feel in a dentist's chair. With a dentist, you get up, and it's over. This is different. I feel so small. I've made such a deal of it because—well, normally I feel in control of my health. And to have someone not listen. It's like the old fears—big eyes bearing down on you, knowing they can get away with anything. And I thought I'd left that behind."

To regain that strength she had already built up, she needed control over her health decisions. To do that, she had to know what was known about menopause, and what was not. Pouring over charts and figures and studies, we discovered how little any expert could decide on

behalf of an individual woman. For example: The addition of progesterone to estrogen offsets the risk of breast and uterine cancer, but also
offsets the good effects estrogen has on bone mass and heart disease. To
remove progesterone from treatment increases the risk of uterine cancer six-fold—yet uterine cancer is so rare that this apparently enormous increase in risk does not lead to great increase in the number of
cases. Moreover, the uterine cancer that is associated with estrogen
treatment is rarely fatal; it occurs in a less serious form than uterine
cancer that occurs in the absence of estrogen treatment. Interwoven
with these issues of life and death are issues of quality of life: Some
women gain weight rapidly while on hormonal treatment, and some
become depressed when they stop the treatment. How can anyone
trust anyone else to ask what matters more, or which risks are more
tolerable to any individual woman?

Together, Audrey and I worked out a way of gaining greater control over her medical decisions. Using the work of Professor Kay-Tee
Khaw, an epidemiologist at the Clinical School in Cambridge, England, who has compiled a survey of studies and risks and figures,[16]
and Audrey's own software program, we made a decision tree, in which
the various risks were mapped out. Then, Audrey compiled a list of
questions, which might be used to assess individual risks. If she could
find the answers to these, then the tree could grow more branches with
delicately balanced answers. These answers would not be foolproof,
but they would be rational, and her own. "It's this sort of thing," she
admitted, "that makes my anxiety just melt away."

IT IS NOT ONLY in the doctor's office, however, that women are
subject to so-called experts' views of menopause. The women I interviewed, whether or not they had yet experienced menopause, engaged
with a forbidding discourse about menopause, wherein they resisted
others' expectation of what was, or would happen to their bodies and
how these changes will affect them. In spite of the proliferation of interest in menopause, in spite of increasing health and longevity that
make midlife precisely that—the pivot between early and mature
adulthood—some of the most recent descriptions of women and menopause are precise replicas of those of 50 years ago. Helene Deutsch
believed that menopause was a "partial death" for women. In 1945,
she wrote, "Everything she acquired during puberty is now lost piece

by piece; with the lapse of the reproductive service, her beauty vanishes, and usually the warm, vital flow of feminine emotional life as well."[17] In 1992, Germaine Greer wrote that menopause is "a time for mourning . . . the menopausal woman should be allowed her quiet time and her melancholy."[18]

The experts on menopause are now women who speak from personal experience—in contrast to the "personal views" on menopause published ten years ago, which were written by men;[19] yet, their voices, too, can drown out other women's individual experiences. I came to understand how eager midlife women were to discuss menopause and express their anger that one woman's voice should over-speak theirs. *The Change* came out in Britain in the autumn of 1991, when I was conducting interviews with midlife women throughout the country. They engaged me in heated dialogues, relieved to have some audience for their resistance to a dominant voice. "I open my mouth after each page and a little bleat comes out," Audrey said. "I do this just to make sure I can still make a sound." She had spoken for her parents when, as a child, she had learned English before they had. She had used these skills in a variety of jobs as translator both of spoken languages and of computer software manuals. But now her experience within the cultural institution of menopause put her hard-won language at risk. Her language, she feared, was losing its impact. She was seen as a member of a group—a menopausal woman—rather than an individual with an individual's range of experiences and potential. Hence, her positive protest came as she gained control over her individual treatment.

Diane Summers, too, at 48, was trying to find her own angle on her experiences, and she felt threatened by the voice that seemed to have the answers. She felt the text of *The Change* was both speaking, and not speaking to her: "We are hearing the same thing again," Diane Summers protested. "The message is: 'It's woman's lot to suffer, and we just have to put up with it.' She has no right to say that. She has no business telling us this. Women don't need to be *more* afraid. This is gibberish . . . these terrible predictions. Menopause isn't some monster that's going to eat me alive or turn me into something else. I don't want to be told again how awful things will be for me, because I'm a woman."[20]

Diane's protest was fired by a need to write her own script. In common with six of the thirteen women in my sample who had not had children, Diane's approach to menopause was guarded. "I'm afraid of being afraid," she explained. "It's not regret—it's worry that I'll come to feel regret."

For most women, the end of their active fertility is not menopause, but the birth of their last child.[21] The mourning of lost fertility that was observed in menopausal women of previous generations[22] is no longer in evidence. This may stem from the contemporary expectation of fewer children, and from the much wider range of roles and activities available to women. In fact, menopause no longer signals the foreclosure of any possibility of pregnancy; yet for women who had never had children, the cessation of fertility associated with menopause could "ring a panic button" as it brought them face to face with their past decisions. Diane felt a "vague threat of accountability." "To whom?" I asked in amazement. She shook her head, unable, quite, to name the judge who might condemn her. Instead, she reviewed, again, the process of her decision:

> I thought I was used to the idea. There were lots of reasons for not having kids. My husband was older, and didn't want any. I had been ill, and the treatment I'd had was not a good indicator for pregnancy. There would have had to be strong reasons for children, and there weren't. The panic I felt was totally irrational. What? That I supposed at 50 I'd decide the time was right! (she laughed). But I was feeling so busy, so happy, and then when quite suddenly at a routine check up I was told I was "menopausal." I was in such a state—that when I did get a period, I thought "Oh, I just missed a few. That doctor didn't know what he was talking about." It was denial on that scale, because of course I knew that menopause doesn't come just like that, with no more periods, but they might be scattered for a while.

The depression Diane described involved a "dark blue mood," a sense of "something like slush rather than blood in my veins." She went about her ordinary life feeling that her smiles and speech masked an awful emptiness inside her. She believed that she acted from habit, that her movements were automated, that they no longer had any human meaning. Each morning, the fact that she had another day to get through was "like a punch in her stomach." Everything that had once interested her seemed to be drifting out of reach. She watched it go, and understood the danger she was in, but felt strangely indifferent. "There's a changing rhythm to my life. I see now—I don't think I noticed this before—but menstruation was a marker I depended on. Not being a mother . . . but this identification of myself as a natural woman . . . But, of course, there are so many dimensions to all this, and that's what I think this depression is—a way of reorientating myself. Not an end—no!" she laughed, "just a change—that all in all is very interesting."

THE SECOND TYPE OF stall some women felt at menopause was in response to changing rhythms—either the hormonal rhythms that brought about fluctuation in mood, energy, and desire, or the objective sign of participation in a monthly cycle. For these women, some menopausal experience was pleasurable as it reminded them that they were part of a natural cycle. Patricia Galen described the charm of those sharp shifts in body temperature, which are often characterized as symptoms in need of treatment. "The sudden spurt of inner heat would send my head spinning. I had to sit back to steady myself. This could be in my studio, in the middle of a class—or once, in the middle of a demonstration, so that I had to grip the sides of the lectern for support. But I felt a marvellous glow of individuality, that I was feeling something no one else in the room felt, and that this was a chapter in my biological history. It had a definite outline, an objective form, which many physical sensations—other than pain, or that intense power of sexual orgasm—simply do not have. There was also the coming together of a universal phase of life and my individual life history. That reaching out to the universal from my immediate sensations was exhilarating."

The very brevity of this touch, rather than its duration, led to depression, as the assurance of some continued participation in natural fluctuations was in doubt. "An intense sadness that pours over me," Patricia said, wherein all the things she wants to do seem to be rushing past her. She cannot reach out to pick one. She lost her ability to concentrate and, for while, spent much of her time, "just sitting in a chair, grabbing its arms with [her] hands" to prevent things from moving too quickly away. There was no specific loss, but a dread that she would not be able to focus, as though the distractions of her earlier life had been essential to keeping her on track. Previously, with her periodic menstruation, she had a sense of a seasonal regulation. She had a rich fantasy life, of purging and newness, of fresh starts and fresh chances, which helped with various projects. "It was lovely to have this cyclical reassurance, of conclusion and renewal. Now I feel pushed to a time frame without the familiar markers—without markers I can as yet see."

Patricia, now 49, had held her first pottery exhibition when she was barely 21, and since then had built up a fairly wide reputation as both a potter and a weaver. She believed that "a kind of easy talent" had "smoothed over" a more rugged vision, but that she had sustained her individuality by drawing from her daily life, and its rhythms. Motherhood, she said, had a range of shapes and textures, as did romantic love and rupture. There had always been strong biological references to her work which "may still be there" she remarked, but she "could not find them."

Margaret Drabble, tackling the question of what lies on the other side of a midlife crisis describes a similar impasse of forty-year-old Kate:

> For the first time, she feels, she has no idea of what will happen next. She has run through what she now recognizes were the expected phases of life . . . and she doesn't know what will happen next, nor how to make it happen, and being an energetic and active person, she strongly dislikes the feeling of helplessness, the lack of direction, that this uncertainty generates. She looks at the component parts of her life—her children, her ex-husband, her ex-lover, her work, her parents—and doesn't know what to do or think about any of them. Her implacable progress has been halted, a link has been broken, and the past no longer seems to make sense, for if it did, how would it have left her here, in this particular draughty open space?[23]

As Patricia feels this edge between a past that made sense and an unknown future, she feels as though she is asked to answer a riddle—one of those mythical riddles in which a correct answer is required to save her life. She feels she wastes time, "coming up with a thousand answers," none of which is right. She feels her deliberate attempts are inefficient, and wonders whether she might do better simply to shift her mind "away from the puzzle." Yet she resists a return to the safety of the pre-crisis awareness. If she denies how things have changed, she will only be "mimicking the person [she] used to be." She has to match the meaning this change has had for her with other meanings. Previously, she had a familiar tool kit from which to choose. Now she has to manufacture her own.

Current research has found no significant changes in anger, anxiety, depression, self-consciousness, or worry about the body between women observed from the time they were premenopausal to the time they had become postmenopausal.[24] This means that, in general, a woman's mood is not determined by menopause; but an individual woman may respond to it with increases in anger, anxiety, depression, or self-consciousness because of how she experiences or perceives its meaning. The depression both Patricia and Diane felt wore a double face: They feel helpless and indifferent to their own well-being, but they have a grim courage, which makes them ride out these feelings. Three months after Patricia had first spoken about her depression, it had deepened. As she went about her normal activities there was a "hole inside her," and it upset her that she "had to ignore" so much of what she was feeling. Diane also felt afraid of her depression. "This could become a part of me, and I don't want it to." For depression has a way of digging itself in deep. "In these moods," Patricia noted, "I start seeing myself in ways that I want to reject. I can see how they are destructive . . . the self-badgering is merely vicious."

Diane, too, protested against the self-criticism that "took [her] out of [her] body, where [she] caught ugly glimpses of [herself]." She seemed to be empathizing with others' views, and then turning them against herself. What sustained her, she said, was the conviction that underneath all these awful feelings "there was a good person." But waiting for this person to emerge, was "like waiting for a fractured bone to heal." And Patricia explained: "I feel I'm just about to drown under all these half-heard recriminations. I feel the water line tickle my lips. If I were to speak my mouth would fill with this warm thick water."

Often, depressed moods just go. People get used to things. There are distractions, or compensations. But the jolt that these women had experienced was not easily absorbed. "I see now the pleasure I got from certain types of admiration. I didn't realize, before, how much that mattered. It was a background hum . . . nice . . . a quiet motivation." This admiration had not ceased magically on menopause, but with the shift in her sense of self came a reassessment of her dependence on how others saw her. Patricia uncovered remaining traces of a patronizing admiration that had begun at the start of her career: "It was, 'Oh, what a clever young woman . . . charming, isn't she?' So there was gallantry in how I was treated. Certainly that has faded over the years, but I was attuned to it. I expected it. What shocks me is that I liked it, and I did not realize that I would be well shod of it."

The patronizing voices that were at one time "nice" and provide a "quiet motivation" were small things in Patricia's life, yet giving them up was confusing. The self-badgering she had thought destructive was ultimately useful. Depression lowered her defenses against self-criticism. Her usual English "stiff upper lip" was loosened; as she acknowledged her negative feelings and negative views, she was able to see the taken-for-granted views that made her vulnerable. The absence of those monthly rhythms, on which she had felt dependent, now could be seen as an opportunity for extending her references. "I can put more things together, absorb different things. What regulated my imagination could—I now see—also limit it. I've begun to do all sorts of things. There's is now a speedy rise in my output. After so many years of just ticking nicely along, I now feel this thrilling release."

To step outside the time-frame—from menarche to menopause—in which others' interest in her is usually confined, is to step into that "open, draughty space" which she can fill as she wants. The "quiet time and melancholy," which some menopausal woman take, is not a space for mourning a partial death, but a rest before the leap ahead, or a time to regain her balance as she drops certain weights. Patricia sees that what she has been carrying all this time thinking it was "nice," may in fact be a burden she is "well shod of."

FOR SOME WOMEN, MENOPAUSE is a catalyst to change and growth: They see the next phase of their lives outside the barriers of others' definition, theirs to be created. For some women, menopause is virtually uneventful, while other women find it a rough passage. Yet the outlook of midlife women is now better than it has ever been. Women in midlife today are less likely to be depressed than they were ten years ago.[25] Fewer menopausal women are depressed than are women with young children.[26] This brilliantly loud-mouthed generation of midlife women is exerting influence on cultural concepts of women, age, and youth. They are rapidly creating an age-heterogenous culture that makes menopause "the leading health issue of the decade"[27] and highlights vast options in their new midlife.

7

Women Who
Cannot Find
the Way Ahead

I n each of the categories so far described—traditional, innovative, expansive, and protesting—different women approach
midlife crisis from different angles and draw upon different resources for growth, while each exhibits a common pattern of development. The crisis begins with realization that certain impulses or
needs had been buried at one of those crossroads in women's development—at the threshold of adolescence as she feels the pressures of sexuality, at the threshold of adulthood as she leaves the protected structures of school and family to make her own way, and at the threshold
of either marriage or maternity, when female roles may overpower her
individual voice. At these danger points, women often bury their own
responses, and instead of being guided by their own knowledge of who
they are and what they could be, are led by ideals of who they should
be and what they should feel. This burial of their own vision and voice,
and the belief that they must meet the many competing ideals that
have beset modern women, deny them adequate control over many of
the compromises they make during their first years of adulthood. At
midlife, as looking-back time allows them to see a life pattern, and as
the pressure mounts to make good use of their future, they confront
suppressed needs and wishes. They then enter a crisis, which seems
catastrophic, but which is in fact a path through to greater power and a
stronger sense of self. As new needs and emotions and knowledge come
to life, anxiety is aroused about how much has to change, and whether

the changes can be tolerated, or whether the newly released knowledge should be buried again. As this anxiety is tested and resisted, new futures are created. For the outcome of this crisis, I have found from these studies, is that women are entering a new midlife with new skill in handling the difficult choices that this special generation of women has had to confront.

In each developmental story, however, there is a range of potential failures. Given the social and personal pressures that often make this development impossible until midlife, given the sheer hard work of this development, it is not surprising that growth is sometimes disturbed, foreshortened, or distorted. There is a clear developmental push among women in their forties, but the paths taken can have wrong turns, or the efforts of the journey may be judged to be too great. In such cases, the flexible concourse between feelings and visions is lost. An increased rigidity prohibits growth. A woman may then look to her youth as the one time she had significance. Her only hope for continued happiness is to believe she will always *seem* young. Hence, she cannot find the path ahead.

Different women face different risks to their midlife development. For traditional women, there is a danger that the revision and rebalance will be stopped by an impulse to deny or minimize their regret. The crisis question, "How could I, for so long, been controlled by others' needs and wishes?" may be replaced by a tableau of satisfaction. She denies regret or anger; the goals or ambitions that have been set aside, and await addressing in midlife are not, she judges, important. She may deny their value—or reality—because admitting it, and changing it, arouses too much anxiety.

For innovative women, the danger lies in diminishing their own values and responses as they enter what was once a man's world. They may insist that they are simply learning the rules of the game as they become "prisoners of men's dreams."[1] For some women, these rules do work well and, in their particular professional circumstances, do not need changing. Women do, after all, have every right to be like men, respond like men, and behave like men, should they wish. But some innovative women do excessive work on themselves to adapt to a world in which they devalue their own impulses and try to learn from others what they should be. They may be reluctant to resist the world they want to join, and so they deny their power to change it.

Expansive women, who are determined to break past patterns and break through to new vistas, may find the changes they desire ultimately too disruptive. Punishments may be meted out by partners, who are frightened by those changes in the status quo. Such a woman then confronts other queries: What might she lose in changing, and how does the potential gain balance against the potential loss? Or, an expansive woman may make a false start, and find that the steps so courageously taken are not the right ones. She may stick to her new goals on principle, believing that there is no other means of change. She may try one tack, and then fail. Discouraged, and frightened of subsequent failures, she may cease trying.

Protesting women, who at midlife try to pick up the strands of a foreshortened youth, may sink into depression as the parallel life they seek to meet evades them. Their greatest challenge is to shift the habitual balance between fear and spontaneity, and trust the impulsiveness that, for so long, has been viewed as destructive.

There were, in a small number of my sample, definite, strong signs of stalled growth. Repeated, virtually compulsive plastic surgery, fanatic grooming, an obsession with appearance—these go beyond the modicum of insanity about our appearance many of us retain in this society, which is financially underpinned by exploitation of women's "vanity" and insecurity.[2] Such behavior may signal terror at being "not young." They are symptoms of stalled growth, as a woman believes that she is nothing beyond her youth. More common and more subtle, however, are psychological stalls to midlife growth—disappointments or regrets or failures that cannot be overcome, habits that will not be broken, and ideals that retain their rule. This type of foreshortened growth cuts across different categories of women in crisis because it seems to prevent even the onset of crisis. It locks a woman into an idealized hope, which both tantalizes her and punishes her with regret; she is obsessed by what she might have been. She is bewildered by others' flexibility, by their capacity for change and by their multiple visions. The symptom of this type of thwarted growth is envy.

Envy: Poisoning Ideals

There is a long-held and wide-spread belief among psychologists that women are more envious than men,[3] and that midlife women are more envious than other women.[4] This has never been supported by any study, nor seriously researched to any degree. It is pure prejudice, and like all prejudice, it is unjust and untrue. On the basis of this study, I am convinced that midlife women are a decidedly unenvious lot. Those who are envious, struggle with their envy in unexpected, unexplored ways. They reveal the frenetic pain of someone who is being smothered, rather than of someone who enjoys another's destruction.

Envy is one of the most unpleasant emotions we can experience. Less painful perhaps than grief, it nonetheless arouses a discomfort both emotional and physical. When Giotto depicted the seven deadly sins for the walls of the Arena chapel, he showed envy as a snake shooting from a sinner's mouth. He shows not only the nastiness, but the gagging discomfort. What is so strange and twisted about envy, in its notorious "meanness," is that it does not actually blind one to others' qualities, virtues, and achievements, but creates a knife-edged sensitivity to them. Instead of appreciating others for their fineness, the envious person feels attacked by them. Envy signals anger against the very things one appreciates. It makes one want to attack what one admires.

In *Othello,* that play about the rampant, pathological destructiveness of envy and jealousy, Iago's grudge against Cassio is: "He hath a daily beauty in his life that makes me ugly." Iago's capacity to see what others are—their greatness and their weakness—gives him both reason to loathe them and power to destroy them. Some awful flaw, some death knell of emptiness persuades him that others' beauty is a measure of his contrasting ugliness. When asked to explain his behavior at the end of the play, he, whose mastery of speech and imagery has such powerful effects on others, cannot explain himself. With a clear-sighted outward eye, he cannot see the inner mechanism that drives him.

Envy has no direct or simple aim. It stimulates actions and provides motives, yet its logic is quite different from the logic of ambition or greed. When we are ambitious or greedy, we have some idea what we want and what we should aim for. When we are struck by envy, we are not aware of what *we* want. We are simply enraged by what *other* people have. Envy's source is dissatisfaction and deprivation. It increases as one's power diminishes. It feels like need or desire, yet it is unclear what could satisfy envy. Largely negative, it feeds on others' downfall and suffers from others' successes. Feeling powerless, the envious person becomes destructive.

ENVY SEEMS TO TAKE on different forms in adults and in young children, who are much better at blending it with other feelings. In her marvellous descriptions of siblings fighting over a mother's lap or a favorite toy, Judy Dunn[5] shows envy in action, but she also shows how envy is only one item in their relationship. It has primacy at one moment, and is submerged at another. It can motivate attacks on a sibling and attention-getting behavior toward a parent, but its innocence seems to reside in the fact that it can, after all, be satisfied (by making a sibling cry, or by getting a place on the mother's lap); then, there is room for a whole new range of feelings. Among girls in middle childhood,[6] envy plays a part in the ways girls organize their friends. One child's envy may lead her to reject another; then other girls act along with her, following the rules set by the clique. They act as though from envy, even though they may not be at all envious. Envy among these children is highly volatile. It revolves around birthdays, holidays, or recently acquired pets. Usually, girls justify their envy on quasi-moral grounds: Someone who arouses envy is considered to be showing off, to think she's so smart, to think too much of herself. Therefore, her exclusion from games, or whatever teasing or taunting or scolding she receives, is seen as justified punishment. In adolescence, friendship and envy sometimes go hand in hand:[7] Amy (aged 14) said that she believed that if she made an effort to get to know a girl and like her, then she could overcome her envy; but another girl (aged 15) said that she wanted to stay friends with Ruth "so that I can keep an eye on her." "What do you need to watch out for?" I asked. "I want to know how worried I should be, like whether she's racing ahead of me." "What do you do if she is?" I asked. "I feel awful," she replied, "but at least I *know*."

"What do you envy about her? I mean—why her?" I wanted to

know, and she shrugged. "She's so pretty, and smart. Like she's always smart. When she walks into the school, everyone feels different. She's really there. Well, if I say these things—they sort of fall apart. They sound silly, but they're not! You know, clothes look different on her. White tennis socks, that red sweater she wears, with it's wide ribbing set against her skirt, and her hair's always so—neat. She'll probably go to Stanford. She's all set up inside. I don't like talking about this. It isn't just one thing, it's everything; but sometimes when I match up to her, like I get a higher grade or something, or when she messes up, I feel relieved. Okay? It just makes me feel better, because I'll know I don't have to envy her today." Her relief at one small break from her envy, registered its pain. But however familiar she was with it, and however articulate she was about the range and details that aroused her envy, she could not locate its cause.

THERE IS POWERLESSNESS IMPLICIT in envy. There is also an idealization of the state that is envied: Whether it is being always smart, or going to Stanford, the implicit belief is that if one had what the other has, then one would have all one needs. There are many confusions imbedded in envy, which makes it difficult to tackle. In envying someone, a person may be envying a state—of being loved, admired, or successful. Sometimes, what one wants is to possess that state oneself; sometimes, what one wants is to be that person who embodies or represents that state; and sometimes, it is an inability to tolerate someone else having those qualities or assets that one envies. Defeat is built into envy: first, because no one can become someone else; second, because the enviable state will not provide the perfection one envisaged in envying it; and, third, because someone else not having enviable qualities won't do the envying person any good. The trouble is logic doesn't banish envy; it has a kind of magical structure, which can't be argued away, and the confusion only makes it hurt all the more. The idealization on which envy breeds remains hidden, and so envy persists.

In the midlife women I interviewed, envy was consistently described as less intense than it had been in their past. This was a common theme; fifteen women spoke of this, some in the guise of being more self-accepting as they got older, or more content, or less concerned about what other people were, or had, or did. Moreover, the older women in the age range of my sample were more likely to de-scribe themselves as "not envious" than were the younger women in the sample: At fifty, a woman has, in general, less problem with envy than at forty. Women could track the change within themselves. Blanche, at 48, described her midlife release from past envy: "My heart used to sink when I saw another attractive woman walk into the room. It must have been when I was in my mid-thirties that I realized I was looking older, and I couldn't feel comfortable just because I was younger than most of the people in my profession. That used to be so important to me—being younger than the rest. And when a colleague would mention a woman I didn't know, and start talking about her work, or saying that she was applying for some grant or position, peck-ing away in my mind was the stupidest question 'What did she look like?' I guess I could afford then to think that it really mattered what you looked like. But I think it's more than worrying about being judged as I judge others. I've felt a real growth in empathy over the last few years. I've stepped out of that awful pecking order stuff, and in-stead, it's a matter of just seeing the other and who they are, rather than worrying whether they're better than you. I don't—sort of pull things apart like that any more. What's the point? You think 'Okay, she feels good about herself.' But then that's just okay . . . It doesn't hang around me like it used to."

Blanche implicitly connects the threat of being marginalized with a heightened concern about the appearance of other women. As she realizes that she is beginning to look older, she worries about being ousted professionally by someone who looks younger. But this occurs when she is in her mid-thirties, and has not yet slipped off the yoke of that particular ideal—the woman who wows people with her work and her looks. She slips this yoke off as she realizes she cannot afford to wear it: The self-dissatisfaction is worthless and inappropriate. As she no longer is magnetized by others' views (asking "What does she look like?" when another woman's work is discussed) she no longer inter-nalizes others' ideals. She can concentrate on her own vision, and her own life.

Many midlife women felt that they had reached, or were reaching, a position of empathy and breadth in which they could overcome envy—which is a decided contrast to standard images of generous youth and grudging age. In distancing themselves from the idea of some perfectly imaged woman, they felt less threatened by others. Others' successes or qualities were constructed not as a perfect whole, but as part of the good things in life to which she too had some access. In all sorts of ways, women in midlife described release from ideals—from what they had expected they should be when they were young adults, from what their mothers thought of them, from coming up to certain standards as a wife or [less often] a mother. In distancing themselves from the ideal, they became more confident of their own vision, and less concerned that another's vision or voice would supplant their own. There was less second-guessing of their responses and decisions, less sense of being shadowed by some judge, fewer of those shapeless fears, which only now, in their absence, did they describe. Release from ideals opened new channels of communication and new responses. They felt an increased capacity for female friendship, and a lessening of their fear of other women, however pretty and however young. Release from envy is part of normal midlife growth. As she no longer idealizes who or what she should be, she no longer craves for or wishes to destroy, an imagined, embodied ideal.

Patterns of Envy

Yet envy was problematic for several women; and when it was, it marked the point at which these women were stalled in development. Something fixed them to one point and kept them blinkered. For them, envy got worse as they got older. As they noted the passage of time, they found themselves unable to make use of it. These envious women loathed their envy and hated who they became under its influence, yet they lacked the psychological tools to remove it.

In my study, only seven women had the current experience of envy as a predominant theme in their conversation, something that they kept coming back to in one way or another. Seven out of 80 is not a high proportion, but it is enough to reveal a pattern. These women saw others' achievements as targeted against them, not only highlighting the absence of their own worth, but somehow deliberately constructed to make them feel bad. Phyllis said that very young people put her "in a flap," that they didn't seem real to her, that she would look at them while they talked and she would be cutting away their youth, like a bruise on a pear: "They don't own their youth any more than I owned mine—they'll see, they'll drop it on the ground and be miles away before they notice, just like I dropped mine." Her resentful predictions were heard within a nearly sensuous chant of appreciation of their youth. She spoke of "skin that's inhuman it's so smooth" or "teeth like they all have these days, right out of an old ad for Macleans."

Youth was by no means the only, or even most common focus of envy. These women were far more likely to envy their peers than they were to envy younger women. Envy was aroused more quickly by a woman with whom another had many points of identification, for they saw the envied woman as someone whom they should be. They envied them for being richer, happier, more self-confident, more successful, more spontaneous, more generous, more likable—but beneath all of this, as I teased out the focus of the envy, and asked, "Well, do you envy this other person, who isn't so rich, or successful or generous?" I discovered that what they envied was another's sense of having achieved something, or of having gained recognition for something, or another's sense of purpose or another's personal resources and self-satisfaction. When they envied another woman's appearance, they were envying the sense of self it seemed to express, or which they guessed must lie behind the appearance. They envied others' self-esteem, or a more general sense of having something in their lives, which was theirs and which they valued. They envied a woman's ability to speak up or be heard. When it came down to precisely what they envied, they were nearly as starstruck as the 14-year-old who brooded over the white tennis socks and red sweater with the wide ribbing set against the skirt. What they focused on, eventually, was how another person felt about herself. They envied her subjective experience (not the reflection in the mirror). Then, once envy got going, so to speak, it would latch on to anything, and just keep rolling. The big issues would collect smaller ones. Whatever another enviable person had became something that could be envied as a stand-in for the person.

THE FEW WOMEN WHO were plagued by envy were not objectively less well off than other women: This wasn't the poor envying the rich, but women who perceived themselves as having failed, envying those they perceived as having succeeded. They had a fairly strong image of a potential self, which they weren't managing to realize. They focused on defeat, and described their lives as a series of disappointments, usually because some long-held aim had gone unrealized. A series of investments and hopes and efforts had not paid off. They had put their energy and placed their hopes into a plan that now seemed defeated. They faced the problems of wasted energy, a cruel comparison between the use they had put their time to, and the pay-off they saw of other people's time. They may have given everything (and, hence, had to give up a number of things) to a marriage that had not worked out or that remained a terrible burden; or they had anticipated success that was not realized. They sometimes resented other, more successful people, for not giving up what they had to give up: "She just dumped her children in child care from the word 'go,' and elbowed her way past me, giving me a kick in the shin for good measure," Phyllis said of another who had "ousted" her from her part-time job, and eclipsed her promotion, as she "marched in the firm with her new woman image, never missed work because of a child's illness, or cared one whit for family obligation."

But such defensive criticism, which is usually thought to be an essential part of envy, was actually rare. What struck me was how peculiarly quick these women were to suppose that another woman was better, more powerful or more successful. Through their envy, they expressed empathy with another's qualities. Two felt overwhelmed by others' confidence and competence: "She opens her mouth, and everyone listens . . . over and over again, I see it happen . . . [someone else] does something, and it really matters, while what I say or do just won't register . . . I can get the words out, but they just hang there, heavy and stupid, not doing anything," Roberta mused. "I see women—especially this one . . . stand up . . . well, this one time she was talking to her mother-in-law, saying how she'd do the shopping for her but not prepare her dinner. It was, you know, I'll do this and not that. It's both those things that floor me—that she can say I'll do this . . . I won't do that . . . It's where she comes from . . . she knows what she wants to give, and what she doesn't, and she can say it, and you know, walk away after, still whole," Nan Hallen marvelled.

Women who envied were threatened by depression, which they could just about keep at bay until envy struck, and then all sorts of negative feelings would flood in. They could construct defenses against negative feelings (dissatisfaction and frustration) until these defenses were struck down by seeing someone else who, they believed, had overcome all obstacles to that good self they envisaged within them.

Two mindsets characterized this small group of women. First was the belief that something had unfairly marked them out. They believed that they were distinctive in their bad luck, that the efforts that, for other women, were fruitful, were for them sterile. Hence, they felt powerless: There was no reasonable link between their efforts and their achievements. This fissure had occurred sometime in early adulthood. At some previous stage, they had felt lucky, in control, on the right track. Then—and they did not know why—something had stopped. Their conversation was splattered with references to nothing having happened, to time standing still, or to their lives racing by without anything to show for the passing of time.

Second, they shared a rigid connection to an outdated self image—usually going back to adolescence. At that time, they had felt themselves successful, and were still stunned by the discrepancy between former expectations and current realities. They were stuck to an ideal plan, and measured themselves in terms of how far they fell short of it. Several had strong, effective personal attachments, good jobs, useful skills, yet none of these achievements touched their rigid and demanding notions of success.

In many ways, these women, who focused on defeat, actually had a strong self-image. They saw themselves as competent and intelligent. Three described themselves as well-educated, and the others who did not hold college degrees considered themselves to be "smart enough" or "one pretty smart lady" or "quick to see what's what." They compared themselves, usually favorably, with other women whose achievements caught their eye—such as an actress, or writer, or talk show host, or a colleague who surpassed them, or a friend or relative who had "done well." But, at the same time that they compared themselves favorably with others, they often denied that another's abilities accounted for her position. The people they admired became people who were no better, smarter, or talented than they. Sometimes this led to resentment. Eventually, these "admired" figures became people who did not deserve their success. They only "filled the bill" or were "at the right place at the right time," or had "caught on." They "knew how to play the game," had "the ruthlessness you need today," were "selfish" or "cold." This perspective led to despair: others get what they want by good luck; when luck, not deliberate action, leads to results, one is powerless, with no control over the outcome.

These women experienced a split between what they thought they were, in some social sense, worth, and how they felt they were perceived. "I know what other people think when they ask what I'm doing now," Phyllis said. "They feel safe, because I'm so uninteresting to them." "I know my friends think I'm just a hanger on," Roberta declared. "The parents who drive up in their smart cars think they're so much better than me," Celia insisted. Some had empathy with these negative views. "I know I'd think the same of someone else," Roberta admitted. "It must be good to see how they've surpassed me," Phyllis mused. But as they compared themselves to others, I was surprised by their narrow field of vision. The population of their mental world was small: Only a few people had qualities or abilities worth envying. In contrast, women who admired lots of people and acknowledged many others' successes were far less likely to suffer envy. Only Alison had a wide-ranging generosity of spirit, which included many other women. When I pointed this out to her she ruefully noted how this actually increased her envy: "Sure, I have lots to choose from. It's like, who's the flavor of the week? And sometimes I'm carrying three or four scoops around all at once." Envy became a past-time, something to be savored—albeit viciously, in self-defeat.

Discounted Achievements

Envious women are expected to be unsympathetic, by nature, mean; but these women were not. None of these women was idle or lazy, and each of them had in their lives what, for others, might well have been a source of pride and satisfaction. Phyllis, 47, had been inspired, by her brain-damaged son, to train, to assess, and to identify children's learning difficulties. Roberta, 45, managed her husband's business, which was involved in setting up large marquees for parties and conferences. She was his "design scout" and would work on new designs for the interiors of marquees. Alison, 44, taught French part time. Celia, 46, gave horse riding lessons and managed a stable. Nan, 40, worked as a freelance copy editor. Certainly, they were all "undervalued" in an objective sense. They had worked steadily, and hard, as most women do, to maintain a standard of competence and to contribute to their families' well-being. But this kind of undervaluing, of being in an insecure and not particularly well-paid job, is so common among women that it does not explain why these seven, among my sample of eighty, suffered from envy. Nor was the problem that they had no outlet for their intelligence and talent, for they did exercise these. They were goal-orientated and, on the whole, hardworking.

Phyllis said that her self-image "had peaked at 25":

> I always assumed I would do well. Everyone assumed that. Life was so easy for me in those days. I did real well in high school. I got into every college I applied to. After graduation I landed a job right away as an editor with a really great publisher—and then one day I was looking around and saying, "Where am I?" You know, suddenly I wasn't going anywhere fast, and I felt this awful free fall. I can't . . . Do you maybe see? It's fifteen years ago, but it might as well be yesterday; there's still this awful, sickly feeling. You're shooting ahead . . . that's how I was, just everything going so smoothly, and then there's suddenly nothing to support you. There was no reason not to give up my job when I had my kid because other people were getting promoted and I wasn't. Suddenly I'd become something different . . . not this wonder girl who would grow into a wonder woman. I couldn't see why. I still don't . . . And for a while my husband was doing so well, and we were doing so well, and then suddenly we weren't, and while other lawyers were getting rich—real rich—he was still an associate, working long hours and getting praise from the senior partner but not much else. And he wanted sympathy, but all I wanted was for him to get ahead. I'm not proud of that. I know that wasn't a helpful way to go about things and that I made things worse. I know I wanted him to be successful because it was suddenly apparent that I wasn't. And then I had this child . . . well you have to accept the hand you're dealt, don't you? And some of the parents I've met since—well, they're an inspiration . . . they should be, but I end up thinking "Why can they rise above this, and I can't." That's what I'm always thinking, I guess . . . why are these other women making it? So many of them. They're not better than me. But there they are, just riding forward and laughing at me as they pass me by.

Phyllis still communes with an internalized set of goals or expectations, which she knows will not be realized. Yet she cannot be released from these expectations, even as she knows that in clinging to them she is harming her relationship with her husband and slighting her child. She feels inferior to those women who have brain-damaged children and can say, "I learn so much from him," or "I love him as he is, and want him to be the best that he is." She could vividly describe the "better" empathy of other parents, while she mourned the inadequacy of her own. Her own dissatisfaction has locked her into an idealizing state vis-à-vis others. Unable to see from within, she is "always thinking" how well others are doing. She cannot see that her disappointments and failures are potentially part of a good meaningful life. She cannot see this because, in idealizing others, she diminishes the validity of her own experience. Like the teenage girl who asks her interviewers whether there is somewhere a girl who has found the perfect fit, both inside and out, Phyllis is bemused by idealized expectations she knows she will never meet. Hence, she feels isolated, discounted within an inferior world. She constructs an external vision that mocks her, believing that those who are more successful are "laughing at [her] as they pass [her] by." Their imagined mockery is a reflection of her own envy.

Roberta, struggling like 14-year-old Amy with her idealization of others, said, "Something about another woman will just spark it off, and I'm burning with fury, asking 'Why *her* and not *me*?' These feelings leave scars, and you never know when they'll open up again. I get so angry, and think and say such awful things. But it makes me ache, just feeling what it's like . . . for a minute you think what being her is like. And getting older—facing fifty!—well that's me locked out, isn't it? I feel trapped in my own life. I just don't see a way out. My friends will ring up and tell me their good news—phew—it's like being battered, one slap after another, and they just keep on. Especially this one woman . . . she's been doing this and that on the Tribune, and suddenly she's become real big, traveling all over the place and covering everything. On and on she goes about what new thing she's going to do. It's a nightmare—she just won't stop, and I want to say: 'Give me a break; can't you just give me a break from all your fucking triumphs.' " Yet I observed Roberta in conversation with her friends, and she prodded them into revelations about their triumphs. She would ask how they were, and what was happening at work, and whether there was

any good news about this or that. I put this to her, and she said "Yeah,
that way I can brace myself for it; it won't jump out at me unawares."
Like young Amy, defeated by her adoration of another girl, Roberta
needs to know about their triumphs, to decide how much envy to ex-
pend in a single day.

Easy Crossings

Both Phyllis and Roberta were stuck at a point earlier in development
at which they had easy successes, which they were now unable to repeat. In her "good" adolescence and early adulthood, Phyllis had been
carried along by others' approval. ("I always assumed I would do well.
Everyone assumed that.") She identified with "everyone's" view, but
felt bereft in adulthood, when she was no longer the "wonder girl." In
coping with her child's (minor) brain damage, she felt an additional
"personal insult, which hardly anyone else has to bear." No longer effortlessly fulfilling others' expectations ("Life was so easy for me in
those days"), she feels dissociated from who she is—for she already was
disassociated from the sources of her own goals and feelings. She no
longer has compensation for this disconnection. Remaining discon-
nected, even in the midst of an active, engaged life, she cannot find a
new link between her life and her ambitions. She feels mocked by others' success (they are "laughing at [her] as they pass [her] by"), just as
she feels cheated by that free fall, which began fifteen years ago, but
which "might as well be yesterday," because the sickly feeling is still
with her.

Roberta, who feels "trapped in [her] own life" and does not
"see a way out" also suffers confusion as to why others can proceed
and she cannot. Having made the perfect transition from girl to adolescent, she feels betrayed by imperfections arising in the reality of
maturity. As she fails to snatch rewarding approval in adulthood, she
wishes she could be someone else who knew how to gather the rewards she still craves. Midlife was threatening ("And getting older—
facing fifty!—well, that's me locked out, isn't it?"), because it locked
the door forever on that wonder girl era. Having once, apparently,
been the embodiment of others' ideals, she cannot thrive without
the reinforcement of others' amazed admiration.

NAN, TOO, LOOKED UPON one crossroads as a perfect meeting point. Her husband had fallen deeply in love with her when she was 19, seeing her as the "Rainbow girl" for whom he had been searching so long. His would be the loving eye that would keep her forever young and cherished. At 40, in an emotionally abusive marriage, she looked upon her husband's lost love for her as a grace that might one day return and amaze her. She would "earn it," she hoped. Though she "couldn't help doing things that make him mad," she would keep trying, and one day she would learn to be better. She half-saw the underworld in which she crept, and in which she savored envy, like a poisonous, half-comforting sweet: "Maybe everyone out there is free of what I live with. I see them spouting their so-called wisdom. Stupid . . . thinking they know about us, thinking they know about anything, when they're only happy because they don't think. But you don't . . . you can't just leave because someone hits you once in a while. Kids, you know, they're hit. Their parents hit them. Families get close . . . you get irritable, partly, you know, because you care so much. And I couldn't leave. Not only because there's nowhere to go. I couldn't be happy with anyone else. I just wish I could be different, so he could be happy with me."

Nan was still trying to pick up the pieces of the shattered mirror and to find therein an ideal image—of her husband's love, of herself as once loved. Women outside her underworld were creatures whose contentment and ease proclaimed them, in her eyes, "stupid." Describing herself as unable to be "happy with anyone else," she saw other women as "only happy because they don't think and they don't know." Her husband's previous idealization of her had been so rewarding and intimate that she kept trying to retrieve it, and failed to develop other goals. As she spoke about her future, she worked hard to deny the reality of her aging. "I think when something really significant happens, it happens forever, and doesn't change, and even if I change for myself and for the world, there will be something between us that's always the same."

So did she not live in time, I asked, like other people, who changed with time?

She looked at me mildly, blankly. Perhaps I was one of the stupid ones, whose view she could discount because "they don't see and they don't know."

"You envy so many other people," I ventured. "Why?"

She still looked at me mildly, blankly, and replied, "Because they can let go. They can change into things."

"And couldn't you?" I asked; but she retreated into her mild despair, and said nothing. Despair and crisis are, for all their common features, strangers.

Rigid Goals

In Alison's determination to "make it" as an actress, she had formed a dream, which guided her life. She had trained in the theatre, spent all her summers in repertory workshops, had dropped every personal attachment when a part in a play, however small, called her to another city or state. The parts on offer decreased rather than increased during her thirties, and she took a rush course in secretarial school, just to get a job. She worked in various offices, but would always drop a job when a part came along. I saw her perform: She insisted that if I were to understand her, I must see her acting "because it's what I really am." She was more than competent; she was as good as many who were far more successful than she. But the enormous part luck played in this highly competitive field worked against her. She said that throughout her twenties and thirties she would often repeat to herself "It only takes one good role" or "I only have to be noticed by one critic." These were chants that persuaded her that some opportunity might one day present itself to her, even as daily, she met with rejections. At 45, she was doing office work and tutoring in French, and still thought of herself as an actress, still taking small parts in small companies, but she described how she had lost hope and saw her future as "a series of broken strings."

I was silly to do what I did. But at the time—when I was making all those crucial decisions about what to do—it seemed like a really fine thing. Maybe it was that environment of the late sixties, when people thought it was really limiting to be planning a career. Can you believe that! Look at them all now—all of them with their strong career lines. I can't understand how it stalled me, and worked as a roller-coaster for most of my friends and sibs. But I suppose acting was, for me, a profession. That's what I thought it would be. It's still an obsession with me. It's strange how one idea can just get hold of you and keep you there for so long. I should have done something sane, something with a ladder you can actually climb. This is all hit and miss, and I've missed. But that was all I could think about, and now it's all I know. Sometimes I get to the point where I'm thinking, "Yes, I can give it up. I should really try for something else," but an hour later I'll slip back to the old mindset where I'm watching someone and thinking "Yes, this is how people look when they're worried about being shortchanged, or this is the precise movement someone makes when she's embarrassed about what she's just said, or this is the way someone sits when she's interviewing someone!" That's how I see the world—as an opportunity to reproduce it on the stage. I wouldn't have to make the big time to be satisfied. It's just the need to do what I want to do. I'm so ashamed of my failure. Everyone else around me—my brother and my sisters, they've done so well. They're all doing different things, and they're all interesting things— things that make sense . . . things that make money! I love seeing them, and my friends, too, but when I hear what they're doing, and see their children, and walk in their houses, my legs buckle under with envy. That kind of rhythm to their lives . . . it's what's behind it all, they don't see . . . I can taste it, even though it's miles away, so I keep asking myself "Why didn't I do that? Why didn't I try something else?" That feeling is so awful, that the only way I can comfort myself is by thinking that if it gets worse, or doesn't go away, I can always kill myself. That's some comfort, isn't it? But it is reassuring to think that I have that if I see nowhere to go, I can always die. So at least I won't feel this.

"What do you feel when you don't get a part you've auditioned for?" I asked. "Does that make you feel the same way?"

She thought for a moment. "When I don't get a part, I feel like this," and she slammed her fist into her chest, "but I immediately start thinking about the next audition. But when someone I know gets one—even one I didn't try for, or when someone else has . . . well, it's then I feel that I just want to die." Envy disrupted sleeping patterns— just as depression does. She would wake at three or four in the morning, and lie awake, knowing she would not sleep, yet would feel a cold night terror as she brooded over others' successes like nightmares. "I think about Marion and the part she's got, and what it will be like, and how she'll feel—and I imagine the sheer bliss of a bullet through my head." As others' achievements drive dissatisfaction into her like gunfire, she longs to destroy all her feelings, so that she will not be suffering this envy.

ENVY ENTERS THESE WOMEN'S lives through the points at which aims and effort were seen to be powerless. Change and growth were not attempted because, so defeated were they by envy, they did not believe they had power to change. They were in mourning for a self they had assumed they could grow into but had lost along the way.

Envy Dissolved

All midlife women, during the changing decades of their adulthood, had confronted and managed difficult choices. They had taken careful stock of past goals in light of their adult experience. Some had maintained themselves and their families. They had faced unfair disappointment and frustration. Yet they had also managed to achieve midlife growth. The hidden challenge, which hedged envious women in, was the sense that somehow, hidden within their lives, was a force that prohibited the growth and advancement they valued most. It was not simply a matter of failing to achieve as much as they had hoped, but of failing to find social reinforcement for anything like the sort of thing they had hoped to achieve. Either from a partner or a select group of friends or an employer or the world at large, they confronted a blank where they craved a reaction. Nan was still caught, buried, in an underground childhood, unable to link up with and make use of an adult reality. Others had all jumped the hurdle that many girls confront at adolescence. They had taken their goals and their self-respect and their ambition through adolescence and into adult life—and then, suddenly, everything had stopped for them. They were bewildered by the clash between previous advance and present stasis. They could not see what had gone wrong for them, and right for others. They could not find any intersection between the self they thought they were, and the self they craved. Unable to find the resources to shatter old ideals, they remained trapped by them, with their sense of inferiority as a constant companion.

Yet psychological growth is always possible. A small event can push one through a mental passage that had once seemed impenetrable. Nearly three years after Alison had so powerfully drawn the connection between envy and depression, she telephoned me to say that something had changed. For Alison, relief came as she obtained a strong supporting role in a long-running play. It took only a modest success to alleviate (temporarily?) the feelings she had thought she could only escape through death. I met her a month after she phoned. She said her problems with envy had "just dissolved."

"As easily as that?" I wondered, for she had had small successes before.

"Yes, I think so. Because this role has been so much fun, and more high profile than anything I've done, that I . . . Well, the difference is . . . now I know what it's like. A kind of success becomes routine, and there's the companionship—or not—of the team, and the steady pay check, and the sense that things are happening. I don't feel that far from everyone else now, not fundamentally different from those above me. It's like—now I know what it's like to feel whole. No, you don't have to bother, asking me the next one, like how I'll feel when this run's over and I wake up in the morning to nothing. Because I don't know. Maybe I won't have to face that. Maybe if I do, I'll find God. But for now, it's a relief not to have that scalpel jab me when I hear that someone else has landed a part. I can now think 'Well, good for her,' without feeling that her success is a scorched earth policy."

This modest success had provided her with the reinforcement she needed to shift the power of an old ideal. Gaining some insight into what success is like, she sees both what it can offer and what it cannot. As she realizes the limitations of what success can give her, she no longer sees herself as fundamentally different from those who do achieve the goals she would so badly like to achieve. Instead, she sees a common struggle, and makes a connection between her own efforts and possible outcomes. "I know that when I'm on stage, if I do my best, then something may come out of it. Feeling that . . . that I have a chance, is so good—and strange! In a way, it's a little thing, and yet it seems to make all the difference." For what makes "all the difference" is the hope that emerges when she gives up her assumption that all her efforts will be ineffective. Instead, she works with the "strange" feeling that she has a chance.

ENVY BREEDS WITHIN A narrow vision and a belief in narrow options. It has been suggested that women may have been more envious of one another because their lives were so similar, and similarly constrained.[8] Since it was only in terms of appearance, dress, and family social standing that they mattered, it was in these that they could readily compare themselves to other women. Having no other outlet for achievement, they jealously guarded their position in the pecking order.

Today's midlife women have no shared standards by which to assess their success. Yet they are under more pressure than any other generation of women. They were taught that they would be the new generation, with vast opportunities, and hence they have high expectations of themselves and their potential. Alongside the pressure and excitement of expectation, however, the actual increases in opportunity have been modest; constraints in fulfilling their goals have been continuous; and the contradictions in ideas of who they should be and what they can be, have been endless. In the first years of their adulthood, many women constructed a new ideal of career achievements, without yet being free of old ideals of feminine grace, beauty, and devotion to others. It is not surprising that some women get stuck by a "failure" to achieve an idealized standard. What is surprising is how few such women there were in my sample, how most women were responsive to that difficult developmental push towards new midlife in which they were free of these external judgments and internal repressers. For most of these women, the special challenges and compromises they confronted in their first years of adulthood as the first generation of "the new woman" was transformed in midlife into the skill of making them their *own* women.

Stalling Points and Signs of Stasis in Midlife Development

Some women have extreme difficulty with the midlife passage. Because they remain enthralled by some past ideal, they see midlife as a dead end—rather than as a crossroads to various futures. The signs of such an impediment may be:

1. insistence on continuous contentment/anxious avoidance of any regret
2. constant focus on the rules of the game/continuous control over oneself to conform to accepted patterns
3. refusal to take further risks, once one effort to change has been unsuccessful
4. persistent depression/bitterness towards others
5. acute and abiding envy—not simply pangs, which come and go— which may be the result of easy fulfillment of one's (or others') ideals in an earlier phase of life, or rigid focus on one goal and a narrow conception of success

Steps towards growth

1. Confront the costs of past compromises. These are inevitable, not shameful. They will lead you to changes you want to make on behalf of your future.
2. Identify the most uncomfortable aspects of your environment at work or at home. Ask whether these can be changed, or whether a different environment would allow more spontaneous self-expression.
3. Failure is an inevitable part of learning. Treat "failure" as a source of information about oneself rather than a sign of inadequacy.
4. Concentrate on at least one thing you really want to change, and develop several strategies for possible change. This will ease depression, and lessen the sense of helplessness that accompanies it.
5. Broaden your sense of what success is. A single goal is unlikely to be realized, but there are many ways to be successful. When you see one thing as the only success, you idealize others and deny the breadth of your own achievements.

8

Love and Experience: What Do Women Learn?

The balance of power within midlife marriages has been observed to change.[1] Women, in midlife, are seen to have more power relative to men than they did in their youth. They gain more power, because they take it. They take it, because they are able to be self-assertive. They are able to be more self-assertive because they are more likely to know what they want and what they feel, to trust their own experience. Bringing this into a relationship can be easier than they had ever dreamed—or it can incur huge costs.

As women change and grow, crucial relationships are transformed—sometimes as a result of midlife development, and sometimes as a necessary prelude to it. The question women ask at the beginning of midlife crisis—"Why did it take so long to trust myself?"—has another version in the context of close relationships. "Why was I afraid to speak out, to state my needs, to show my feelings?" is posed as women negotiate their development within existing relationships of love and sexuality. In a more drastic vein, she may also ask, "Why didn't I know what I felt?" As her own perceptions and feelings become the source of her knowledge, the location of power within a relationship shifts. Many women in my sample were bewildered as to why it took them so long to bring more of themselves—their voices, vision, goals, and desires—into the relationship.

The balance of power in adult relationships is seldom a matter of brute force. Power does not simply press down upon a passive receptor. Dominance and dependence emerge as partners share perceptions of who has more say, whose pleasure counts more, who sets standards of what is acceptable and what is not. Power in personal relationships is highly subjective. Partners construct myths about the location of power. They may disguise from themselves either their control or their submission. False power stories are commonly told: A husband jokes about his wife being "boss," when the scope of her influence is minimal and trivial. In John Mortimer's "Rumpole" stories, the barrister privately refers to his wife as "She who must be obeyed," suggesting that he is subservient to her. But Hilda Rumpole issues orders only because she cannot engage her husband's attention. He does not want to exchange views with her; he has no interest in her; and he lets her have her way because he wants to avoid contact with her. Like so many people who shout because no one will hear them when they speak, Hilda has to be forbidding because she is discounted. Women who nag or cajole or flatter may be thought to have power because they can influence a partner; but the means by which they gain influence proves their powerlessness. A woman who nags is a woman whose normal voice in unheard. A woman who wheedles gifts from a partner lacks direct control over financial resources. A woman's "wiles" are powerful only when she is powerless.

Questions about love and power are not newly hatched in midlife, but they are addressed anew as the skills a woman is likely to acquire in midlife growth allow new questions to be asked and new answers to be given. As her own feelings and her own experience become a more constant source of knowledge, the fear she may have had of being rejected or abandoned is quelled. She may still value the relationship, she may still be afraid of loneliness or loss; but the fear can now cease its domination, as the costs of self-suppression are judged too high. As she realizes how much energy has gone into pleasing her partner, or embodying some ideal of lover and helpmate, she realizes how she has foregone the power that could be hers. Questions of power in close relationships are very difficult to judge. They are mingled with those strong needs we have for a partner to flourish, and the simple necessity of compromise and accommodation within a partnership. Instead of a stark scale, questions of power and questions of care can only be measured with highly subjective gradients. Among traditional woman, a husband's ambitions, needs, and desires can structure her life. What has she given up, and on the basis of what beliefs? a woman may ask herself. Among innovative women, who pursue careers as demanding as those of a husband with a traditional wife, a partner's share in domestic tasks may diminish as his resistance seems more powerful than her requests.[2] These women then must ask themselves how forcefully they want to instigate change, or whether it is easier, and safer, to bury their own needs and deny the extend of their compromises? Among expansive women, the route to change may be blocked by a partner's disapproval. Does an expansive woman with a punitive partner bow to his disapproval, or does she make changes in spite of it? Among protesting women, the premature catapult into adulthood may have created an ambivalent dependence: fear of dependence resides beside a profound need. Does a protesting woman criticize all forms of sexual and romantic intimacy as versions of old constraints, or does she construct relationships that allow her to be as spontaneous and "irresponsible" as she wants?

As a woman's strengthening vision highlights these forks in the road ahead, she may face the task of reconstructing more than she had planned.

The Starting Point: Seduction and Betrayal

Some time ago, while I was preparing a course about women literary characters who had been "discarded" or abandoned by husbands or lovers, I was trying to trace a book whose title, I was convinced, was something like *Love and Women*. Though I had not read the book for over ten years, some sentences stood out so clearly that I felt I had the pages in front of me. Yet the more I searched for this book, the more certain it seemed that it would forever elude me. I could remember the distinctive voice, speaking about women's strength, ego, drive, and endurance. The love plots of women's lives were rich with pain, but not defeat, and the struggle ended with increased control over their futures.

I knew further that this same author wrote elsewhere about the breakup of her own marriage to a well-known poet,[3] of how she experienced the emergence of a new self that was no longer part of "we" or "us." I could recall the unexpected force of self-respect thriving in the midst of loss and loneliness. But I could not remember the author, and either I had mis-remembered the title, or the library's computer was too lazy to conduct a thorough search.

The more I thought about this book, the more I knew I needed it. Here was a text that portrayed lost love as a prelude to self-transformation rather than self-annihilation. Here was a voice that would counter the assumption that in losing a relationship a woman lost her self. Here, the voice of a middle-aged woman stood alone and abandoned and fully self-identified, fully prepared both to experience unhappiness and to mark the transition to a single but whole self.

I needed this book to balance my students' persistent interpretations of a female character's response to lost love. They were increasingly impatient with those novels in which a story ends with a good marriage, promising a good life. In their youthful hubris, they were brusquely dismissive, too, of the passive shock of Jean Rhys's female characters who, when abandoned, lose all focus and will and hope. They were searching for a new language of loss and love, which could accommodate the individual knowledge and experience they were working so hard to achieve themselves. This book would offer a midlife woman's voice, which was all too often absent from their texts. It was my eager, hidden agenda to prove to them that a woman, through lost love, could find within herself a source of knowledge beyond either the tragic or pathetic. Moreover, by unearthing a strong midlife voice, they could read younger women's stories in a different light.

But nothing I keyed into the University Library computer would offer me access to this book—not "love" or "loss" or "women." Eventually, a chance reference gave me the name of the literary woman who had supplanted my "abandoned" woman as wife of the famous poet; and from that point, I was able to discover the name of the poet husband and the name of his first wife.

The title of the book I had been searching for was not *Love and Women,* or any such permutation of those terms, but *Seduction and Betrayal.*[4] When I described my relief at finally tracing the book to a colleague and explained how my memory had been caught in that useless loop, his laughter—louder and longer than is normally heard in the Library coffee room—made me see the humor, and hence the logic, of my mistake. The far more specific title of Elizabeth Hardwick's book had been filed in my memory according to a more general

heading. Not all stories about women and love involve themes of seduction and betrayal, but they are commonly enough linked for memory to slip in one in place of the other. The life-long challenge is to
break this link, to establish a love that is empowering rather than limiting, that instills courage rather than fear. This task is not easily
achieved, and it is rarely achieved early.

THE STORY OF LOVE and women all too often *is* a story of seduction and betrayal, of cruel submission and terrible loss. Such stories
involve more than love, passion, and lust: They occur within a context
of women's perceptions of what they need and how they might com-
pensate for loss. When a woman is seduced, and her seduction "dam-
ages" her or curtails future options and social status, then the emotional force of the seduction is intensified. When she is dependent
financially on a partner, the bonds of love, when broken, ensnare her in
a different kind of bondage. When she sees herself with a lover's eyes,
she loses her own vision when she loses him. Love and dependence,
like seduction and betrayal, are structured by the social realities in
which they occur.

Throughout the past twenty-five years—the years of today's midlife women's adulthood—love has less and less often been seen as an
answer to women's problems and the end of her story; more and more
often, love is seen as the beginning of difficulty and the source of conflict. This changed perspective rests on the growing understanding that
love is not "woman's whole existence,"⁵ but an important part of a
very different whole.

What may, initially, put women at a disadvantage in achieving
equal power within a love relationship is their overriding fear of isolation, abandonment, and loneliness. A basic psychological difference
between boys and girls is thought to center on differences between feeling oneself linked to or connected with others, and seeing oneself as
separate, bounded, and distinct from others.⁶ The different weight
given to independence and connection involves different ideas of what
is safe and what is dangerous. It has been repeatedly found that girls
and women fear isolation and see intimacy as a point of safety; whereas
boys and men are likely to feel that in coming close to another person
they put themselves—a self they see as essentially separate and distinct—at risk. "For men," Lillian Rubin writes, independence is "al-

most universally something to be desired; for women, it's generally something to fear."[7]

Whereas girls and women see lost relationships as a danger, boys and men, apparently, see closeness as the danger. When boys and girls were asked to write stories in response to a picture showing a man and a woman seated side by side on a bench near a bridge, their stories expressed widely different themes. The stories adolescent boys told involved tales of conspiracy, jealousy, and betrayal, whereas girls told stories about the figures' proximity, which involved protection, comfort, and hope. The closeness of the seated figures inspired fear in boys and signaled safety for girls. Maggie Scarf, writing about women and depression, recounts a discussion with Marcia Guttentag shortly before her death. Guttentag had analyzed major themes in men's and women's popular magazines and found that the stories for men primarily concerned adventure, achievement, and triumph over difficult odds, whereas the central theme of the women's stories was coping with loss.[8] The centrality of relationships in women's lives, and women's sense of self as connected to others, make them vulnerable to loss. As relationships are damaged or destroyed, a woman may feel that her essential self is threatened.

This fear of loss, blinding her to potential dangers within the relationship, may be the starting point of women's loss of power within a partnership. Carol Gilligan has noticed a pattern than emerges in the emotional development of some girls and women. They start with the universal human urge to make connections with others, but as they continue to forge these bonds, they are pushed on a route from disturbance, to despair, to dissociation.[9] As the need for attachment promises to be met, a girl or woman may hear disturbing things within the relationship. She may learn that she is not heard, that her opinions do not count, that her emotions do not structure their joint lives in the ways a partner's do. Even worse, she may hear disparagement of what she is worth, what she is likely to attain, what she has a right to think and do and say. She may discover that her feelings will not matter in this relationship, that her role is subservient to someone else's purpose. Yet so greatly does she value the attachment, that she does not wish to leave it, even as she learns these things. She may protest, but her protests, in a context in which she is de-voiced, will be ineffective. As she stays within a relationship in which her own needs are silenced, she feels despair: Both connected, and isolated, she is at an impasse. She may be unaware that she is bereft of power. When she does see how her own feelings are submerged, she can begin to repossess her voice and her power.

Self-Assertion versus Loss

Few women forgo love in midlife, but few women find their loving relationships unchanged. Major questions are raised by even minor changes in a significant relationship. At forty, many women reported becoming more sensitive to the ways in which their negotiations—over a kitchen design, or a holiday, or child's clothing, or grocery shopping—might be outmaneuvered. This greater sensitivity often led to ambivalent feelings. Was it worth fighting for their preferences, they would ask themselves. "We visit the schools together, but he asks the questions." Subeta, explained. "Of course I have a say [in choosing a high school for her son] but my 'say' just gets hit down if it's different from his. Not that he's disrespectful, but he just has more to say. A longer list of reasons! So I guess he cares more. It matters more to him, you know? But when it's something I do care about, I have to step out of things. Instead of listening to each point, I have to remind myself: 'He's like this; he's going to go on for a bit; but there will be point for me to come back, as long as I don't give in . . . ' because, he doesn't see us as disagreeing, since I usually do give in. Like, 'O.K., O.K.,' just because he keeps on."

Even in secure, generally positive relationships, women noticed an imbalance, which needed correcting. For Subeta, the realization came in a critical moment. "I was about to do the usual—'O.K., O.K., if it matters so much to you . . . '—but before the words were out of my mouth I felt this nausea . . . like, I don't want to say that. So I keep talking, and he gets angry, like 'Why are you arguing? Do you really want to argue?' Oh, I was feeling worse. See now," she held out the palm of her hand for me to examine, "I sweat just thinking about it. What got me was how afraid I was—seeing that was worse than the fear. And here I am, a grown woman, afraid of a little argument? It didn't make sense. So I said, 'Yes, I'm willing to argue because I want you to listen.' Am I just a stupid kid, or do other people go through these dramas every day? Because I was really afraid, sick to my stomach

. . . like he was going to hit me or leave me or just chew me up in his mind, hating me. And you know him and me—this isn't what the relationship is really like, except on some level I guess it is, and this isn't right."

The exaggeration of her response is characteristic of midlife development: As women begin to notice their fears, as they begin to feel what has been suppressed, they magnify it in order to see it more clearly. Subeta can see how she once would have seen this as unimportant—a funny habit her husband had, one of those peculiar tricks he had of getting his own way. Now, however, under pressure to see herself as a mature woman, she calls up a childhood stage, making use of one aspect and resisting another. In wondering whether she is "just a stupid kid," she allows the buffeting emotions of childhood to emerge, but looks at them with her woman's eye. She sees the child's fears—of being struck, abandoned, hated—but she sees them as inappropriate. These fears, however, cannot simply be dismissed with a magic wand. It has been, after all, at points like this one—wherein she is de-voiced and threatened with retaliation—that she has responded with the despair of silence ("like O.K., O.K., because he just goes on"). Seeing the pattern, she still feels afraid ("I sweat just thinking about it."). What frightens her, however, is the process enacted within her—the self-silencing, the shame of giving in because she is inappropriately frightened. Argument now seems the best way forward, and she challenges her husband's assumption—previously their mutual assumption—that they do not want to argue. She is willing to, she declares, in order to have a real say.

Changes in relationships, however, require more than one crisis moment: Changes in the status quo need constant reinforcement. Six months later, and then a year later, I interviewed Subeta, and "shadowed" her in her home. "I don't know what it was with me," she reflected. "I can't really name the fear—just some awful dread, if he would think . . . I don't know, it's strange . . . just something bad of me."

"Does it come back?" I asked. "Just once in a while?"

She paused for thought, unwilling to make a slick denial. "It's sometimes there," she began, "but it seems so far away. What's creepy is how far away it is now, when it was so close before."

The objections she had heard were strongly felt but vaguely imag-

ined ("just something bad of me"). These vague whispers of a mascu-
line, critical judge had wielded a force that she could not notice until
she was able to overpower it. Several women in their fifties had similar
recollections of past constraints. Jennie, at 55, reflected: "I guess it
was—well, it was ten years ago, because I remember it was when we'd
moved to this town, and there were all these decisions to make. Some
of them real small, but I could still feel anxious—things like choosing
an oven, or deciding which electrician to use . . . and then, there were
different ones, but the feeling was the same, about whether to apply for
a job, whether I wanted it, should I take it, that sort of thing. And
every time I was just about to make a decision, I had to put everything
on hold, and get Mark to say something. Even if he didn't care, I had
to hear him, to help me through this undergrowth. Because I kept
hearing these jabbering doubts. And once you hear them, once you're
aware, you see just how ridiculous they are, because all they're doing is
holding you back. I was forcing Mark to have ideas or objections because—well, I think I was worried that somehow if I didn't make the
right decision—whatever that is—that I'd disappoint him, or he'd
blame me, or I'd somehow be punished . . . . "

The micro-thoughts that had once given a kind of density to her
decision-making processes now seemed illusory. She recalled the power
of the Over-Eye, which dictated standards and threatened sanctions
should she fail to meet those standards. The process of reclaiming capacities for independent decisions was, in these healthy relationships,
simply a matter of shifting perceptions and persistent enacting of what
they now saw to be sensible and right. Molly Ann, at 53, looked me
directly in the eye, and explained: "Yes, my relationship with my husband has changed. It's new, and we both see the difference. Before, I
held in my mind some imaginary scale. Everything I did for him or for
the family went on one side, and everything I didn't do went on another. Do you get the picture? There I am, trying to decide whether to
go to a meeting on Thursday, and what I'm thinking is that if I have
this time to myself on Thursday, then I'd better drive him to the Metro
on Tuesday and Wednesday, and maybe then, it will be all right to do
my own thing on Thursday. Now I'm talking about something that
went on for years, questions about how selfish I was, how much I was
neglecting either my husband or my son, how much I was asking my

husband to do for the house or our kid—this nitpicking was a constant activity. And I can see it in younger women, pushed to the hilt with their thinking that they have to work and still have to contribute a hundred-and-one per cent to the family. I look at them and I see it, this constant measuring up of what they do and what they don't do."

Free of the imagined objections and imaginary measures, she now marks her decisions with a far more direct reference to what it is she wants to do. Like Jennie who, at 55, can cut through the undergrowth of "jabbering doubts," which used to "slow her down," there is a new capacity to address her own feelings without fear.

Gaining self-assurance and the power of self-assertion even within a secure and strong relationship can be difficult. It is far more difficult to find a new strong voice within a relationship that may be destroyed by it. The women who banished these jabbering voices, who cut through the undergrowth that slowed them down, who found a direct line to what they saw, realized that their fears the relationship might end were groundless. A power was theirs for the taking. What about women who were threatened with loss? Were midlife women better or worse at dealing with it?

Change can be dangerous. As the balance of power in a couple shifts, the relationship may topple. As one partner tries to change, the other may answer with punitive control. Among expansive women who returned to school, we saw how a woman's gathering strength could threaten her partner. Some women, for the sake of marital harmony, suppressed their excitement and intellectual growth while they were at home, and gave it free rein only with their fellow students. But such disguises can be dangerous: A woman may find that she cannot, after all, lift her disguise, and she instead silences her growth. Sometimes the path ahead can only be found once a woman leaves a relationship.

Like Subeta, Jennie, and Molly Ann, Charlotte Cohen believed, at 42, that she had the capacity to change the balance of power within her relationship. Five years after her first marriage ended, she felt ready to start again with a new partner. "I knew the patterns—I thought so, anyway. I thought I knew how things happened, so this time, I thought I could prevent . . . being bulldozed into this or that. You see it coming and you can prevent it—right?"

But Charlotte could not find a way to avoid "being bulldozed into this or that."

> I thought I was going into this relationship with my eyes open. I thought I knew who I was. But when he started shouting . . . when I heard the names and felt his anger, it was like being a child again. Things could hurt so much—shouting and stuff like that. He's so disappointed when I don't want to do something, when I'm not willing to change my plans to suit him, and when he starts shouting, my throat hurts—it really hurts when your feelings are hurt. Maybe things take time to settle down and you have to stay in something to work at it, work things out, because that's what I know my friends would tell me. And they know and I know how bad it can feel being alone, how difficult it is to get to this point, and feel ready to make a commitment. But coming so far—through a marriage and divorce, and all the while struggling with my career and the children, always balancing things and struggling. How can I go back to being that suffering child? Even if things are some day going to get better, it feels so awful that I don't want it. He says I'm getting worse, but it's just passive resistance, and I hate it. You just start feeling ambivalent about everything. If I were younger—yes—I'm sure I would try harder, and maybe get some professional guidance—maybe he'd listen to someone else, because he doesn't listen to me, or to himself with me, he doesn't see how he punishes.

Charlotte has begun with the assumption that being forewarned is forearmed: She is old enough to see how power might be taken away from her, and she thinks that therefore she can prevent it. She finds, however, that in this relationship, her attempts to retain—or gain—power are punished. This punitive process casts her back into the role of a suffering child, whose throat hurts with that choking pain of rejection and criticism. She sees how she might at one time have made the choice to suffer in the hope of subsequent improvement. This view, which she rejects, she nonetheless aligns with the commonsense view, the advice she is sure her friends would give her. But in being "patient," she dissociates herself from her own feelings. Using her feelings as a source of knowledge, she does not "want it." But looking ahead to potential loneliness, she wonders whether she should "pay attention" to her own suffering. What she notices is that now she has the power of choice, as she might not have when she was younger.

Then an interesting twist occurs in her train of thought. Propelled by anxiety, she scans each problem. But as she considers how difficult it is to get to the point at which one is ready to make a commitment, the meaning of a difficult journey changes. She reflects on how far she herself has come, through marriage and divorce, and the constant struggle as a single mother with her career and her children. The value of her relationship with her new partner, and the point to which it has come, is then contrasted with the journey she herself has undertaken in daily struggles, which has given her the measure of her own feelings, which she does not want to bury.

"What are you going to do?" I asked.

Her tense face broke, momentarily, in a smile. "I don't know. I've—decided. Yes, I think I've decided, that this won't work, because I'm not willing to work at it. I don't have the patience, because I so dislike what I feel . . . what I feel I am when we argue. But there's all—all this other stuff. You know, telling the children and my friends, and—'Oh, there she goes again, jettisoning another lover.' I've decided—but not worked it out."

Listening to her reflections, I was reminded of Huck Finn feeling guilty about doing "bad" things, such as helping Jim escape, relieving his pain and sharing companionable pleasures with a slave. As some judge criticizes her for her lack of patience and condemns her for "jettisoning yet another lover," Charlotte half-thinks she is wrong to act upon her own feelings. Even as she mouths conventional attitudes, she resists the social construction of a woman's goodness and gives the greatest weight to her feelings.

THOUGH CHARLOTTE AT TIMES doubted how much weight to give her feelings, she never doubted what she felt. Some women approach midlife so badly dissociated from their emotions that they do not know what they feel or trust what they see. Doubt about our own judgment locks us into a nightmare of uncertainty. It thrusts us into the world of tragic fantasy, in which we have no means of checking up on perception, no means of knowing whether what we see is truth or illusion. Bad judgments get worse as they accumulate. For a woman at forty to see that she was "still as stupid as at seventeen" is a terrible blow. Instead of seeing what has long been known but not realized, and demanding of herself, "Why did it take so long to trust myself?" a woman may ask, "How long do I have to wait before I can trust myself?" or "How can I know what I feel?" Many women who posed this question sought psychological therapy: They needed some point of reference outside their own.

> You feel yourself in slow motion. You're not in contact with what you're doing—except that you are. You know, what you do matters but you yourself aren't linking it up. The worst part is when you forget that you are an underwater creature, and you think you're in sync with the real world, and then something awful happens—you find yourself involved with someone you know after five minutes is a real jerk, but you don't see what you can do about it. And it gets worse as you get older because you know you've been here before, but you don't know how to get out. I'm used to waiting for it to end. I can't do that again. Just wait. The waiting and the panic. How much time do I have left?

As she confronts her lack of control and her inability to grow, Bonnie Jean Simon, at 42, pivots towards despair: There is, she feels, no way out, no point at which she can begin to link up with an Inner-Eye, since she does not trust what she sees. She enlists help by appealing to "an expert who can make more sense of this than me." As she acknowledges this impasse between her responses and her judgment, she seeks but cannot find access to her own voice, buried by confusion and fear since puberty, when her mother, instead of locking her into a tower like Rapunzel, eloped herself and left her children, who discovered her "escape" as they returned from school to an empty house "with all her things gone. I couldn't believe it. I couldn't think what to do. I always turned to [my mother] for advice—for anything. Now there was no one to turn to." Yet it is not until midlife that she identifies that "big hole which squeezed everything else to some dark edge," and seeks help to avoid thinking that "every man who smiles at me is going to balloon into the right one—this time, the right one."

She sees both the ideal and its falsehood as she reflects upon the patterns of her relationships, but she cannot see them together, both at once. She knows that in the past she has been wrong, but each time she meets someone new, she thinks that, this time, it might be right. She thinks both that this time might be different, and that she is stupid to think so. As a result, Bonnie Jean spent an enormous amount of time and energy treating small details of ordinary life as though they were part of an elaborate puzzle. After one of my shadow days with her, she was walking with me to my car, and seemed reluctant for me to go. "What do you think of us, then?" she asked.

I was already seated in the car, and mentally plotting the route home. Her question upset me, going to the heart of my ambivalence about interviewing people who believe that a researcher's groping questions will provide answers for their own problems. "What do I think of you?" I echoed, hoping that the question would crumble as I repeated it.

"I mean, what should I do to keep things together? Because don't you think that this is really good? And I don't want to ruin things. But I don't know how to keep them together."

I thought of Jeri Coppersmith and her realization that she could "ruin" the relationships she craved. But I also felt this was different, because Jeri had been sound in love, just too frightened to believe in it. I had seen nothing much between Bonnie Jean and her friend—nothing other than a man who had dropped in to drink some beer and mend a fuse, in whose company she laughed a lot.

"What do you think this needs?" she persisted.

"Just be yourself," I answered lamely.

Her presumption that relationships were terribly fragile bothered me. I kept seeing some delicate glass key that would splinter as soon it was slipped into a lock. When I rang her two months later, she could barely remember the man who had momentarily stopped by during my shadow day. Instead, it was someone else, a new recruit at her work. When we met again, four months later, she said, "I can see myself manufacturing these love affairs out of nothing, and then hating the guy because his agenda was different. I can see what it was to him, and that makes me sick, because it was so different to me. But I can only see things once they've passed."

Anticipating a subsequent interview a year later, I was nonetheless optimistic. Most of the women were marching forward during these years, with clear strides away from that "girlishness" that, as Anita Brookner had noticed,[10] was their enemy, while retrieving that young girl's skill in observing and accepting the imperfect panorama of human emotions. Bonnie Jean was, after all, in therapy, and was in touch with her problem, even if she had not quite grasped it. She seemed to anticipate my curiosity, for she launched immediately into an explanation of her advance—and her stall: "There are these little squares in my life that I just can't see through. They're painted, and I see the things on them as real, so I don't always know where the squares are that are covering the real world." She meant that some of her experience was a source of sound knowledge, but some of her experience persistently misled her. The challenge was not to distrust all her experience, just because she was partially sighted; and the trick to meeting this challenge was to identify points of blindness—those squares painted so that what was on them looked real to her. "It helps me to know this," she continued, "because I can learn where they might be. And since every guy I like is bound to be painted onto one of those squares, I have to go easy. I now go by a few rules, because when you know you can't see something, you just need a guide."

When that key to growth—trust in her own experience—was slow to come so, too, was her advance; but she was nonetheless progressing, no longer struck by the ideal of the man who would balloon into a perfect fit for the hole inside her.

IN SOME WOMEN, THE fear of loneliness, which Charlotte eventually confronts as the lesser of two dangers, and the self-distrust, which Bonnie Jean was beginning to overcome, can combine with anxiety at wasted time and emotion. The awareness of time passing pressed upon Kathy Selby the necessity of seeing, "that if I keep going on this way, I'll get further and further away from any place I really want to be at. But the funny thing is, as soon as you say this to yourself, you can take one step, and you're where you want to be. It felt real strange at first. It still feels strange, like the dizziness you feel, you know, when you stop spinning. But that doesn't mean you'd feel better if you start spinning again, does it?"

Kathy had, for the past five years, a relationship with a man whose "marriage was always about to come to a this time final end." She and her lover, both 44, had once been colleagues. He had moved to a different firm, and the relationship continued, but gradually became lower and lower key. "There was this instinct to hang on. Such a strong impulse," she reflected. She was never his mistress in the conventional—though somewhat dated—sense of being financially supported or indulged by him. But there were many trappings of the conventional mistress/lover arrangement, with secrecy, with rules for telephoning that applied to her phoning him, but not to him phoning her, with arrangements that were commonly cancelled because of family commitments, which took priority over promises to her.

"Something happened when I hit 42," she explained. "A delayed response to being 40, because I at first felt forty wasn't so bad. But it doesn't go away, does it? I was going to get older, and that was that. I could no longer believe that things would work out one day, that everything would just switch around and be suddenly good. No matter how young you feel, there's this idea of yourself that's changing. And I saw what I guess everyone else would have seen a long time ago—that there just wasn't any future in this."

The ideal future crumbles, and in its wake she is released from persistent humiliation. "I had to end it—I had to deal the final blow. I was seeing him less and less, but thinking about him more. I had to think about him because I was always wondering why I wasn't seeing him and when I would see him. I'd be out for a few minutes and when I came in I was rushing to that phone machine, staring at the little red light to see if it was flashing. Nothing could stand between me and that answering machine. Once I discovered it wasn't working and I went wild. I'm ashamed of it now—it's funny I guess—and I was ashamed of it then—shouting into this empty room because I did not know whether he called while I was out. I'm proud that I ended it. I'm really proud, and after work I can just go out in the evening. I don't think about whether he wants to visit that evening. I can just go. I'm far less lonely now than I was with him."

Often, when someone describes a binding situation, the listener wants to ask "Why did it take so long to see the constraints and do away with them?" How much could one phone call have given Kathy for her to "shout into this empty room" as she tried to catch past echoes of a ringing phone? Why did she have to be forty, then forty-one, then forty-two before she could stop "spinning"? There is an awful temptation to say—perhaps like Oprah, confronting a woman who is beaten by her partner—"Girl, why don't you *leave?*" I tried to take Kathy back to the time when she could not step off that spinning ground, to discover what kept her there, and why she had been able to change.

She did not answer right away. The question was difficult: It involved seeing what she had tried to put aside for so long. It also meant, now, seeing what had been good in the relationship, why she had felt so dependent on it, and realizing, again, that she did not have it.

It's never been easy for me, finding someone I'm interested in, who's also interested in me. For ten years, there really hasn't been anyone important. So though I knew all the time that the Stephen I loved was only a small part of the real Stephen, I felt that he was all I'd have, all I'd ever have. And once you feel that—well, that's it. You put up with anything in order to keep it. And the thought of losing it is terrible. So when people—and you're not the only one—ask me why, I feel we're talking from different sides of the moon. Other people—my friends, my parents—would say, "He's not the only fish in the sea." But that meant nothing to me. Where are these other fish anyway? So I couldn't comfort myself with the idea that there would be someone else . . . but feel my way around—it's like feeling in the dark, feeling things without knowing what they are—and see how maybe there was a string I could tie to this—say, my work—and maybe a string here to this, like a good movie—or this, like a fine meal. And I just keep going until it seems stable enough. And that isn't something that was easy for me . . . because it was always easy to fall back to him. So that's it—why it took so long, because it was hard, and I had to see that, really, staying put was going to be harder . . . and that I could do it.

Women do fear loneliness on a very deep level, and this fear may color their decisions, but the crisis questions midlife women asked concerning their ability to use their own perceptions and feelings as sources of knowledge, help to limit this fear. More dangerous than loss and betrayal, are the costs love exacts. In my sample, I found no women in their fifties who had a problem of "loving too much." It may be little consolation to anyone who has "wasted" emotion in a relationship, that at fifty she will probably have the resources and the courage to step off that "spinning" ground, but it is interesting that the developing strength of women has been systematically ignored. "My happiness is suddenly more precious," Lydia explained, after describing how she had ended a relationship that made her feel "like a crushed limpet." "I guess it sounds strange to say that because I want to be happy I don't want love! But that was it—love wasn't making me happy. I don't know why it took me so long to see that. Well, I'm 55 now, and that seems like an achievement. I want to match it with other parts of my live—because I've achieved things in my work that I'm really proud of . . . what I mean is . . . I want to peg the best part of me with the other parts. All that dependence . . . it just stopped making sense."

Love lessons may be the hardest to learn because they engage such a range of emotions and have so many ramifications. A greater impulse toward connection may delay women's knowledge of what boys learn early—that intimacy can be dangerous, and that love is not a story of safety but of potential betrayal, wherein they can betray themselves as easily as they can be betrayed by another. Love is dangerous because, through love and the hope that love engenders, a woman may be expected to give too much and may be willing to offer too much. Women are more likely to see a failed relationship as a betrayal because they feel betrayed in two senses: let down by a relationship, which they once trusted, and let down by themselves for having given too much or compromised too much.

Dealing with Loss

As women take risks, giving voice to their perceptions and feelings, they may also have to ask, "What will it be like outside the relationship?" As women addressed this question, there was distinctive layering of response—memories of loss, of recovery, observations of others' loss, all blended to make midlife love-loss much more likely to be a task of deliberate self-rearrangement, rather than the devastating displacement it is popularly conceived to be.

> You think you're over it. You think you've learned what men are—or what you become with men. But there's that eternal recurrence—is it always the same? You feel that fire in your belly, and think "I've been there before." But maybe that's the difference. You

know something about the lay of the land. So he's going, packing up, and you ask yourself: "What am I most afraid of?" And when it comes down to it, maybe all you're afraid of is being alone—getting used to being alone. For some it's the extra money. I've never been so lucky. Men and money don't seem to go together for me. But what I do—I'm an old hand, you see—I think a year ago, maybe only six months ago, I didn't have him. I can go back to where I was. Where I was hasn't always been great, but it's never been unlivable. And that's what you do for the next month or so. It's not like the first bust up, or divorce after a twenty-year marriage. Going back to B.C. ['before Chris'] isn't such a big jump.

For Carlene Dasilva, 48, past experience offered a promise of recovery. With greater self-diversity, she also knows that everything is not tied up in one person. "Maybe the pain's as bad as it ever was, but you just can't think, at this age, that the world's going to end because of it. And when you see that, other things start working for you. There's this motor which keeps on running." She could trust other things to take over, other interests and needs and habits to keep her life running, while one segment temporarily stopped. And, like so many women, she saw her experience more clearly as she saw it mirrored in her daughter:

Only eighteen months ago I was sitting right here on this sofa telling my daughter that the world wasn't coming to an end just because her boyfriend dumped her. I felt like this far away from her pain. (her hand made a sweeping gesture, waving to something in the far distance) I sympathized, sure, but part of me just couldn't take it seriously. I see this kid with her life ahead of her and she's crying her heart out because of someone she'd probably throw over in a month or so anyway. When she thought things were wonderful it was funny—it was really funny. Singing and swinging on the bannister, and I wanted to warn her. I wanted to say, "Honey, this thing is not going to last—you better keep something back for yourself." But what warning from me is going to do anything other than prove to her that I don't know a thing. So I watch and wait and try to hold her together when it all goes wrong. I could see it happening. She knows it's falling apart. Her eyes are hard and her mouth quivers and she's not telling me anything because, oh boy, I'm going to say I was right. So she keeps up the bravado, until I come home one day and her little body's shaking like a leaf, and then I could hug her, and boy it's hard to keep from laughing a little, while that just makes her boil. But there she is, young and more strong than she knows, and I know this is going to hurt and I know this going to pass. But here I am, over thirty years on, and still feeling the same thing, crying myself and shaking, just like my 16-year-old daughter. Except it's not quite the same, because even while it's hitting you, punching away at your guts, you can just about see around the edges. It's not much, is it— thirty years, and this is how you creep a tiny bit forward? But it's not nothing, either, is it?

The split between the controlled empathy she felt for her daughter's pain and the immediate experience of her own, allowed Carlene to see both the depth and the limitation of her plight. She speaks of herself as a knowing "I" when she describes her daughter's pain, but them switches to some general representative "you" as she observes herself. Cautiously, she both experiences her pain and seeks ways of seeing beyond it. And, as so often in midlife women, the daughter's or son's experience inspires self-knowledge. The key to recovery from a lost relationship is seeing that the self outside that relationship is still resourceful, still energetic, still able to engage with other people and in other activities in meaningful ways. Younger women, of course, can and do recover from lost relationships, but in so doing they also face dangers and difficulties, which older women are remarkably good at avoiding. For Carlene draws upon two different resources as she explains the limits of her pain. She knows from experience that life goes on—in particular, that her life will go on; and second, she sees her daughter's pain and despair. She distances herself from her daughter's feelings because she sees her daughter's life as so much larger that her present suffering. She sees that her daughter believes that she has lost her self; but Carlene knows she has not. By seeing the density of her daughter's life, she is reminded of her own, and her own potential recovery.

Jealousy

Jealousy, like envy, is thought to be a special problem for midlife woman. Younger women stalk the prestige and wealth of their partners who, in turn, race into the honeyed trap of the nubile female. Midlife women, it is supposed, have more to lose when they lose a partner. A younger women has "horizons," a midlife woman sits at the edge. Her chances for remarriage are deemed slim. Hence, she jealousy guards whatever male she possesses. But does she?

It is difficult to measure how jealous a woman is because jealousy is not always present. Unlike envy, jealousy is aroused in a specific context. Envy is the inability to tolerate other people's pleasures or successes. It stems from a sense of deep inadequacy: When one feels powerless to reach one's own goals, the power, or luck, or vitality of others causes one pain. Jealousy, however awful, is simple in contrast to envy. It is aroused when something one has—a partner, a relationship, a position—is disrupted or possessed by someone else. The three women who spoke about jealous love had just cause. Beth Wilson's husband of twenty years was having an affair with another, slightly younger woman. Gail Heiss's lover had left her for a friend. And Christiane Jacbobson's husband, after a year's separation, had remarried and was starting a new family.

Each woman spoke about jealousy as a conflict between different parts of her self. Her history and those she loved were part of her—now the parts had been flung wide, and she had to reassemble. Beth, at 40, was at the brink of midlife growth. Having just begun to think about the changes she would like to make in her career, she discovered her husband's infidelity. "There is no stable point to my life—or my feelings now," she explained. "I'm crushed, and frightened, and angry—I want him back, and I don't. I want her to die, but I don't care. I feel divided because I'm devastated—and also, there's something inside that's untouched. This is the strangest feeling—that I'm not destroyed."

Such recoveries are slow. No midlife growth, however rapid and broad, can protect us from human pain. But jealousy took on a distinctive form; it was layered, like the midlife self. Beth saw facets of emotion, so that the untouched part of herself could function alongside those that were "crushed." The self-security was new, unexpected ("This is the strangest feeling . . . "). Her suffering is layered by a continuing empathy: "I know how much fun it is for him, getting to know another person . . . having that fun . . . all those unexpected discoveries, and the excitement. But it's still hard for me . . . very hard." Unhappy, she feels his happiness, "because you're so used to caring for him, you often forget how it's hurting you."

For Gail, 46, the humiliation seemed to spur her to a resolution of her crisis: "I've been mulling over so much lately—wondering about whether I might do things that I've wanted to do for a long time—little thing, just going places, and buying things. They sound like nothing— except to me, just looking around a city I've heard about, is more than recreation. It heals something. And what I feel in the center of everything else . . . I feel a will to survive and forget this and not be too hurt. I was so worried about it—before he really left me—it seemed so awful—so dirty, somehow, that's how I felt, that dirty feeling you have when you're guilty—something like that. A nightmare sense—so thick that you keep expecting it to drop away and you'll be flooded with relief. But now—there's nothing, almost as though the pain wasn't there. And the jealousy, too . . . it's just not that strong. I never thought I would feel so little, now that it's over. And I want to celebrate—not because I'm happy, but because I'm still here."

Her loss and jealousy slotted into the midlife flow, a reminder of mortality, alongside her knowledge of potential. In contrast to previous experience, when she remembered "wanting to carve [a rival's] face with the knife that was in [her] stomach," she now felt less vengeful because she was not focusing on how they saw her—or failed to see her. "Because at that time, if I imagined them thinking about me, I felt puny, because of the way they were seeing me. If I thought they weren't thinking about me, then I felt obliterated." Still attached to the gaze of her boyfriend, she had felt defined by what he saw. As he found happiness elsewhere, she had felt there was no place for her in the world. Discovering that, at 46, she could weather all that, she wanted to celebrate being "still here."

Christiane Jacobson, 49, whose husband had recently left her and was now living with a much younger woman, described "hot spots of awful jealousy," and she envied the woman who was now receiving her husband's love, but that was only "one item" among a whole host of feelings. Most of the women whose divorce or separation had been instigated by a partner's attachment to another felt, at some time, both jealous and envious: They wanted to repossess the partner's love and to regain that important place in his life, and they envied the good things—the closeness, the alliance, sometimes even the fresh excitement of the new love. "It's like a whirlpool, all this . . . Just sitting, I sometimes feel I'm sucked into it. I guess I forgot how much things could hurt. But it's clear very early on that you can turn one way or another. You can look towards them—you know the happy couple—or you can turn away and look ahead at your own life. That's really the choice—what I feel anyway. For me, I get out of breath just thinking about them, and you go over and over it and it gets worse and worse. What they must think of you, how you're nothing to them. You don't want their sympathy, that's just making it worse again, turning you into something—you know, what can I be from their point of view? So I turn away from all that, and all the other stuff—the finances, the house, the objects, piles and piles of stupid objects that used to be simple things, with no meaning . . . it just adds to that weight I'm carrying around, and I just keep going, trying to look forward."

As Christiane switches from seeing herself as "you" ("You don't want their sympathy"), she distinguishes herself from that you ("You know, what can I be from their point of view") and then takes charge ("So I turn away from all that . . . "). This spinning drama is likely to recur. It is not a single act, with a final resolution, but it shows the skill of turning away from jealousy and envy, and towards her self, which is the only way forward. What she assesses in this tale of pain and conflict is that thinking about "the happy couple" pulls her away from recovery.

Jealousy could threaten long after divorce, even when the new attachment was unrelated to the split. Christiane suffered a recurrence of jealousy when her former husband's child was born. The feeling, she explained was "just physical," a "pang" and has "nothing to do with what I really want now. The last thing I want is another baby, and yet when I heard about the birth I felt like a whip struck me. Don't ask me why. I can't say why, if you think in terms of my wanting to be her, or be like her, or even have him back. It's just like part of you is suddenly somewhere else, doing other things. You can't just snap off your past, can you?"

Having lost a husband, she felt one part of herself was residing somewhere else, and she could not disconnect her sense of belonging— even to his child by another partner. The startling realization of some other life linked to hers, but doing quite different things, can "strike like a whip." But then this realization turns into something else, as the whiplash becomes a reminder of her past, part of her unique history. She first feels, and then recognizes the pain—like Virginia Woolf's wonderfully realized midlife Mrs Dalloway, who, in dealing with the bitterness of a broken relationship with Peter Walsh, "felt herself everywhere; not 'here, here, here'; and she tapped on the back of the seat; but everywhere—. . . so that to know her, or anyone, one must seek out the people who completed them. . . ."[11] Since she no longer sees herself as "a single point," as a suitable object either of pity or derision, the intensity of jealousy—with its insistence on possession and its links with shame or humiliation—eases. The midlife, multilayered self is actually better equipped to deal with jealousy.

Sexuality beyond Sexiness

All too often, a young woman's sexual initiation involves awareness of herself as an object of desire, rather than awareness of herself as feeling desire. Adolescent girls notice, first, their changed appearance, then the changes in other's responses to them—and only much later do they register changes in their own feelings. Their desires are pegged to the desires of others. Young men, believing that a woman will be seduced by admiration, may further deaden the line to her own feelings. This process is wonderfully described by Doris Lessing's novel *Martha Quest*:

> She was ready to abandon herself, but he continued to kiss her, murmuring how beautiful she was. Then he smoothed her skirt up to her knee and stroked her legs, saying over and over again, in a voice troubled by something that sounded like grief, that her legs were lovely, she was so lovely. Her drowning brain steadied, for she was being forced back to consciousness. She saw herself lying there half

exposed on the bed; and half resentfully, half wearily partook, as he was demanding of her in the feast of her own beauty. Yes, her legs were beautiful . . . Yes, but this is not what I want, she thought confusedly: she was resenting, most passionately, without knowing that she resented it, his self-absorbed adoration of her, and the way he insisted Look at yourself, aren't you beautiful.[12]

Martha Quest is excluded from her own feelings as she is introduced to a man's desire. She is conscious of every curve in her body—not because she feels it anew, but because she is "scrutinizing it with his eyes." She feels cold and hostile as he refers to her breasts as "them"; but "some kind of guilt, like a tenderness, made her slide obediently into the curve of his arm."

The eye of the lover distracts her so that she cannot see what she feels: being "womanly," she shows tenderness because she feels guilty. Her subjective sexual feelings are subservient to an awareness of herself as seen by her lover. If this imbalance continues in midlife then she may find her own sexuality deleted: No longer the paragon of male desirability, she may believe there is no other path to desire.

Is this why Germaine Greer said that the midlife woman who no longer has any interest in sex is lucky?[13] Do the complications of sexual love linger too long and remain too messy? Does she want to avoid forever the "thick" unhappiness, the "dirtiness" of which Beth spoke as she foresaw the end to her relationship? Is she asking, perhaps, the question the teenage girl asked Carol Gilligan and her co-researchers: "If the long journey does not end with perfection, what is all this expended energy about and for whose benefit?" For, in the context of sexual love, we will never be perfect and never be simple and never be final.

The thrust of Greer's remark, however, forces home an unexpected perspective. Greer tosses out the assumption that sex is essential to a good life. She highlights the fact that women have every right to lose interest in sex, and that when they do they should not be labeled as inadequate or unhealthy. If sex is a desire for pleasure, then it is pointless to try to keep the desire going when it fades. If sex ceases to be pleasurable, then why pursue it?

Sexual desire is not a desire like hunger, which signals our need for food. When we do not feel hungry we may still need to eat. Loss of desire for food is a problem because we then lack appropriate signs for our body's needs. Hence, anorexia—or loss of appetite—is a symptom, or an illness itself. When we do not want to eat—ever—we need medical treatment. But if sex ceases to tempt us, why bother with it, why "correct" our desires? If we have no appetite for sex, then we endanger nothing by failing to feed it. A woman who does not have sexual urges simply has fewer needs to satisfy. Why, Greer implies, can she not be left alone with this new simplicity?

This provocative remark was made with reference to menopause, which involves hormonal changes, which, in about 5% of women, leads to changes in their enjoyment and desire for sex. As the production of estrogen slows down, the vagina shrinks, changes shape, and its walls thin. As the production of testosterone diminishes, sex drive, or desire to have sex, may also decrease. The most common reaction, on hearing descriptions of "discomfort" (which is often extreme pain, causing 51-year-old Michelle to "sweat with pain for over an hour after sex") or diminished sex drive, is to suggest ways of easing the pain or stimulating arousal. The vaginal changes that accompany menopause can be easily prevented, or even reversed by replacing the estrogen that is lost at menopause. But are we too quick, as Greer suggests, to assume that someone who does not enjoy sex needs medical intervention? Are we not overlooking a woman's right not to be sexual? Are we not putting the burden on the woman to accommodate her partner's sexual drive, rather than on him to accommodate hers, whether it be high or low?

Greer goes further, as is her custom, to suspect a medical conspiracy, which endorses woman's sexuality at the cost of her health. In emphasising the (small, but persistent and problematic) risks associated with hormonal replacement therapy, Greer insists that the medical practice of offering hormonal replacement therapy rests on the desire to keep women sexually serviceable to men.

What this ignores is the meaning a woman's sexuality might have to her, and the context in which sexuality and sex occur. Sonya Friedman, interviewing Greer on her show *Sonya Live,* drove home this telling point: "Surely," Sonya asked, "the issue is whether a woman who wants sex is able to have it."

For some women, sex and their sexuality are nuisance factors, which they are indeed pleased to be released from. Most women, however, continue to value not only their sexual expressiveness and activity but also the dimension these add to some relationships. What will allow a woman to grow stronger in midlife is not release from sexuality, but new ability to read her own sexuality and to act on it, rather than fear rejection or loneliness or disapproval.

It is not pleasure alone that makes sex so deeply rooted in our lives. The desire to have sex is generally, in our complex human world, more than a desire to have pleasure satisfied. Good sex rests on the assumption that one's partner wants it, too, and will take pleasure in it and will carry some good feeling away after it. None of us always keeps this balance perfectly. Sex is one of many human feelings that has a tendency towards selfishness or submission. But for most of us it remains an involvement we want to sustain. It expresses and enforces connection. There was no difference I could see between post-, peri- and premenopausal women of comparable ages. The proportion of women who remained interested in sex was roughly the same for each group—between 68 and 72 percent. Menopause did not bring a woman's sexuality to a close—nor did it change it. In a few cases, women used menopause as a reason for bringing sexual activity to an end—but only because they had previously found it either distressing or distasteful. The only relation I could find between menopause and sexual interest was that midlife women were more willing to act on their feelings: Hence, the presence or absence of sexual desire was more likely to determine their sexual activity—whereas, previously, a woman's sexual activity may have been more closely linked to the desire of her partner. The physical changes of menopause, which sometimes made sex more difficult, were problems to be overcome. A woman was lucky if she no longer cared for sex only if, for other reasons, she preferred celibacy.

SEX IS NOT ONE thing, or one need, or one desire. There is no single answer to the role it plays in our lives or to the importance is has for us. Many young women say that the physical closeness—the cuddling—is more important than sexual pleasure.[14] Many teenagers describe sexual experience as the result of being led by a partner's desire or insistence, and find their own sexual desire either incidental or irrelevant.[15] For women—especially very young women—the roles and relationships that are associated with sex are more important than the sexual act itself. As adolescent girls grow aware of their sexuality, they are more likely to focus on the different relationships for which sexuality gives them potential.[16] Whereas adolescent boys are more likely to focus on their new ability to make love, girls focus on their ability to be a lover.

Throughout adulthood, in this respect, women change less—or more slowly—than men. As a man matures, he is more likely to increase his sensitivity to the emotional implications and complications and responsibilities of sexual intimacy. The challenge to a man's sexuality is to integrate his sexual feelings, which often arise through impersonal fantasies, with an emotional attachment to another person. A woman is more likely to start off with an awareness of the relational power of sex; in midlife, she often feels more adept at separating sex from the profound vulnerability that entangled it since adolescence. Sex often became a new kind of pleasure. Women said that they were more focused on the act and the satisfaction than on the mass of feelings that had struck them before. "Sex is now a source of fun, rather than hope and terror," Grace said. "I no longer worry about what I look like, what I seem like. I know—I've been married for thirty years so maybe I'm a bit slow. But who isn't? And who says this is sane? But it feels better." Other women enjoyed sex more because its impact was more limited: "I don't feel so shaken up by it," Lynn explained. "It doesn't spill over into my life the way it used to." For as women take charge of their subjective sexuality, the ghostly control of ideals and images, the doubts about a partner's pleasure or approval, the anxiety about meeting someone else's ideal, can be silenced.

A renewed interest in sex can have ambiguous consequences.

I appreciate young men's bodies in ways I never did before. The sheer luxury of a nice male body—I never noticed when they were all around me, and I was resisting and choosing. Now I take more initiative sexually—I'm after the sex, you see, not after promises or security or even love, though I'm quite moved by whatever affection I get. I guess you could say I'm using some of these guys. I do want them for the sex—though I also enjoy their company, and just being with them. Sex isn't just the screwing part. I feel ashamed of myself. No—I feel maybe I should be ashamed. But I'm fairly careful not to hurt anyone. I see for the first time how sweet these young men are. You know, they're vulnerable, too. Maybe if I had sons I would have

learned that a long time ago. But I didn't—. I realize how I've
changed. All those warnings about boys when I was in college—.
Now maybe their mothers should be warning them against me. All
that time I wasted being so suspicious of men. Oh, I had boyfriends.
I even had a husband for many years; but I was so wary. It wasn't just
my mother, of course, it was the way I experienced liberation in my
early adult life. And now I feel this strange thing—a sexual appreciation and a warm sympathy. I enjoy it, too, I know, because I'm the
one who has the power. But these relationships are not about
power—they're about sex, very pure sex!—it's just that I enjoy the
fact that they don't have power over me. It's sweet when they ask too
much—I guess I see it as sweet and funny, because I know I'm not
going to give them any more than I want to.

Sasha Newson took a long time to speak so directly. She started
and stopped several times, hinting at this or that, then turning away to
pursue another topic. She kept testing her limits, both wanting to describe her situations and wondering just how strange it would sound.
The flow of her humor seemed to push her to uncustomary disclosures.
The sexual awakening or heightening was both her and not her, both
something strange and something long missed. She found it much
easier to integrate this sexuality into her life because it was "contained"; it did not color every aspect of her life. She felt more like a
man pursuing younger women, and yet she also understood that the
sexual hunter was not all bad, was not necessarily cruel and had sympathies that extended beyond the sexual.

She was also expressing something else: a shift in her sense of
where power in the relationship lay. Love is supposed to be a meeting
of equals. Both men and women know it seldom is. Love and sexuality
touch our deepest, most primitive needs and our greatest fears. They
expose us to new dangers and activate extravagant hopes, which we
cling to even when we cease to believe in them. Young women and
even adolescent girls see the dangers of love, intimacy, and sexuality,
but often bury their knowledge. Hence, they love too much, and trust
too much. Their story about love is often one of seduction and betrayal, whether betrayed by a man, or another woman, or by herself.
The challenge, for midlife women, is not to avoid love's dangers, but to
participate in them and withstand them, to find within themselves

something uncompromised and bound to survive. As women bring into relationships more and more of their own thoughts and feelings, as they regain old skills in weathering the imperfections of attachments, they break the links between *women and love* and *seduction and betrayal.*

9 Love and Disengagement: Adult Daughters and Their Mothers

I n the final chapter of *Fierce Attachments*, Vivian Gornick's descriptions of her mother's stubborn love take on a surprising reversal as she hears her own voice in an argument that has become more soliloquy than dialogue. The mother's voice is now "remarkably free of emotion"; it is "detached, curious, only wanting information," while the child within the adult daughter launches one more campaign on behalf of some idealized independence. "Why don't you go already?" the mother asks. "Why don't you walk away from my life? I'm not stopping you."[1] The daughter, now in midlife, acknowledges her own clumsy attempts to resolve the permanent tension between them. She recognizes that her battle is directed not against her mother's current attempt to constrain or control her, but against all the different mothers of her past. Her mother has played many useful roles: as model, advisor, and supporter—and antagonist. She has grown by pitting her wits and energy against that elemental maternal reality. Now her efforts have a redundant clumsiness, but habit persuades her to persist yet one more time. Wearily admitting her own psychological choice in this argument, she says, "I know you're not, Ma." Yet enlightenment does not provide liberation. She still stands "half in, half out" of the mother's room.

The ideal of maturity is another ideal that fades in the maturity of midlife. A child's idea of what it is to be an adult is fixed and final. The adult seems to inhabit a different world, firmly bounded and secure.

This is the world we expect to enter as adults. In young adulthood, women often believe they should stand quite firmly and quite separately on their own two feet and look level-eyed at their mothers. They may chastise themselves—or their mothers—when this magical position is not achieved: They may blame either their own weakness or a mother's interference. But as the barriers of the different parts of the self are weakened, as the ideal of independent maturity gives way to acknowledgment of a flexible, layered self, they accept the variations in their own responses.

MOTHERS PLAY SUCH AN important role in their daughters' development that even the mature daughter may look upon her solely through the lens of her own needs, wishes, hopes, and disappointments. Steadfast in her subjectivity, she may remain blind to her mother's own experience. As Marianne Hirsch listened to her friends' conversations about their mothers on the one hand, and their conversations about their children on the other, she spotted a sharp contrast.[2] She heard "opposing voices which we each in various ways contained and could not combine. We found, in retrospect, that when we spoke as mothers, the group's members were respectful, awed, helpful in the difficulties of formulating maternal experiences. When we spoke as daughters about our own mothers, the tone and affect changed and we all giggled knowingly, reverting back to the old stereotyped patterns of discussing a shared problem—our 'impossible mothers'." The complex effort, love, and hope, which women in early adulthood experience as mothers, does not open their eyes to their own mothers' feelings. The sympathy they offered to one another as mothers could not be extended to their own—until they themselves were in midlife.

Some women in this generation of midlife mothers, especially those who sought different, innovative goals, dreaded having children because they were afraid they would become just like their own mothers. Sometimes having a daughter poses a special threat: A daughter will, she imagines, transform her into her own mother.[3] Most women are pleasantly relieved: Their individuality remains intact in spite of the onslaught of maternity. Later, as women and their children grow, the two channels of maternal images come crashing together as they see their own child looking back at them with the anger they felt toward their own mothers. In defense, they feign the self-righteous certainty they believed their own parents felt. They glare back at their children, furious not only at the current transgression, but also at being cast as a stolid, punitive parent.

The comic aspects of this reluctant recognition—of oneself as the authoritative parent one vowed one would never be—have been explored in Roseanne Arnold's television show. As Rosanne and Dan experience those distinctly parental feelings—of disapproval, anger, and loving control—they are overpowered by the fear of becoming the parents they remember. They battle with their children and feign self-confidence, while sympathizing with that brazen youthful anger raging against them. They are caught in the play their own family is now (re)enacting. The Conner family provides a mocking contrast to those well-known television families of the 1950s and 1960s, those of *The Donna Reed Show* and *Leave It to Beaver,* when each parent knew her place and his place; where, in their neatly separate ways of knowing, each knew best; where the parents, having reached that mythical plateau of maturity, were different kinds of beings from those funny children. "We have to be parents," Roseanne explains to her dubious husband when she sends Becky to her room. "We don't have to be *our* parents," Dan counters as they are faced with the task of chiding their daughter for making an obscene gesture in a class photo. The sincere determination to be a just and fair parent disintegrates under the more concrete irritations of having to visit the school principal, where they are kept waiting, and then admitted, only to be chided for their imperfect parenting skills. The mother becomes her child's "savior" only when her own humiliation finds an opportunistic expression in the discovery of her daughter's "innocence." Mother does know best, as she must in any acceptable TV family comedy, but the trajectory of her knowledge is hit and miss. Surely our generation of mothers has clearer memories of its adolescence than did our own mothers? We may assume the mask of maturity, but not with a straight face.

Midlife Children

According to traditional theories of child development, our feelings for our parents in adulthood should be easy and generous, cleansed of anger, resentment, and ambivalence. In light of how we do tend to feel, as adults, this theory about maturity, well-established within the psychological profession, is quite surprising. According to standard development theories, the maturing child, during adolescence, snaps those infantile bonds of love, admiration, idealization for the parents. The rebelliousness, restlessness, and moodiness sometimes associated with adolescence arise, it has been thought, from ambivalence. The adolescent, on the one hand, wishes to divorce herself from her love and dependence; on the other, she continues to love and need her parents. The adolescent fights her parents in order to destroy those internal parental images that hamper her maturity—a maturity that is conceived as self-made and self-bounded. Her attacks on her parents arise from two different complaints: to protest that they are not what they should be, and to sever her own expectations and idealizations. Adding to the conflict, and undermining the determination with which she battles, is an abiding loyalty; she wants to think well of her parents and to avoid hurting them. The quick turnaround in adolescent children between mature and infantile behavior is a symptom of a determined resistance against them on the one hand, and a continuing need not only for their love, help, and support but also for their own internal idealizations of the parents, on the other.

Eventually, it is thought, the maturing adolescent resolves this battle. Her parents shrink to human size. She accepts them as they are, no longer needing them to be what thy are not. Emerging from adolescence as a distinctive, independent self, she no longer needs such infantile props. Then she is able to reengage with her parents on better footing, forgiving them for the faults that at one time seemed unforgivable, and dissolving the rage and irritability that were based upon her great but immature dependence.

This theory has a pleasing narrative, punchy in its simplistic optimism. It gives a theatrical structure to a period of development that sometimes does seem like a drama enacted within a hidden context. There are many problems with the story, however—especially when the leading character is a daughter. Girls are known to be less committed to drawing self-boundaries, and less keen to define themselves through separation.[4] They are also more vulnerable to identification with their mothers, to being shadowed by her history and compelled by her approval. The "mature" person, graciously equipped to forgive parents their foibles and failings, purged of dependence and need for parental approval, unthreatened by past wishes, hopes and pressures, is not a real life character.

As I observed, for a previous project, mothers interacting with their teenage daughters,[5] I spoke to women about their own mothers. I was amazed by the passion aroused: anger, resentment, disappointment, as well as continuing love. This relationship was still in progress, still active, often unresolved, and above all, important. "Until I was in [my] forties," Virginia Woolf wrote, "the presence of my mother obsessed me. I could hear her voice, see her, imagine what she would do or say as I went round my day's doings."[6] Woolf's own history with her mother, who died when she was 13, may not be representative, but this, "haunting" by the mother up to middle adulthood, has a wide resonance. Though her "obsession" is linked to her mother's early death, the echoes of speech and action that are more intrusive than comforting, commonly sound in the most independent of women. Our parents do eventually shrink to something like mere human size, but the process is gradual and piecemeal and never complete. What we find instead, is an ability to function as though we were fully independent of them, but there remain hot underground springs of child-emotion, which, in various circumstances, gush forth, unadulterated by maturity.

Many women feel stuck in an adolescent pose vis-à-vis a mother. They still need her approval, and still criticize the approval she offers, because it isn't quite right, quite to the point, or quite what they wanted in the first place. As soon as they feel ready to forgive their mothers for some past transgression, they find themselves at her throat again, complaining of a look, a turn of phrase, an assumption or expectation that threatens the stability of their hard-won ground. And in the midst of their continuing battles against the mother, they discover her final triumph—the sound of her voice in theirs as they speak.

These discoveries, once, made many women feel that the mother's female personality and feminine history, were enemies to individuation and fulfillment. "Hating one's mother," Elaine Showalter has said, "was the feminist enlightenment of the 50's and 60's." Showalter explained what many mother-hating women knew well: that it was "only a metaphor for hating oneself."[7] But the metaphor was also a cause: Women resented certain feminine traits within themselves, and they blamed their mothers for them. They wanted to change themselves and they saw they were not changing as rapidly as they thought they should. They felt hampered both from within and from without. Their mothers had, as they saw it then, bequeathed them a defective feminine nature. They had colluded with a society that restricted and even punished their attempts at self-correction. They were complaining of the mother's bequest, just as Virginia Woolf had forty years before, in what remains the most famous feminist text: "What had our mothers been doing then," wonders Woolf as she experiences the Oxbridge patriarchy, which excluded women from college lawns, from ancient libraries, from High Table luxury, "that they had no wealth to leave us?"[8]

This era of anger toward the mother has, I hope, had its day. Those "enlightened" voices of complaint and hatred are now in midlife, and some have turned—again as Showalter has noted—"beyond matrophobia to a courageously sustained quest for the mother." The sound of the mother's voice in our own has warned us of the necessity of extending our sympathies. Self-preservation advises forgiveness. Yet more than that, the "sustained quest for the mother" replaces the impulse to complain about our inheritance with the need to understand it. We acknowledge the need to understand her, to hear her story, because we see that what she is reflects what we are. In accepting her, we may be accepting our own femininity—which we can do when we feel strong enough to mold it to our own values and needs. The tension between this need to discover our female history through our mother, and the wish, which so many of us live with for so long, to free ourselves from her shadow, was brutally and brilliantly described by Dorothy West, when she wrote that, at her mother's death, she and her sisters were "finally bereaved, free of the departed" and therefore "in a rush to divorce ourselves from any resemblance of her influence."[9] Yet, gradually, the sisters hear their mother's voice in one another's and shout, "You sound just like her!" until, instead of the hot sisterly denial "I do not!" they say "So what?"

The crux of that life-long "adolescent" task then becomes not a freeing of the daughter's psyche from the mother's, but an acknowledgment that "some part of her is forever embedded" within us, and "we are not the worse for it."[10] The supplementary realization seems to be that we were focusing on the surface all along, and that the real depths of our mothers' lives, which we felt so familiar with, were in fact hidden by our self-preoccupation. As we accept her part in our lives we also feel how little we know of hers. We hear her silence at the same point we recognize the sound of her voice in our own. This is the strange, reverberating resolution we come to at midlife. We do not win an adolescent battle, but accept the blurred boundaries, which are less threatening now, as the self becomes more layered and flexible. We acknowledge the connection, and its implacable permanence, but no longer feel bound and constrained by it. We may also feel a new need for a different closeness, as we try to hear her story anew.

Dependence Sustained

The gothic twists in the mother/daughter plot will always hold our interest, but they are neither inevitable nor usual. General research offers no confirmation for a conflicted and anxiety-producing relationship. That "great unwritten story," which Adrienne Rich described as "essential, distorted, misused"[11] and, which other writers, from Helene Deutsch onwards,[12] have depicted as normally and permanently one of conflict, wherein the growth of one produces anxiety in the other, when the sexuality of one breeds envy and hatred in the other, has another side wherein the well-being of the mother and the daughter are intermeshed, where each needs to understand the other if she is to understand herself, where the progress of one depends upon the progress of the other.

Grace Baruch and Rosalind Barnett, who have for some time been researching the conditions under which adult women thrive, studied women between the ages of 35 and 55 to discover how a woman's overall well-being was related to her relationship with her mother.[13] Were women who were fully independent from their mothers better off? Did self-esteem increase according to distance from a mother? Baruch and Barnett found that adult women were psychologically better off when they had good relations with their mothers: They had higher self-esteem, felt less anxious, less depressed than did women who were at odds with their mothers. Not only did they benefit from good relations, but also they valued them—and at the same time they valued them, they knew that their continuing love and persistent "dependence," were unfashionable: "I know it sounds silly," admitted one woman who said that when she felt down, she still, at 50, felt comforted by being with her mother. Often the mother was seen by adult daughters as a source of comfort, and still, even in midlife, the mother could be "the primary person from whom affirmation is sought."[14]

The "dependency," in which adult daughters continue to "need" mothers, is not a dependency in which they fail to achieve capacity for independent action and thought. It is a dependency formed through attachment, through the need to sustain the attachment, and to maintain its good working order. The "girl within" the woman does not diminish her maturity, but contributes to her individuality, providing a self-awareness that extends across various life phases. The adult daughter acknowledges some continuity of need and attachment and resource, rather than something stunted, warped, or rigid, when she allows the girl within to speak and to say she still wants to "be with Mom" when she is "down."

The life-long attachment to the mother continues to make a difference to a daughter's well-being, but the nature of this attachment shifts. During adolescence, she individuates herself from the mother, seeking out, discovering, and forging differences, while she watches out for, anticipates, and criticizes her mother's and father's responses, finding signs that her developing self is validated through their (positive or negative) responses, or legitimized through their admiration and understanding.[15] Much of the tension that frequently characterizes mother/daughter relationships during adolescence is linked to this special love and need; for it is through her love for her mother that a daughter is sensitive to disappointments and frustrations in the relationship. However different she becomes from her mother, or from the adolescent girl who developed through her mother, her mother's responses remain a point of reference.

The independent identity a daughter seeks never sets hard, though in her early adult years she often checks it, expecting to find that it has. The internal persistence of the maternal gaze is experienced as an intrusion: "Why doesn't my mother leave me alone?" she protests, when she herself is the author of these "intrusions." What may release further energy is another shift in that internal gaze: She can now be released from the ideal of the perfect daughter, or the perfectly mature woman, perfectly independent from her mother.

S E V E R A L   M I L E S T O N E S   C H A N G E   A   woman's relationship with her mother. She may use distinctive events to mark new differences in her relationship, whereby she seeks out new dimensions of equality. Sexual initiation or marriage or pregnancy may make her feel part of a "woman's club" and give her new access to a mother's knowledge or status. Sometimes a new job, a promotion, a success, or even a new home is viewed partly in terms of what it should mean to the parent, and what status, vis-à-vis the parent, it gives her. Sometimes the daughter makes such a claim, or bid for equality, only to be reminded that the distance between the two women (in terms of equality, understanding, wisdom, or perspective) has not changed. "I came home for a visit after I had been working in Denver for eight months," 18-year-old Amy complained, "and there was my mother treating me as though I couldn't cross the street safely unless she hurled advice after me."

While daughters, well into adulthood, often expect some change within themselves to effect a sudden, dramatic change in their relationship with their mothers, negotiations in the relationship often remain piecemeal and gradual. Painstakingly, and often with irritation at her slow pupil, the adult daughter "teaches" the mother precisely what a new role or new position or new achievement or direction means. Sometimes the roles the daughter takes are very different from what the mother expected or even what she, having come to adulthood in a different time, thought possible. Many women, whose mothers never thought of working outside the home, who never conceived of achievement outside traditional female roles, still try to offer up their own professional achievements like a gift. This offering, with its abiding supposition that achievement is given depth and reality through a parent's endorsement, is often spiked with criticism. The parent—so the child judges—has not been sufficiently impressed, or pleased, or appreciative. A daughter who wants a very different life from her mother's is no less concerned to gain her mother's attention and appreciation than is a woman who chooses her mother as a role model. Both women who admire their mother's lifestyle and life choices, and those who feel highly critical of a mother's values and choices, have to work in the same way toward release from concerns about pleasing her or impressing her.

FORTY WAS OFTEN CITED as the magic age whereby a woman no longer cared in the same way about what her mother thought. Forty was the time, finally, to grow up. This age was a marker both because women observed change within themselves, and because being forty has such symbolic impact. Though a few women said they still "heard a mother's running commentary" as a "companion reel to [their] own responses," they were now able either to confront it and stop it at will, or "let it go on running, without really caring about it." This "lack of care" was often linked to a different kind of care: As a woman no longer tried to please her mother she often felt a new concern not to hurt her.

At 40, Chris Lu explained that visits from her mother no longer create a "mini-crisis of self-doubt." She did not now feel pressured by her mother's traditional conception of female housekeeping. "When she comes to visit, I don't worry whether the kitchen floor has been washed, or whether the children are wearing clean jeans, or whether she thinks I look like a slob. It doesn't even bother me when she launches into some eulogy about [my cousin] who is really her dream girl—always 'well turned out' and pleasant and on top of things."

As Chris notes her indifference to what she supposes is her mother's ideal daughter, she also expressed a wish to "show her love and appreciation and not to hurt her." There is a shift away from the pressure of meeting a mother's expectations: As women themselves were no longer daunted by their own ideals, they were no longer shadowed by what they thought their mother's ideal was. Yet there is no lessening of the connection and the desire to preserve it. The greater release Carol Shaeffer, 44, felt with her mother was mirrored by a corresponding change in her mother: "I can now talk to my mother like a real person, without worrying that whatever comes out of my unguarded mouth will be impaled on a spear and held up to ridicule while she wails about the kind of person her daughter has become. It was hard—real hard—for her to accept my divorce and to realize I wasn't desperate to remarry and that I really wanted to think about other things and that I have a viable life as a single woman."

The new ability to "talk like a real person" was an opportunity she took up at a signal from her mother. "We were clearly getting nowhere. I was miserable in the marriage, and she kept offering to pay for joint therapy. And by 'therapy' she meant medicine for the marriage, not for my little lost soul. That wasn't what I wanted, and that wasn't what I believed in. It was getting so that I felt worse talking to her than I did fighting with my husband! But I didn't want to divorce *her*. So I told her, 'Look, this is how I feel. I want this divorce.' She couldn't really understand that, until I shouted it out plain as day. Maybe she still can't, but she does a good job at listening."

The development toward an equal exchange of views between mother and daughter is mutually reinforcing. As the daughter learns to speak up ("Look, this is how I feel"), the mother then has the opportunity to see the daughter's feelings "plain as day." As Carol sees how her mother's view changes in response to her own self-assertion, she learns that she herself can shift her mother's expectations. This makes her feel far less constrained; the flexibility and fluidity of self that Carol is achieving is answered by her mother's responses, and this opens further paths of communication. Whatever her past suppositions about what her daughter should be, the mother is motivated to be more flexible—mothers, too, seek "a common base for relating."[16]

The transition Carol describes sounds reasonable and natural enough. Children of any age frequently exaggerate the rigidity of a parent's hopes or expectations: They may work hard to resist ideals that the parents do not actually embrace. A woman thinks her mother needs her to be wonderfully successful, but the mother only wants her to be happy. A daughter thinks her father would like her to be beautiful, but in fact he only needs her to feel good about herself. But some expectations about what will make a daughter happy or what is essential to her well-being may be so persistent that tension arises around these issues. Between mothers and daughters, marriage can be a sore point, and divorce can create upheaval. Some researches have concluded that women who feel best about their divorce, and who are able to sustain self-esteem throughout its awful process, are those women who are not close to their mothers and who do not sustain good relations with them. This may be the exception to the general finding that adult women are better off when they have good relations with their mothers.[17] I found that mothers tended to be more sympathetic to daughters in young adulthood who were getting divorced than they were to midlife daughters who decided to divorce. Mothers had greater expectations of compromise and self-control for an older daughter, and the lack of sympathy for her "stubbornness" or tendency to be "too exacting" or "not trying hard enough" was imbedded in the mother's assessment of the daughter's diminished chances, in midlife, for remarriage. For other mothers, the sight of their daughter's lives being "ruptured" gave them "a broken heart," and their lack of support seemed to arise within the context of their own pained involvement. Most women want to be able to talk freely to their mothers, and to present their genuine identity, without the censorship many felt was necessary to "keep things smooth between us" or "to keep her from worrying" or to "prevent her interfering." Yet, well into their forties, many women feel their communication with their mother is blocked or limited, and they are unable to reveal their complexity and rough edges. Grace Baruch found that when she suggested to her women patients that they bring their mothers into the therapy session, they reacted with dread. "Competent, successful women are terrified at the prospect of talking openly with their mothers."[18] Baruch found, however, that the most efficient way of overcoming this reluctance was to talk to the mothers and explain the daughter's continuing need of them. To this appeal the mothers were highly responsive and, as she describes it, they "lost their rigidity"—that is, their ability to hear only a range of problems, their fear of hearing what is outside the boundaries of the acceptable, their wish to deny their child's inchoate emotions and pain. At a daughter's invitation for participation in her psychological recovery, a mother was likely to put the achievements of her own midlife passage on display.

THE RELATIONSHIP BETWEEN MIDLIFE women and their mothers is new. These are very different generations, surprising one another, puzzled by one another, tracking one another, seeking understanding, while wary and critical. This "continuous negotiation" between mothers and daughters has been brought about, too, by increased life expectancy, especially for women. Though men now live longer, extending the time they may have in relationships with adult children, women still have increased life expectancy. The special relationship between adult mothers and their daughters has its own progression, as both mothers and daughters make varied use of this extension.

The absorption of these changes into the psychology of need and connection can be seen in the markedly different ways women of 30 and women of 50 respond to a parent's death. In Anne Stueve and Lydia O'Donnell's study of daughters of aging parents,[19] their case studies show how, at different points in adulthood, daughters frame the prospect of a parent's death in very different ways and concentrate on different aspects of their loss. A woman in her thirties said that without her parents, she would be "lost": "They've helped me through many, many hard times. I really wouldn't know what to do [if they died]. I don't even want to talk about them leaving because I just want them around forever. I just kind of block that right out of my mind. When my father had the heart attack, it scared me half to death."[20]

This woman, not yet in midlife, still speaks of her parents in terms of her own need for them, her own need still to talk to them, to hear them say "straight out and tell [her] what they think," and her dependence on their understanding as a resource for strength and comfort. Later, closer to midlife, the typical focus on a parent's death has changed. Lauren, nearly forty, with much older parents, speaks of her father: "If he dies today, I would feel very comfortable with it—beyond the missing him—but I would have no regrets. I've said what I wanted to say."[21] Here, at the threshold of midlife—and with an older father, for the life-phase of the parents also influences the expectations of the daughter and the context in which she views a parent's loss—the daughter feels that the ability to communicate her love and appreciation has brought about a resolution of the bond. The effect on her is mentioned almost as an aside ("beyond the missing him") so that this is acknowledged but is not seen as the central issue it is for the younger woman, who cannot bear to contemplate it.

A third woman, more than ten years older than Lauren, speaks about the death of a mother in terms of her hope that she will die happy, without pain or discomfort or regret: "I hope that she won't be uncomfortable . . . And I hope that she will just go and not be frightened at the time . . . If they told me that she would die tomorrow, I think I'd be very, very happy because I'd know that she had a happy life to the last moment."[22]

There is a gradual shift from a personal need for the parent in young adulthood, for the comfort and understanding and continued closeness. In early midlife, the focus is on resolution and expression, and later, well into midlife, the focus is purely parent-centered, with no talk of missing the parent, but only of seeing her life comfortably completed. The concern for a parent continues after that magical resolution, but the "need" has a different focus. These three examples show a progression from a continued need for the parents in a woman in her thirties, who cannot conceive of stability or comfort or security in the absence of that relationship, to a recognition of a woman nearing 40 that the relationship, though of supreme importance, has its limits: her account of resolution suggests the possibility of completion. In one sense, the relationship is finished; it has served its purpose, and has a retrospective stability. The fifty-year-old woman steps outside a perspective in which her parents are seen in terms of her own needs, and she assesses a "good" death from the parent's point of view. At the other end of the midlife passage, the battle that began in adolescence can be put to rest, and the need that makes this relationship so powerful and tense can be eased into a disinterested love.

AND YET, BENEATH THESE healthy shifts in mourning remain a daughter's abiding child-love. Even the most independent woman, fifty or over, can experience a child-terror at a parent's death. When Pauline Perry spoke in public about her violent, unanticipated grief at her mother's death, she was flooded with responses from other women who, in their fifties and sixties, shared her feelings. They, too, felt that no preparation for such a loss was possible, and that abiding grief at a mother's death was inevitable at any age. I remember when my mother's own mother died, when she was forty. Her panic seemed unwholesomely dramatic. I felt a cold withdrawal from the theatre of her grief, in which a grand announcement that she was "coping" was followed by an outburst of tears. Her grief was flung at me like a brick. I could not understand what she was grieving for, so brittle and angry did their relationship seem to me. Her mother was a problem, something to control. Their frequent phone conversations were filled with arguments. Every meeting was followed by a new spate of criticism. Why this excess of mourning when an old woman died?

Several women described a sense of "panic" or "terror" when their mother died. Jessica, 45, said that she walked out of the hospital, having made the arrangements for her mother's burial, and longed to embrace to "every kind-faced person on the street" to gain comfort. She felt "helpless," and kept forgetting she was grown-up and independent: "I might as well have been ten years old—those were the feelings

I had. I kept seeing myself as ten, and not having a mother to go home to." Julia, 43, said that she kept hearing her mother call out to her, "like she's asking for my help and I can't give it to her because I don't know where she is." The twin fears of being abandoned, and of being the abandoner, haunted their period of grief. And when the intensity of mourning subsided, they were left with a changed self, a self that they now felt had been pushed into true middle age, decidedly mortal.

In speaking about their grief, women in their forties still revealed how closely they saw themselves and defined themselves in relation to their mothers. "I spent so much time countering what she would say, pin-pointing the ways she was undermining me—what picky fights we had! Now I have that non-interference I was fighting for! Much good it all does me. My thoughts drip into an empty bucket. No resonance."

Other women in their forties could anticipate that these battles were coming to a close. Eliza Gale, 44, whose mother died during the course of my interviews with her, could just about spot the future development on the horizon. "I fought her for so long, far longer than was necessary. I had already got the independence I'd wanted. I pushed her away because she seemed threatening me, long after she really was. If she had lived for a few years longer, I might have been able to learn this before it was too late for me to share it with her. I was just beginning to feel it—the end of that long adolescent resistance. I regret being unable to offer this forgiveness."

The Father's Return

When I wrote about adolescent girls' attitudes towards their mothers and their fathers, I found that they were far more articulate about their feelings for their mothers, far more tuned into a mother's feelings, and had greater access to the different aspects of the positive and negative emotions that bound them to their mothers.[23] They usually admitted loving the father, and they often found him "fun"—though the structured activities they preferred doing with him—the hiking, sailing, camping, woodworking—were often tiring, and they sometimes felt that being with him was a "burden," whereas they felt able to relax and "just hang out" with a mother. It was puzzling, then, to hear from adult daughters just how important their fathers had been to them in adolescence, given the short shrift teenage girls often give a father, describing him as "issuing orders" and "laying down the law." "Talking to my Dad," said one girl whom I reinterviewed recently in a small study of teenage daughters and fathers,[24] "means sitting down and listening to what he has to say." Girls often protected themselves from the coldness of a father's authority—from his failure to listen to them—by withdrawing, by foreclosing their intimacy. This distancing can escalate, as fathers often believe that a daughter has a right to more privacy, especially in adolescence, and the daughter then interprets his acceptance of her reticence as further rejection, and retaliates by increasing her distance from her father.

This tendency to punish a father by being "cold," by "keeping a low profile," by "not exposing" herself, however, does not shut off the powerful emotional flow between father and daughter, nor does it block the influence that a father has on a daughter's adult goals and self-esteem. The emotional richness of the relationship is often put on hold. In a recent seminar, Carol Gilligan suggested that a father's "rejection" or self-distancing from a teenage daughter may arise as a daughter, growing all too wise, responds to the vulnerability he wants to hide—from both her and himself.[25] Afraid that she is getting too close to understanding his weakness, he responds with increasing authority.

Fathers no longer try to hide their vulnerability when their daughters reach midlife. This ability to disclose a wider range of feelings, to step out of rigid roles, has an enormous impact on the father/adult daughter relationship. The father may have once rejected such sympathy—out of a wish to protect his daughter and to be strong for her—but now, seeing a daughter's strength, he is apt to feel grateful for her reengaged sympathy.

Midlife women frequently experienced a new closeness with their fathers, increasing an intimacy that had begun in early adulthood. Sandy Hersch, at 46, felt she was recapturing in her relationship with her father something she had missed during her adolescence. "When I look at [my father] now, I see several different things. It's not the way it is with my mother . . . there everything comes together . . . everything's there together, all the time. But I get these images of my father—memories of him, how the whole atmosphere of the house changed when he came home, how self-important he was. And now when I sit down with him, I sometimes want to have this out with him . . . 'Hey, Dad, why did you play those silly games, with your white dentist's coat and your shiny shoes?' But he just looks at me with his mild eyes, and I don't know whether he meant to pretend to be strong, or that was just me, seeing him that way, but even when he pulls the same stunts— with his frown or his voice going real low . . . there's just a person in all that. Maybe his smile's changed, but when I start getting edgy, he backs away—because he's hurt, and I don't think I ever saw that before. It's so touching . . . well, it's really touching the way he starts to smile when I begin to accuse him—usually of something that's gone right out of his mind, it happened so long ago. And it can be so good being with him now, and maybe when I was a kid he used to take that kind of pleasure, too, but I wasn't able to see it, at least not when I was a teenager."

This new ability to see the vulnerable person behind the "dentist's coat and shiny shoes" confirmed the reality of her connection with her father. It revealed a mutuality she had once thought lacking. Carol Schaeffer, who had worked so hard to create a mutuality with her mother, described a similar process with her father. "Sometimes I think about how my mother used to talk about him—you know, the man carrying all the financial burdens, problems at work, that sort of thing . . . and that meant I shouldn't stir things up, and I should work hard. Well, that has no reality anymore for me, and seeing who he is behind all that—it's a surprise. Well, it's a real surprise. I feel I've found a treasure. We talk—and I see a thousand responses in him that were just buried before. It can feel so alive—I'm this and that to him. I took that for granted with my Mom—all that variation in the contact. I didn't realize I had it with him, too."

The discovery of the "treasure" of a father's vulnerability and the flexible mode of communication revitalizes the relationship ("It can feel so alive . . ."). As a woman's relationship with her mother attains that long-sought balance between people whose dependencies on one another are past, the difference between a daughter's response to her father and to her mother, so pronounced in adolescence,[26] becomes muted.

When Parents Won't Shrink

A significant minority of women—a little over 10% in my study—
were not dealing with love, expression, and resolution, but with disengagement. Even as well-functioning adults, they saw distance from a
parent as essential to sanity, self-esteem, or simple equilibrium. They
knew that anger against a parent, and the despair a child feels in face of
parental injustice, would always be part of them: their only hope was to
feel it less rather than more. These women, in midlife maturity, still
could not summon up that magnanimous forgiveness and acceptance
of a parent, which is traditionally thought to mark the end of adolescence.[27] Typically, it was a mother whose past "crimes" bound them in
rage.

What they remembered still was the pain of the mother's anger,
the "terror of her yells reeling across the kitchen," the "knife-like
darts" of the angry eyes, the mean set of the mouth as the mother's
anger pounded upon them. They described a childhood anxiety,
focused on a mother's unpredictable moods. "I woke up every day and
opened the door of my room and took a deep breath as the knot in my
stomach tightened, knowing I was about to face my mother," explained Toni. Three of these women, whose mothers were now dead,
described "sheer relief" at her death: They were better off without her;
they felt a much wider scope for growth and self-acceptance; life was
simply more enjoyable because she was gone.

These were women who knew that their mothers had loved and
cared for them. They knew their mothers had wanted the best for
them, been proud of them, and helped them thrive. Nor had these
mothers inflicted severe physical pain on them—though 47-year-old
Gabriel Speirs described how her mother had repeatedly hit her with
the wooden side of the hair brush when she, as a girl, had flinched at
the severe brushing of her hair. Gabriel reported ruefully that her
mother had later proudly reminisced that she had "never raised a
hand" to any of her children. The slap of the hairbrush against the
skull had gone unrecorded in the mother's memory, while its stunning
effect on the daughter meant that even today, in expectation of that
wooden crack against her temple, she flinched at sudden movements.

Explaining her response to her mother's death eight years before, Toni Bryce, now 52, said that she repeatedly dreamed about visiting her mother in hospital, or seeing her mother returning in a boat. In her dream, she realizes that the symptoms of the mother's illness are subsiding and that she has not, after all, died. "These dreams wake me with a start. I know they sounded like wish fulfillments. They seem to be saying, 'See, it's all right, your mother is still alive.' But there's only one catch—" she laughed, and turned from pink to red as she watched my reaction. "To me these dreams were nightmares! I wake up, really confused, and then the relief comes in a rush as I realize she is truly dead and gone." Clare Lazlo, at 49, made a meticulous distinction as she explained her response to her mother's death nine years before: "I could grieve for the unhappiness she felt, but I could not grieve for having lost her."

It is so difficult to say why, for some people, a mother's remembered anger was a simple, limited thing, whereas for others it remains large and fierce, its bark and bite as effective today as it had been forty and fifty years before. It is impossible, from retrospective accounts, to get an objective gauge of a mother's anger. The child's perspective magnifies the anger, responds to it like an animal responds to danger, whereas for a parent it may be water off a duck's back. The reality of the mother's anger, for the child, may have no objective measure, save in the meaning it had to her. Were the mothers whose anger inflicted a pain that was neither forgotten nor forgiven, really more brutal than other mothers, whose anger was judged to be ordinary and forgivable?

In the absence of any observation of those bad times, with the one-sided evidence of a daughter's recollections, I can only suggest why forgiveness seems impossible, and why grief at her death is distorted into relief. These were not hard women, nor were they women who had no respect for good strong feeling. They all felt that this emotional closure endangered their integrity or their sense of their own goodness. They were all mothers themselves and worried that their own children might one day turn upon them with similar accusations. They felt, too, that this lack of forgiveness and, for those whose mother had died, the inability to perform a daughter's proper mourning, exacted a cold price: They were hurt by their own rejections of their mothers, yet they knew they would never relent.

The mothers these women described combined high expectations of their daughters with vehement and unpredictable responses. They had encouraged the daughters' drive and determination, but they had not rewarded it. The mothers had typically been strict and controlling, yet simultaneously dismissive and neglecting. Or, their pride had been intermittent—so that one moment the child was "wonderful" but the next moment some unwitting offense destroyed the good image she had earned. The women who, in midlife, still felt unable to forgive their mothers had had to compete for her approval, winning competitions only to discover that, somehow, their wins were not good enough.

Gabriel's sister was a successful opera singer, and this high-profile achievement had obliterated—in Gabriel's account—her mother's appreciation for her own lower key but nonetheless substantial academic attainments. Toni said that her younger sister had achieved every distinction she herself had worked so hard to achieve "but two years earlier." The mother's apparent preference for the younger sister linked up with that menacing image of a highly determined, driven competitor galloping behind her.

A more devastating rival than a sibling could be a mother's frustration or depression. Clare said that, for her mother, "domesticity was a real trap, and I don't think she ever understood how she stepped into it." This brittle disappointment created an arena in which her own voice was little more than an echo; she could not search out the warmth she needed to feel whole. The exposure to a mother's bitterness, combined with an inability to succeed *for* her mother (that was her sister's privilege), created a sense of exclusion through which forgiveness was unlikely to emerge.

For Toni, whose dreams about the mother's magical return to life suggested horror rather than comfort, the "unforgivable parental act" was really a network of thoughts, assumptions, and perspectives, which she felt threatened her own sanity. Her mother had always involved her in her own wide-ranging battles and grudges. These were against neighbors (regarding common walls) or employers (regarding lack of promotion and then dismissal) or with dressmakers (who had not, in her view, delivered the desired article). Unlike Clare's mother, Toni's had not been trapped in a traditional domestic lifestyle. She had trained as a surgeon at a time when she stood out as the only woman resident, and she had fought a male hierarchy single handed. By the time the women's movement gathered strength, Toni's mother was already well-established, but her adversarial personality, which had probably been formed within the context of "the myriad of insults and slights which she'd recite to us, daily, at the dinner table," prevented her from getting its support. After some initial participation in the women's movement, she withdrew on the grounds that her talents were "not sufficiently appreciated."

Though Toni believed that many of her mother's complaints had some legitimate basis, she wanted to withdraw from the rage and antagonism with which her mother managed these problems. Since her mother tended to alienate so many people outside the family, Toni was one of the very few people available as a companion or as someone to listen to what she called her mother's "tirades." Having suffered the brunt of her mother's anger when she was younger, Toni had learned to avoid confrontation with her, and she had valued the good relations between them, but maintaining them had been a strain. She "never knew when [her] mother would start pecking away at [her]." When her mother was not directing anger at her, she was still expressing anger towards others. "She lived in some mean murky world, where everyone was sneering at her," Toni explained, and "it was hard work to maintain my own, more human perspective." Her mother's death from cancer freed her from the obligation to stand by a difficult, isolated woman, and allowed her "to take [her] own perspective for granted, and not have [her] optimism continually under siege."

WOMEN WITH POOR RELATIONSHIPS with their mothers had to find special routes through or around them. As they saw that the battle was continuous, they tried to develop strategies that would help them—"not once and forever, like I used to dream of, but enough to get me through each meeting, and not make me rage after." "Anything could set my mother off," Gabriel said. "Things were fine and then from nowhere came this anger which was really amazing. It had its own momentum, so sitting tight and keeping still wouldn't help. I'd go all rigid inside. It was really like waiting for a storm to pass, because you couldn't touch it. I'd see my other friends say things—simple little things you shouldn't have to think about—like 'I'm sorry,' to their mothers, or start to offer explanations or excuses—but I wouldn't ven-

ture anything like that with mine. I couldn't pour water on the fire—
anything I did would just make it flare up again. An apology would be
fuel! I'd try not to breathe. I understood that she was angry with me, all
right, but I never understood what she was angry about. It had to do
with her conception of 'the world.' It's taken me a long time, and more
than a little therapy, to get over my own fears, and to understand that
anger isn't a necessary response, or even a natural one. I know her voice
will always be inside me. Sort of like a room in my mind with the
drapes all torn up. But as long as I can keep that door closed, and recognize it for what it is, I'm all right."

Whereas most midlife women sought a deeper understanding of
their mothers, these women felt that their mother's perspective threatened their stability. "I don't even want to try to understand her," protested 44-year-old Leslie Feinberg, who insisted that she could tolerate
her mother only if she could "guard" her mind "with a portcullis. You
run the risk of being invaded by lunacy if you follow her through her
own corridors of thought." The natural tendency to try to see things
from a mother's point of view was, in self-defense, deliberately resisted.

Bound as these women still were to their mothers by both love
and fear, they tread a line between the desire to sustain some closeness to their mothers and to protect themselves. Grace Hogan
wanted to help her mother move into an apartment after the death of
her father, but in order to do so, she had to put a barrier between
herself and some of her mother's stock responses: "The pessimism of
my mother—she sits there, stewing over every last item on her list of
life, and she cannot see that her depression has nothing to do with
her immediate situation, that her worry about the plumber charging
too much and the car battery being low doesn't add up to a ruined,
useless life. I can feel my own pessimism revving up when I'm anxious about something, and I have to stop and think and say—no,
there's something I can do about this."

As Grace remembers that she is strong and she can step out of the
pattern that she feels is being set for her, she realizes, too, that she had
fought her mother "long after it was really necessary." Yet these unnecessary battles linger in the shadow of fear.

Beyond Disengagement

Most women were far more interested in a new engagement with a mother. Their hope was to remain attached or to reattach. The impetus varied from reparation to deprivation: from regret at past unruly behavior, to the fear that a mother's life was passing away, and she had not yet "got to know her properly" or "understood things from her point of view" or "listened to her story."

Joann Mason, facing difficulties with her own daughter, reflected in new ways on an old relationship. "I gave her hell when I was a teenager, and now I look at her and just can't see what I saw then. I thought she was my jailor, and I thought she was standing in my way. That's all I saw of her—some great big shadow blocking my path. And now when I feel how mild she is—well, I look at her and suddenly my heart will start thumping because I'm afraid of how I used to rage against her. Sometimes I think she's expecting me to lay in on her like I used to. It's just—you turn around and suddenly she's a different person. I want to show her that I'm grateful she's stood by me, and didn't give up hope that one day I might say a nice word or two to her." The adult relationship provided new opportunities for expressing good will.

For other women, the need to keep close and get closer involves the wish to rediscover the mother and to explore her perspective and, through their voices, validate their mothers' lives anew. African-American women writers, especially, have used their skills to unlock the stories of their mothers' lives.[28] Silenced by powerlessness and illiteracy, these older women may barely know that they have a self whose history can be narrated. Their daughters employ their own strength and talents to discover the subjective reality of the women who have formed them.

Looking back on their childhood, midlife women expressed a new curiosity about what things were like for their mother, how her hopes had been formed and then transformed, and what role the daughter herself had played in fulfilling or hindering those hopes. Sometimes a woman would seek a new closeness, or initiate a new discussion with a sister or brother to help her reconstruct the neglected drama of a mother's life. "I spent many hours telling her, and analyzing with my sister, what was wrong with her life," Kari Reis realized. "Maybe it's time now I let her speak for herself."

This new appreciation of the mother's subjective reality (what it felt like being her, and how she would explain herself) frequently occurred at the death of another parent or relative. The death of one parent changes and intensifies a child's relationship with the existing parent.[29] In part, the adult child responds to the surviving parent's need, but also, realizing she may not have much more time with the surviving parent, she feels a new commitment to the relationship.[30]

How Women in Their New Midlife Care for Elderly Parents

The confusion and ambivalence of that middle-aged woman, standing "half in, half out" of the mother's room, catch on a range of changes and puzzles. Changing life spans make crucial differences to adult relationships with a mother. In previous generations, people in midlife had already experienced the death of their parents, but today they expect many more years "together" as they remain attached and live apart. Several women in their forties, whose parents had died, described themselves as "orphans"—thus borrowing an image of a forlorn, uncared for, unprotected child, whose appropriateness was symbolic rather than actual. They felt deprived of a bond, which no one born a century earlier would have imagined laying claim to. Yet today, in spite of the rhetoric about the family's decline, increased life expectancy leads to continued expectations of continuity, which abides in spite of much "bending and stretching" necessary to accommodate individual and societal change.[31]

TO THE FRICTION AND pleasures of this continued bond are often added new burdens and responsibilities. Midlife adults are sometimes called the generation in the middle, since they are often still responsible for the parenting of their own children but can become, in addition, responsible for the care of elderly parents. Though most elderly people want to remain independent and self-sufficient, though they resist dependency as long as they possibly can, and though most parents realize that they themselves have taught their children the virtues of self-sufficiency and self-reliance, they nonetheless, if they live long enough, face the reality of new dependencies and new needs.[32]

Daughters and daughters-in-law, rather than sons, are expected to respond to these new needs. Women remain "the linchpin of family contact,"[33] the "kinkeepers" who keep track of birthdays and anniversaries, who organize family meetings, who carry a "worry burden" through their concern for a parent's health, well-being, and comfort.[34] This seems to be one area in which no changes have been made. The idea that the woman as daughter should nurture needy relatives still holds. And because an elderly person in need of care cannot be cajoled to pitch in (as a child can), to share tasks (as a partner can), she seldom feels justified in rejecting an ailing parent's needs. Though the spouse will respond more immediately than any other relative to the needs of his or her partner, the nearly eight-year difference in life expectancy between men and women, combined with women's relative youth at marriage, means that most elderly parents without a spouse to care for them, are mothers. Hence, the parent who becomes childlike, in need of the adult child's parenting, is more often the mother; and the child who provides the parenting is usually the daughter.[35]

The definitions of "care" and "help" and the mutual expectations and demands involve a new and varied vocabulary. Though most parents want continued contact with their adult children, and indeed more contact than they have, very few expect more.[36] Though most parents and their children believe that the child has some duty to offer an elderly parent emotional support and a reasonable amount of companionship, there are huge differences among classes, cultures, and individuals regarding obligations of the child to provide financial or instrumental help. One study has revealed that those people who believe midlife people should offer a parent financial support, or a place in the child's home, were not themselves providing such help—and those who did help support a parent, or had a parent living in their home, were those who thought that children were not suitable sources of intensive personal help.[37]

Caring for a parent is a complex task, stirring up a medley of divided loyalties, doubts, new variations on a woman's well-worn question about what she owes to whom, and how much (of her time, her energy, her attention) she has a right to claim for herself. The burden of duty and obligation was universally felt by women who saw their parents in need—whether or not they believed "objectively" that they were duty-bound to respond to those needs. Though some general patterns seemed to hold (in working-class families, for example, the daughter was likely to offer an elderly parent more help, and to take the parent into her home), each woman struggled with her decision. The struggle was heightened as she knew that, in this relationship, as a daughter of a mother in need of care, she might be judged with a special severity. The jumble of emotions a parent arouses, and their volatility, could give the image of the caring or careless daughter continued power. Whereas all the women who faced this issue dwelt on similar thoughts—about what was best for the parent, what was best for their families, what would work for them, and whether their decision would allow them "to live with [themselves]," they came to widely different conclusions.

Renee Collins was only 39 when her mother came to live with her. At that time, her mother was fit and healthy. Her father had died eighteen months before, and though her mother was coping well, Renee was worried that her mother was depressed. "I encouraged her to come because I didn't want her to get worse. In many ways, I thought her coming to live with us was insurance against her growing even more dependent on us." Renee's children were young when her mother came, and they had recently moved to a new house, to which the mother had contributed a substantial sum to the down payment. The house, however, wasn't large, and the mother/grandmother shared a room with Renee's nine-year-old daughter. This provided the daughter Emma with some perks: she was given a television and phone in her own room, which her brothers saw as a distinct advantage. While Emma played with her friends in the bedroom during the day, the grandmother was usually in other parts of the house, so they were seldom in each other's way. When, five years later, her mother had a stroke, there was no way, Renee explained, that she could put her mother "out to pasture now."

When Renee weighed up the costs of her mother's presence and the new duties it brought upon her, the balance sheet mentioned other family members. "My husband has ulcers that turn to his advantage. 'Don't rile me. The doctor says I mustn't get upset,' he keeps saying, so he can keep a pretty low profile, which I let him get away with as long as he doesn't complain too much about being neglected. But it was always hard on Emma, sharing a room with Mom, and looking back, I think I was awfully selfish, letting her come the way she did. You know it's sometimes real easy just to turn a blind eye to a child—especially the youngest. You're so used to hearing them complain that you can't really take it seriously, and they always want so much and don't seem to understand what it must be like to be old and alone. There's some part of me calculating the whole time: Who can take this? Who's had to take that? Who can give the most? It's like a metronome sometimes, and I'm sick of it, but I'm stuck with it. When Mom had her stroke— well, I knew she was growing downhill pretty quick, but I kept thinking maybe she's just under the weather—and then this thing. I felt black—not blue you know, but black inside. What was I going to do now? Emma is 15, and though she's pretty good most of the time about having Mom in there with her, it must be a strain. It's not what I want for her. I guess I'll try to arrange some room for Mom downstairs, or something. I don't want us to blow up over this. My husband's O.K. Tim [her 17-year-old son] is O.K. But the three of us— Emma, Mom, and I—are on pretty shaky ground. Mom's got to stay here, but somehow I have to find a way to make things good for Emma. I look at that pouting face, and I want to tell her I feel the same, and then if Mom goes further downhill—well, I don't think I'll manage."

The circle of thoughts outlined here is: I want Mom to be well; I want to be fair to my family. But issues of scarcity make fairness impossible. Fairness to herself is put on the back burner as she tried to deal evenly with everyone else. Her thoughts, too, kept catching on the nail of her mother's financial contribution to the house purchase, and the unwritten obligations of that contract. No narrative of mothers and daughters is simple, or "clean" of unspoken gifts of exchange.

Rose Mathieson described how she began doing little things for her mother, and then she did more and more. She said that she had weighed up various options, and she decided that she could not face the guilt she would feel if she did not look after her mother. So the decision was based on the discomfort she would suffer if she resisted her mother's need. Justine Bassey, from a similar self-knowledge, yet a different assessment of her tolerance, said, "I know I'll feel awful, telling my mother she can't come here, and I don't know how we'll sort it out, but I know what I'll become if I do look after her, and so I'll have to say 'no'."

Yet this "hard-hearted woman" helped move her mother into sheltered accommodation and provided her with a list of phone numbers and activities to help her reestablish a new independence, given her now limited energy and mobility. Her "toughness" was based not on neglect, but on her decision to take a stand and say: "I will do this, and no more." The ability to do this, she concluded, resulted from her own awareness of mortality. "If she just bullied me with her weakness, and I felt real strong, then I'd have no choice, even though caring for her could make me into a monster. It helps that I know one day I may be old and in need, and that I can honestly say 'This is how I'd want my kid to handle things.' And I just don't shudder at being called 'selfish' like I used to. 'Selfish' only bites so deep now. I've given a lot to others. Of course you can never say 'That's enough, forget the rest,' but you can trust yourself to be reasonable about giving to others. So when I feel that I'm doing enough, I don't feel I have to answer this other little voice that's accusing me."

Here, the tender gains of maturity show both their strength and their uncertainty. Rose feels justified, but stands on a narrow perch as she holds her ground. At 53, she feels better equipped to do this—to be "hard" and to be "fair." On the whole, the older a woman was, the more directly she handled those tricky problems of guilt, duty, and commitment. Some women in their forties skirted the moral issues as "too big and too bothersome and they don't have answers anyway," and instead sought out other commitments as a protection against a parent's demands. Being in full-time employment could provide protection against others' demands on their time, and some women noted this advantage of being in paid employment. "When I was made redundant, because the company I worked for folded, I was in a panic," explained 46-year-old Teresa, who had three adolescent children at home and an elderly father living nearby. "I thought: 'Anyone can ask anything of me now!'—and I ran for the next job as though the devil himself was in pursuit." Paid employment outside the home offered her a legitimate range of excuses. It was easier for an employed woman—especially one in full-time employment—to say "No, I can't do that today," or to "shave" domestic commitments. She could phone her father rather than visit him, or "stop by for a few minutes on my way to work, rather than feel I have to spend several hours with him just because I've taken a seat. And with the money I earn I can send him to his doctor's appointment in a taxi, rather than take him myself."

While sons who work full time are seen by elderly parents to be busy and occupied, they seldom excuse a daughter who works.[38] Many older women think that working daughters should adjust their schedules to help out an elderly parent.[39] Nor do elderly women in general expect as much from a son as from a daughter. Liz Blakeny, at 52, explained that she had to make a very inconvenient journey each February, often on icy roads to visit her mother on her birthday. Her brother, however, simply sent a card. "If he even remembers to do that," Liz laughed, "she's delighted, and thinks he's a caring son, whereas if I didn't turn up in person, with flowers and candy and kisses, she'd feel hurt and neglected."

What may sound like an idiosyncratic example of a mother's biassed expectations, is actually typical. Parents do tend to expect more from daughters than sons. Elderly mothers are much more likely to express resentment towards the amount of care and attention they receive from daughters than from sons. Though daughters tend to give them more care and attention, the elderly mother may expect more— and more.[40] Midlife women, preserving their own time and energy and their own sense of fairness, look double-eyed: "I harden myself to this," Liz explained, "I feel it, and it hurts. But I know she's wrong. I give her what I can. That's enough for me. I don't expect it to be enough for her."

Rewarding Care

For many women, however, the circumstances in which they make decisions about care and selfishness are more supportive. The ambivalence or anger towards the care an elderly parent required was often "on the surface" compared to the importance of maintaining the bond with them. Many women were very glad to help care for a parent, and proud of their coping ability, and eager to "take my turn at giving her something."

On the whole, caring for a parent strengthened the affection. One women said, "I used to be jealous of my older sister. She did so much, and was so witty—my mother was always laughing at things she said. Now she comes to visit, and I see her chatting away, and instead of feeling jealous when Mom's eyes light up at her jokes, I'm pleased because they're both happy, and I know this generosity has come from my being able to look after Mom."

Many women loved the idea of contributing to their parents' lives—by helping them keep up with a changing society (one woman taught her elderly father how to keep track of his finances on a computer), by discovering social networks of friends or services they could make use of. Such things contributed to their own sense of competence. Other women barely noticed what in fact they did do to help care for a parent. Carol insisted, "Oh, my mother's very independent and can do most things herself," yet this was followed by a list of exceptions: "she just needs help now and then getting to the post office," or "I only need to shop for her when she's feeling unwell," or "I just take her out sometimes, so she can see some old friends." These acts of care, slotted into a normal schedule, were counted as "nothing."

However heavy the burden of care, however careful a woman was to control it, to say "I will do this, and no more," the strength and quality of the relationship mattered. When the elderly mother did not appreciate what the daughter did for her, when the elderly parent did not enjoy being cared for, the emotional cost to the daughter was severe. The worst thing for the daughter was the feeling that the past she and her mother had shared, and the relationship they had built up, no longer counted, when things between them were "dead, and there's just one more job after another."

At times, duty and obligation and "repayment" or "just plain decency" were enacted within a continuing and even strengthening bond; but, sometimes, the adult daughter negotiated a delicate path between love and care, on the one hand, and the stress of self-preservation, on the other. Tending her mother, who was badly afflicted with Alzheimer's disease, Miriam Bennet said that her goal was "to keep sane." Most women dreamed of a society that made better provisions for an elderly parent. Yet most women deeply mourned even a troublesome parent when she died. "I turn to my daughter for comfort," Pat said when her problems were "resolved" by her mother's death. "Emma can't give me back my mother, but she reminds me what I had with her, and how I still can have it."

The myth of independence from the mother is abandoned in midlife as women learn new routes around the mother—both the mother without and the mother within. A midlife daughter may reengage with a mother or put new controls on care and set limits to love. But whatever she does, her child's history is never finished. Here, in this passionate and complex relationship, midlife women feel remnants of the Over-Eye—that severe judge of feminine ideals; though this is now in contact with the lens of the Inner-Eye. Liz notes that layered perspective: "I do all this because she expects it of me—not because I want to think I'm good, not even because I want to placate her, but because I don't want to hurt her. Something in me just prohibits that further battle. But when she asks too much, I'll have to gather enough courage to resist."

The Third Shift: Passing It On 10

There remains a gap in the stories I have told of women's midlife growth. As individual styles and problems have been described, as their battles with the balance sheet of attachment and expansion have been assessed, as their resistance to the marginalization process has been explored, the focus has been on the fierce privacy in which each woman forges the shape of her life. We have seen the resources that she is able to draw upon in midlife. We have seen how new energy is released as the control and maintenance of past ideals no longer interfere with her own thoughts and desires. We have seen how her sense of being self-responsible for her life, combined with the accumulated experience that enables her to spot patterns, give her new control over her choices. A further resource, which she draws on anew, and which she stocks anew, is friendship.

In every other developmental phase, friends and peers play an important role. A child's friendships open to her the social world beyond that of the family. They provide irreplaceable channels of creative communication and awareness of herself as a social being—as a person among peers. In the playground, she learns hard lessons in both inclusion and exclusion. She experiences peers' kindness and protection alongside their cruelty and neglect. Outside school, she learns about companionship and the flexible structure of play, mutually created. In adolescence, friends help her with the self-questioning, self-doubt, and self-discovery that are essential to further development. Friends inspire her as models, filling her with hope; or, they make her despair because she can never be like them. The world of friendship informs her of her contemporary world and provides her generational identity. But, in early adulthood, its significance slips. Friendship falls behind the new priorities of romantic attachment and the creation of families and careers.

In early adulthood, friends, whatever their importance, lose their centrality. They remain as reference points established at previous stages of life, but they no longer provide that crucial developmental impetus. At this stage, when women are learning how difficult their lives really are, how unrealistic some of their youthful optimism may have been, they tend to draw on their own energy and ingenuity, pumping themselves dry in the process of adapting to their realities without giving up too much. Often, during this stage, women begin to feel isolated from other women, whose lives arouse either wonder or derision. How, they may ask, can another woman do all this, while they themselves feel under such constraint and bear such burdens? Or, seeing other women fail to fulfill their expectations, they take a step back: Knowing all too well the conflicts that threaten the fulfillment of their own plans, they may deny, in self-defense, a commonality. While young women track the progress of their friends with varying degrees of wariness and interest, their emotional life tends to be centered elsewhere.

In a textual analysis of interview material,[1] I found that women in early adulthood have far fewer references (less than half) to friends and friendship than do girls and adolescents. Perhaps this is to be expected: Women with jobs, women with families, simply do not have time for girlish chatter. But friendship is not mere child's play. Its importance recurs. For when women between 40 and 53 spoke about their lives, there were nearly as many references to friendship as there were in the conversations of adolescent girls.

THE ROLE OF FRIENDSHIP in women's lives changes as they change. At one time, the support women could offer one another was based upon the similarity of their lives. As she mourned the loss of a community built up by traditional women, Patty Anselli remembered the friendships that worked so well for women, providing them with support and establishing an environment in which their children could be safe. Women in her neighborhood were friends because their lives were pegged to the same routines, the same troubles, and the same constraints. "Our friendships grew from the other things that were important to us—our children, our neighborhood, and our homes. We were friends with women who had children the age of our children. We compared our kids. We worried about them together, and we reassured each other. We felt safe with each other."

In Patty's view, friendship is based on shared life patterns and life events. She and her friends could look at one another and gain a sense of being right—or not; together, they tracked the developmental of their children.[2] The stability and security they felt with each other was based upon the stability and security of their lives. They could be depended on not to surprise one another, not to change too fast, not to step out of line. Though such stability might look nice from afar, it has potential for cruelty, as women who change may be seen to betray friendship.

This generation of women shares no notional time line, or what Ravenna Helson calls a *social clock pattern,* which sets targets for milestones, such as marriage, the birth of children, writing one's first book, being promoted, and so on. Within a single generation, women have suddenly lost that comfortable—and constraining—inevitability, which their mothers were more likely to share. And this changes the face of friendship.

The new variation of women's lives weakens the thrust of all easy comparisons. "I know exactly what you feel," or "I know just what you're going through," are utterances that have never before had such little truth. But it is more than an easy understanding of another woman's circumstances that is at stake. Common experiences provide the basis for comfort, encouragement, and advice. Painful events—such as the death of a parent or a spouse—are less painful when they are considered normal—on time, rather than off time. Even more positive events—such as marriage and childbirth—feel better when they are "on time." Researchers have found that life events that occur at their socially expected times are less stressful than those occurring at "non-normative" times. Expected, or "normative," events are more easily accommodated by support networks. Friends going through similar experiences can offer more immediate, practical comfort.[3]

Women in midlife have discovered new things in comm

beyond their diversity. This took time. As women's lives cease to have that stable commonality, communication can become more difficult. What is shared? What isn't? What has to be explained? What is understood? Who is critical of whose lifestyle? How can friendships be established on ground that isn't shared? These are questions newly asked by this generation of women. They are forced to ask this by the hunger for friendship that strikes them in midlife.

Friendship now involved a dance in which sympathies were tested gingerly, like steaming bath water. "One word can shut me up," Katrina Pieters admitted, "and I give up—just start to go through the hoops of social talk." At 45, with many of her previous friendships "flat," she felt a new urge to connect with women. "It can happen quickly—just like it did when I was fourteen, when on one school bus ride someone became your friend. And that was that. It's like that—but it's more than a few words. You have to be sure she's going to listen, and not judge, and not tell me what I should do. But understand."

For Patricia Galen, friendship was established by "exchanging rhythms." With some people, conversation was "stilted" and would not "flow." "What I say sometimes just rolls over someone. It's an awful feeling, when you're trying to talk, and nothing happens. I may barely know whether something makes sense, and just try it out. And then sometimes it's picked up—you see the flash in the eyes . . . it's taken in and it means something. The feeling that ideas matter—which is difficult when you're talking about difficult things. Who it is who understands? Not someone who just thinks they know what you mean, but someone who sees it and wants to see it more."

For Katrina, friendship returned to that intense adolescent phase in which trust meant listening and not judging. Since she was on the escape route from the pressure of conforming to others' ideals, she did not want to face them again in a friend, who would tell her what she should do. For Patricia, understanding meant caring about her experience, rather than sharing it. As she experienced the layering of the midlife self, she wanted to feel the effect of different meanings, things she "barely knows" and is unsure of. She, too, returns to the pleasures of adolescent friendship in which her responses are validated.

But midlife friendships are not merely a recurrence of adolescent friendships. Women's descriptions of how their friendships, especially with women, had changed, commonly involved the word "relief." They described their relief at being "unhampered by self-doubt and envy," or relief from "worrying what she's thinking about me," or "no longer hemmed in by what she's going to say about me." Not only did women feel freer from concern about how other women judged them, they expected other women to judge them more leniently and view them more favorably. They were less concerned about a friend's opinion, and more optimistic about what the opinion would be. They felt relief both on the giving end as well as the receiving end. Not only did they feel a new ease and optimism in their expectations of friends' responses to them, but their own feelings were "better," more generous, less defensive and suspicious. They trusted other women more. They were far less worried about being hurt by them or betrayed by them. Hence, they could reveal themselves without feeling exposed. The feminine "fronts" many women described could now be set aside. The messy room, the dusty shelves, the scruffy hair, the imperfect mother, the cracked marriage, the stalled career—these did not have to be hidden; these were no longer the sore points of vulnerability as they had once been—even to women who deliberately resisted the feminine mystique.

Whereas women recalled, in adolescence and young adulthood, putting effort into hiding their vulnerability from friends—even as they sought comfort—the areas of vulnerability now were free of shame. Moreover, as friendships were no longer characterized by small cliques, women felt less vulnerable to gossip. "I hate to think what the past few years would have been like without my close friends," said Beth Geist. "I was having all this trouble at work.[4] I felt *embattled*. I could see the hard edges that others were drawing around me. It was good, of course, to go home, and be just 'old Mom'—nothing special, nothing awful. But what amazed me—like a gift out of the blue—was the way my friends rallied round me. I started doing things like having lunch with them, meeting them in the evening—not just one, not a best friend like it used to be, but a whole river of them, women who were willing to talk like I can't remember talking since my pajama party days. And they had so much to offer, more than I ever knew they had in them. What I got was not just 'ooh, how beastly'—the sort of easy sympathy you can get when you trade horror stories about work. There was a real listening . . . so that makes it better than a family. And what surprised me about myself, was what I said—how freely I spoke. And I realized how guarded I used to be with women friends . . . as though they might do something with the negative information I gave them—even if it was only feeling better because I was having such trouble at work."

Beth touches on a number of issues, which emerged repeatedly as women reassessed the importance of friendship and noticed how it had changed since early adulthood. It is as fun as it was during adolescence (her "pajama party days"), but it is more fluid: Friendships are no longer ruled by a clique, wherein one alliance can threaten another; instead, she has a "whole river" of friends. The significant friend was no longer someone "to whom I can tell my secrets" or someone who "can be trusted not to say stuff behind my back";[5] for the concern was no longer with that precarious "trust" that was inevitably betrayed by teenage friends.[6] This was not because she assumed her midlife friends would have more discretion or be less prone to gossip, but rather because she was not concerned with "what they might do with the negative information." The focus was not on a friend taking possession of some information, which could then do her harm, but an appreciation of other women's ability to "listen" and to give back "more than I ever realized was there."

This startled realization was echoed by Monica Selleck, who found "buried treasures in women I thought I knew for years." "I was always so defensive—like they'd got their act together when I'd really messed up mine. So maybe that's why for so long I didn't really talk to them, just presented this brave face. Even to good friends, who'd done a lot to help me, I don't think I came clean with . . . you know, about how down I could feel about myself and sometimes my daughter. So to hear how they were really feeling their way, too, in this mess we're handed when we try to make a good life while we're stuck with being a woman—like the good life is somehow cleansed from womanly things . . . so to hear how they were often down, too, on themselves, on their kids and their husbands, and to see how they were dealing with these things—I don't know, it was just an eye-opener, and such a relief, to feel that they were feeling some of things I felt, that they could understand—not because they were 'lady bountifuls'—but because they were in the same boat. So now I can begin to talk to them without thinking that they're going to think they're superior."

Whereas Beth found friends supportive in her crisis at work, as the actual conditions of her job edged her against the constraints of her ideal as a career woman, Monica found friendship important in edging her away from the ideal that haunted her—the ideal woman who had not "messed up" her life, who never felt "down on herself, her kids and her husband." As her friends unearthed their "buried treasures" of struggle and empathy, Monica realized that her own struggles were not isolated instances, worthy of shame and derision, but part of that tricky task of constructing a "good life" without being "cleansed" of "womanly things." In seeing that other women did not adhere to the ideal that shadowed her, she was able to feel less "down" on herself and also was able to increase her communication with others ("I can begin to talk to them without thinking that they're going to think they're superior") and hence increase her sense of "belonging," she said later, "to a whole group of women who are really great and not fundamentally different from me." Her renewed appreciation of other women went hand in hand with self-acceptance. This handclasp spreads: As more women silence the ghostly chattering of the ideal to hear their own voices, the more directly they can speak to one another and inspire in others the assurance of "belonging to a whole group of women who are really great."

Reticence and Revelation: Working at Friendship

The diversity of women's lives creates an essential privacy, which often makes contact among women more difficult, more reserved, more scarce. Friendship now requires work. "It isn't easy now. There's a new feeling of separate worlds," Olga Pearce reflected. "Or maybe I just notice it more now—well, it's noticing . . . what isn't being said. There's this tremendous good will . . . I see it in other women, and I feel it in myself. But there just isn't the time to make use of it." A second change in women's lives has further threatened the power of women's friendships: Time, in which friendships are made and maintained, is now a scarce resource.

Friendship among women, which once filled in empty time, now has to be set aside, deliberately and with difficulty. Katrina Pieters had seen a lack of friends as a sign that she was not in control of her life. It was a signal that change was needed, and she needed friends to help her effect the change. "There's this hunger for other women. We meet—and marvellous things seem to happen. It takes a while, but what you see is that it isn't just you, and that other people are working on things, too, trying to deal with these feelings. There's no record of them—not one I know anyway—and it feels so much better, groping together."

In isolation, she feels her doubts as a personal flaw. She retreats to a pre-midlife stance, in which her own experiences do not "count." In the company of other women, however, her experiences are validated. They are her, but not "just her"—that is, they are not the result of some personal inadequacy, but of a generational struggle. In identifying this, she feels a communal creation.

But to get to this point, many women had to struggle with that sense of being separate. Kay Plackett took some time to notice that she was enforcing this separation. Fearing envy, she showed only her "pliant, nonthreatening" side to her friends. She noticed her voice: "It was flat, controlled, somebody else's." She also noticed an emptiness in her friendships, as she (implicitly) insulted her friends with the assumption that they would be daunted by her success. She becomes ashamed of how she added to this sense of separate women, which "made me feel so different, so that I didn't see how much I was trying to mold myself into my idea of a good, safe woman. Seeing them as more like me, I could be more like myself." While Monica was relieved to see that her friends did not look down on her and the "mistakes" that had constrained her, her friends may have been trying, like Kay, to break the defensive barriers between them.

ONCE THIS IS DONE, the connection should be maintained—more carefully than it had been in the past. "I used to drop people when the going got rough," Nicola Campbell explained. "Now I say—Hey, I want to talk about this. You see more and more that friendships aren't easy. But it also hurts more when they end. I mean, once I'd get annoyed by someone—then just drop her. It could be over nothing. She just said something that annoyed me, and I stopped liking her. I remember that . . . just stopping a friendship, feeling I didn't like someone any more. But now I wouldn't. I meet so many people, and only sometimes does something real happen. And when it does, it is real—because it used to be half real—there was this, well, we're two young women here, so we'll stick together, but there could also be something else. Now when there's something else, I make an effort. It's so hard, but I do. Because you can't be careless with friendship."

Time is a scarce resource, but so is friendship. Therefore, time and patience have to be used to maintain the friendships. The diversity of women's lives and of their values and of their communication styles means that meeting many people does not always result in friendship. When it does, Nicola feels she has to be careful with it and not let it break for small reasons.

As traditional women felt edged out by their busier friends and marginalized in the ethos in which working hard and working long in the workplace has glamor, innovative women resisted the time constraints that prevented them from welcoming a visiting friend or taking time to listen to her. Expansive women, seeking radical change, often explained that one motive for embarking on a continuing education course or retraining program was "to meet other women." Not only had that drawn them there, but the support and encouragement of other women kept them there. Protesting women often formed passionate friendships in which, together, they built a counterculture in which they exulted, explained Patricia, in appearing "too loud, too bawdy, and too sexy." Friendship developed into a form of resistance—against feeling marginal, against a machinelike dedication, against self-doubt, against social images of midlife. Friends were often perceived as necessary to growth—the "groping together" was far more constructive than groping alone. But it was not only support and comfort and understanding friends could offer; they were also the source of power.

The Women's Room

When, in their youth, today's midlife women made the first giant step into the male bastions of the workplace, they were disconcerted by a silent network—a network supplying information and support, a network to which they had no access. Somewhere behind the scenes, somewhere outside both the formal and informal meetings, was a center of activity, which aided and abetted men's progress. As women felt their exclusion, they labeled this network "the men's room": There, in the men's toilet, from which women were reasonably barred, information, casually exchanged, decisively shaped men's careers. The term came to refer not only to the limited number of events that actually took place in the men's room, but to the entire system of knowledge to which men had access and from which women were excluded.[7]

Preparing to enter a difficult world in which they would have to compete to succeed, many women were disconcerted to see how men often did not have to compete with one another. Instead, men befriended one another, mentored one another, supported one another. What many women experienced was not the cutthroat environment they had expected, but a cozy club. When they tried to join it, they were ostracized, by both the men and the women. Trying to be "one of the boys" was a loser's game. Either she failed, and the men ridiculed her; or she succeeded, and women saw her as "sleeping her way to the top."[8] There could, at that time, be no comparable women's network. In the workplace, women were too scarce, or too divided, or too defensive, to band together and empower one another.

In early adulthood, women's experience of women together was characterized by rivalry as much as by bonding. At times, the rivalry seemed to threaten the fabric of women's progress. Competition and conflict among women is still an issue many find difficult to address. As Nicola noted, the end of a friendship "hurts more" as it is valued in all its rarity. Several women, returning with "relief" to friendship in midlife, described the sense of doom they experienced as members of a women's group engaged in conflict. "It would start with just one person—saying how the conversation was really getting her all upset and all sorts of nasty notions were buzzing around the room—and then the different armies would group. Over and over, there would be people who were 'in' and people who were 'out,' and someone who was way beyond criticism one week, would be in for it the next."

As Olga reflects on past divisions, she describes the format of girls' cliques: They are volatile and mean. But, unlike a young girl who keeps going back to the same friends, explaining to her dismayed parents that she has made up with them because "they are not mean all the time,"[9] the women in their twenties and thirties avoid contact in order to avoid the pain of divisiveness. "I gave up going," she explained. "It was a battle station, not a group." In more personal circumstances, too, conflict with friends, during early adulthood, was avoided. The "Mommy Wars," or the defensive stances between traditional and innovative mothers, is well-documented,[10] and women described the ending of friendships in young adulthood based on implied criticism of life choices. Monica felt her former classmates looked down on her. Mai, too, felt that her roles were "belittled by people at college who had struggled so much to make the grade." She understood how their struggles separated them from her: "They see my life as cushy—which in some ways it is, but then they don't see how I have real problems, too." Joann was haunted by the memory of how "smug" she felt when her friends' marriages broke up: "That isn't what I would have said at the time—but I did . . . I felt smug, like 'poor her, and lucky me.' The kind of support I got from my friends was a surprise—and made me regret my old feelings."

But friendship is not only about similarity and support. It is about passionate difference and clashing moods. One of the hardest things in regaining friendship was learning how to disagree—how to fight as freely as they did as children, and make up as readily. "I still feel that dread—" Olga explained, "when something goes wrong—just a disagreement, like you're talking and—wham!—there you are with no way forward. It's an awful feeling. But what do you do? Say, 'Oh, I agree,' when you damn well don't? I guess I try to hear it. That's how it is for her, and I mull over that. But I don't agree. And then when something does go wrong, I try to pick things up again. I'll phone. We'll meet. You don't have to get stuck on these points."

Conflict among women is frightening partly because of its echoes with constraints. Much of the competition among women, as they have previously known it, is competition of women who have no power—the competition of women in a patriarchy. What is so disturbing about this type of competition and conflict is that it reinforces the circuits of patriarchal power. When women believe that social norms are inevitable, they constrain—even cripple—themselves and other women.[11] In the recent Chinese film *The Red Lantern*, one wife introduces her child to her husband's new wife as "a girl—how useless," thus accepting the value system that oppresses her.[12] Believing that power lies with men, she plots against other women who threaten her attachment to a man, rather than plotting alongside women to take possession of their own power. In failing to see how male power is supported by her belief in it, she reinforces that male power, and destroys potential women allies.

The crisis question, "Why did it take so long to trust myself?" or "Why did it take so long to see what I know?" reveals the role a woman may herself have played in enforcing constraints upon her. As women see the part they sometimes play in keeping themselves back, they also see how other women have joined them. It is often through other women, rather than men, that they learned about the importance of their looks. It is often other women, rather than men, who ostracized them for not caring enough about how they look. It is with other women that they learn to analyze their face in the mirror. It is through other women that they often felt most awed by the tasks of balancing their expansive and affiliative needs—feeling "selfish" or "selfless." It is through other women that they felt most criticized for their choice to pursue careers or stay at home. It is against other women they measure how much they have "aged." It is often other women who help sustain those ideals of the woman who has found the "magical spot in which everything comes together." In adhering to the rules of a patriarchy, they compete against one another for scarce and indirect accesses to power.

This is changing, and the change is registered by midlife women's realization that they can bond together without rivalry. It is registered by midlife women's understanding that conflict between them, which is inevitable, does not necessarily involve rivalry, which can so easily be destructive. As, together, they refuse to hide their doubts or bury their knowledge, they reinforce the power they have gained.

Midlife friendships have a new instrumentality. As I shadowed these women, whose time was scarce, whose future growth depended upon amassing energy for themselves, I noticed that friends' needs were routinely prioritized. Whatever a woman learned about her self or her society or her profession was rapidly shared. "Now when I see my friends—my women friends," Kay explained, "I'm looking for ways in which I can show what I do and why and how I feel about it. So much of all this was done through them—because I started to see how they would understand, that they were working with something, too. This, you know, is so different . . . from hiding what I was, and feeling so different. All sorts of things which I had to smooth over, I now see, and talk about. I don't know why it took me this long."

As Kay learns that a new generational language can be spoken—that different women share patterns of doubt, conflict, and desire—she can accept those rough edges. As women shared their hard-won skills in linking up with their own knowledge, they established a future in which they find themselves at the center, not the margin. Given this generation's distinctive battle, subsequent generations of women, learning from them, may find that this does not take so long.

Epilogue

A woman's fifth decade is a turning point, wherein she frees herself from the weight of external images and expectations. As the crisis of midlife is resolved, she is able to cease those internal arguments and conflicts that have absorbed so much energy. Though she may not have a blueprint for the rest of her life, or an answer to every question about herself, or a precise scale to assess her competing needs and responsibilities, she has new skills for achieving, and creating, the second half of life on her own terms.

It is not surprising, after all, that the human psyche, so intricately adaptable and deviously clever at surviving, should find ways to resist social and cultural voices that tax its vigor. Nor is it surprising that women do not, until midlife, harness this psychological strength. Whereas younger women often see themselves as resisting all constraints and walking freely along a self-chosen road, these very women are likely, later, to see that at least some of this confidence was blind, that at least some of their contentment was forced by others' wishes, and that at least some of their goals were shaped by others' aims. Midlife triggers an independent outlook, which shatters the ideals—both feminine and feminist—that shadow women throughout adolescence and young adulthood. As women like Mai and Nell and Amy leave their "shadow voices" behind, they gain greater control over the whole of their lives. Through this control, they see more clearly the patterns

in which they participate. Through this control, they gain further assurance that their own wishes and needs and desires carry weight.

This does not mean that woman go through the first half of their
lives blindly or foolishly or thoughtlessly. This does not mean that,
before forty, women are helpless in making choices. On the whole,
women of this distinctive generation have been more deliberate, more
reflective, more determined to reshape their lives in their own vision
than any previous cohort. This determination has led to new demands,
and these demands have all too often been supported by new ideals,
many of which are contradictory or superficial. Some, like Kay Plackett, are amazed that they have "got away" for so long with speaking in
another person's voice, working either—as Kay did—on a pliant, nonthreatening facade, or, as Grace did, to match the "hard male model
younger women exaggerated."

Throughout adulthood, women try in various ways to realize the
ideals they have formed in adolescence. They test them out—on society at large, on the people close to them, on the institutions in which
they work. In the first half of life, fulfillment seems to reside with the
realization of these ideals. At midlife, when our futures are balanced by
our pasts, when we are aware of our remaining potential and feel a new
urgency to utilize it, the context in which we have been acting comes
under harsh scrutiny. "Looking back, I shudder to see the compromises I made—or the terms on which I made them," Mai Collins reflected. "But there is no wood when you're young—just some nice
green trees. There was a time when I felt bang in the middle of a for-
est—no way out. And so, what's been invigorating about these past few
years is relief from worrying about how wrong I've been, and just being
able to move forward." And Rosa Cortes, feeling "something within
[herself] that has to be answered," steps back from a husband's protectiveness to overcome an inhibiting sense of inferiority. Midlife is not a
time at which punishment is necessarily meted out for mistakes made,
but a time when those mistakes can be revised, revisioned, to become
points of departure.

But a woman does not have to see her past as mistaken or misguided in order to see the need for change. As she recenters her vision,
what seemed solid may now appear fragmented. Innovative women
often realize that much of what they saw in their youth as promising

fulfillment and freedom was motivated in part by misshapen ideals. Hence, Katrina Pieters was stunned by the imbalance of her life. "Anyone else pursuing this lifestyle could have seen what I didn't see. Anyone going before might have shown me a better way. It seems so inefficient—that everyone has to get through on her own." But this is everyone's plight—and everyone's challenge and delight: that each of us does live in the highly specific context of her own life, with all those attachments that seem inevitable and all those occurrences that may be mere chance. From this, she has to fashion the story that means the most to her—the story of her own life, its effect on others, its potential for achievement.

In youth, the belief that one is unique often leads to a conviction that one can manage easily what others have failed to contend with. Micky Riley recalled how convinced she was that things would be different for her, because "when you're young the world seems safer." Now, at 46, she reassures the caution she had once thought was needless, and hears her mother's voice with a midlife woman's ear. "My mother was always saying that I had to 'be careful.' Big things, small things: it didn't matter. There was always the underlying message that I didn't know how dangerous things were. So I couldn't walk on my own at night. I had to take care how I presented myself and what I led others to believe. What a *worrier,* I thought. 'Against life,' I labeled her. So my friends and I would walk the streets of New York at all hours, proving our mothers wrong. She hadn't achieved as much as I thought she should have because she was afraid. That's what I thought—that her fear had held her back. We wanted to show that our mothers were wrong because we had to believe we were safe if we were to go through life the way we wanted to."

Normal adolescent rebellion—and a normal adolescent's skewed assessment of risk—was now seen by Micky as unwillingness to admit how difficult—and dangerous—her life might be. Just as women, before they have children, underestimate the time involved in child rearing;[1] just as women, before they marry, overestimate the amount of time a partner will devote to domestic chores;[2] just as women at early stages of their careers underestimate the occupational prejudice against them and overestimate their chances for promotion;[3] just as the younger feminists of today believe their ideological mothers have overemphasized the constraints on women,[4] so, too, does each woman re-quire experience of living as a woman in this world before she can mea-sure and confront her own inhibiting accommodation to others' ideals.

The crisis of midlife comes as women see they will need to be dif-ferent if they are to move forward. For, if women, however liberated, are still enthralled by "the beauty myth,"[5] then how much more so are they caught in the web of the myth of woman's middle age. Still, it is "good copy" in *When Harry Met Sally* for a 32-year-old woman to en-vision forty as a "dead end." Still, it is feasible to see midlife as a phase ruled by menopause.[6] A healthy resistance to this marginalization spurred these women to savor a secret freedom. As Monica Selleck in-sisted, when she turned forty, "What I felt was relief. I was not what others expected I would be, or what I always expected being forty meant. And for a few years that was me—riding high on relief." Many women found something else within that relief: "I felt stronger than I'd ever been, and younger than I'd ever been," Jeri Coppersmith said, "but a little way down the road I noticed how I was stumbling in the same old way." The strength of that relief, however, prepares women for facing their stumbles, and making the effort to modify their pace. Linda Gerson, wondering why "I create these problems for myself," corrects her vision as she notices it: If she sees through her own eyes, then the pressure of others' vision will be lifted.

The new strength women find in midlife should not, however, be overestimated. Life's problems cannot be resolved solely from within. For women to change, they had to effect a shift in their relationship with others—especially in the subtle play of power. They had to change their daily lives—sometimes radically, sometimes with fine-tuning. They had to make new decisions about how accommodating they should be to the occupational cultures in which they were pursu-ing their goals. They had to find new forms of expression. They had to forge new terms of friendship. And since the context of each woman's life is so different, and because each woman became more and more sensitive to her lived context, she had to find her own way. Guideless, they shared a secret mission, but each cleared a single path.

No other generation has faced greater challenges in "getting through it on her own." Whereas other generations of women might well have been less fortunate as they faced predictable impediments to their potential, this generation has had a greater puzzle to solve. There is no one stumbling block, no single set of dangers, but rather a slalom course. Some women are experts on the first leg of the track, yet suddenly find they cannot negotiate what others, having fallen badly earlier on, find simple and sure. "I started out so sure of what I wanted, and I was so sure I could get it. That determination—" Patricia Galen laughed as it loomed up before her. "And it isn't that now I see I was wrong or too idealistic—it's not that. No, I wasn't wrong, and I'm very pleased about what I've achieved, and how all that I've done will help me to do more. But as you get older—but it's more than getting older, isn't it? Yes, and it's certainly not getting old. No—there's a process— isn't there?—that you don't want just to call 'maturity.' It's as though the whole texture of your life changes, and you get better at touching it."

As Patricia and I shared enjoyment in her investigative description, I thought about the aptness of her terms, which blended problems in her work as a sculptor with life issues; but I also heard her utter what each of the women going into crisis and resolving it knew: that she had undergone a journey during which she had changed in specific, ordered ways. The question that remained was: Why, since each woman saw the psychological work she had done, was the story of midlife development so sparsely reported?

The silence of which my friend Pamela had spoken at that crucial meeting in a London airport—when she said that every woman undergoes change at around forty, but keeps this process secret—had been the starting point of this research. Now, five years after that initial conversation, I saw that the "silence" was single-sided. Women did not silence this development within themselves—on the contrary, its power resides in the fact that this development is enacted. Women did not hide this change from one another. On the contrary, their ability to speak to one another creates new capacities for friendship. Its silence stemmed from others' inability to hear—an inability that all too often stemmed from lack of interest. The social marginalization that stimulated this change also ignored it.

But was this privacy necessary to this development? Did women, knowing they were in some sense no longer in the cultural spotlight, use this darker space to achieve greater psychological freedom? Could it be that, as the decks were cleared of any consequential theory about who they should be, they had greater freedom in finding who they were? And, if so, would anything be endangered by its disclosure?

I put this question to Pam, who was once again passing through England, though this time she was able to stay longer. First, she smiled: Her gut reaction to my questioning discourse was amusement. But then she focused on the query. "I don't think so. Anyway—we are in the limelight now, because there are so many of us, because we're doing so much, and because we are forever talking about who we are and who we want to be. Our cover's blown—," she laughed suddenly at her own phrase. "But it's always threatening to come back, as though we'd be better off in disguise."

"Do you think we would? I mean, would we be safer in disguise, since we can no longer go unnoticed?"

She cast me her sideways glance. "You mean—as crones or superwomen on a hormonal high?" As I nodded, she considered her own question. "No—we can't get away with those disguises for long. Besides, we've all become too—articulate. It's time to risk a revelation."

Notes

INTRODUCTION

1. This model of women's crisis in midlife is close to that of Wilfred Bion's concept of catastrophic change in which a new phase of development is achieved only by a breakdown in the previous structure of the self. Wilfred Bion, 1965, *Transformations: Learning to Growth*. In her 1994 seminar series in the Cambridge Psychoanalytic Forum, Meg Harris Williams beautifully consolidated Bion's concept of catastrophic change.

2. For example, Arlie Hochschild and Anne Machung, 1989, *The Second Shift*; Harriet Harman, 1993, *The Century Gap: Twentieth Century Man and Twenty-first Century Woman*.

3. For example, see Anita Shreve, 1989, *Women Together, Women Alone*.

4. I was writing *Working Women Don't Have Wives: Professional Success in the 1990s* while conducting the interviews that formed the basis of this book.

5. Arlie Hochschild and Anne Machung, in *The Second Shift*, 1989, describe accommodations of conflicts about housework. Julia Brannen and Peter Moss, in *Managing Mothers*, 1991, describe women's "cognitive manoeuvres" as they try to manage their regrets at cutting down on their work for family reasons.

6. The study of working mothers in early adulthood was begun in 1981, but was then updated in 1992–93. In the meantime, I had begun, in 1990, my study of midlife women. This alerted me to the different ways in which conflicts were managed.

7. Joyce Carol Oates, 1993, *Foxfire*.

8. Orville Brim and Jerome Kagan, 1980, "Constancy and Change: A View of the

Issues," in Orville Brim and Jerome Kagan, eds., *Constancy and Change in Human Development,* pp. 15–16.

9. Mathilda White Riley, 1976, "Age Strata in Social Systems," in R. Binstock and E. Shanas, eds., *Handbook of Aging and the Social Sciences.*

10. Arlene Skolnick, 1991, *Embattled Paradise: The American Family in an Age of Uncertainty,* p. 161. Maturity has been transformed in the past hundred years. Whereas in 1850, only 2% of the population lived past the age of 65, now about 75% of all people die when they are past 65. This increase in life expectancy has virtually all occurred since 1900: Two-thirds of the total increase in longevity since prehistoric times has taken place since 1900, and has occurred most markedly in the past three decades (S. H. Preston, 1976, *Mortality Patterns in National Populations: With Special Reference to Recorded Causes of Death,* p. 153).

11. L. S. Wrightsman, 1988, *Personality Development in Adulthood.* This has also been the finding of the MacArthur Foundation Research Network on Successful Mid-life Development (MIDMAC) set up in 1989; reported by Grace Bradberry and Justine Hancock, "Mid-life: A Drama Not a Crisis," *The Daily Mail* (London), May 24, 1993, pp. 28–29.

12. Gloria Steinem, 1991, *Revolution from Within: A Book of Self-Esteem.*

13. Germaine Greer, 1992, *The Change: Women, Aging and the Menopause.*

14. See Germaine Greer, 1989, *Daddy, We Hardly Knew You.*

15. Gaily Sheehy, 1992, *The Silent Passage.*

16. See, for example, Carl Jung, 1969; Lillian Rubin, 1979, *Women of a Certain Age.*

17. John Clausen, 1993, *American Lives: Looking Back at the Children of the Great Depression.*

18. See George Vaillant, 1977, *Adaptation to Life,* and Daniel Levinson, 1978, *The Seasons of a Man's Life.*

19. Lyn Mikel Brown and Carol Gilligan, 1992, *Meeting at the Crossroads: Women's Psychology and Girls' Development.*

20. Jamaica Kincaid, 1986, *Annie John* (New York: Plume).

21. Susanna Kaysen, 1993, *Girl, Interrupted,* p. 167.

22. Michèle Roberts, 1993, *Daughters of the House* (London: Virago).

23. Doris Lessing, 1990, *Martha Quest* (London: Paladin).

24. Jung Chang, 1991, *Wild Swans* (London: HarperCollins).

25. Another exception is Nadine Gordimer's *The Lying Days,* which was also written when she was 30. But she sees the girl's rage against hypocrisy as being led by love and male strength—and so writes a very different plot from the others discussed here.

26. Sylvia Plath, 1963, *The Bell Jar* (London: William Heinemann).

27. See Lyn Mikel Brown and Carol Gilligan, 1992, *Meeting at the Crossroads.*

28. Mary McCarthy, 1963, *The Group* (New York: Harcourt, Brace and World).
29. Gloria Steinem, 1991, *Revolution from Within;* Germaine Greer, 1992, *The Change;* Angela Davis, 1990, *An Autobiography* (London: Women's Press).
30. Freud, 1965, "Femininity."
31. They do this undisturbed partly because few adults realize how much young children know, so they leave this knowledge uncontrolled.
32. Terri Apter, 1990, *Altered Loves: Mothers and Daughters during Adolescence.*
33. Lyn Mikel Brown and Carol Gilligan, 1992, *Meeting at the Crossroads,* p. 230.
34. For this reason I have not specifically stated the race or ethnic background of the women in my sample. I have resisted this because I believe that to the extent that these features of a person's life are relevant to my study, they are clear. I have resisted because these characteristics can become labels, which imply presumed differences that were not borne out by my study.
35. As of 1988, in an attempt to stop the rise in Medicare costs, the Federal government changed its payment procedure for hospital care. Instead of covering the hospital bills—subject to deductions—Medicare now pays a flat rate for specific illnesses and medical procedures. Since hospitals receive the standard payment even if their costs are below that amount, there is an incentive to save money on Medicare patients by sending them home as soon as possible. Since the new payment system was set up, the average length of hospital stay by Medicare patients has decreased by two days. This means that more of the nursing of convalescent patients is being done at home. See Marilyn Power, 1988, "Women, the State and the Family in the US: Reaganomics and the Experience of Women," in Jill Rubery, *Women and Recession.*
36. The Center for the Study of Social Policy investigated whether women were less willing to work as a result of changes in welfare rules that frequently penalized women for working. Many women took on extra jobs and worked longer hours (12% in Georgia and 16% in Michigan), and the majority of women expressed the desire to work longer hours if only work were available. Center for Study of Social Policy, 1984, *Working Female-Headed Families in Poverty,* Washington, DC: March. Cited in Marilyn Power, 1988, "Women, the State and the Family in the US". Moreover, though at any one time 16% of women on welfare are in work, in the course of a year, 88% have worked, which shows that they are not simply depending on welfare and giving up attempts to work.
37. Carolyn Heilbrun, 1989, *Writing a Woman's Life.*

CHAPTER   1

1. Helen Franks, 1981, *Prime Time.*
2. Judith Paige and Pamela Gordon, 1991, *Choice Years.*
3. Even Gail Sheehy, in her wonderfully empathic book, *The Silent Passage,* some-times follows this fashion. One woman she discusses is "an elegant European," another is a "sizzling redhead."
4. Pauline Bart, 1971, "Depression in Middle-Aged Women."
5. Judith Viorst, 1986, *Necessary Losses.*
6. Arlene Skolnick, 1991, *Embattled Paradise,* p. 162.
7. Germaine Greer, 1992, *The Change.*
8. Germaine Greer, 1992, *The Change.*
9. John Dryden, 1966, *Secret Love: or, The Maiden Queene,* Act III, Scene 1, *The Works of John Dryden, Plays,* John Loftis, ed., Berkeley: University of California Press.
10. Carolyn Heilbrun, 1989, *Writing a Woman's Life* discusses the paucity of midlife women's voices in fiction; Germaine Greer, 1992, *The Change* repeatedly chafes under the insult of midlife women's invisibility.
11. Sigmund Freud, 1965, "Femininity," pp. 134–35.
12. Carolyn Heilbrun, 1989, *Writing a Woman's Life.*
13. Nonhuman animals, with the exception of one species of ape, do not recognize the shape in the mirror as themselves.
14. Jacques Lacan, 1979, *The Four Fundamental Concepts of Psycho-analysis.* For Lacan, the mirror stage signals a child's entry into the world of language. As the child realizes that the reflection stands for himself, who is other than the reflection, he understands the possibility of symbolism and, hence, of language. For girls, however, this leap in understanding of the reflection as symbol plays a specific role in their development as they learn the pressure that reflection can exert upon them.
15. Sandra Gilbert and Susan Gubar, 1979, *The Madwoman in the Attic;* see also Ellen Cronan Rose, 1983, "Through the Looking Glass: When Women Tell Fairy Tales."
16. Anne Frank, 1989, *The Diary of Anne Frank,* pp. 566–67.
17. Lyn Mikel Brown and Carol Gilligan, 1992, *Meeting at the Crossroads.*
18. See some fathers' response to daughters in Terri Apter, 1993, "Altered Views: Teenage Daughters and Their Fathers."
19. Dana Crowley Jack, 1991, *Silencing the Self.*

20. From interview material collected for Terri Apter, 1990, *Altered Loves*.

21. Gloria Steinem, 1991, *Revolution from Within*, p. 227.

22. E. Jane Dickson, interviewing Doris Lessing, 1992, "City of the Mind," *The New York Times*, Sunday, 10 May, Book Review, p. 7.

23. In Margaret Atwood's *Cat's Eye*, Elaine reflects that she "never got used to the Queen being grown up" and is convinced that the "matronly facade does not fool" her, that the girlish Princess Elizabeth is "in there somewhere" (p. 399). She denies the reality of what she sees.

24. Anita Brookner, 1991, *Brief Lives*, p. 75.

25. Dana Crowley Jack, 1991, *Silencing the Self*, p. 94.

26. John Berger, 1973, *Ways of Seeing*, p. 46.

27. Anita Brookner, 1991, *Brief Lives*, p. 195.

28. Robin Lakoff and Raquel Scherr found that women who denied their interest in their appearance simply repressed it, or were defending themselves against it: they did not overcome it. Serious women are slow to speak to one another about it. They feel that quite simply they are beyond it, and they never admit their feelings and concern about it to one another (Robin Lakoff and Raquel Scherr, 1984, *Face Value*, p. 284).

29. Gloria Steinem, 1991, *Revolution from Within*.

30. "A Day in the Life of Angela Carter," *The Sunday Times* (London) *Magazine*, August 25, 1991, p. 50.

31. Women under the age of 24 are more likely to want to undergo surgical change than older women. Elaine Hatfield and Susan Sprecher, 1988, *Mirror, Mirror*.

32. Erik Erikson, 1965, *Childhood and Society*, pp. 252–53.

33. Germaine Greer, 1992, *The Change*, p. 433.

34. Virginia Woolf, 1967, *Mrs. Dalloway*, p. 42.

35. Neil G. Bennet and David E. Bloom, 1987, "Why Fewer Women Marry," p. 18; and the report of the demolition of these statistics in Susan Faludi, 1991, *Backlash*.

36. Susan Sontag, 1972, "The Double Standard of Aging," pp. 29–38.

37. Simone de Beauvoir, 1984, *The Second Sex*, pp. 587.

38. Simone de Beauvoir, 1984, *The Second Sex*, pp. 587–88.

39. Robin Lakoff and Raquel Scherr, 1984, *Face Value*.

40. See Roger Gould, 1978, *Transformations*.

41. David Gutmann, 1987, *Reclaimed Powers*.

42. Martin Martel, 1968, "Age-Sex Roles in Magazine Fiction (1890–1955)."

43. Alice Rossi, 1980, "Life-Span Theories and Women's Lives," pp. 4–32.

44. Judith Todd, Ariella Friedman, and Priscilla Wanjiru Kariuki, 1990, "Women Growing Stronger with Age," pp. 567–77.

CHAPTER 2

1. Julia Brannen and Peter Moss, 1991, *Managing Mothers.*
2. Arlie Hochschild and Anne Machung, 1989, *The Second Shift.*
3. I have since learned that Dr. Rosemary Jackson was also a member of one of Germaine Greer's classes during that time, and like Olga, she described herself as the one traditional woman hearing this advice about revolutionizing women's lives to gain their freedom. Jackson was much younger than Olga at the time, yet she, too, had a child, whom she eventually left, as Greer was encouraging women to do. Yet Jackson is now writing about the enormous problems, psychological and social, for women who leave their children. Greer has since then changed her assessment of the meaning children have to women's lives, but it would be interesting to know how many of her students had the secret thought that she was the only traditional female in the class.
4. Virginia Woolf, 1925, *Mrs Dalloway,* pp. 44–45.
5. Nor Hall, 1980, *The Moon and the Virgin* (New York: Harper & Row).
6. Dana Crowley Jack, 1991, *Silencing the Self,* p. 192.
7. Lyn Mikel Brown and Carol Gilligan, 1992, *Meeting at the Crossroads.*
8. This term is taken from Kathleen Gerson, 1985, *Hard Choices.*
9. Arlie Hochschild, 1983, *The Managed Heart.* Hochschild's discussion of emotion management is highly innovative and entertaining. One problem I have with her study, however, is that as an all too frequent flyer, I rarely see flight attendants exhibiting their famous smile and cheerfulness. Instead, they handle passengers by issuing brusque orders and indicating that there is nothing to be done about a given situation. Hochschild studies the flight attendants' response to their training and to the passengers. It may well be that people highly overrate their own ability to manage their feelings and to control others through this management. Moreover, seeing someone manage his or her demeanor in order to control you can be highly infuriating. When you are angry, it may increase your frustration to feel that someone is "handling" you and your anger rather than responding efficiently and accurately to your complaint. Left out of Hochschild's account, then, is the frequent failure of emotion management, and the responses that obvious emotional management and controlling behavior may arouse in others.
10. Margery Spring Rice, 1981, *Working Class Wives,* 2nd ed. (London: Virago).
11. Jane Rogers, 1987, *The Ice Is Singing,* pp. 35–36.
12. Roger Gould, 1978, *Transformations,* p. 310.

13. Lillian Rubin, 1979, *Women of a Certain Age.*
14. Pauline Bart, 1971, "Depression in Middle-Aged Women."
15. Bernice Neugarten, 1968, "The Awareness of Middle Age."
16. Lillian Rubin, 1979, *Women of a Certain Age;* her demolishment of the empty-nest myth was preceded in academic literature by Leonard Pearlin and others.
17. Marjorie Fiske Lowenthal, Majda Thurnher, and David Chiriboga, 1975, *Four Stages of Life.*
18. Bernice Neugarten, 1979, "Time, Age and the Life Cycle," pp. 887–94.
19. See Katherine Newman, 1993, *Declining Fortunes.*
20. Ravenna Helson, Valory Mitchell, and Geraldine Moane, 1984, "Personality and Patterns of Adherence and Nonadherence to the Social Clock," pp. 1079–96.

CHAPTER 3

1. Margaret Carlson, "The Most Powerful Woman," *Time,* May 10, 1993, pp. 29–37.
2. See, for example, Colette Dowling, 1981, *The Cinderella Complex.*
3. Judi Marshall, 1984, *Women Managers,* p. 3.
4. Juliet Schor, 1992, *The Overworked American.*
5. William Whyte, 1956, *The Organization Man.*
6. Terri Apter and Elizabeth Garnsey, 1994, "Enacting Inequality: Structure, Agency and Gender," pp. 19–31; Elizabeth Garnsey, 1987, "Working Hours and Workforce Division."
7. Juliet Schor, 1992, *The Overworked American.*
8. Lotte Bailyn, quoted by Kathleen Hirsch, 1992, "A New Vision of Corporate America."
9. See Shulamit Kahn and Kevin Lang, 1987, "Constraints on the Choice of Work Hours: Agency vs. Specific Capital," p. 14; Robert Moffit, 1982, "The Tobit Model, Hours of Work and Institutional Constraints," pp. 510–15. Both cited in Juliet Schor, 1992, *The Overworked American,* p. 128.
10. Rosanna Hertz, 1986, *More Equal than Others,* p. 122.
11. See Katherine Newman, 1993 *Declining Fortunes.*
12. See Linda Davies, 1993, "A Raw Deal," pp. 30–37.
13. Terri Apter and Elizabeth Garnsey, 1994, "Enacting Inequality"; Elizabeth Garnsey, 1993, "Exploring a Critical Systems Perspective," pp. 229–56.
14. Judi Marshall, 1984, *Women Managers.*
15. See Kathleen Gerson, 1985, *Hard Choices;* Arlie Hochschild and Anne Ma-

chung, 1989, *The Second Shift;* Liz Roman Gallese, 1985, *Women Like Us* (New York: Morrow).

16. Judi Marshall, 1993, "Patterns of Cultural Awareness as Coping Strategies for Women Managers," in S. E. Kahn and B. C. Lang, eds., *Women, Work and Coping: A Multidisciplinary Approach to Workplace Stress* (Montreal: McGill-Queen's University Press); also Judi Marshall, 1989, "Re-visioning Career Concepts: A Feminist Invitation," in M. B. Arthur, D. T. Hall, B. S. Lawrence, eds., *Handbook of Career Theory* (Cambridge: Cambridge University Press), pp. 275–91; Terri Apter, 1994, *Working Women Don't Have Wives.*

17. Judi Marshall, 1984, *Women Managers.*

18. The inability to predict women's future careers from early adulthood aims has also been noticed by Kathleen Gerson, 1985, *Hard Choices,* and Judi Marshall, 1984, *Women Managers.*

19. Terri Apter and Elizabeth Garnsey, 1994, "Enacting Inequality," pp. 19–34.

20. The Equal Opportunities Commission, with its forecast (in its report published on April 14, 1994) for 38% of women managers by the end of the decade, believes that similar means of downgrading the position of manager will occur in Britain.

21. George Akerlof and Janet Yellen, 1986, *Efficiency Wage Models of the Labor Market.*

22. Terri Apter, 1994, *Working Women Don't Have Wives.*

23. Jill Rubery and Roger Tarling, 1988, "Women's Employment in Declining Britain."

24. Rosabeth Moss Kanter, 1989, *When Giants Learn to Dance* (New York: Simon & Schuster), p. 62.

25. Rosabeth Moss Kanter, 1989, *When Giants Learn to Dance,* p. 63.

26. Rosabeth Moss Kanter, 1989, *When Giants Learn to Dance,* p. 43.

27. Patricia Aburdene and John Naisbitt, 1993, *Megatrends for Women.*

28. Terri Apter, 1994, *Working Women Don't Have Wives.*

29. See Terri Apter, 1990, *Altered Loves.*

30. These two different methods of protesting against an unsatisfactory organization were defined by Albert Hirschman, 1970, *Exit, Voice and Loyalty.*

31. See Frances Conley, March 1992, "Unmasking Sexism: One Doctor's Diagnosis," pp. 20–22.

32. Age discrimination is not illegal in Britain.

CHAPTER 4

1. Margaret Atwood, 1991, *Cat's Eye*, p. 13.
2. Margaret Atwood, 1991, *Cat's Eye*, p. 400.
3. Paul Wink, 1992, "Three Types of Narcissism in Women from College to Midlife," pp. 7–30.
4. Heinz Kohut, 1977, *The Restoration of the Self.*
5. Of the twenty radical women in my sample, seven were returners to education, and nine returned to the workplace. These new steps were sometimes combined with other external changes, such as divorce or the death of spouse. Six of the women who returned to education had been "waylaid" from education earlier in life, as had four of the women returning to or new to the workplace. The remaining radical women sought change through relocation, some constantly in the form of travel, as they hoped to learn more by seeing more.
6. Alice Koller, 1983, *An Unknown Woman,* p. 135; quoted in Mary Field Belenky, Blythe McVicker Clinchy, Nancy Rule Goldberger, and Jill Mattuck Tarule, 1986, *Women's Ways of Knowing.*
7. Rosalind Edwards, 1990, "Mummy Mode and Student Mode: Connecting and Separating the Family and Education in the Lives of Mature Mother-Students."
8. Rosalind Edwards, 1990, "Mummy Mode and Student Mode."
9. This was one of the "drier" projects from which this book emerged.
10. Most women prefer part-time work, and eighty percent of part-time workers earn less than $11,000 a year. See Katherine Newman, 1993, *Declining Fortunes;* see also Elizabeth Garnsey, 1987, "Working Hours and Workforce Division."
11. For a description of marriage as a fair economic exchange, see Gary Becker, 1965, "A Theory of the Allocation of Time" and Gary Becker, 1981, *A Treatise on the Family;* for a critical view of its implications, see Terri Apter, 1994, *Working Women Don't Have Wives.*
12. Eighty percent of part-time workers earn less than $11,000 per year (Juliet Schor, 1992, *The Overworked American*).
13. Many women have to endure the economic effects of divorce on their children. Many men are only compelled to support children under the age of 18, hence, a women may find that her wealthy ex-husband refuses to pay college fees.
14. See Kathleen Gerson, 1985, *Hard Choices;* Terri Apter, 1994, *Working Women Don't Have Wives.*
15. In America, discrimination on the basis of age is unlawful, but it is very difficult to enforce. All sorts of reasons can be given, especially with many qualified appli-

cants, for giving a job to one younger person rather than another. In Britain, age discrimination is perfectly legal, and many job advertisements carry age limits. It is very common to have age limits of 30 or 35 on many posts, which women in midlife might see as reasonable reentry or late-entry spots.

16. See Arlie Hochschild and Terry Arendall, *Mothers and Divorce;* and Lenore Weitzman, 1985, *The Divorce Revolution.* But how far and deep is the financial fall? According to one study, the income of the American woman, whatever her economic class, decreases by 73% when she divorces, while that of her ex-husband decreases by 42%. The husband, however, tends to have fewer expenses after divorce (he usually does not need to accommodate his children) and has greater earning power—at least his earning power is not decreased by the divorce (Lenore Weitzman, 1985, *The Divorce Revolution*). Recently, this finding has been challenged not only for its accuracy, but for its participation in a conspiracy (Susan Faludi, 1991, *Backlash,* p. 26)—perhaps to frighten women off divorce, but also to complain about the "no fault" divorce laws, which, in America, may leave the wife exposed and without compensation for her timely investments in the family, which have distracted from her pursuit of a career: if neither partner is at fault, a judge may reason, then a woman should not be compensated for loss of income.

More recent assessments of the woman's fall in income after divorce describe a 30% decrease (Greg Duncan and Saul D. Hoffman, 1988, "What Are the Economic Consequences of Divorce?", p. 641), and women work hard to improve on this. After heading their family or being single mothers for four years, the women who had regular work experience before their divorce were now earning about 80% of the family income when they were married. Even women who had not worked at all before their divorce had, four years later, incomes of slightly less than half their average pre-divorce *family* income (see Lee Rainwater, 1984, "Mothers' Contribution to the Family Money Economy in Europe and the United States," in P. Voydanoff, ed., *Work and Family* (Palo Alto, CA: Mayfield), quoted in Terry Arendall, 1986, *Mothers and Divorce* (Berkeley: University of California Press)). Furthermore, many women who had been head of their families for several years spoke of enormous advantages. Three women felt that they were more than willing to confront the lower wages available to women and the restricted opportunities in order to protect themselves and their children from what they saw as the antisocial behavior of their former husbands. "When people see these three big strapping boys I'm in charge of, I get lots of pity. 'Single mother' they mouth, and I laugh in their faces. There's rough and there's rough in this life, and my rough is a whole lot smoother than any rough with a man." Five years after divorce, the women were convinced that images of inadequacy were a myth.

17. Cited in Arlie Hochschild and Anne Machung, 1989, *The Second Shift.*

18. Ravenna Helson, Valory Mitchell, and Geraldine Moane, 1984, "Personality and Patterns of Adherence and Nonadherence to the Social Clock."

19. Lenore Weitzman, 1985, *The Divorce Revolution,* p. 346.

20. See Grace Baruch and Rosalind Barnett, 1983, "Adult Daughters' Relationships with Their Mothers" for emotional recovery; Greg Duncan and Saul Hoffman, "A Reconsideration of the Economic Consequences of Marital Dissolution," in *Demography, 22* (1985): 485.

21. Grace Baruch and Rosalind Barnett, 1983, "Adult Daughters' Relationships with Their Mothers," pp. 601–606, found that the average time of healing was five years; and seven years after divorce, women who were employed and had children scored very high on self-esteem and did not report many symptoms of anxiety or depression.

22. Greg Duncan and Saul D. Hoffman, 1988, "What Are the Economic Consequences of Divorce?"

C H A P T E R   5

1. Arlene Skolnick, 1991, *Embattled Paradise.*

2. A. A. Cambell, 1968, "The Role of Family Planning in the Reduction of Poverty," pp. 236–45.

3. It may be that the "exceptions" to this prediction are vast, and that the midlife forecast for teenage mothers has been overly pessimistic. More extensive research into adult development has shown that "the stereotype of the teenage mother . . . belies the diversity in outcome as well as in strategies for overcoming an unplanned and potentially disruptive life event" (Jean Brooks-Gunn and Frank F. Furstenberg, 1989, "Long-Term Implications of Fertility-Related Behavior and Family Formation on Adolescent Mothers and Their Children," pp. 319–39).

4. Reference in Margaret Morganroth Gullette, 1986, *Safe at Last in the Middle Years.*

5. See Sara Ruddick, 1989, *Maternal Thinking.*

6. Grace K. Baruch, 1989, "Reflections on Guilt, Women and Gender," p. 7.

7. Sara Ruddick, 1989, *Maternal Thinking,* p. 72.

C H A P T E R   6

1. Germaine Greer, 1992, *The Change; Newsweek,* May 25, 1992.
2. Gaily Sheehy, 1992, *The Silent Passage;* Gail Sheehy, 1993, "The Flaming Fifties."
3. See Carl Jung, 1969; Carolyn Heilbrun, 1989, *Writing a Woman's Life;* Judith K. Brown and Virginia Kerns, eds., 1985, *In Her Prime;* Rhoda Metraux, ed., 1979, *Some Personal Views: Margaret Mead* (New York: Walker Pub. Co.).
4. See Margaret Morganroth Gullette, 1993, "What, Menopause Again?" pp. 34–37.
5. Alice Rossi, 1992, "The Menopausal Transition in Midlife."
6. The incidents of flushes, sweating, and general discomfort at menopause are known to vary widely in different cultures. See Kay-Tee Khaw, 1992, "The Menopause and Hormone Replacement Therapy"; Mary Walsh, 1987, *The Psychology of Women.*
7. Peter Schmidt and David Rubinow, 1989, "Menopausal Mood Disorders: Past and Future Research Strategies."
8. Ann M. Voda, 1982, "Menopausal Hot Flash," in Ann M. Voda, Myra Dinnerstein, and Sheryl R. O'Donnell, eds., *Changing Perspectives on Menopause,* cited in Alice Rossi, 1992, "The Menopausal Transition in Midlife."
9. Cited in Alice Rossi, 1992, "The Menopausal Transition in Midlife," p. 10.
10. Germaine Greer, 1992, *The Change.*
11. Kay-Tee Khaw, 1992, "The Menopause and Hormone Replacement Therapy," pp. 615–23.
12. Kay-Tee Khaw, 1992, "The Menopause and Hormone Replacement Therapy," pp. 615–23.
13. Ann Kent, April 17, 1992, "Propaganda or the Simple Truth?" *The Times* (London), Life and Times sec., p. 6.
14. Three doctors were interviewed in England, and three were interviewed in America. Aside from each following different procedures, there was no difference in attitude.
15. Kieran Sweeny, 1994, "Stop, Look and Listen."
16. Kay-Tee Khaw, 1992, "The Menopause and Hormone Replacement Therapy."
17. Helene Deutsch, 1945, *The Psychology of Women,* pp. 459, 461.
18. Germaine Greer, 1992, *The Change,* pp. 314–15.
19. Dr. Eleanor Birks, at the Evelyn Hospital in Cambridge, England, was, in 1982, delighted to open a government publication addressed to doctors, which con-

tained two articles on menopause subtitled, "A Personal View." "Finally!" she thought, and opened the journal eagerly, only to find that the "personal view" of menopause was written by two men.

20. The anger and anxiety of these women were not always linked to a particularly accurate view of Greer's argument. Some women were angered by her attack on hormonal replacement therapy. ("If one woman suffers from osteoporosis because of what she says, then she'll have to answer for it," Paula, 51, declared.) Other women were confounded by her dismissal of their lives up to menopause ("It's as though we never had any choice up till then, that we're just a bunch of stooges till our periods stop.") or her descriptions of menopausal women as free to do as they liked ("You think people stop taking bites out of my day-to-day life just because I've stopped menstruating? Where exactly does this sudden freedom to do as we like come from?") Other women discounted her relevance: She did not speak for them, not for their generation or their lifestyle or their needs or their hopes.

21. Alice Rossi, 1992, "The Menopausal Transition in Midlife," p. 5.

22. Paula Caplan, 1987, "The Myth of Women's Masochism."

23. Margaret Drabble, 1980, *The Middle Ground,* p. 16.

24. Alice Rossi, 1992, "The Menopausal Transition in Midlife," p. 4; K. A. Matthews, R. Wing, L. Kuller et al., 1990, "Influences of Natural Menopause on Psychological Characteristics and Symptoms of Middle-Aged Healthy Women," pp. 345–51.

25. C. Bird, 1979, "The Best Years of a Woman's Life," pp. 20–26.

26. L. Radloff, 1979, "Sex Differences in Depression: The Effects of Occupation and Marital Status," pp. 249–65; J. Meyers, M. Weissman, G. Tischler et al., 1984, "Six-Month Prevalence of Psychiatric Disorders in Three Communities," pp. 959–67; T. Hallstrom and S. Samuelsson, 1985, "Mental Health in the Climacteric," pp. 13–18.

27. Jane Brody, May 19, 1992, "Menopause: The New Awareness," *The New York Times,* pp. C1, C8; and Alice Rossi, 1992, "The Menopausal Transition in Midlife," p. 8.

CHAPTER 7

1. See Suzanne Gordon, 1991, *Prisoners of Men's Dreams.*

2. Susan Faludi, 1991, *Backlash;* and Naomi Wolf, 1991, *The Beauty Myth,* wonderfully describe and analyze this exploitation.

3. Max Scheler, 1961, *Resentment.*

4. Helene Deutsch, 1945, *The Psychology of Women.*

5. Judy Dunn, 1984, *Brothers and Sisters.*

6. Terri Apter, 1993, "Young Girls' Friendships and Cliques."

7. Terri Apter, data for study of adolescent girls, 1990, *Altered Loves.*

8. Rom Harré, 1986, *The Social Constructions of Emotion.*

CHAPTER 8

1. Judith Todd, Ariella Friedman, and Priscilla Wanjiru Kariuki, 1990, "Women Growing Stronger with Age," pp. 543–66; B. J. Reinke, D. S. Holmes, and R. L. Harris, 1985, "The Timing of Psychosocial Changes in Women's Lives: The Years from 25 to 45," pp. 1353–64; B. L. Neugarten and J. W. Moore, 1968, "The Changing Age-Status System," pp. 5–21.

2. See Arlie Hochschild and Anne Machung, 1989, *The Second Shift.*

3. Elizabeth Hardwick, 1979, *Sleepless Nights.*

4. Elizabeth Hardwick, 1974, *Seduction and Betrayal.*

5. For example, Byron, *Don Juan.*

6. Nancy Chodorow, 1978, *The Reproduction of Mothering.*

7. Lillian Rubin, 1985, *Intimate Strangers,* p. 120.

8. Maggie Scarf, 1980, *Unfinished Business.*

9. Carol Gilligan, June 15, 1993, "Remembering Iphigenia."

10. Anita Brookner, 1991, *Brief Lives;* discussed in Chapter One.

11. Virginia Woolf, 1925, *Mrs Dalloway,* pp. 168–69.

12. Doris Lessing, 1964, *Martha Quest* (London: Picador), p. 298.

13. Germaine Greer, 1992, *The Change.*

14. Maggie Scarf, 1980, *Unfinished Business.*

15. Sharon Thompson, 1990, "Putting a Big Thing into a Little Hole: Teenage Girls' Accounts of Sexual Initiation," pp. 341–61.

16. Terri Apter, 1990, *Altered Loves;* James Youniss and Jacqueline Smollar, 1985, *Adolescent Relations with Mothers, Fathers, and Friends.*

CHAPTER 9

1. Vivian Gornick, 1987, *Fierce Attachments.*

2. Marianne Hirsch, 1989, *The Mother/Daughter Plot,* p. 26.

3. Nancy Friday, 1977, *My Mother/My Self* explains her inability to decide to have children as she feared becoming the mother of a daughter.

4. Carol Gilligan, 1982, *In a Different Voice;* Nancy Chodorow, 1978, *The Reproduction of Mothering.*

5. Terri Apter, 1990, *Altered Loves.*

6. Virginia Woolf, *Moments of Being,* 2nd ed., ed. Jeanne Schulkind (New York: Harcourt Brace Jovanovich, 1985), p. 80.

7. Elaine Showalter, 1985, "Towards a New Feminist Poetics," p. 135.

8. Virginia Woolf, 1929, *A Room of One's Own,* p. 21.

9. Dorothy West, 1989, "My Mother, Rachel West," p. 382.

10. Dorothy West, 1989, "My Mother, Rachel West," p. 383.

11. Adrienne Rich, 1976, *Of Woman Born,* p. 225.

12. These writings about mother/daughter conflict focus on the negative feelings of the mother to a daughter's adolescence and young adulthood. Other writings—in particular Nancy Chodorow, 1978, *The Reproduction of Mothering*—focus on connection in infancy and very early childhood, and though these accounts suggest potential conflict, they do not present the relationship as essentially limiting. Instead, they focus on how female identity is structured by the relationship with the mother.

13. Grace Baruch and Rosalind Barnett, 1983, "Adult Daughters' Relationships with Their Mothers," pp. 601–606.

14. Grace Baruch and Rosalind Barnett, 1983, "Adult Daughters' Relationships with Their Mothers," p. 347; Ruthellen Josselson, 1987, *Finding Herself,* also found that the adult women she interviewed continued to feel close to a mother and valued a friendly relationship.

15. For an extensive analysis of this process, see Terri Apter, 1990, *Altered Loves;* for an account of validation, see Linda Bell and David Bell, 1983, "Parental Validation and Support in the Development of Adolescent Daughters," in H. D. Grotevant and C. R. Cooper, eds., *Adolescent Development in the Family* (San Francisco: Jossey-Bass), pp. 27–42.

16. Gunhild Hagestad, 1984, "The Continuous Bond: A Dynamic, Multigenerational Perspective on Parent-Child Relations Between Adults," pp. 129–58.

17. Grace Baruch and Rosalind Barnett, 1983, "Adult Daughters' Relationships with Their Mothers."

18. Grace Baruch and Rosalind Barnett, 1983, "Adult Daughters' Relationships with Their Mothers," p. 349.

19. Anne Stueve and Lydia O'Donnell, 1984, "The Daughter of Aging Parents," pp. 203–25.

20. Anne Stueve and Lydia O'Donnell, 1984, "The Daughter of Aging Parents," p. 211.

21. Anne Stueve and Lydia O'Donnell, 1984, "The Daughter of Aging Parents," pp. 212–13.

22. Anne Stueve and Lydia O'Donnell, 1984, "The Daughter of Aging Parents," p. 211.

23. Terri Apter, 1990, *Altered Loves*.

24. Terri Apter, 1993, "Altered Views: Teenage Daughters and Their Fathers."

25. Carol Gilligan, June 15, 1993, "Remembering Iphigenia."

26. James Youniss and Jacqueline Smollar, 1985, *Adolescent Relations with Mothers, Fathers, and Friends;* Terri Apter, 1990, *Altered Loves*.

27. Lily Pincus and Christopher Dare, 1978, *Secrets in the Family*.

28. See Alice Walker, 1983, *In Search of Our Mothers' Gardens* (New York: Harcourt Brace Jovanovich), and Toni Morrison, 1988, *Beloved* (London: Picador).

29. Grace Baruch and Rosalind Barnett, 1983, "Adult Daughters' Relationships with Their Mothers," p. 204.

30. Grace Baruch and Rosalind Barnett, 1983, "Adult Daughters' Relationships with Their Mothers," p. 205.

31. Gunhild Hagestad, 1984, "The Continuous Bond," p. 141.

32. Margaret Clark, 1969, "Cultural Values and Dependencies in Later Life," p. 71.

33. Gunhild Hagestad, 1987, "Parent-Child Relations in Later Life: Trends and Gaps in Past Research," p. 413.

34. V. W. Marshall, C. J. Rosenthal, and J. Synge, 1983, "Concerns about Parental Health."

35. Though many women in midlife feel the pressure to look after elderly parents, the pressure on midlife women today is far less than it will be on the midlife women of the next generation. This generation of elderly parents gave birth to the baby boomers, and hence have several children to share the burdens. The baby boom generation has had far fewer children, and their children will face far greater pressures in looking after the elderly population when they are in midlife.

36. W. Hawkinson, 1965, "Wish, Expectancy, and Practice in the Interaction of Generations."

37. Elaine M. Brody, Pauline T. Johnsen, and Mark C. Fulcomer, 1984, "What Should Adult Children Do for Elderly Parents? Opinions and Preferences of Three Generations of Women," pp. 736–46.

38. Eleanor P. Stoller, 1983, "Parental Caregiving by Adult Children," pp. 851–58.

39. Elaine M. Brody, Pauline T. Johnson, and Mark C. Fulcomer, 1984, "What Should Adult Children Do for Elderly Parents?", p. 419.

40. Gunhild Hagestad and R. Snow, 1977, "Young Adult Offspring as Interper-

sonal Resources in Middle Age," Paper presented to the annual meeting of the Gerontological Society, San Francisco, CA; cited in L. Troll, S. Miller, and R. Atchley, 1979, *Families in Later Life* (Belmont, CA: Wadsworth), p. 97.

CHAPTER 10

1. This calculation in the number of references to friends was based on a textual analysis of my interviews with adolescent girls (see *Altered Loves*), working mothers in their thirties *(Working Women Don't Have Wives),* and the midlife women I interviewed for this book.

2. Bernice Neugarten, 1968, "The Awareness of Middle Age"; see also Ravenna Helson, Valory Mitchell, and Geraldine Moane, 1984, "Personality and Patterns of Adherence and Nonadherence to the Social Clock," pp. 1079–96.

3. F. Furstenberg, 1976, *Unplanned Parenthood: Social Consequences of Teenage Childbearing* (New York: Free Press); R. Hogan, 1982, "A Socioanalytic Theory of Personality," in M. M. Page, ed., *Personality: Current Theories and Research* (Lincoln: University of Nebraska Press), pp. 55–89 (cited in Helson, Mitchell, and Moane, 1984); also Leonard Pearlin and Morton Lieberman, 1979, "Social Sources of Emotional Distress," in Roberta Simmons, ed., *Research in Community and Mental Health* (Greenwich, CT: JAI Press). These researchers have also found that many negative events, such as divorce, are more stressful because they are nonnormative. Some events are always nonnormative, that is, outside an expected framework. Divorce, however common, is never an expected or predicted or planned event, like marriage, childbirth, returning to work, retiring. Losing a parent early, having children "too" early or late, one finds that adjustment and change and support are more meager, and stress more likely.

4. This is discussed in Chapter Three.

5. Terri Apter, 1993, "Young Girls' Friendships and Cliques."

6. See Ruthellen Josselson, 1992, *The Space between Us;* Margery Harness Goodwin, 1991, *He-Said—She-Said: Talk as Social Organization among Black Children* (Bloomington: Indiana University Press); Terri Apter, 1990, *Altered Loves.*

7. Even now many women feel that the informal network of male friendships is more detrimental to their progress than family demands or overt bias against them. See Terri Apter, 1994, *Working Women Don't Have Wives.*

8. See cases discussed in Terri Apter, 1994, *Working Women Don't Have Wives.*

9. See Terri Apter, 1993, "Young Girls' Friendships and Cliques."

10. For example, see Lynda Richardson, "The Mommy Wars," *Chicago Tribune,*

February 7, 1993, sec. 6, p. 4; and Anita Shreve, 1989, *Women Together, Women Alone.*

11. Elizabeth Garnsey, 1993, "Exploring a Critical Systems Perspective."
12. I am grateful to Elizabeth Garnsey for pointing out this incident and its relevance. See also Terri Apter and Elizabeth Garnsey, 1994, "Enacting Inequality."

EPILOGUE

1. S. Prendergast and A. Prout, 1985, "Education for Parenthood," Cambridge: Child Care and Development Group.
2. Arlie Hochschild and Anne Machung, 1989, *The Second Shift.*
3. Judi Marshall, 1984, *Women Managers.*
4. See, for example, Katherine Roiphe, 1993, *The Morning After* (Boston: Little, Brown); and to a lesser extent, Naomi Wolf, 1992, *Fire with Fire.*
5. Naomi Wolf, 1991, *The Beauty Myth.*
6. Germaine Greer, 1992, *The Change.*

References

Aburdene, Patricia, and John Naisbitt. *Megatrends for Women.* New York: Random House, 1993.

Akerlof, George, and Janet Yellen, eds. *Efficiency Wage Models of the Labor Market.* Cambridge and New York: Cambridge University Press, 1986.

Apter, Terri. *Working Women Don't Have Wives: Professional Success in the 1990s.* New York: St. Martin's, 1994.

Apter, Terri. "Altered Views: Teenage Daughters and Their Fathers." In *The Narrative Study of Lives,* edited by Ruthellen Josselson and Amia Lieblich. San Francisco: Jossey-Bass, 1993.

Apter, Terri. "Young Girls' Friendships and Cliques." Paper presented to the Human Development Group, Graduate School of Education, Harvard University, February 9, 1993.

Apter, Terri. *Altered Loves: Mothers and Daughters during Adolescence.* New York: St. Martin's, 1990.

Apter, Terri, and Elizabeth Garnsey. "Enacting Inequality: Structure, Agency and Gender." *Women's Studies International Forum* 17, no. 1 (1994): 19–31.

Atwood, Margaret. *Cat's Eye.* London: Virago, 1991.

Bart, Pauline. "Depression in Middle-Aged Women." In *Women in a Sexist Society,* edited by Vivian Gornick and Barbara Moran. New York: Basic Books, 1971.

Baruch, Grace. "Reflections on Guilt, Women and Gender." Working paper no. 176, Wellesley College, Center for Research on Women, Wellesley, MA, 1989.

Baruch, Grace, and Rosalind Barnett. "Adult Daughters' Relationships with Their Mothers: The Era of Good Feelings." *Journal of Marriage and the Family* 45, no. 3 (1983): 601–606.

Bateson, Mary Catherine. *Composing a Life*. New York: Plume, 1990.

Becker, Gary. *A Treatise on the Family*. Cambridge: Cambridge University Press, 1981.

Becker, Gary. "A Theory of the Allocation of Time." *Economic Journal* 75, no. 299 (1965): 493–517.

Belenky, Mary Field, Blythe McVicker Clinchy, Nancy Rule Goldberger, and Jill Mattuck Tarule. *Women's Ways of Knowing: The Development of Self, Voice, and Mind*. New York: Basic Books, 1986.

Bennet, Neil G., and David E. Bloom. "Why Fewer Women Marry." *Advertising Age*, January 12, 1987.

Berger, John. *Ways of Seeing*. New York: Viking, 1973.

Bion, Wilfred. *Transformations: Learning to Growth*. London: Heinemann Medical, 1965.

Bird, C. "The Best Years of a Woman's Life." *Psychology Today*, June 1979, 20–26.

Bradberry, Grace, and Justine Hancock. "Mid-life: A Drama Not a Crisis." *The Daily Mail* (London), May 24, 1993, 28–29.

Brannen, Julia, and Peter Moss. *Managing Mothers: Dual Earner Households after Maternity Leave*. London: Unwin Hyman, 1991.

Brim, Orville, and Jerome Kagan. "Constancy and Change: A View of the Issues." In *Constancy and Change in Human Development*, edited by Orville Brim and Jerome Kagan. Cambridge, MA: Harvard University Press, 1980.

Brody, Elaine M., Pauline T. Johnsen, and Mark C. Fulcomer. "What Should Adult Children Do for Elderly Parents? Opinions and Preferences of Three Generations of Women." *Journal of Gerontology* 39, no. 6 (1984): 736–46.

Brookner, Anita. *Brief Lives*. Harmondsworth, England: Penguin, 1991.

Brooks-Gunn, Jean, and Frank F. Furstenberg. "Long-Term Implications of Fertility-Related Behavior and Family Formation on Adolescent Mothers and Their Children." In *Family Systems and Life-Span Development*, edited by Kurt Kreppner and Richard M. Lerner, 319–39. Hillsdale, NJ: Lawrence Erlbaum Associates, 1989.

Broverman, I., et al. "Sex Role Stereotypes and Clinical Judgments of Mental Health." *Journal of Counseling and Clinical Psychology* February (1970): 34.

Brown, Judith K., and Virginia Kerns, eds. *In Her Prime: A New View of Middle Aged Women*. South Hadley, MA: Bergin and Garvey, 1985.

Brown, Lyn Mikel, and Carol Gilligan. *Meeting at the Crossroads: Women's Psychology and Girls' Development*. Cambridge, MA: Harvard University Press, 1992.

Cambell, A. A. "The Role of Family Planning in the Reduction of Poverty." *Journal of Marriage and the Family* 30, no. 2 (1968): 236–45.

Caplan, Paula. "The Myth of Women's Masochism." In *The Psychology of Women: Ongoing Debates,* edited by Mary Roth Walsh, 78–96. New Haven, CT: Yale University Press, 1987.

Chodorow, Nancy. *The Reproduction of Mothering.* Berkeley: University of California Press, 1978.

Clark, Margaret. "Cultural Values and Dependencies in Later Life." In *The Dependencies of Old People,* edited by Richard Kalish. Ann Arbor: Institute of Gerontology, The University of Michigan, 1969.

Clausen, John. *American Lives: Looking Back at the Children of the Great Depression.* New York: Free Press, 1993.

Conley, Frances. "Unmasking Sexism: One Doctor's Diagnosis." *Stanford Magazine,* March 1992, 20–22.

Davies, Linda. "A Raw Deal." The Magazine, The Sunday Times, July 4, 1993, 30–37.

De Beauvoir, Simone. *The Second Sex.* Translated and edited by H. M. Parshley. Harmondsworth, England: Penguin, 1984.

Deutsch, Helene. *The Psychology of Women.* Vol. 2, pp. 459, 461. New York: Grune and Stratton, 1945.

Dowling, Colette. *The Cinderella Complex.* New York: Summit, 1981.

Drabble, Margaret. *The Middle Ground.* Harmondsworth, England: Penguin, 1980.

Duncan, Greg, and Saul D. Hoffman. "What Are the Economic Consequences of Divorce?" *Demography* 25, no. 4 (1988): 641.

Dunn, Judy. *Brothers and Sisters.* London: Fontana, 1984. (Published by Harvard University Press as *Sisters and Brothers,* 1985)

Edwards, Rosalind. "Mummy Mode and Student Mode: Connecting and Separating the Family and Education in the Lives of Mature Mother-Students." Paper delivered to the Women and Psychology Conference, Birmingham, England, July 14, 1990.

Erikson, Erik. *Childhood and Society.* New York: W. W. Norton, 1964.

Faludi, Susan. *Backlash: The Undeclared War against American Women.* New York: Crown, 1991.

Frank, Anne. *The Diary of Anne Frank: The Critical Edition.* Edited by D. Barnouw and G. van der Stroom, translated by A. Pomerans and B. M. Mooyaart-Doubleday. London: Viking, 1989.

Franks, Helen. *Prime Time: The Mid-life Woman in Focus.* London: Pan, 1981.

Freud, Sigmund. "Femininity." *The Standard Edition of the Complete Psychological Works of Sigmund Freud.* Vol. 22. Edited and translated by J. Strachey. New York: Norton, 1965.

Friday, Nancy. *My Mother/My Self: The Daughter's Search for Identity.* New York: Delacorte, 1977.

Garnsey, Elizabeth. "Exploring a Critical System Perspective." *Innovation in Social Science Research,* 6, no. 2 (1993): 229–56.

Garnsey, Elizabeth. "Working Hours and Workforce Division." In *Flexibility in Labour Markets,* edited by Roger Tarling. London: Academic Press, 1987.

Gerson, Kathleen. *Hard Choices.* Berkeley: University of California Press, 1985.

Gilbert, Sandra, and Susan Gubar. *The Madwoman in the Attic: The Woman Writer and the Nineteenth-Century Literary Imagination.* New Haven, CT: Yale University Press, 1979.

Gilligan, Carol. "Remembering Iphigenia." Seminar, Cambridge Psychoanalytic Forum, June 15, 1993.

Gilligan, Carol. *In a Different Voice.* Cambridge, MA: Harvard University Press, 1982.

Goodwin, Margery Harness, and Charles Goodwin. "Children's Arguing." In *Language, Gender and Sex in Comparative Perspective,* edited by Susan Philips, Susan Steele, and Christine Tanz. Cambridge and New York: Cambridge University Press, 1987.

Gordon, Suzanne. *Prisoners of Men's Dreams.* Boston: Little, Brown, 1991.

Gornick, Vivian. *Fierce Attachments.* New York: Straus, Farrar, and Giroux, 1987.

Gould, Roger. *Transformations: Growth and Change in Adult Life.* New York: Simon and Schuster, 1978.

Greer, Germaine. *The Change: Women, Aging, and the Menopause.* New York: Alfred Knopf, 1992.

Greer Germaine. *Daddy, We Hardly Knew You.* London: Hamish Hamilton, 1989.

Gullette, Margaret Morganroth. "What, Menopause Again?" *Ms.* July–August, 1993, 34–37.

Gullette, Margaret Morganroth. *Safe at Last in the Middle Years.* Berkeley: University of California Press, 1988.

Gutmann, David. *Reclaimed Powers: Toward a New Psychology of Men and Women in Later Life.* New York: Basic Books, 1987.

Hagestad, Gunhild. "Parent-Child Relations in Later Life: Trends and Gaps in Past Research." In *Parenting Across the Lifespan: Biosocial Dimensions,* edited by

Jane Lancaster, Jeanne Altmann, Alice Rossi, and Lonnie Sherrod, 405–33. New York: Aldine de Gruyter, 1987.

Hagestad, Gunhild. "The Continuous Bond: A Dynamic, Multigenerational Perspective on Parent-Child Relations Between Adults." In *Minnesota Symposia on Child Psychology,* vol. 17, edited by M. Perlmutter, 129–58. Hillsdale, NJ: Lawrence Erlbaum Assoc., 1984.

Hallstrom, T., and S. Samuelsson. "Mental Health in the Climacteric." *Acta Obstet. Gynecol. Scand.* 130 (suppl.) (1985): 13–18.

Hardwick, Elizabeth. *Sleepless Nights.* New York: Random House. 1979.

Hardwick, Elizabeth. *Seduction and Betrayal: Women and Literature.* New York: Random House, 1974.

Harman, Harriet. *The Century Gap: Twentieth Century Man, Twenty-first Century Woman.* London: Vermilion, 1993.

Harré, Rom, ed. *The Social Construction of Emotions.* Oxford, England: Blackwell, 1986.

Hatfield, Elaine, and Susan Sprecher. *Mirror, Mirror.* Albany, NY: State University of New York Press, 1988.

Hawkinson, W. "Wish, Expectancy and Practice in the Interaction of Generations." In *Older People and Their Social World,* edited by A. Rose and W. Peterson. Philadelphia: F. A. Davis Co., 1965.

Heilbrun, Carolyn. *Writing a Woman's Life.* New York: Ballantine, 1989.

Helson, Ravenna, Valory Mitchell, and Geraldine Moane. "Personality and Patterns of Adherence and Nonadherence to the Social Clock." *Journal of Personality and Social Psychology* 46, no. 5 (1984): 1079–96.

Hertz, Rosanna. *More Equal than Others: Women and Men in Dual-Career Marriages.* Berkeley: University of California Press, 1986.

Hirsch, Kathleen. "A New Vision of Corporate America." *Boston Sunday Globe Magazine,* April 21, 1992, 16.

Hirsch, Marianne. *The Mother/Daughter Plot: Narrative, Psychoanalysis, Feminism.* Bloomington: Indiana University Press, 1989.

Hirschman, Albert. *Exit, Voice and Loyalty: Responses to Decline in Firms, Organizations, and States.* Cambridge, MA: Harvard University Press, 1970.

Hochschild, Arlie. *The Managed Heart: The Commercialization of Human Feeling.* Berkeley: University of California Press, 1983.

Hochschild, Arlie, and Anne Machung. *The Second Shift.* New York: Viking, 1989.

Jack, Dana Crowley. *Silencing the Self: Women and Depression.* Cambridge, MA: Harvard University Press, 1991.

Josselson, Ruthellen. *The Space between Us.* San Francisco: Jossey-Bass, 1992.

Josselson, Ruthellen. *Finding Herself.* San Francisco: Jossey-Bass, 1987.

Jung, Carl. *The Structure and Dynamics of the Psyche.* Translated by R. F. C. Hull. London: Routledge, 1969.

Kahn, Shulamit, and Kevin Lang. "Constraints on the Choice of Work Hours: Agency vs. Specific Capital." National Bureau of Economic Research Working Paper 2238 (May 1987): 14.

Kaysen, Susanna. *Girl, Interrupted.* New York: Turtle Bay Books, 1993.

Khaw, Kay-Tee. "The Menopause and Hormone Replacement Therapy." *Reviews in Medicine* 68 (1992): 615–23.

Kohut, Heinz. *The Restoration of the Self.* New York: International Universities Press, 1977.

Koller, Alice. *An Unknown Woman.* New York: Bantam, 1983.

Lacan, Jacques. *The Four Fundamental Concepts of Psychoanalysis.* Edited by J.-A. Miller, translated by A. Sheridan. New York: W. W. Norton, 1981.

Lakoff, Robin, and Raquel Scherr. *Face Value: The Politics of Beauty.* London: Routledge, 1984.

Lever, Janet. "Sex Differences in the Games Children Play." *Social Problems* 23, no. 4 (1976): 478–87.

Levinson, Daniel. *The Seasons of a Man's Life.* New York: Alfred Knopf, 1978.

Lowenthal, Marjorie Fiske, Majda Thurnher, and David Chiriboga. *Four Stages of Life.* San Francisco: Jossey-Bass, 1975.

Marshall, Judi. "Patterns of Cultural Awareness: Coping Strategies for Women Managers." In *Women, Work, and Coping: A Multidisciplinary Approach to Workplace Stress,* edited by Bonita C. Long and Sharon Kahn. Montreal: McGill-Queen's University Press, 1993.

Marshall, Judi. *Women Managers: Travellers in a Male World.* Chichester, England: John Wiley, 1984.

Marshall, V. W., C. J. Rosenthal, and J. Synge. "Concerns about Parental Health." In *Older Women,* edited by Elizabeth Markson. Boston: Lexington, 1983.

Martel, Martin. "Age-Sex Roles in Magazine Fiction (1890–1955)." In *Middle Age and Aging,* edited by Bernice Neugarten. Chicago: University of Chicago Press, 1968.

Matthews, K. A., R. Wing, L. Kuller, et al. "Influences of Natural Menopause on Psychological Characteristics and Symptoms of Middle-Aged Healthy Women." *Journal of Consulting and Clinical Psychology* 58, no. 3 (1990): 345–51.

Meyers, J., M. Weissman, G. Tischler, et al. "Six Month Prevalence of Psychiatric Disorder in Three Communities." *Archives of General Psychiatry* 41, no. 10 (1984): 959–67.

Moffit, Robert. "The Tobit Model, Hours of Work and Institutional Constraints." *Review of Economics and Statistics* 64, no. 3 (1982): 510–15.

Neugarten, Bernice. "Time, Age and the Life Cycle." *American Journal of Psychiatry* 136, no. 7 (1979): 887–94.

Neugarten, Bernice. "The Awareness of Middle Age." In *Middle Age and Aging,* edited by Bernice Neugarten. Chicago: University of Chicago Press, 1968.

Neugarten, Bernice, and J. W. Moore. "The Changing Age-Status System." In *Middle Age and Aging,* edited by Bernice Neugarten, 5–21. Chicago: University of Chicago Press, 1968.

Newman, Katherine. *Declining Fortunes: The Withering of the American Dream.* New York: Basic Books, 1993.

Oates, Joyce Carol. *Foxfire: Confessions of a Girl Gang.* New York: Dutton-W. Abrahams, 1993.

Paige, Judith, and Pamela Gordon. *Choice Years: How to Stay Healthy, Happy and Beautiful through Menopause and Beyond.* New York: Random House, 1991.

Pincus, Lily, and Christopher Dare. *Secrets in the Family.* London and Boston: Faber and Faber, 1978.

Power, Marilyn. "Women, the State and the Family in the US: Reaganomics and the Experience of Women." In *Women and Recession,* edited by Jill Rubery. London and New York: Routledge and Kegan Paul, 1988.

Preston, Samuel H. *Mortality Patterns in National Populations: With Special Reference to Recorded Causes of Death.* New York: Academic Press, 1976.

Radloff, L. "Sex Differences in Depression: The Effects of Occupation and Marital Status." *Sex Roles* 1 (1979): 249–65.

Reinke, Barbara J., David S. Holmes, and Rochelle L. Harris. "The Timing of Psychosocial Changes in Women's Lives: The Years from 25 to 45." *Journal of Personality and Social Psychology* 48, no. 25 (1985): 1353–64.

Rich, Adrienne. *Of Woman Born: Motherhood as Experience and Institution.* New York: Norton, 1976.

Riley, Mathilda White. "Age Strata in Social Systems." In *Handbook of Aging and the Social Sciences,* edited by Robert Binstock and Ethel Shanas. New York: Van Nostrand Rheinhold, 1976.

Rogers, Jane. *The Ice Is Singing.* London and Boston: Faber and Faber, 1987.

Rose, Ellen Cronan. "Through the Looking Glass: When Women Tell Fairy Tales." In *The Voyage In,* edited by Elizabeth Abel, Marianne Hirsch, and Elizabeth Langland. Hanover, NH and London: University Press of New England, 1983.

Rossi, Alice. "The Menopausal Transition in Midlife." Symposium, Development in Midlife: Biopsychosocial Perspectives, American Psychological Association, Washington, DC, August 15, 1992.

Rossi, Alice. "Life-Span Theories and Women's Lives." *Signs* 6, no. 1 (1980): 4–32.

Rubery, Jill, and Roger Tarling. "Women's Employment in Declining Britain." In *Women and Recession,* edited by Jill Rubery. London: Routledge and Kegan Paul, 1988.

Rubin, Lillian. *Intimate Strangers.* New York: Harper and Row, 1985.

Rubin, Lillian. *Women of a Certain Age.* New York: Harper and Row, 1979.

Ruddick, Sara. *Maternal Thinking.* Boston: Beacon Press, 1989.

Scarf, Maggie. *Unfinished Business: Pressure Points in the Lives of Women.* Garden City, NY: Doubleday, 1980.

Scheler, Max. *Resentment.* Edited by Lewis Coser, translated by William Holdhein. Glencoe, IL: Free Press, 1961.

Schmidt, Peter, and David Rubinow. "Menopausal Mood Disorders: Past and Future Research Strategies." In *Premenstrual, Postpartum and Menopausal Mood Disorders,* edited by Laurence Demers et al. Baltimore, MD: Urban and Schwarzenberg, 1989.

Schor, Juliet. *The Overworked American: The Unexpected Decline of Leisure.* New York: Basic Books, 1992.

Sheehy, Gail. "The Flaming Fifties." *Vanity Fair,* October 1993.

Sheehy, Gail. *The Silent Passage: Menopause.* New York: Random House, 1992.

Showalter, Elaine. "Towards a New Feminist Poetics." In *The New Feminist Criticism: Essays on Women, Literature, and Theory,* edited by Elaine Showalter. New York: Pantheon, 1985.

Shreve, Anita. *Women Together, Women Alone.* New York: Fawcett, 1989.

Skolnick, Arlene. *Embattled Paradise: The American Family in an Age of Uncertainty.* New York: Basic Books, 1991.

Sontag, Susan. "The Double Standard of Aging." *Saturday Review,* Sept. 23, 1972, 29–38.

Steinem, Gloria. *Revolution from Within: A Book of Self-Esteem.* London: Bloomsbury, 1991.

Stoller, Eleanor P. "Parental Caregiving by Adult Children." *Journal of Marriage and the Family* 45, no. 4 (1983): 851–58.

Stueve, Anne, and Lydia O'Donnell. "The Daughter of Aging Parents." In *Women in Midlife,* edited by Grace Baruch and Jeanne Brooks-Gunn, 203–225. New York: Plenum Press, 1984.

Sweeny, Kieran. "Stop, Look and Listen." *The Times,* April 14, 1994.

Thompson, Sharon. "Putting a Big Thing into a Little Hole: Teenage Girls' Accounts of Sexual Initiation." *Journal of Sex Research* 27, no. 3 (1990): 341–61.

Todd, Judith, Ariella Friedman, and Priscilla Wanjiru Kariuki. "Women Growing Stronger with Age." *Psychology of Women Quarterly* 14, no. 4, (1990): 567–77.

Vaillant, George. *Adaptation to Life.* Boston: Little, Brown, 1977.

Viorst, Judith. *Necessary Losses.* New York: Fawcett, 1986.

Voda, Ann M. "Menopausal Hot Flash." In *Changing Perspectives on Menopause,* edited by Ann M. Voda, Myra Dinnerstein, and Sheryl R. O'Donnell. Austin: University of Texas Press, 1982.

Walsh, Mary Roth, ed. *The Psychology of Women: Ongoing Debates.* New Haven, CT: Yale University Press, 1987.

Weitzman, Lenore. *The Divorce Revolution.* New York: The Free Press, 1985.

West, Dorothy. "My Mother, Rachel West." In *Invented Lives, Narratives of Black Women, 1860–1960,* edited by Mary Helen Washington. London: Virago, 1989.

Whyte, William. *The Organization Man.* New York: Simon and Schuster, 1956.

Wink, Paul. "Three Types of Narcissism in Women from College to Mid-life." *Journal of Personality* 60, no. 1 (1992): 7–30.

Wolf, Naomi. *The Beauty Myth.* New York: Morrow, 1991.

Woolf, Virginia. *A Room of One's Own.* New York: Harcourt Brace Jovanovich, 1929.

Woolf, Virginia. *Mrs Dalloway.* London: Hogarth Press, 1925.

Wrightsman, L. S. *Personality Development in Adulthood.* Newbury Park, CA: Sage, 1988.

Youniss, James, and Jacqueline Smollar. *Adolescent Relations with Mothers, Fathers, and Friends.* Chicago: University of Chicago Press, 1985.

DATE			